GLOBAL
CHURCH
PLANTING

GLOBAL CHURCH PLANTING

Biblical Principles and Best Practices for Multiplication

Craig Ott and Gene Wilson

Baker Academic

a division of Baker Publishing Group
Grand Rapids, Michigan

Published by Baker Academic
a division of Baker Publishing Group
P.O. Box 6287, Grand Rapids, MI 49516–6287
www.bakeracademic.com

Printed in the United States of America

Library of Congress Cataloging-in-Publication Data

Ott, Craig, 1952–
    Global church planting : biblical principles and best practices for multiplication / Craig Ott and Gene Wilson.
        p.   cm.
    Includes bibliographical references (p.   ) and index.
    ISBN 978-0-8010-3580-7 (pbk. : alk. paper)
    1. Church development, New. I. Wilson, Gene, 1953– II. Title.
BV652.24.O88 2011
254′.1—dc22   2010021084

11   12   13   14   15   16   17   7   6   5   4   3   2   1

Contents

Part IV: Critical Factors

Foreword

The church is the most brilliant concept ever created. It has outlasted cultures, governments, skeptics, and enemies from within and without, and it will continue to do so until Jesus returns. We must love the church as Christ does, and that love is at the core of *Global Church Planting* by Craig Ott and Gene Wilson.

These authors and experienced church planters remind us that our churches are growing, living organisms and therefore will naturally reproduce. If we're not reproducing, it's a sign something is unhealthy in our congregations. Ultimately, a church's health is measured by its sending capacity, not its seating capacity.

In light of the Great Commission Jesus gave to the church, any definition of fruitfulness for a local congregation must include growth by the conversion of unbelievers, including the planting of new congregations. Saddleback began as a church plant, and then we planted another church during our first year. We've continued to plant new congregations every year since then.

Global Church Planting offers a comprehensive, biblical foundation for starting new churches, but it also gets down to the nitty-gritty of finding funding, developing a sense of the local culture, and pulling together the team that best meets the specific needs of the community where the church is being planted.

Ott and Wilson rightly insist that any church plant must be based on the centrality of Jesus Christ and his Great Commission. We grew Saddleback by reminding people that "a great commitment to the Great Commandment and the Great Commission will grow a great church." Ott and Wilson teach that church plants should seek help and support from other churches and/or their denomination. This allows the church to grow within a Great Commission community of cooperation.

Jesus doesn't expect us to produce *more* than we can, but he does expect us to produce *all* that we can by his power within us. This book will help you to do that. It should be read by anyone thinking about planting a church, but it should also be read by anyone in church leadership—because even if you are not part of a church plant, your congregation should be involved in initiating and then supporting church plants. And that's another thing I like about this book; it teaches that church planting is not consigned to some subgroup, for those with a pioneering spirit. Instead, all believers are called to plant churches as we reproduce the life of Christ in others and follow the Great Commission.

Jesus has given the church a job to do, and we must obey the Great Commission or, regardless of what else we do, we will fail at fulfilling our purpose for existing, which is helping Jesus bring others into the kingdom of God. May this book inspire you toward Great Commission thinking, even as it shows you what steps to take as you establish new congregations in the body of Christ.

Rick Warren
Senior Pastor
Saddleback Church

Preface

The growth of global Christianity at the end of the twentieth and beginning of the twenty-first centuries is nothing short of astonishing. Hundreds of millions of persons, especially from Africa, Asia, and Latin America have been welcomed into tens of thousands of new congregations, some in the most unexpected places (such as China) and in the most unlikely shapes and forms (such as Christian ashrams). The subject of church planting has also received much attention in recent years, with a growing awareness that evangelism apart from church planting is an incomplete approach to fulfilling the Great Commission. Disciples are made in communities of believers that are best able to reach others of their ethnic or social group. Such communities become God's instrument for kingdom impact on individuals, families, neighborhoods, and society.

Yet roughly one-third of the residents of Planet Earth are still without a local church that can share with them the gospel of Jesus Christ in an understandable and meaningful manner. The need for church planting, especially pioneer church planting among unreached people groups, remains an urgent task and a formidable challenge. In many places, such as urban centers, there are too few churches able to evangelize all the communities and various segments of the population. In other places churches with long membership rolls exist, but their members understand little about the Christian faith, do not attend church, or exercise a syncretistic mix of Christianity with other religious beliefs and practices. Well-prepared church planters, both local and expatriate, are still greatly needed.

In North America the cause of church planting has gained new momentum. Denominations have promoted it, church-planting networks and training institutes have emerged, resources abound, church-planting conferences flourish, and numerous books have been published. This is a welcome development. However, with few exceptions most of the energy and resources are geared to the needs and context of church planting in North America. The appearance of David Garrison's widely read study *Church Planting Movements* (2000) not only sparked renewed interest in church planting but also raised awareness that the most effective methods are likely to be very different from those practiced in the past by most missionaries and church planters. Church planters and missionaries working outside North America are left without much guidance. In most settings more than simple adaptation or tweaking of Western methods will be necessary to be effective, especially if the church planter is working cross-culturally.

Our primary goal is to combine sound biblical principles with the best practices from around the world to provide a practical guide for church planters working in a wide variety of cultural contexts. The teachings and example of the New Testament church provide the foundation for our approach. Whereas the biblical goals and principles never change, the world does, and therefore so do the specific methods. Thus we seek to also learn from careful research that will contribute to fulfilling those biblical purposes in a variety of settings. We have chosen not to focus on one particular model of the church (such as the house church) or a single methodology of church planting (such as incarnational versus attractional). Instead we have sought to examine church-planting efforts and movements, great and small, from diverse contexts and avoid the temptation to derive a single formula for success. The reader will need to thoughtfully and prayerfully evaluate the various methods, models, and examples that we present in these pages to discern which ones are best suited to his or her particular situation.

Having said that, we must add that we have devoted much of our discussion to what we call apostolic church planting, following closely the example of the apostle Paul. Such planters work more as itinerant or catalytic agents and less as pastors of the churches they plant. They seek to reproduce themselves in the local believers and plant churches that can reproduce and multiply on the basis of local leadership and resources.

The task of planting and reproducing churches, especially in cross-cultural settings, involves a comprehensive array of topics, skills, and challenges that deal with virtually every aspect of Christian ministry and mission. It is impossible in one volume to cover every aspect adequately. We have attempted to provide an overview of the key issues and include numerous references to further literature and resources that will help the reader to explore topics of interest in greater detail. (Citations from non-English original sources were translated by us, the authors.)

The book has been structured in four parts: Part I, "Biblical Foundations," examines the task, importance, and New Testament beginnings of church planting. Part II, "Strategic Considerations," takes up decisions that must be made early in the planning process, including the nature of church multiplication and indigeneity, the role of the church planter, contextualizing the shape of the church, and the models and approaches to church planting. Part III, "Developmental Phases," describes the phases that most church plants undergo, with very practical guidelines for leading a church plant from inception to reproduction. Finally, part IV, "Critical Factors," considers factors that undergird effective church planting: the personal life of church planters, teams, development of leaders, wise use of resources and partnerships, and developing churches with kingdom impact.

We write not as armchair theoreticians but as those who have experienced firsthand the challenges of cross-cultural church planting. Gene served eighteen years as a church planter in Quebec, Canada, and ten years as a church-planting coach in Latin America; he now works with church planters and their coaches globally. Craig served twenty-one years in Germany as a church planter, trainer, and church-planting consultant throughout Central Europe. We have both continued to teach, consult, and coach church planters in over forty countries. Most examples in this book that are not attributed to another source come from our own personal experience, observation, or interviews with church planters. Furthermore we have both taught church planting in formal academic settings and been involved in research of church planting. Our hope is to combine the best of these practical and biblical insights into a helpful volume for church planter practitioners, trainers, coaches, and teachers as well as mission leaders and leaders of local churches who partner with global church planting efforts. We have also written with the hope of providing a resource for the many grassroots church planters and trainers of church planters who work in Africa, Asia, and Latin America.

Such a work would not have been possible without the help and encouragement of many others. ReachGlobal, the mission agency with which we have served, has generously supported and encouraged us in this endeavor. Ben Sawatsky, a passionate church planter, keen strategist, and missionary statesman, has been an inspiring and encouraging mentor to us both. The research and experience of many of our students, particularly those at the Akademie für Weltmission (Korntal, Germany) and at Trinity Evangelical Divinity School (Deerfield, Illinois), have directly or indirectly contributed many of the insights shared on these pages. We are particularly grateful to Jim Kinney and his colleagues at Baker Academic for their competent assistance, and to our research assistant Ben Stevens for his efforts behind the scenes tracking sources, gathering data, and editing the manuscript. Last but not least, we thank our life partners, Linda and Alice, for their support, patience, and encouragement, which played no small part in bringing this work to completion.

For more information and resources to help apply the principles and practices found in this book, visit www.globalchurchplanting.net.

Prologue

The Parable of the Apple Trees

Once upon a time there was a land where many people were starving. It was a terrible time of suffering, and no one seemed to know what to do. The apple trees of the town were moved with compassion, especially as they saw the many hungry children with gaunt faces. They decided that they could be part of the solution. Each tree would try to increase its harvest to provide more food.

One particular tree had an especially great vision to become the largest and most productive tree that could feed hundreds of people. He determined to extend his branches wider and sink his roots deeper. And he did. He grew greater and stronger, with broad and graceful branches. His trunk was stately as a Corinthian column, his roots sinuous and muscular. He became very productive, the envy of all other apple trees, doubling, even tripling, the number of apples that he could grow, feeding more and more people. And the apples that he bore were the tastiest and largest apples to be found. He was also very concerned that no fruit go to waste. So he developed a way to hold on to his fruit until the harvesters arrived, not letting a single apple drop to the ground. It was a brilliant plan. Many children were nourished and survived the winter thanks to him.

This tree became quite a sensation among apple growers and was admired by everyone in town for his commitment to feeding the hungry. Soon apple growers were coming from far and wide to discover how this tree could produce so much and such wonderful fruit. He became known as "Mega-tree."

But Mega-tree gradually became frustrated. His branches grew so wide and heavy that each year when the fall winds would blow large branches would crack. Some would come crashing down, wasting precious fruit and slowing production. These would have to be regrown if the same number of apples were to be harvested next year. One year the winds were so strong, and Mega-tree had grown so large, that he was nearly uprooted altogether. That gave him a pretty big scare. But what disturbed Mega-tree most was his realization that he had reached his productive capacity. No matter how hard he tried, he just couldn't increase production any more. And worst of all, he realized that there were many hungry people he still could not feed.

Mega-tree remained faithful to his task and continued to produce many good apples, but the once-grand vision faded and his joy began to wane. Over time his trunk became gnarled, and his fruit wasn't quite as sweet as in the early years. Apple growers stopped visiting him and looked for other large, productive trees from whom they could learn.

Meanwhile there was another apple tree in town. This tree was also moved with compassion and wanted to feed as many hungry people as possible, but he was rather small and unseemly. His fruit was not very sweet, and sometimes it was even a bit wormy. And he didn't produce a tenth of the harvest that Mega-tree produced. He was embarrassed by the fact that his fruit often fell to the ground and rotted before it could be harvested, so of the little fruit that he did bear, less still went to feed the hungry. Apple growers of course took no notice of him and would walk right past him on the way to visit Mega-tree. So unbeautiful was this tree that he received the nickname "Twiggy."

Twiggy began to feel sorry for himself. "You're a poor excuse for a tree," he would woefully say to himself over and over, shaking his boughs sadly. "You'll never be able to feed many of the hungry." Looking over at the elegant and expansive branches of Mega-tree, he'd see the many crates of large, beautiful apples being harvested, and that made him feel even more like a failure. It also made him a bit jealous, which he didn't like to admit to himself. Sometimes he'd make excuses for himself: "It's the soil. If I had the soil that Mega-tree has, I could do what he does." But he knew in his heart it wasn't really true.

One day as Twiggy's eyes were cast toward the ground in a sulk, he noticed something quite odd. There not far from his roots grew a little plant. Upon closer inspection, it proved in fact to be a little baby apple tree. At first he thought, "Oh no! That's just what I need now—someone with whom I have to share this lousy, unfertile soil! I'll probably bear even less fruit once he grows up. His roots will probably get tangled with mine. He might even block my sunlight."

Twiggy's resentment grew toward both Mega-tree and Baby-tree until suddenly he was struck by a thought, as if stuck by lightning (and for a tree that's a pretty shocking experience). He realized that Baby-tree was a result of one of Twiggy's apples falling to the ground. As if that thought wasn't earthshaking enough, another followed quickly: "If I just keep letting some of my apples fall so that their seeds grow into trees, there could be lots of new apple trees bearing fruit and feeding many more people." Though Twiggy was not very good at math, he knew enough to reason, "In fact, the sum of all those apples on trees growing from my seeds will be more, yes, *much* more, than even Mega-tree is producing. We could feed many more people."

"But wait!" Twiggy mused further. "What if my baby trees also let some of their apples fall to the ground? Then they would grow into even more new trees bearing even more fruit and feeding even more people. And then those trees could also drop some fruit, and then . . . by golly, we could feed the whole world at that rate!" And so it was that Twiggy gladly began letting some of his apples fall to the ground. Some passersby sneered, "How wasteful! You'll never amount to anything." Or they jeered, "Why don't you take a lesson from Mega-tree?" But Twiggy just kept on quietly, faithfully letting some apples fall, and as he had hoped, some of his offspring followed his example. Soon enough there were apple trees growing throughout the whole land. And though none of the new trees ever was as impressive as Mega-tree, no children or grownups ever needed to go hungry in that town.

The moral of the story: If you want to feed more people, don't merely grow more apples, bigger apples, and sweeter apples; rather, plant more apple trees that in turn can reproduce yet more apple trees to grow exponentially more fruit. And if we want to feed a spiritually hungry world, we must seek to not merely grow bigger and better churches that reach more people (though that is certainly a good thing to do) but to plant churches that in turn reproduce more churches, that reach exponentially more people.

Part I

BIBLICAL
FOUNDATIONS

1

The Task of Church Planting

Many church planters are enthusiastic about their calling and the challenge of launching into such an exciting endeavor. Because church planters often have pioneering and entrepreneurial personalities, they sometimes have little patience for defining goals or answering fundamental questions about the nature of the task. But not doing so is like setting out to build a house without blueprints. Even allowing for unexpected developments and creative freedom, it's essential to have a good idea of the nature and goal of the task if it is to be fulfilled.

Years ago a cartoon frequently shown on German television depicted a character shooting an arrow rather randomly at a wall, then walking to the wall and drawing the bull's-eye around the point where the arrow struck. Such a method ensures that you're always on target! Oddly enough, some church planters do seem to shoot first and draw the target later. Given the growing number of church planters who have had little formal biblical or theological training, the need is all the greater to begin by defining terms and becoming clear about the nature of the church and what it thus means to plant a church. This is particularly important when one is planting a church in another culture. Of course entire books have been written on the nature of the church. This chapter maps in summary fashion a theological blueprint for the practical work of church planting.

What Is a Church?

Defining the church is the first obvious step in understanding church planting. Our natural tendency is to envision planting congregations that look and act something like our home church, even though the church may be planted in another culture or under very different circumstances. One tacitly assumes that this is the best or only biblical form of the church.

However, a careful look at the New Testament reveals that the first-century churches took a number of forms, meeting in various places and with differing emphases and structures. The church in Jerusalem, for example, which included members who were "zealous for the law," continued to observe many Jewish practices such as participation in certain temple rites (Acts 2:46; 5:42; 21:20, 26). The predominantly Gentile churches had no such practices and met primarily in homes. Yet all were legitimate New Testament churches suited to their contexts.

Many elements of church life with which we are familiar at home may be neither biblically necessary nor culturally appropriate in a different setting. Does a congregation have to have a paid pastor, own a building, celebrate weekly Sunday morning services, or have legal status including a formal constitution and bylaws to be a "real" church? These may be desirable, but by New Testament standards they are hardly essential. Many of the churches planted by Paul would not meet what many today might consider a minimal standard for being an established church. Nevertheless, he addressed even the most problematical congregations as "the church." This forces us to consider more carefully what genuinely constitutes a local church in the biblical sense.

Every leader in a church-planting team should judiciously study the Scriptures and seek to answer these and many other questions about the life and nature of the church. One must distinguish between that which is biblically mandated and essential and that which is nonessential. The Scriptures allow great freedom in the details of church life and polity. Cross-cultural church planters must take extra care not to impose foreign expressions of church life, but to creatively develop the new church in ways that fulfill biblical purposes in a culturally appropriate manner. At the same time the church should demonstrate the countercultural values of the kingdom of God.

Church planters must clarify their ecclesiology in their own minds prior to launching a plant. A biblical study on the nature of the church should be included in the early teaching of any church plant,[1] allowing local believers to help determine what forms the church should take to fulfill biblical purposes in the local context. While there is no substitute for turning directly to the

---

1. Consider studying for example the book of Acts on evangelism and church life, Ephesians on nature of the church and biblical metaphors of the church, the Pastoral Epistles on church order and leadership, or 1 Peter 2 on the continuity of the people of God in Old and New Testaments.

Scriptures for our understanding of the church, there is also much value in becoming familiar with historical teachings on the church and learning how the church has taken shape in other contexts (see chapter 6 on the shape of the church and contextualization).[2]

We must begin by understanding the essential *nature* of the church. A summary of various understandings of the essence of the church is found in table 1.1. First and foremost, the church is a *spiritual* entity, conceived by the Father (Eph. 1:3–6), built by Christ (Matt. 16:18), and indwelt by the Holy Spirit (Eph. 2:19–22). The church is God's primary vehicle for manifesting the nature of the kingdom of God in this age and among all people. This biblical vision of the church should capture our imagination and stir our hearts. What a glorious and holy privilege to be God's servants in the planting and establishing of local churches!

The early church fathers often spoke of the church as the fellowship of the saints. Emphasis was rightly placed on the church as a people rather than as an institution. Essential attributes of the church were summarized in the Nicene Creed (AD 381) as *one* (unity), *holy* (sanctified life), *catholic* (universal, for all people), and *apostolic* (based upon teaching of the apostles). These attributes have been variously interpreted through the history of the church,[3] but they are confessed by nearly all Christians. The Reformers focused more on essential *marks* of the church, in an attempt to discern what constitutes the true church in contrast to false expressions of the church. Luther spoke of the *right preaching of the Word* (doctrine) and *faithful administration of the sacraments* (baptism and the Lord's Supper) as the two essential marks. Reformed churches added the *exercise of church discipline*. Free churches emphasized the *personal regeneration and piety* of their members.[4]

2. People of other cultures often appreciate the importance of past wisdom and are rightly skeptical of innovations that have little continuity with history. Craig Van Gelder writes, "All thinking about the church, all ecclesiologies, reflect to some extent the historical circumstances of the eras in which they were developed. . . . All ecclesiologies must be seen as functioning relative to their context. There is no other way to be the church except within a concrete, historical setting. . . . New contexts require new expressions for understanding the church" (2000, 40–41).

3. For example *apostolic* has been taken by Roman Catholics to refer to apostolic succession, whereas some Protestants interpret it in terms of the apostolic-missionary sending of the church. Van Gelder writes, "For the church to be holy, it must seek to appropriate the redemptive power of God in its midst. For the church to be catholic, it must organize itself to be flexible and adaptive to new contexts. For the church to be apostolic, it must organize itself to be missional within all its ministry functions and through all its functions. For the church to be a communion of the saints, it must promote the building and strengthening of relationships through the exercise of both the fruit and the gifts of the Spirit" (2000, 52).

4. The term "free church" is used here generally for non–state churches—that is, churches such as Baptists or Pentecostals in contrast to churches such as the Catholic, Episcopal, Orthodox, or Lutheran churches. See discussion in Van Gelder 2000.

Table 1.1
The Essence of the Church

Nature	Marks
One	Right doctrine
Holy	Faithful administration of the sacraments
Catholic (universal)	Church discipline
Apostolic	Personal faith
Purpose	**Metaphors**
Witness, *martyria*	People of God
Fellowship, *koinonia*	Body of Christ
Service, *diakonia*	Flock of God
Proclamation, *kerygma*	Bride of Christ
Worship, *leiturgia*	Temple of God
	Royal priesthood

A more practical approach is to define the church in terms of its *purpose* and *work*. Acts 2:42 describes the basic activities of the church in terms of apostolic teaching, fellowship, breaking bread (and baptism), and prayer, to which are added worship and evangelism (v. 47) and then later the intentional sending of missionaries (Acts 13). Theologians have also spoken of the church's witness (*martyria*), fellowship (*koinonia*), service (*diakonia*), proclamation (*kerygma*), and worship (*leiturgia*).[5] Rick Warren's popular book *The Purpose-Driven Church* lists outreach (to evangelize), worship (to exalt), fellowship (to encourage), discipleship (to edify), and service (to equip) as biblical purposes that should be kept in balance and give the church direction. Yet another way to view the church is in terms of its *relationship to Christ*. Highly relational cultures, especially in Majority World settings, may find such an understanding more helpful than other approaches:

- confession of Christ as Lord (baptism)
- witnesses to Christ (evangelism)
- remembrance and fellowship of Christ (Lord's Supper)
- Spirit of Christ (filling, fruit, gifts)
- love of Christ (worship, devotion)
- Word of Christ (preaching, teaching)
- family of Christ (fellowship, community)
- sacrifice of Christ (stewardship, service)
- suffering of Christ (faithfulness, perseverance)

Note how the key biblical metaphors of the church also place the church in relationship to Christ—for example:

5. See, for example, Bate 1994.

- Christ as head of the body
- Christ as the good shepherd of his flock
- Christ as foundation, cornerstone, and builder of his church
- Christ as the door to the sheepfold

Based on this discussion we offer the following practical definition of a local church as we will be using the term in this book. *A local church is a fellowship of believers in Jesus Christ committed to gathering regularly for biblical purposes under a recognized spiritual leadership.* This very basic definition includes several key elements:

- *Believers.* The church is composed of persons who have experienced salvation through repentance and faith in Jesus Christ according to the gospel and confessed in baptism. They desire to be faithful disciples of Jesus Christ, regenerated and enabled by the Holy Spirit. They are the new people of God.
- *Gathering.* These believers are committed to meeting together regularly to serve God and one another.[6] They are the family of God. As a missionary people, they gather in preparation to be sent as agents of God's mission in the world.
- *Purpose.* Their fellowship gathers to fulfill biblical purposes that include prayer, worship, evangelism, instruction, edification, service, celebration of the ordinances of baptism and the Lord's Supper, exercise of church discipline, and the sending of missionaries. They embody values of the kingdom of God.
- *Leadership.* They submit to recognized spiritual leaders. Leaders provide a minimal form of structure under Christ's headship. In a spirit of servanthood they give direction, spiritual oversight, and care, teaching and equipping the body of believers.

This might be considered a minimal list of practical characteristics defining a church for the church planter. Isolated believers, special interest meetings, or unstructured gatherings alone do not constitute a church.

This definition leaves much room for flexibility. A paid pastor is not essential, but recognized leaders are. Church buildings are not necessary, but regular meetings are. Adherence to a particular creed or denominational distinctive is not required, but faithfulness to biblical truth and purposes is. Deep spiritual

6. See Robert Banks's (1994) discussion of the Greek term for the church, *ecclesia*, which in its profane usage primarily means an assembly. He argues that in Paul's early usage "the term is applied only to an *actual gathering of people* or the group that gathers as *a regularly constituted meeting* and not, as in today's usage, to a number of local assemblies conceived as part of a larger unit" (1994, 29–30).

maturity is a goal, but more essential is the believers' fundamental commitment to obedience in following Christ.

What Do We Mean by "Church Planting"?

Having defined what we mean by *church*, we can simply define church planting as that ministry which seeks to establish new churches. Normally this will be through evangelism, discipleship, and gathering of these persons into a functioning congregation. Most church planting will also have the longer-term goal of multiplication. We thus offer this definition: *Church planting is that ministry which through evangelism and discipleship establishes reproducing kingdom communities of believers in Jesus Christ who are committed to fulfilling biblical purposes under local spiritual leaders.*

Planting is a term used by the apostle Paul to describe his ministry of establishing new churches in 1 Corinthians 3:6: "I planted the seed, Apollos watered it, but God made it grow." Though Paul had a variety of gifts and ministries, here "planting" refers to his pioneering apostolic ministry of establishing new churches in locations and among people where there was no preexisting church. He makes this clear in Romans 15:20: "It has always been my ambition to preach the gospel where Christ was not known, so that I would not be building on someone else's foundation."

Complementary to planting or pioneering ministries are "watering" ministries such as that of Apollos noted in 1 Corinthians 3:6. Paul had sent him to Corinth to further instruct the church there (1 Cor. 16:12). Whereas the ministry of planting involves primarily evangelism, discipleship, and congregating, the ministry of watering involves further teaching and strengthening churches that have already been gathered. Both planters and waterers are essential to the long-term goal of establishing healthy, reproducing churches. When we speak of "church planting" in this book we are broadly referring to the entire process of planting (in the sense of pioneering) and early watering leading to the establishing of healthy new churches.

Church Planting as a Spiritual Undertaking

Most of this book will discuss the process and practical methods of church planting. But we must keep foremost in our minds that church planting is essentially a spiritual undertaking, done primarily by spiritual means. Jesus is the real church planter, as he promised, "I will build my church" (Matt. 16:18). The Great Commission as recorded in Matthew 28:19–20, to go and make disciples of all nations, is sandwiched between the affirmation that all authority in heaven and on earth is given to Jesus (v. 18) and the promise of Jesus's presence with the disciples until the end of the age (v. 20). Only through "remaining in Christ" can our ministry bear fruit; indeed, apart from Jesus we can do nothing (John 15:5). John's Gospel furthermore recalls Jesus's promise that the Holy Spirit would convince unbelievers of sin, righteousness, and judgment and thus of their need for salvation in Christ (John 16:8).

Luke's Gospel ends with Jesus's command to wait in carrying out the Great Commission until they have been "clothed with power from on high" (Luke 24:49). Nothing could be clearer from Luke's second volume, the book of Acts, than the centrality of the enabling and empowering work of the Holy Spirit in the spread of the gospel and establishment of churches. For example:

- power for witness and preaching (Acts 1:8; 4:8)
- granting boldness in the midst of persecution (Acts 4:31)
- strengthening and comforting the churches (Acts 9:31)
- guidance in decision making (Acts 16:6–10)
- calling and sending missionaries (Acts 13:2–4)
- confirming the apostolic preaching through signs and wonders (Acts 2:43; 4:16; 5:12; 6:8; 8:6, 13; 14:3; 15:12; 19:11)

It was the Lord who added new believers to the church (Acts 2:47) and the Lord who opened the hearts of those who heard the gospel (Acts 2:37; 16:14). Luke also writes of the growth of the church in terms of the Word of God increasing, spreading, and multiplying (Acts 6:7; 12:24; 13:49; 19:20). Human agents play a subordinate role.

The same emphasis can be found in letters of the apostle Paul. God's power to save is in the gospel itself, not in the messenger (Rom. 1:16; 1 Cor. 1:18). The message must be proclaimed in the power of the Holy Spirit (Rom. 15:18–19; 1 Cor. 2:4–5; 1 Thess. 1:5). The church in Corinth had become divided by concentrating on various workers and particular spiritual gifts. To correct this Paul redirects their attention in 1 Corinthians 3:5–10 to the more central truth that ultimately it is God who is at work through the people and their gifts (accented via italics below):

> What, after all, is Apollos? And what is Paul? Only servants, through whom you came to believe—as the *Lord* has assigned to each his task. I planted the seed, Apollos watered it, but *God* made it grow. So neither he who plants nor he who waters is anything, but only *God*, who makes things grow. The man who plants and the man who waters have one purpose, and each will be rewarded according to his own labor. For we are *God's* fellow workers; you are *God's* field, *God's* building. By the grace *God* has given me, I laid a foundation as an expert builder, and someone else is building on it.

The advance of the gospel will face spiritual opposition. The expansion of the church in Acts encountered persecution, demonic opposition, and human failure.

Paul writes of the spiritual nature of much opposition (e.g., 2 Cor. 10:2–4; Eph. 6:12). Yet Scripture makes equally clear that Christ has overcome all spiritual principalities and powers (e.g., Rom. 8:35–39; Col. 1:16). Though we have no assurance that every individual attempt to plant a church will succeed, we do have the promise that ultimately the cause of Christ will prevail with his words: "I will build my church; and the gates of Hades will not overcome it" (Matt. 16:18).

These truths should give church planters great confidence that the fruitfulness of their efforts is ultimately dependent on God's working. This does not excuse us from preparing well, working hard, and evaluating carefully. But it frees us from unnecessary pressure to produce results and from a needless sense of failure when, after giving our best, we see little visible fruit of our labors. It equally guards us against pride and boasting when we experience great blessing in our ministry. Walking and working by faith should characterize our attitude in ministry. Full dependency on God should be the "method behind the methods." Finally, these truths should move the church planter to greater prayer. Prayer or praying is mentioned twenty-six times in the book of Acts. Paul's letters to his churches abound with examples of how he prayed for them and their spiritual growth (e.g., Eph. 1:15–23; 3:14–19; Phil. 1:3–6, 9–11; 2 Thess. 1:11–12). These serve as wonderful examples of how church planters can pray for their church plants and people.

Church planting is a thoroughly spiritual endeavor. We may employ the most proven methods—and methods *are* important—but they are no substitute for prayer and deep dependence on divine guidance and working. It is possible by human means to establish an institution that has all the outward appearance of a church. But a true church is the creation of the Holy Spirit.

Church Planting—An Undertaking Demanding Wisdom and Insight

Church planting is not only a spiritual undertaking; it is also a complex human undertaking. Many a church planter has been passionately committed but practically unprepared and naive, leading to unnecessary frustration and often failure. Proverbs 19:2 reads, "It is not good to have zeal without knowledge, nor to be hasty and miss the way." God has given us the capacity for insight and understanding so that we might better understand his ways and exercise greater wisdom in his service. There are several ways we can seek to be better informed, discern God's wisdom, and be better stewards of our energy in the ministry of church planting.

- *Biblical teaching.* Though the world of the New Testament was very different than the world today, we can still glean many important principles from the example of the first Christians as they spread the gospel and planted churches.

- *Prayer.* James 1:5 gives us the promise: "If any of you lacks wisdom, he should ask God, who gives generously to all without finding fault, and it will be given to him."
- *History.* We can learn lessons from the history of missions and church planting, discovering some means God has blessed and some pitfalls to avoid. The adage is all too true: if we fail to learn from history we are condemned to repeat it.
- *Social sciences.* The social sciences help us understand human behavior and societies. If we want to serve people well, we must understand them deeply. Social sciences help us overcome blind spots and discover in a disciplined manner factors that will lead us toward effective ministry, addressing people's deepest needs in both biblical and culturally appropriate ways.
- *Best practices.* Some of the most helpful insights are gained as church planters share with one another and seek to discern together best practices for church planting. One caution here is that effective methods in one setting may have little application to another.

There is a difference between sound wisdom and crass pragmatism in which the end justifies the means. Further, the best methods are no guarantee of success—only Christ can build his church. But God works through human means, and he generally chooses to work through well-prepared and informed servants who are humble and teachable and who make use of every available means to advance his cause.

When Might a Church Be Considered "Planted"?

How does the church planter know when his or her job is done? When should the church be considered "planted"? At what point does the church planter and/or the church planting team move on and entrust the church fully to local leaders? The Bible does not give us a checklist to use in answering these questions. Missionary church planters have been notorious for staying too long, dominating the church, and having the attitude that local believers are never quite far enough along to survive without the missionary. The opposite extreme occasionally occurs as well: the church planter, having failed to develop local leaders disengages abruptly and the church withers and dies.

Some writers looking to the example of the apostle Paul suggest that a church should be considered planted very shortly after the first believers have been congregated (e.g., Allen 1962a, 3). Indeed, in most cases Paul left the churches within only a few weeks or months after their initial establishment. In Asia Minor he and Barnabas even installed elders in the churches shortly after the initial evangelization and then considered the work "completed"

(Acts 14:23, 26).[7] Thus a qualified and recognized local leadership seems to be essential.

However, concluding that missionary involvement should be curtailed quickly after the gathering of the first converts overlooks the larger biblical picture. Paul's quick departure was often prompted by persecution, not by plan. Paul remained over two years in Ephesus, where God had opened up to him a "great door for effective work" (1 Cor. 16:9), thereby postponing other pioneering work. The biblical report also makes clear that continued assistance was given to these fledging congregations through follow-up visits, letters, and sending of additional coworkers. Thus more careful analysis of the Bible reveals that planting healthy churches involves much more than short-term campaigns that leave new congregations to fend for themselves. Paul's church-planting method installed local leaders and entrusted responsibilities to them quickly, but various forms of longer-term assistance were also provided to the young churches.

From the example of Paul and his coworkers, we discover that disengagement from a church plant can be viewed as a process of shifting emphases and responsibilities as the church matures. Rather than an abrupt withdrawal, missionary phase-out can be a gradual process with various team members serving in differing capacities and with diminishing levels of contact and assistance. The biblical examples also demonstrate that various gifts and talents are needed during the progressing phases of planting and establishing churches.

In keeping with our definition of a church, we suggest the following short-term goals as a measure for phasing out the church planter's or church-planting team's involvement:

- Persons from the locality or focus people have been led to faith in Christ, discipled, and congregated into a fellowship of mutually committed believers meeting regularly.
- A qualified local spiritual leadership team (ideally from the focus people) has been called and recognized by the congregation. They guide, teach, and appropriately apply the Scriptures in their lives and society.
- Culturally appropriate structures for fellowship, worship, evangelism, service, and governance are functioning.
- Local believers have internalized biblical values and goals. Kingdom purposes for the church are being progressively lived out.

The church might be considered "planted" when the above short-term goals are achieved. However, the longer-term development of the church must be

---

7. Paul considered the work in Crete "unfinished" because qualified elders had not yet been appointed (Titus 1:5), but we are not sure how long the church in Crete had existed when this was written.

kept in view if genuine kingdom communities are to be established. After his or her departure, the church planter may continue to encourage the church toward the attainment of longer-term goals. Such goals would include the following, among others:

- church multiplication by planting daughter churches, sending church planters, and sending or supporting missionaries[8]
- the establishment of local ministries that demonstrate kingdom values of compassion and justice
- initiation of specialized ministries to ethnic groups, subcultures, or special-needs persons
- creation of contextualized practices relating to local customs, traditions, and ceremonies
- being linked to or helping to form a national or regional fellowship of churches (see "interdependent fellowships" below)
- participation in local or regional initiatives with other churches

Attaining such goals is rarely possible during the pioneering phase. But the values and vision for such longer-term goals must be instilled early in the planting of the church.

What Kind of Church Is to Be Planted?

Unfortunately many books on church planting and growth give little attention to the kind of church that is to be planted. However, if churches are to be planted as we have attempted to biblically define them, they must adhere to more than some minimal definition or denominational standard. They must be *kingdom communities*, *healthy congregations*, *reproducing organisms*, *indigenous churches*, and *interdependent fellowships*.

Kingdom Communities

A biblical understanding of the church will lead us to plant churches that are *kingdom communities*. New Testament scholars and evangelical missiologists alike recognize the centrality of Jesus's teaching on the kingdom of God for our understanding of the church and mission. Kingdom communities are congregations of Christians who embody and live out kingdom values as Jesus taught them. Their essence is found first in their relationship to the King, Jesus

8. Stuart Murray goes so far as to claim, "Self-propagation, or reproduction, is not just an admirable quality of some churches, but integral to the definition of the church" (1998, 60).

Christ, and second in their obedience to the will of the King explicitly stated in the Scriptures. Simply stated: they are Christ centered and Bible based.

Kingdom communities are formed of people who are born of the Spirit, who enter God's kingdom with childlike faith, and who are poor in spirit.[9] They are characterized by the values of the Sermon on the Mount. They strive for personal holiness.[10] They know that they may experience suffering and tribulation in this world, but they live in the hope that the fullness of the kingdom will appear when Christ returns.[11] Kingdom communities become a transforming, countercultural witness and movement having an impact on persons, families, communities, cities, and nations. The power of the gospel becomes active in them, and they become the salt of the earth and light of the world.[12] No church is perfect or without sin, but every church should be a sign and foretaste of the kingdom of God. David Shenk and Erwin Stutzman write,

> Church planting is thus the most urgent business of humankind. It is through the creation (or planting) of churches that God's kingdom is extended into communities which have not yet been touched by the precious surprise of the presence of the kingdom of God in their midst. . . . The transforming grace of God recreates the visible presence of the kingdom of God in that cluster of people who are committed to Jesus Christ as Lord and Savior. (1988, 23)

In chapter 19 we will discuss further the nature of churches that have kingdom impact.

It will not do to merely plant churches focused narrowly on their own private concerns or confined to routine Christian programs. Church history is replete with tragic lessons of what happens when churches fail to live out their kingdom calling. In light of the hundreds of thousands of Rwandans killed in tribal warfare in a country supposed to be predominantly Christian, one observer wrote:

> One of the "facts" we loudly proclaimed was that 20,000 or so Africans were becoming Christians every day. Of course, no one denies the phenomenal turning to Christ in recent decades all across sub-Saharan Africa. But in the midst of this ingathering of souls, apparently we have not stopped to consider our long-term biblical mandate, which is not simply to gather converts but to assimilate them into churches where their character will be shaped by biblical values and standards. We have not paid sufficient attention to serious warnings about the high risks of a truncated understanding of our mission. (Reapsome 1995, 4)

9. Matthew 5:3; 18:4; 19:14; Luke 18:17; John 3:3–7.
10. Matthew 5:20; 7:21; 1 Corinthians 6:9–10; Galatians 5:19–21; 2 Peter 1:10–11.
11. Matthew 5:10; Acts 14:22; 2 Thessalonians 1:5; Titus 2:13; Hebrews 9:28.
12. Matthew 5:13–16.

Other historical examples might include the Crusades of the Middle Ages, racism in churches of North America, uncritical acceptance of Hitler's National Socialism in German churches, and apartheid in many churches of South Africa.

Healthy Congregations

In recent years considerable attention has been given to the topic of church health. In Revelation 2–3 Jesus himself examines the seven churches of Asia Minor, gives his assessment of their health—their strengths and weaknesses— and declares what corrective measures are to be taken. As churches are being planted, it is important to keep in view indicators of church health that not only serve to identify symptoms of unhealthy developments but can also give positive direction for church life. Various lists of church health indicators have been formulated (see table 13.1 for examples).

Unhealthy churches rarely reproduce, unless they reproduce through conflicts that result in church splits. Church health is normally a reflection of the spiritual health of the leaders. However, sometimes churches develop in unhealthy ways simply because of blind spots, ignorance, or circumstances that are beyond the control of the leaders. Healthy congregations are congregations with a healthy relationship to Jesus, a healthy understanding of the gospel, a healthy commitment to their calling, and a healthy (and honest) assessment of their strengths and weaknesses. Such churches will have kingdom impact and are in the best position to reproduce.

Reproducing Organisms

One of the consistent themes throughout this book is the importance of planting churches that reproduce. Reproduction is a part of life: all healthy living organisms reproduce. The church is not an institution but a living organism, the body of Christ. As we shall see, reproduction was a characteristic of New Testament churches and central to the apostle Paul's missionary strategy. Only as churches reproduce can the world be reached with the gospel. In chapter 7 we will discover many different ways that churches can reproduce. Church planters must seek to plant churches that have in their very DNA the vision and commitment to reproduce and ultimately multiply. Having this as a goal has far-reaching implications for the methods church planters use. Thus the methodologies that we recommend in these pages seek to keep this longer-range goal in view.

Indigenous Churches

Churches that we plant are to be *indigenous*. In chapter 4 we will discuss in greater detail the nature of an indigenous reproducing church. An indigenous church is one that is primarily composed of and led by local believers. It has become rooted in the local culture in such a way that under the guidance and power of the Holy Spirit it develops its life and ministry in culturally appropriate ways. A palm tree will not thrive and reproduce in Alaska, and a fir tree will wither and die in the desert. They are not indigenous to the local climate and environment and are unable to adapt. Similarly, an indigenous church must be suited to and rooted in its cultural environment in such a way that it can thrive in the local setting while at the same time living out countercultural kingdom purposes. A church that is foreign dominated or foreign in nature will generally have difficulty thriving and reproducing.

The history of missions is replete with examples of missionaries who disregarded local culture, planted foreign-looking churches, established ministries that were not locally sustainable, and became closely associated with foreign powers. The churches planted were sometimes like David in Saul's armor: encumbered with structures, forms, and ministries that fit another time and place but were inappropriate in theirs. Local believers were sometimes viewed as cultural traitors, or worse, as instruments of subversive foreign influence. Furthermore, missionaries have often had condescending, paternalistic attitudes toward local believers, denying ordination to them for decades, underestimating the work of the Holy Spirit in their lives, and exercising power over them through control of finances or by retaining positions of authority. The stated goal of self-governing churches remained something for the distant future because the local leaders never seemed to be quite ready.

Like the goal of reproduction, this basic goal of planting indigenous churches has far-reaching implications for both the methods of church planting and the attitudes of the church planter. The cross-cultural church planter must spare no effort to understand the local people and culture, plant the church in a culturally relevant way, with locally sustainable structures, and empower local leaders for ministry.

Interdependent Fellowships

In many situations the question arises whether the new church should become affiliated with a preexisting association of churches or denomination. Missionary church planters often partner with an existing national church. To what extent should the church cooperate with local ecumenical associations, ministerial fellowships, or an evangelical alliance? These are important questions that need to be addressed at the outset of a church-planting ministry. Sometimes they will be answered by the sponsoring agency. Other times they must be answered by the church planter or local believers.

All too often church planters have worked in a spirit of independence or even competition. Sometimes other Christians and churches in the locality or region are simply ignored. Cross-cultural church planters might assume that they have little to learn from the local believers and do not need their assistance. They may think they have all the answers that they learned in seminary, in the home church, by having read the latest book, or by attending the latest seminar. The churches they plant are, not surprisingly, also independently minded, having little connection with others either locally or internationally.

Jesus, however, prayed for his disciples and those who were to follow, "that all of them may be one, Father, just as you are in me and I am in you. May they also be in us so that the world may believe that you have sent me" (John 17:21). Evangelicals are often quick to note that in this prayer organizational unity is not primarily in view. Yet some form of visible spiritual unity is to be evident if the world (i.e., unbelievers) is to notice and recognize that Jesus was sent by the Father. In other words, demonstration of Christian unity and fellowship has implications for evangelism!

The churches of the New Testament were not independent but interdependent in various ways. Though they did not have denominational structures in the modern sense, neither were they fully autonomous. The predominantly Gentile church in Antioch submitted to the leadership and decision of the Jerusalem Council (Acts 15:30–31). The predominantly Gentile churches planted by Paul were expected to assist the Jerusalem church in famine relief (1 Cor. 16:1–4; 2 Cor. 8). Paul recruited coworkers from the various churches that he planted, and they ministered, at times exercising authority, in other churches. No church should exist entirely in isolation from other churches. A spirit of unity and cooperation with other believers locally, nationally, and internationally should be instilled. Such relationships may be very informal or may be quite binding. This will depend on local circumstances and theological convictions.

Missionary church planters have often sought to create a new denomination or movement reflecting particular doctrinal positions or methods of ministry from the sending church. This has resulted in an unfortunate proliferation of denominations and independent churches throughout the world. One of the positive developments in recent decades is a greater spirit of partnership between foreign mission efforts and national church bodies in host countries. Mission agencies and cross-cultural church planters are increasingly seeking like-minded partners in the host country who share compatible doctrine, lifestyle, and vision. There are many advantages to such partnerships in church planting:

- Unity in the body of Christ is demonstrated.
- Better stewardship of resources and gifts is achieved.
- Missionaries and nationals can form joint church-planting teams.
- Expatriate church planters can do internships under national pastors or church planters and thus better adapt and understand ministry in the culture.

- Identification with a national association or fellowship of churches can give the church plant identity, credibility, and legal status.
- Local believers have a greater sense of being a part of the larger church of Christ and not merely an isolated or foreign religious sect.
- The national church may receive new impetus for evangelism and church planting through its relationship with the foreign missionary.

We shall return to effective methods for forming international congregation-to-congregation partnerships and the use of short-term mission teams in chapter 18. Such partnerships require time, patience, and commitment, but they can result in great rewards and true synergy in mission.

2

The Reasons
for Church Planting

During recent decades there has been a renewed focus on church planting in evangelical missionary activity. Church planting appears in the vision and purpose statements of many mission agencies. Concern for unreached peoples—that is, ethnic groups without a viable Christian witness and local church—has spawned new efforts to "adopt a people" and to undertake pioneer church planting among them. Denominations have come to recognize that church planting is essential to the long-term growth and health of a movement. Church planting has become a topic of interest even among mainline churches in Europe, amid growing awareness that the society has become post-Christian and even nominal church membership is dramatically falling. And yet the theological reflection on and rationale for church planting has often been rather shallow.[1] In this chapter we present first the biblical mandate and then the practical reasons for church planting.

The Biblical Mandate for Church Planting

Church planting is more than a practical necessity. It is a biblical mandate! Roman Catholic theologians have long affirmed the centrality of church plant-

---

1. Several writers in Great Britain have developed a theological rationale for church planting, such as Martin Robinson and Stuart Christine (1992), David Dunn Wilson (1996), Stewart Murray (1998), and Tim Chester (2000). But in North America few have taken notice of these writers.

ing.[2] The earliest Protestant to seriously reflect on mission was the Dutch Reformer Gisbertus Voetius, who formulated a threefold purpose of mission as conversion, church planting, and glorification of God's grace (Jongeneel 1991). This formula has influenced numerous missiologists since. Though church planting was not always a stated objective of Protestant mission agencies, it has always been a practical necessity. Numerous mission leaders and theologians have advocated church planting as central to the task of mission.[3] For example, Georg Vicedom, in his classic *The Mission of God*, concluded, "Therefore the goal of mission is the proclamation of the message to all mankind and gathering them into the church" (1965, 103).

However, theological writings and conferences in recent decades have seldom mentioned church planting as in any way central to mission. Evangelical missiologists have increasingly emphasized holistic mission and the kingdom of God while rarely even mentioning church planting. While this emphasis may reflect a correction of earlier imbalanced evangelical views, the neglect of church planting in current theologies of mission is also in need of correction. Because the church itself is central to God's mission, church planting must be central to that mission.

Mission practice and theology have grown apart, and this is a dangerous development. With the short space here we can only sketch the primary biblical reasons for church planting. Though there is no explicit command in the Bible to go and plant churches, the biblical record leaves no mistake that church planting is essential to God's salvation purposes and the fulfillment of the Great Commission.

Church Planting as Part of Salvation History

Salvation history is the story of God's redemptive acts, including his calling a people—not merely individuals—to be his instruments in carrying out his plan of redemption. As one writer states it, "God's way of relating to his troubled world has been to seek out a community of people who will dedicate themselves to fulfilling his compassionate and liberating will for all, on behalf of all" (Kirk 2000, 31). This call began in Genesis 12 with Abraham, who was to become a great nation bringing blessing to all nations (Gen. 12:3). The promise is passed on to the people of Israel, who were to be the instruments of God's salvific purposes in the world. Unfortunately Israel failed. The Messiah would, however, come and fulfill the role of "light for the Gentiles (or nations)" and "servant of the LORD" (Isa. 42:6; 49:3–6).

2. See for example the discussion in Oborji 2006.
3. These include among others Robert Speer (1902, 39–40), Roland Allen (1962a, 81), H. W. Schomerus (1935), Hendrik Kraemer (1938, 287), Walter Freytag (1961, 2:184), and David Hesselgrave (1980, 29, 33).

Based on the redemptive work of Christ, a new people of God, the church of Jesus Christ, is formed in the New Testament. They are to carry on his salvific purposes and spread the news of his kingdom, becoming a "light for the Gentiles" (Acts 13:47). One becomes a part of this new people not by natural birth but by spiritual birth (John 3:3–5). The continuity of God's purposes through a people is nowhere more clearly and beautifully stated than in 1 Peter 2:9–10: "But you are a chosen people, a royal priesthood, a holy nation, a people belonging to God, that you may declare the praises of him who called you out of darkness into his wonderful light. Once you were not a people, but now you are the people of God; once you had not received mercy, but now you have received mercy." Peter echoes terms used of Israel in the Old Testament (Exod. 19:5–6), applying them to the church. The church becomes the instrument of God's glory and eternal plan, as Paul writes, so that through it the wisdom of God may become manifest, not only to the nations but to rulers and authorities in heavenly places (Eph. 3:10).

The book of Revelation describes the culmination of salvation history, emphasizing that God will bring into the kingdom persons from every people, nation, tribe, and tongue (Rev. 5:9; 7:9). The marriage supper of the Lamb, when Christ receives the church as his bride, will be a time of great rejoicing (Rev. 19:6–8). This will be one of the culminating events of salvation history. Church planting is the ministry of proclaiming the gospel and forming kingdom communities among every nation, tribe, people, and tongue to glorify God in time and eternity! Tim Chester rightly summarizes, "If the church is at the heart of God's work, we need not be embarrassed about making it the heart of mission" (2000, 29).

Christ Loves the Church and Desires to Build His Church

Christ states his explicit will regarding the church in Matthew 16:18: "And I tell you that you are Peter, and on this rock I will build my church, and the gates of Hades will not overcome it." We cannot enter into a full discussion of this passage in all its complexity here. But one thing is clear: for Christ to build his church, he must plant his church—churches must be called into existence. We should be cautious about interpreting this text in an overly abstract manner. The *ekklesia* is simply the assembly of God's people. Matthew's only other use of the term *ekklesia* occurs in a very practical context of church discipline in 18:17. Specific assemblies of believers are in view, and these collectively comprise the universal church. Christ will build his universal church by planting and building local communities of believers.

The church planter can be assured that to engage in the task of church planting is to obey the expressed will of Christ. Christ himself will be the church builder. The passage also indicates that spiritual opposition is to be reckoned with. However, Christ will prevail. Individual church plants may fail, but the ultimate cause of building Christ's global church, his kingdom people, will not.

The church is *Christ's* own church, not ours. As George Eldon Ladd comments on this passage, "Jesus' announcement of his purpose to build his *ekklesia* suggests primarily . . . that the fellowship established by Jesus stands in direct continuity with the Old Testament Israel. The distinctive element is that this *ekklesia* is in a peculiar way the *ekklesia* of Jesus: 'My *ekklesia*'" (1974, 110).

A second passage indicating the value of church planting is Ephesians 5:25–27: "Husbands, love your wives, just as Christ loved the church and gave himself up for her to make her holy, cleansing her by the washing of water through the word, and to present her to himself as the radiant church, without stain or wrinkle or any other blemish, but holy and blameless." The church is Christ's bride. He loves her. He gave his life for her. Not only has he purchased the church through his work of redemption on the cross, but he is sanctifying her. Though she has many flaws and blemishes today, one day she will be beautified and perfected as she is received into Christ's eternal presence. Thus Christ both builds his church and sanctifies his church.

From these passages we see that church planting and church edification is the work of Christ himself. This is a most noble undertaking, one near to the heart of God, both mandated and empowered by Christ. Church planting is not merely a "method of evangelism." Indeed evangelism should lead to the building of the church. The church is not an afterthought, not merely a place where individual Christians happen to meet for mutual encouragement. It is the object of Christ's love and the instrument of his service in the world.

The Great Commission Entails Church Planting

Two aspects of the Great Commission as formulated in Matthew 28:18–20 entail church planting: the command to baptize and the command to teach obedience to all that Christ commanded. These are virtually impossible to fulfill apart from planting churches. The command to baptize reminds us that conversion includes entry into the new community of Christ. Baptism is often viewed as an individualistic event. Indeed it is a public confession of personal repentance and faith, but beyond this it indicates reception into the body of Christ, the new kingdom community. "For we were all baptized by one Spirit into one body—whether Jews or Greeks, slave or free—and we were all given the one Spirit to drink" (1 Cor. 12:13). Similar to proselyte baptism among the Jews, early Christian baptism indicated identification with a community—a meaning that we have largely lost today. In other words, to baptize is to enfold into a Christian community, the church.[4]

Christ calls us to make disciples who obey all that Jesus commanded. The command to teach obedience also assumes committed participation in the new

---

4. Hans-Werner Gensichen writes of the command to baptize in Matthew 28, "Enfolding in the church is assumed as an integral part of mission" (1971, 134). The only biblical example we have where this is not clearly the case is the baptism of the Ethiopian eunuch in Acts 8:38–39.

community of Christ. Preaching the gospel and converting the lost only begin to fulfill the Great Commission. The commands of Christ cannot be kept by one individual alone, and the kingdom of Christ cannot be demonstrated in isolation. Where there are no communities of disciples, they must be created. Mission must be considered incomplete without the planting of churches among every people. Because disciples are to be made of all nations, the work of church planting cannot be considered completed until communities of disciples have been established among every people.

Acts: New Churches Are the Normal and Necessary Result of Biblical Mission

Everywhere in the book of Acts, where evangelism occurs, churches are created.[5] Believers are found meeting together in homes or in public places for prayer, fellowship, the breaking of bread, and the apostles' teaching. They simply don't go their individual way. These small congregations are placed under local spiritual leadership, exercise spiritual gifts, care for the poor, and preach the gospel. George Peters writes,

> The apostles seemingly did not go out to "plant" churches. They were not commissioned to launch out toward that goal. They were sent forth to preach the gospel. Yet wherever Acts 1:8 was faithfully discharged, a church was born. The functional tie between gospel preaching and church planting, nurture and growth, is clearly established. We may confidently state that the church is germinal in the gospel as evangelism is germinal in a New Testament church. (1981, 20)

The language of Acts makes it quite clear that as persons came to faith in Christ, they became part of the local church community. For example, Acts 2:41 reads, "Those who accepted his message were baptized, and about three thousand were added to their number that day." "Added" (*prostithemi*) is a term used in early Jewish proselyte literature to indicate being gathered to or joining a fellowship, implying a break with the former community—for example, Gentiles being joined to Israel (Reinhardt 1995, 99–100; cf. LXX Esther 9:27; Isa. 14:1). We find the same terminology in Acts 2:47; 5:14; and 11:24.

In Acts 2:47 we read, "And the Lord added to their number daily those who were being saved." Here it is significant that being added to the church is concurrent with being saved.[6] "Their number" is a reference to the local

---

5. Only two possible exceptions are to be found: the Ethiopian eunuch and perhaps the few believers in Athens.

6. "The force of the Present participle *tous sozomenous* [τους σωζομενους] . . . is iterative, suggesting that they were added *as* they were being saved" (Longenecker 1981, 291–92). See also Bruce 1965, 102.

church and is sometimes translated as such.[7] Later in Acts 11:24 the term is used again in a parallel formulation, "and a great number of people were brought [i.e., added] to the Lord." Being "brought to Christ" and being "added to the church" are virtually equivalent expressions.

Biblically speaking, becoming a believer, being saved, and belonging to the Lord all include being added to a local church, a community of believers, Christ's body. Once again, we must avoid thinking of the church in this context in an abstract manner; the church is a local assembly of believers (cf. Banks 1994, 27–31). Being a believer is not to be separated from participation in a local church. Biblical evangelism leads to believers' being gathered in communities—that is, church planting and growth.

Only in churches do new believers receive the encouragement and teaching they need to grow in faith and service. Only in mutual accountability and fellowship can true discipleship occur. Only in communities of believers can kingdom values be realized. This is one of the challenges facing specialized parachurch organizations that emphasize evangelism apart from the enfolding of new believers into local congregations. The fruit of evangelism is generally lost.

Biblical evangelism cannot be separated from the church, and where churches do not exist they must be planted. As Howard A. Snyder states it, "To do justice to the biblical understanding of evangelism, we must go a step further and say that the goal of evangelism is the formation of the Christian community. It is making disciples and further forming these disciples into living cells of the Body of Christ—new expressions of the community of God's people" (1975, 331).

Church Planting Is Central to Paul's Understanding and Practice of Mission

As we have seen in Acts, Paul worked as an evangelist gathering new believers into churches. In the Pauline correspondence we do not find the formulation of an explicit mission strategy or methodology. However, in Romans 15:18–25 we do read of Paul's working principle: in the power of the Holy Spirit he seeks to preach the gospel where Christ is not yet known. He does not want to build on another's foundation, that is, work in churches that others have founded. Granted, Paul's concern did not end with the planting of churches.

---

7. "The phrase επι το αυτο, which is common enough in classical Greek and in the Septuagint, acquired a quasi-technical meaning in the early church. This meaning, which is required in [Acts] 1.15; 2.1, 47; 1 Cor. 11.20; 14.23, signifies the union of the Christian body, and perhaps could be rendered 'in church fellowship.' Not perceiving this special usage of the word in verse 47, scribes attempted to rearrange the text, either by moving the phrase to the following sentence (3.1) or by glossing it with an equivalent phrase, εν τη εκκλησια" (Metzger 1971, 305). The term *epi to auto* reads *en te ekklesia* (in the church) in the Western text.

He clearly continues to minister to churches already planted through letters, visits, and prayers, even postponing further pioneer work to strengthen existing churches. Nevertheless, his calling and purpose is to evangelize new regions and found new churches.

In Romans 15:18–25 Paul makes a remarkable claim, that "from Jerusalem all the way around to Illyricum, I have fully proclaimed the gospel of Christ" (v. 19) and that "there is no more place for me to work in these regions" (v. 23). Paul considers his pioneering work in this region completed. But what could he have meant by these words? Certainly a church had not been planted in every town, much less had every person heard the gospel in this enormous region from Jerusalem through what is today Turkey, Greece, and the Balkan states. Paul apparently considered his missionary ministry in the region complete because churches had been planted that would *further preach the gospel* to those who had not yet heard and would *further multiply* by establishing churches in as yet unreached regions. The seeds of the gospel had been adequately planted in strategic centers. These churches would in turn continue to evangelize and reproduce, planting additional churches and thus completing the evangelization of the region.

In the New Testament we find several examples of churches Paul planted that evangelized and reproduced throughout their region. In Acts 13:49 we read that because of the church in Pisidian Antioch, "the word of the Lord spread through the whole region." Of the Thessalonian church Paul writes, "The Lord's message rang out from you not only in Macedonia and Achaia— your faith in God has become known everywhere. Therefore we do not need to say anything about it" (1 Thess. 1:8).

Perhaps the clearest example is the church in Ephesus. Paul remained in Ephesus for over two years because there, in his words, "a great door for effective work has opened to me" (1 Cor. 16:9). According to Luke, the result of Paul's teaching in Ephesus was that "all the Jews and Greeks who lived in the province of Asia heard the word of the Lord" (Acts 19:10). As a result of dramatic conversions, "the word of the Lord spread widely and grew in power" (Acts 19:20). Even critics claimed that "Paul has convinced and led astray large numbers of people here in Ephesus and in practically the whole province of Asia" (Acts 19:26). From Ephesus, churches were eventually planted throughout the province of Asia. These included the other six churches of Revelation 2–3 (Smyrna, Pergamum, Thyatira, Sardis, Philadelphia, and Laodicea), Colossae, and Hierapolis (Col. 4:13). Probably none of these churches were planted by Paul; rather they were most likely the fruit of a dynamic church-planting movement launched from Ephesus.

Numerous biblical scholars draw the same conclusion regarding the centrality of church planting to Paul's mission. For example, W. P. Bowers argues, "Paul's missionary vocation finds its sense of fulfillment in the presence of firmly established churches" (1987, 198).[8] Andreas Köstenberger and Peter O'Brien write, "The activities in which Paul engaged as he sought to fulfill his missionary commission included not only primarily evangelism through which men and women were converted, but the founding of churches and the bringing of believers to full maturity in Christ" (2001, 184). Eckhard Schnabel concurs: "Paul's missionary work did not end with the oral communication of the good news of Jesus Christ and the conversion of individuals. Paul established churches, communities of men and women who had come to faith in Jesus the Messiah and Savior" (2008, 231–32). This confirms Roland Allen's statement in his classic *Missionary Methods: St. Paul's or Ours?* "Paul did not go out as a missionary preacher merely to convert individuals; he went to establish churches from which the light might radiate throughout the whole country" (1962a, 81).

This is how Paul understood his pioneering work, and it was for him the guiding principle. Mission for Paul meant not only to preach the gospel but to also plant churches, and his mission could not be considered completed apart from planting churches that would *multiply*. Only then could a region be considered "reached."[9] Evangelism leading to the planting of reproducing congregations will complete the full preaching of the gospel not only in a region but throughout the world.

An Integration Point for Ecclesiology and Missiology

Church planting is where missiology and ecclesiology intersect. Unfortunately many missiologists and mission practitioners have a weak ecclesiology, as if mission could exist without the church or as if the church were a practical but imperfect and bothersome necessity. On the other hand, many standard systematic theologies and ecclesiologies devote few pages, if any, to the topic of mission. A missionless church is no church, and a churchless mission is not biblical mission. In the words of Lesslie Newbigin, "An unchurchly mission is as much of a monstrosity as an unmissionary Church" (1954, 169). The church is God's instrument in mission. Planting new churches is essential to the goal

---

8. See also O'Brien 1995, 43; Wedderburn 1988, 97.

9. This understanding of mission is similar to the modern "unreached peoples" concept: a people group is considered reached only when an evangelizing church is present within it. However, churches in "reached" areas may still need nurture and maturing in order to become multiplying churches able to evangelize whole regions. Even Paul's pioneering mission did not abandon weak churches for the sake of further pioneer work (cf. Bowers 1987). But once healthy churches were established, he did in fact seek to pioneer new regions. Writers such as James Engel and William Dyrness (2000) emphatically reject any attempt to measure completion of the Great Commission and claim that the Great Commission can *never* be truly fulfilled, because we will never come to the place of having truly obeyed *all* that Jesus commanded us. Such a view seems to overlook Paul's understanding of mission. Paul considers his work in a region completed once healthy, multiplying churches are established.

of mission. In the words of Michael Quicke, "At its best, church planting has the capacity both to recall the church to its primary task of mission and to remind mission strategists of the significant role of the church" (1998, x).

It should be evident from the discussion thus far that the church, and therefore also church planting, is essential to God's kingdom purposes and the fulfillment of the Great Commission. Church planting is not an end in itself in the sense of propagating religious institutions for their own sake.[10] But church planting *is* an end in the sense that it is God's chief instrument for expanding his kingdom, bringing redemption to the nations, and forming a people who will manifest his glory. Church planting and growth, while not synonymous with the kingdom of God, are nevertheless essential to the spread of the kingdom. It is not merely a question of more churches being planted but also of the *kind* of churches being planted.

The task of mission can be formulated as *the creation and expansion of kingdom communities among all the peoples of the earth to the glory of God.*[11] The chief means of creating such communities are evangelism and discipleship, which lead to the planting, growth, and multiplication of churches that manifest the reign of God in word and deed. Having discussed the theological reasons for church planting, we now turn to practical reasons for planting churches.

Practical Reasons for Church Planting

The need for church planting is obvious in regions and communities where no churches exist. However, critics often argue that in all but the most remote parts of the world enough churches already exist to complete the Great Commission. Not *more* churches are needed, so the argument goes, but *healthier* and *larger* churches. Similarly, some argue that rather than numerous small churches, fewer larger churches would be more effective for evangelism and ministry. Planting new churches where other churches exist offends Christian unity and creates unnecessary competition, weakening existing churches.

---

10. Stuart Murray, one of the few writers to seriously discuss the theological foundations of church planting, states it this way: "[Church planting] *may* be a significant means of advancing the mission of God. It *may* facilitate evangelism, peace-making, action for justice, environmental concern, community development, social involvement and many other mission ventures. But it is likely to function in this way only if it is set within the right framework. Church planting seen as an end in itself, or simply as an evangelistic methodology, may fall short of its potential and distort our understanding of God's mission and the nature of God's kingdom" (1998, 26). Murray goes on to subordinate church planting to the kingdom of God: "Neither church growth nor planting are ultimate goals. Both are subordinate theologically to the advance of the kingdom" (1998, 45). We, however, argue that the church is instrumental to the spread of the kingdom. For a similar and fuller critique of Murray, see Chester 2000, 31–35.

11. For further discussion see Ott and Strauss 2010, 156–61.

These arguments are indeed valid in many situations. A mere numerical proliferation of small, competing, and struggling churches will not necessarily advance God's kingdom purposes. Larger churches can have greater impact than smaller churches in many ways because of their greater resources, ability to carry out specialized ministries, and higher public visibility. Often wise stewardship speaks for investing in existing churches and against planting new ones. Some communities are already well served by numerous biblically sound churches, while other communities are underserved. Wise stewardship will focus church-planting resources and energy on locations of greatest spiritual need and strategic opportunity.

However, framing the issue in terms of larger churches *versus* church planting, an either-or option, poses a false dichotomy. Many large churches plant daughter churches and continue to grow. It should also be remembered that even the largest churches were once small when they were planted! In fact, Ed Stetzer and Phillip Connor (2007) studied some 2,080 church plants from twelve denominations in North America and found that church plants that in turn planted a daughter church within the first three years of their establishment grew *faster* on average than churches that did not plant a daughter church.[12]

The impact of small churches (as opposed to large churches) should not be underestimated. For example, house churches in many parts of world, though hardly visible to the public, are having a tremendous influence in their societies, much like the effect of leaven in Jesus's parable of the kingdom (Matt. 13:33). Planting new churches where other churches exist needn't necessarily involve competition or weakening of those churches. In most locations there is a need for both more churches and larger and healthier churches.

One sometimes hears the argument that most new church plants fail within the first few years of existence, thus wasting resources and energy. Various studies have proved this to be a popular myth. Stetzer and Connor's massive study on "church survivability" found that "68 percent of church plants still exist four years after having been started" (2007). Survival rates have been demonstrated to increase when the church planter is assessed and various support systems are provided. A study of all 4,339 congregations in the Church of the Nazarene revealed that the closure rate of churches five years or older (3.6 percent) was virtually the same as that of church plants five years or younger (3.5 percent; Olson 2002, 5).

New Churches Grow Faster and Reach More Non-Christians

There is growing statistical evidence that new churches, generally speaking, not only grow faster than established churches but also grow more through

---

12. Such churches had an average attendance of 130 after the fourth year, whereas churches that did not plant a daughter church had an average attendance of less than 80 (Stetzer and Connor 2007).

evangelism. Studies in North America demonstrate that baptisms per hundred members can be four times higher in new churches than in older churches (see Wagner 1990, 32–33). Net membership growth in the Church of the Nazarene in 1995–96 also demonstrated that the churches eighteen years old or younger grew by 40 percent, nearly double the average growth rate of older churches (Sullivan 1997, 25; see also Olson 2002). In one district of the Free Methodist Church with forty churches, five churches were less than five years old. But these five churches accounted for 25 percent of the total church attendance and 30 percent of all conversions, and they produced 27 percent of persons entering vocational ministry in the district (Mannoia 1994, 18–19). A study by the North American Mission Board of the Southern Baptists found that churches less than three years old averaged ten conversions per hundred members per year, churches three to fifteen years old averaged five conversions per hundred members per year, and churches over fifteen years old averaged only one and a half conversions per hundred members per year (cited in Harrison, Cheyney, and Overstreet 2008, 60).

Similar evidence can also be found in Europe. For example, membership statistics of Free Evangelical churches in Germany revealed that churches more than five years old received an annual average of one new member through conversion for every 102 members, while churches less than five years old receive one for every 38 members. Growth through conversion began to drop significantly in churches over twenty years old. Churches with more than two hundred adult members experienced not only a lower percentage of total growth but also a lower percentage of conversion growth. Similar trends are seen in other denominations in Germany.[13] Wolfgang Simson (1995, 69–71) believes that 30–56 percent of people in new churches are seekers who can be better integrated into such churches.

We must be cautious about generalizing this principle to every context. As a case in point, Allen J. Swanson's (1986) random sample study of 113 churches in Taiwan showed that churches less than five years old actually grew slower and had a lower percentage of conversion growth than older churches. Yet Christian Schwarz's (1996, 46) data on one thousand churches in thirty-two countries showed that generally, over a five-year period, smaller churches had a significantly greater percentage of growth than larger churches.

One explanation for this phenomenon is that newer churches are planted in newer, growing communities, while older churches are typically in older neighborhoods that are stable or decreasing in population. Persons new to a community are often more open for new relationships, personal change, and the possibility of attending a new church where others are also new. However,

13. For example, German Baptist churches also reported significant growth among home mission churches. See "Baptisten Gemeinden wachsen um bis zu 10%," *Idea Spektrum* 21 (2001): 10.

new churches usually also evidence greater evangelistic zeal and are more intentional in reaching out and integrating visitors into the life of the church. Newcomers don't go unnoticed. Members of church plants tend to be more aware of their purpose and more focused and motivated to evangelize. They realize that if they don't evangelize, they probably won't grow. New believers receive more personal attention. As a church grows and becomes established, more energy is usually devoted to meeting the needs of the members and less on outreach.

Church plants are often more flexible in their methods. They can be creative without disrupting older church traditions and without robbing other ministries of workers. They are freer to adapt worship, develop outreach, and create ministries that respond directly to the needs of the community. There is often a contagious sense of anticipation and boldness among team members of a church plant. This all contributes to more effective evangelism and church growth.

All Churches Eventually Plateau in Growth

Though many churches experience consistent growth over many years, eventually every church plateaus. No church can continue to grow indefinitely. Churches that experience decades of uninterrupted growth are rare exceptions. In the United States and most countries the majority of churches plateau with a Sunday attendance of under two hundred.[14] Sometimes this is because of the unresponsiveness of the focus population. More often it is because the energy of the church is diverted from evangelism to the needs of members. Also the church structure, the gifts of the leaders, expectations of members, location, and other limitations do not allow for consistent growth beyond a large family–sized church.

This reality is not necessarily to be bemoaned. It does, however, accentuate the need for continually planting new churches as a way to reach new people.

14. One national random survey in the United States found that the average size of a Roman Catholic congregation is 716, but for mainline Protestant churches average size is only 125, and for conservative Protestant churches only 123 congregants (Woolever 2005). Another national study found that "71% of US congregations have fewer than 100 regularly participating adults" (Chaves, et al. 1999, 468). The median average membership (half larger and half smaller) of churches in Indianapolis is 150, and 30 percent have 400 or more members (Farnsley, n.d.). Southern Baptist churches have a mean Sunday worship attendance of 80 persons, and "47.1 percent of the congregations are growing, 20.2 percent are plateaued, and 32.7 percent are declining" (Jones, n.d.). In the Presbyterian Church USA the mean congregational membership is 212 and the median 107 (PC(USA) 2005). Average membership in Church of the Nazarene (USA and Canada) congregations is 104 (Crow, n.d.). In Great Britain the 2005 English Church Census revealed that the average English church has a Sunday attendance of only 84 (Evangelical Alliance Information and Resources Centre 2006). In the Free Evangelical Churches of Germany (Bund Freier evangelischer Gemeinden) the median average membership is 64 adults. A church-planting movement in India with over 5,400 churches has an average membership of 85 believers (Garrison 2004a, 47).

Figure 2.1
Cumulative Growth through Planting Daughter Churches

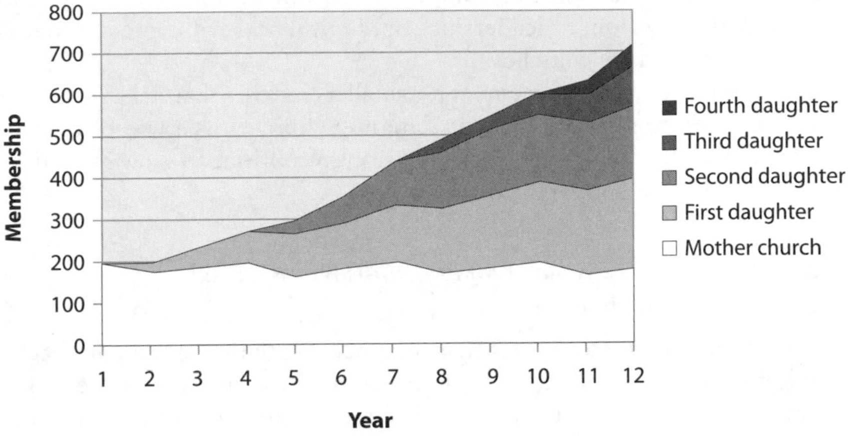

A church with one hundred members can give twenty members to form a daughter church; a church with five hundred can give many more. Experience demonstrates time and again that after giving members to start a daughter church, the mother church will begin to grow again and will regain or even surpass its plateau size, while the daughter church will also grow. On the whole more people are reached. The growth pattern might look something like the graph in figure 2.1. The mother church has plateaued at two hundred members. If it gives twenty or thirty members to start a daughter church every three years, the total movement grows. After starting a daughter church, the mother church resumes growth to its natural plateau of two hundred. The mother church has never broken the two hundred barrier, and none of the daughter churches experienced dramatic growth. But a cumulative movement with over seven hundred members has been launched, more than tripling its initial size in eleven years. If the daughter churches had also started new churches, the growth could have been exponentially larger.

This pattern can be illustrated throughout the world. In many movements the growth is much more dramatic (see Garrison 2000). But even with ordinary gifts and resources, relatively small churches can launch multiplying movements.

For example, in Germany, where church growth is generally slow, a congregation in Bonn with just over 300 adult members gave a total of 118 members between 1989 and 1996 to start five daughter churches. During that period the daughter churches nearly doubled their membership, growing to a total of 214. Meanwhile the mother church grew by more than the 118 members it had given to the daughters. Total church attendance for the movement grew from 420 to 690, and the number of home groups grew from 24 to 55.[15] This is an example of growing a movement through church planting with ordinary gifts and modest resources in a somewhat resistant region. The key was the mother church's visionary leadership, bold faith, and willingness to release members to plant new churches.

This should be an encouragement for smaller churches that struggle to break growth barriers to consider starting daughter churches as a way of reaching more people. Often the mother church will even continue to grow after giving members to launch daughter churches.

New Churches Can Reach People Groups Not Reached by Existing Churches

This is particularly the case when churches are planted among unreached people groups. It has been estimated that as much as one-third of the world's population of six billion people are still not within reach of a local church able to effectively communicate the gospel to them: "200 major ethnolinguistic peoples each have over 100,000 unevangelized ethnoreligionists in their midst," and there are "1,192 unevangelized ethnolinguistic peoples who have never been targeted by any Christian agencies ever" (Barrett, Johnson, and Crossing 2008). According to another study approximately one-quarter of the world's population, over 1.6 billion people, live in 5,837 people groups with under 2 percent evangelicals and no active church planting within the last two years (Holste and Haney 2006). Unless new churches are planted, it is highly unlikely that these people will have any contact with Christians or hear the gospel in a way that they can understand (see Wood 1995).

Not only do existing churches plateau in growth, but they tend to reach relatively homogeneous groups of people. New churches can focus on reaching additional social groupings, subcultures, and ethnic groups. Existing churches may be inaccessible to sectors of the population because of transportation difficulty or social barriers. For example, in Eastern Europe the Roma (commonly called Gypsies) are typically looked upon with disdain by the general population. In one Eastern European city numbers of Roma were coming to faith in Christ, but they were made to feel very unwelcome in the existing churches. There remained, unfortunately, no other way to disciple these believers apart from establishing a new church for them (LOP 43, 2005).

New churches can reach out in local neighborhoods in ways that geographically more distant churches cannot. Furthermore, older churches have often exhausted their natural evangelistic contacts through family, friends, and

---

15. Data based on membership records of the Bund Freier evangelischer Gemeinden in Deutschland and personal report of the leading pastor.

colleagues of their members. New churches often are able to develop new contacts in the community and thus reach new people.

New Churches Are Necessary to Saturate Cities and Regions with the Gospel

It has been the strategy of organizations such as DAWN (Discipling a Whole Nation, Montgomery 1989) and the Alliance for Saturation Church Planting to saturate cities and regions with new churches so as to reach more people. Their goal is one church per thousand residents or, in rural areas, within easy traveling distance of every person. The rationale is that the average church will only be able to personally reach and evangelize effectively about one thousand persons. A study in Munich, Germany, in 1993 demonstrated that to attain the goal of even one evangelical church per ten thousand residents, one hundred new churches would have to be planted! The study further revealed that the fastest-growing churches were all under five years old and were not centrally located but located in communities where they had immediate contact with residents (Ott 1994). The experience of the Christian and Missionary Alliance churches in Guinea, West Africa, illustrates this point well (see case study 2.1).

New Churches Are Necessary for Long-Term Growth and Discipleship of New Believers

As demonstrated in case study 2.1, until new churches are planted, large numbers of persons who have made professions of faith do not continue in discipleship. Reports are sometimes heard of large movements of "church-less" Christians, for example among the Tamil in India. Such persons may not attend existing churches because they do not feel welcome or because the social barriers are too great for new believers to overcome. Sometimes the existing congregations are geared to the needs of Christian populations but not contextualized to meet the needs of new Hindu-background believers. In other cases traditional church buildings quickly became too small to hold the large numbers of new believers, or traditional leadership structures could not adapt and care for the needs of the growing church. David Garrison (2004b) found that there is a 50–80 percent attrition rate among new believers who do not become integrated into a church fellowship.

New Churches Stimulate Established Churches to Greater Evangelistic Activity

While church planting is sometimes viewed as a form of competition with existing churches, members of older churches often observe how new churches are reaching people for Christ using creative methods. This can in turn stimu-

Case Study 2.1

Church Planting in Macenta, Guinea

For years evangelistic campaigns in the district of Macenta had produced large numbers of "decisions" for Christ. The membership in churches, however, had not grown for twenty-five years. Something was wrong! A strategy was created to begin planting churches in locations geographically more easily accessible to the persons becoming Christians. This would facilitate follow-up, decentralize spiritual nurture, and mobilize lay church planters. Ideally every church would plant a new daughter church every year, and every Christian was encouraged to lead one other person per year to Christ. In order for such an ambitious plan to work, lay leaders for the churches would have to be trained through a program of theological education by extension (TEE) and practical church planting experience. If traditional theological education and ordination were expected for the leader of every new church, the plan would be doomed from the start.

The program was launched in 1992. By 1996 the number of churches had grown from 25 to 150 (many were house churches in the villages). Even more dramatic, the membership had grown from 1,000 to 6,000, demonstrating that the church-planting plan was indeed facilitating more effective evangelism and follow-up, which was resulting in increased church membership and genuine discipleship. The number of ordained pastors had not changed, but ninety lay pastors had been trained and mobilized. This all occurred in the midst of considerable opposition and even persecution (Pfister 1998).

late them to renew their evangelistic efforts. The old phrase "That won't work here" is regularly disproved by new church plants! Existing churches often become comfortable with the status quo, lag in evangelistic motivation, or are discouraged about evangelism. Numerous stories could be told of how a new church plant gave impetus to joint evangelistic efforts together with the other churches in a region or city. Ultimately more believers and more churches are mobilized, more people are reached, and all churches benefit, not just the church plant.

When an established church gives members to begin a daughter church, the remaining members suddenly notice empty seats in their own building. They observe the evangelistic zeal of the daughter and often begin to rethink their own evangelistic strategy. The status quo has been shaken! The mother church has renewed evangelistic zeal.

New Churches Mobilize More Workers

Church plants typically begin with a small team of workers. Not only are these workers highly invested, but as the church plant grows the new members are naturally plunged into ministry. In a church plant everyone knows that he or she must contribute and serve. Everyone is needed. Workers are stretched and challenged to develop new skills, take on responsibilities, and discover gifts that they never would have considered in an established church. The excuse "Someone else can do it better than I can" doesn't apply in a church plant, because there often is no one else! God graciously supplies gifts and talents as workers step forward in faith and service.

Schwarz's (1996, 48) international research revealed that, on the average, in churches with under one hundred members, 31 percent of worshipers are actively serving in the ministry of the church. That percentage drops consistently with the increasing size of the church; churches with over one thousand members have only 17 percent of worshipers serving. Our observation is that church plants (normally very small at the start) often have as many as 75 percent or more of the members serving. On the other hand, when a mother church gives members and workers to plant a daughter church, a vacuum is left behind where former members served. There also new workers must be trained and mobilized to carry on ministry.

New Churches Are Key to Social Change

As kingdom communities are planted, societies will be positively affected. Church growth experts have long observed that "social lift" occurs as people become Christians: as people from the poor and lower classes become Christians, and as they adopt biblical lifestyles, they rise in social standing and standard of living (McGavran 1980, 295–313; Wagner 1981, 42–46). For example, fathers take more responsibility for their families, with the result that money is spent on education instead of alcohol or gambling. A work ethic is adopted, and human dignity is instilled in place of despair and inferiority.

Advocates of holistic ministry, such as Tetsuano Yamamori of Food for the Hungry, include church planting as a part of a total urban strategy to minister to the poor (Yamamori 1998, 9; see also Grigg 1992). As communities of hope and help are established among the poor, they become empowered to improve their lot in life. The Thailand Report on Christian Witness to the Urban Poor stated, "We believe the basic strategy for the evangelization of the urban poor is the creation or renewal of communities in which Christians live and share equally with others" (LOP 22, 1980, 16). Various relief and development organizations have found that partnering with local churches is one of the most effective ways to support communities not only for spiritual transformation but also for social, educational, and economic betterment.

Unfortunately, many, if not most, existing churches tend to neglect the poor or have difficulty accepting and serving the poor. Conversely, the poor often feel neither welcome nor comfortable in churches of higher social classes. While we should seek to correct this difficulty in existing churches, planting new churches among the poor may remain the only realistic option if they are to be reached with the gospel. One of the most dramatic examples of this is the sensational growth of the Gramin Pachin Mandal movement among the Bhangi Dalits in India. Started in 1984, the movement grew to over 700,000 baptized believers by 2004. The Bhangis are the lowest of the low caste, rejected by the general population and relegated to the most demeaning work such as cleaning latrines. Only when a highly contextualized movement was launched that gave them dignity and allowed them to exercise their own leadership was a growing Christian movement possible (see Pierson 2004).

Furthermore, churches among the middle and upper classes must be planted with a vision to become voices of justice and compassion in society. Unfortunately, established churches have often become complacent with the social status quo. New churches can play a significant role in both practically assisting the poor in meeting immediate needs and working toward social change at the systemic level. Nairobi Chapel, for example, has determined to plant two churches among the poor for every church it plants among the middle or upper classes (Muriu 2007). In Manila a middle-class Evangelical Free Church released workers to help plant a church in a squatter district; various social programs to help the poor were part of the new church from the very beginning. Churches must become "salt, light, and leaven" in society, advocating education, equal opportunity, protection of human rights, land reform, safe and reasonable working conditions, fair treatment and equal opportunity for the underprivileged and marginalized. We will return to this topic in chapter 19.

What about Planting Churches in Communities Where Churches Already Exist?

Planting a church in a locality where other churches already exist is a sensitive matter. As noted above, such a church plant will likely reach new persons and contribute to the evangelization of the area. But it could also potentially empty other churches as Christians change their allegiance to the new church. Is such a church plant a violation of Christian unity? How can one determine if such a plant is justified in communities where other churches already exist? We do not advocate church planting everywhere and at any cost. Competition, denominational "flag raising," and sheep stealing should never characterize a church-planting effort. A church should never be planted at the cost of another. But neither should "denominational turf," personal kingdom building, or maintenance of a dying religious tradition be motivations for opposing new church planting in a community.

In many parts of the world a majority of local residents formally belong to a church but neither actively participate in church life nor personally adhere to

When Planting Churches Where Other Churches Exist

1. Honestly evaluate the spiritual needs of the community.

Are the spiritual needs of the community being adequately met by the existing churches? Do particular segments of the population such as ethnic groups, social classes, or neighborhoods remain unreached or underserved? What is the proportion of Christians to non-Christians in the community? What is the geographical distribution of churches in the area? Are existing churches evangelizing effectively? Decide to plant only where there is genuine need.

2. Consider how many churches are enough.

There is no fixed rule for determining the optimal number of churches for a region. Missiologists sometimes consider a region adequately reached where active Christians make up 10 percent of the general population. However, even in such areas there may still be pockets of the population who remain unreached by existing churches. The existing churches may also be geographically unevenly distributed. Furthermore, existing churches may be entirely ingrown, have no interest for outreach, and fail to influence the community for the kingdom. Murray summarizes the point quite well:

> How can the mission of the church in contemporary society be accomplished? If this mission can be accomplished through the churches that already exist, then church planting is unnecessary. But if this is not feasible, because of the location of these churches, their inability to communicate with the surrounding community, or simply because there are not enough of them, then church planting is crucial. (1998, 14)

3. Inform existing churches of your intentions and assure them of a cooperative spirit.

Open communication is the first step to demonstrating respect, goodwill, and unity with other churches. Make clear the purpose and nature of the church plant, and indicate that your intent is not to "steal sheep" or proselytize but to evangelize and serve the community in new ways. This will avoid misunderstanding and ease negative suspicions. The presentation of demographic data clearly indicating the spiritual needs of the community may open the eyes of existing church leaders to the importance of a new church.

4. Carry through with promises to cooperate and not to proselytize.

Participation in local ministerial fellowships, the Evangelical Alliance, or similar groups as well as cooperation in prayer weeks, evangelistic efforts, or other joint ministries will demonstrate a spirit of unity and cooperation. Should an active member of another church begin attending the church plant, it is usually a good policy to contact a pastor of that church and openly discuss the situation. Other ways to foster good relations include informing other churches regularly of public events, supporting them in their initiatives, and refraining from criticizing others.

From this discussion it should be more than evident that church planting is not only biblically mandated and central to fulfillment of the Great Commission but also a practical necessity in many, if not most, places, even where other churches are already present. Church planting is at the very center of a biblical understanding of mission. It is the key to launching Christian movements among unreached people groups as well as saturating "reached" regions with the gospel.

even the most basic Christian beliefs. While only God can judge the heart, for all practical purposes such nominal Christians must be reached or re-reached with the gospel and won to a living faith in Jesus Christ. Existing churches that see no need to do so have no right to forbid a new church to attempt to reach out to such nominal Christians. Many of these churches are dominated by a theology that denies the power of the gospel and the authority of Scripture.

> The presence of church buildings or even congregations in an area where church planting is being considered does not necessarily preclude the possibility of planting new churches. Introverted or socially isolated churches, churches concerned only with their own spiritual development, churches with nothing to communicate to their neighbours, churches speaking in terminology that cannot be understood, churches that speak much but do little, churches that fail to incarnate what they are proclaiming, may be making no positive contribution to *missio Dei*. (Murray 1998, 37)

Sidebar 2.1 lists a few guidelines for church planting in communities where other churches exist.

3

New Testament Beginnings

Though the New Testament is not a church-planting manual, it does give church planters principles and parameters to guide them in their efforts. Charles Chaney (1982, 20–35) has written that the three pillars of church planting are the nature and purpose of God, the nature and purpose of the church, and the need and condition of contemporary humankind. If this is true, we should find not only strong motivation for cross-cultural church planting but also enough biblical principles to guide us in the task. There are no doubt hundreds of lessons that can be discovered to guide church planters. In this chapter we can highlight only the most salient features and lessons by examining conceptual foundations for church planting in the Gospels, early church realizations in Acts, and reflections in the Pauline Epistles.[1]

Gospel Foundations

Many students of church planting begin their study in the book of Acts because the apostles are not sent out and empowered to make disciples and form churches until after Jesus's resurrection and ascension and the outpouring of the Holy Spirit (Acts 1–2). There may be theological reasons for this, but starting with Paul's ministry has certain disadvantages. The one who said "I will build my church" also prepared his followers to participate in its estab-

1. We refer readers to more detailed biblical studies on early Christian mission and the expansion of the early church, such as Ramsay 1982, Bruce 1969, Green 1970, Longenecker 1964 and 1971, Banks 1994, Riesner 1998, and Schnabel 2004 and 2008.

lishment and provided seminal concepts that can serve as foundations for any church-planting ministry today.

Another weakness with using Pauline church planting as a starting point is that significant reproducing churches were planted apart from Paul's ministry. The church in Jerusalem (Acts 1–8:3) and the church in Antioch (Acts 11:19–30; 13:1–3) are obvious examples. From them the church spread to Galilee, Samaria (Acts 8–9, particularly 9:31), Syria, Phoenicia, Cyprus, and Cyrene (Acts 11:19–20). This was in many ways an expansive lay evangelization movement (initially as a result of persecution) that produced many new churches—*Jesus communities* made up of those who had come to know him as Savior and Messiah. These communities were centered on Jesus's person and teachings; thus the seeds of any Jesus movement today must look to his own teaching for its roots and character.

When the disciples in Jerusalem received power from on high, they already knew why they had been sent out in the world; they also had experienced the *koinonia* the Master intended for his church. They proclaimed the gospel, made new disciples, and gathered them in kingdom communities without receiving additional instructions to guide them in their church-planting activities, except through the leading of the Spirit. A vast number of churches emerged throughout Judea and Samaria.[2] Therefore we are justified in looking to the Gospels for the church-planting foundations that would shape the early church's ministry and later be carried to the Gentiles through the traveling ministry of Paul, the other apostles, and their coworkers.[3]

Jesus—Master Builder of the Church

In a sense, Jesus is the church planter par excellence (Matt. 16:18). We can affirm this historically in that he established the first Christian community, built on his teaching and empowered by his Spirit to fulfill his mission in the world. Jesus considered the company of disciples an embryonic community or church.[4] We know this because he calls them *ecclesia* in Matthew 18:17 when

2. In Acts 9:1–2 the "followers of the Way" are still found in the synagogues. It would appear that the persecution and the preaching of Philip, Peter, and other apostles (Acts 8–10) contributed to the creation of new kingdom communities distinct from the synagogues throughout Judea, Galilee, and Samaria (Acts 9:31). Luke tells us that these communities were growing numerically (ibid).

3. F. F. Bruce points to additional evidence that Jesus intended to found a prototype church that would be a new Israel: the choice of twelve men who would one day "sit on thrones judging the twelve tribes of Israel" (Luke 22:30). He writes, "But the designed coincidence of their number, twelve, with the totality of the tribes of Israel, implied that there would be an 'Israel' for them to lead" (1969, 177). They were careful to replace Judas to maintain the twelve.

4. "At quite an early stage, it appears, this community was designated by one of the terms which in the Old Testament are applied to the whole assembly (*qahal*) or congregation (*edah*) of Israel" (Bruce 1977, 206). Bruce also points out that the resurrection faith, not Pentecost,

he gives them instructions about how to deal with offenses. Stuart Murray points out clues to the functioning of pre-Pentecost kingdom communities from Matthew 18:15–20: "[Jesus] describes a community which is serious about discipleship; a community characterized by open and loving relationship; a community that recognizes it is comprised of imperfect people and develops a style of life that remains faithful to the highest standards but realistic about failure; a community that balances individual responsibility and corporate action; a community in which there is no hint of clericalism; and, arguably, a community small enough to operate in such a way" (1998, 85).

In the other Matthean reference to *ecclesia* Jesus promises to build his church (Matt. 16:18) based on the truth, affirmed by Peter, that he is the Messiah. The reference to *ecclesia* is primarily used in a future sense, but it is rooted in the present. The church is founded on the apostolic proclamation of who Jesus is (rock), lives under apostolic authority (power of keys), and stands victorious over satanic opposition (gates of Hades). Thus the advance and expansion of the church is guaranteed, and its foundation is none other than the person and work of Jesus Christ spread by apostolic teaching. The company of disciples before Pentecost was embryonic and somewhat fluid but nevertheless exhibited the traits that Jesus expected of his followers.[5]

Foundational Concepts for Church Planting in Jesus's Teaching

There were at least four themes in Jesus's teaching that provided a conceptual framework for the disciples and apostles as they proclaimed the name of Jesus and gathered believers: (1) expanding the kingdom, (2) sowing and reaping, (3) gathering true worshipers, and (4) making disciples.

EXPANDING THE KINGDOM

In the Gospels the establishment of the church is announced and prepared by Jesus's teaching of the kingdom. Although the kingdom of God cannot be equated with the church, the church is God's primary instrument in this age to advance his kingdom as a sign of and witness to the kingdom that will one day come in fullness. Jesus's announcement of his kingdom is centered on the spreading of his Word and the calling out of a people subject to his Word

---

"brought the scattered followers of Jesus together again, and within a few weeks after his death they appear as a coherent, vigorous and self-propagating community in Jerusalem" (ibid).

5. This company of committed followers grew beyond the apostolic band and included believers from many classes of society—women like Mary and Martha, religious leaders like Nicodemus and Joseph of Arimathea, loyal friends like Lazarus, Mary his mother, James, and his other natural brothers (Acts 1:14; 1 Cor. 15:7), and additional unnamed disciples totaling at least 120 (Acts 1:15). And there were others, perhaps more loosely connected to the Jerusalem community, because a company of more than five hundred believers witnessed one of Jesus's early postresurrection appearances (1 Cor. 15:6).

and rule, in anticipation of the birth of the church. Philip Steyne describes the relationship well:

> In the process Christ inaugurated a new age for God's rule over His people. The Lord brought a new people into being who would demonstrate His righteous and just rule, modeling on earth what God does in heaven (Matt. 5–7). His kingdom was to be a present reality, already having been initiated in this age, but not fully here until He returns. . . . His citizens were to live under a "kingly rule" with an understanding of community (Matt. 8:8–11). In the fellowship of true community they had all things in common, their faith as well as their means. . . . His kingdom would exercise influence through its citizens upon lives and structure. His kingdom possessed men. It came upon them and delivered them from alien powers (Matt. 12:28; Luke 11:20), resulting in a different perspective on life. (1992, 244–45)

The expansion of the kingdom is also evident in the parables. Through Jesus's illustrations the disciples learned that the amount and rate of growth would depend on the people's receptiveness but that the gospel seed must be sown in any case (Matt. 13:1–23). Kingdom growth would be surprisingly powerful and expansive like that of the mustard seed (v. 31–32), penetrating and transforming like that of yeast in a lump of dough (v. 33), and would continue until the day of judgment (vv. 24–30). The growth itself is clearly the mysterious work of God, although humans have a responsibility to sow the seed (Mark 4:26–29).

Jesus's kingdom teaching brings a qualitative dimension to church planting, as illustrated by the effects of salt and light (Matt. 5:13–16). James Denney, a nineteenth-century Scottish theologian, expresses this eloquently:

> He called men who were living in the world, in all the various lines of life, into the Kingdom. He associated them with Himself and with one another in the consciousness of being the citizens and subjects of the Kingdom. . . . There is in the kingdom a real union of persons, who are conscious that they have what binds them to each other, and what separates them from the world; but there is nothing formal or institutional about it. . . . It is destined to carry to all that law of love which Christ has revealed, and, as it does so, to transform, or rather to transfigure them. The kingdom of God becomes a conquering and transfiguring power—the leaven exerts its virtue, the salt its savor—in proportion as the citizens of the kingdom are intensely conscious of their new relation to God, and of the new obligations it imposes. (1976 [1895], 175–76)

This qualitative dimension is embodied in our understanding of church planting as the establishment of new kingdom communities. The kingdom emphasis also underlines a holistic, integrated view of church growth and corrects a production mentality that would put the primary focus on numbers.

Sowing and Reaping

In Peru church planting is called "sowing churches" (*el siembro de iglesias*). In the parable of the sower, the seed represents the Word of God, the soils illustrate people who are receptive to varying degrees, and the sower himself is the proclaimer of the Word. Finally the Spirit, the Lord of the Harvest, superintends the whole process and gives life to new disciples and kingdom communities. Jesus underlines the disciples' responsibility to spread his Word and prepares them for the different responses of the hearers, as well as the counteroffensives of the enemy (Matt. 13:3–8; Mark 4:3–20; Luke 8:5–8).

This theme takes us back to a seminal Old Testament passage, Isaiah 55:9–13. Isaiah begins with the Messiah as witness to all nations (vv. 4–5) and an appeal to seek him while he may be found (vv. 6–8). He then focuses on the unfathomable, powerful, and living Word of God, which accomplishes his purpose. The emphasis on the powerful Word, which is taken up in Acts (see Pao 2002), serves as an important reminder to church planters that their primary responsibility is to sow the Word and trust God to work through it:

> The four essentials for all church planters are: Spirit, Seed, Sower, and Soil. Without any of these, New Testament church planting is impossible. . . . The common access to the essentials makes church planting a possibility for more people than generally thought. Churches can be planted without big finances or elegant buildings. Churches can be planted by ordinary people who are filled with a vision and the Holy Spirit. The secret is no longer bound to a religious title or degree. The necessary resources are available to multitudes. (Brock 1994, 30)

Gathering True Worshipers

The idea of gathering worshipers into the new messianic kingdom is an important motif for church planting in the Gospels. Jesus used the illustration of a harvest field to emphasize the urgency of gathering true worshipers (John 4:22–42). He instructed his disciples to pray for more laborers to be sent to the harvest field that people might know the Lord of the Harvest (Matt. 9:37–38).

When the harvest is ready, the grain should be cut, bound into sheaves, and carried to the storehouse. In the same way, when a group of people responds to the gospel, they are brought into the fellowship of the local church to worship God.[6] In the parable of the great banquet, when the invited guests would not come, the master commanded the servants to "make" another group to join the spiritual feast (Luke 14:23).[7] Thus the Lord's parables implicitly point

---

6. The harvest analogy is used in an eschatological sense for the judgment day in Matthew 13:30 and elsewhere but in Matthew 9:38 and John 4:35–42 it has this sense of gathering the saved.

7. Although the primary reference is to the invitation extended to the Gentiles, who are invited (although unworthy) after the Jewish people rejected the same invitation, we underline

to the responsibility of bringing people into the Christian fold from every nation. These parables also underline the inevitable expansion and growth of the kingdom, giving the church planter assurance that the greater cause will not fail.

MAKING DISCIPLES

Finally, we see church planting in the mission Jesus gave the disciples.[8] Jesus sent them out the same way the Father sent him to earth (John 20:21) and demonstrated to them the incarnational character of their mission. He charged them to go and take the gospel to people, living out its power while teaching its emancipating truth: "The Christ will suffer and rise from the dead on the third day, and repentance and forgiveness of sins will be preached in his name to all nations, beginning at Jerusalem. You are witnesses of these things" (Luke 24:46–48). Before his ascension, in Galilee he explained that they were to baptize those who repented, teach them all he had taught, and bring them into a community of disciples. They were to form new communities of believers that shared the same essential characteristics as the original community of Jesus and his disciples.

Thus Jesus's teaching on the church (though limited) and the disciples' seminal experience of community provide the conceptual framework for the expansion of the church in Acts. The Holy Spirit brought these things to memory and guided the church (John 14:26; 16:13–15). The spontaneous growth of the church is really a continuation of what Jesus began with his disciples, a realization of the mission he gave them, and an extension of the church he established among them (see Coleman 1987, 9–16).

Early Church Realizations: Patterns and Principles from the Book of Acts

Most branches of evangelical Christianity have come out of a restoration movement that looks back to the New Testament church, either as a norm to be restored or as an ideal to be followed. Luke's narrative not only chronicles the past but also serves to encourage believers, teach moral behavior, exalt God, and defend godly people and practices.[9] God put his seal of approval

---

the repeated use of the ingathering-incorporation motif in opposition to Western individualistic notions of salvation.

8. See chapter 2 for a discussion of Matthew 28 and the implicit command to plant churches.

9. See Liefeld 1995 and "Acts: The Problem of Historical Precedent" in Fee and Stuart 1982 for more hermeneutical principles dealing with narratives. Liefeld cautions: "There does not seem to be any indication within Acts itself that Luke was writing to provide a paradigm for Christian evangelism, missions, and church life" (1995, 32). Yet he later allows for the establishment of biblical principles from Acts under certain conditions: "In short, those who seek guidance from Acts can certainly find principles that are appropriate in

on these accounts through inspiration so that the church would have positive examples and prototypes of how the Holy Spirit led the early believers.[10] In order to avoid normalizing narrative accounts excessively or inappropriately, we can distinguish three degrees of relevance for practices from narrative portions—*prescriptive*, *descriptive*, and *representative*.

Some things are clearly *prescriptive* for the church. Jesus taught that his disciples should observe everything he commanded them (Matt. 28:18–20). The practices in Acts explicitly taught elsewhere in the New Testament, such as the ordinances, the command to love each other, and the preaching of the gospel, would also fall in this category. However not everything in Acts can or should be replicated. Some reports are merely *descriptive*: events like the casting of lots to find a replacement for Judas have a historical value (see discussion in Liefeld 1995, 117). Others are particular to the culture and context, like meeting in the temple courts, or Paul's custom of preaching the gospel first in the local synagogue. We should not try to replicate the unique signs that accompanied the initial outpouring of the Holy Spirit at Pentecost or the writing of divinely authoritative letters.

In a third category we place those consistent patterns that carry *representative* value (Fee and Stuart 1982, 101–2). By the use of repetition, literary emphasis, and other devices the author makes them stand out as normal (customary, typical) practices, even if they are not given normative (absolute, authoritative) force. Patterns with representative force (1) are repeated consistently (thus only one pattern is found), (2) stand in harmony with the rest of Scripture, and (3) are not unique to a particular context or culture. In this chapter we will call them *church-planting patterns*.[11] This chapter highlights some of the more salient principles that can, in our judgment, be generally applied to church-planting efforts. These consistent patterns can be used to develop *ministry principles* provided they are (1) based on clear parallels between the contemporary situation and the biblical context and (2) adapted to current ministry realities in their application. In short, we do not seek to *imitate* the events and methods of Acts, but we do seek to

---

similar situations, but may find that conditions are too different to allow invitation of some normative pattern. This may seem as though we are imposing an external guideline on the interpretation of Scripture. Rather, we are recognizing the fact that guiding principles for activities that mesh with culture, such as missions, may be transferable, but only with great care and wisdom" (124–25).

10. Sometimes narratives have special didactic force, as seen in Paul's use (1 Cor. 10:6–13). Jesus used a Davidic narrative as a justification of his disciples' conduct during the Sabbath (Mark 2:23–28). Certainly narrative sections are included when Paul writes that all Scripture is "profitable for teaching" (2 Tim. 3:16).

11. Coleman attributes special significance to patterns in Acts that apply Jesus's example: "This present study purposes to discern how the apostolic church carried out His mandate. Primarily using the Acts as reference, my design has been to see an unfolding pattern, especially noting principles of Christ's example in their witness" (1987, 14).

continue in the same *trajectory*, in continuity with the dynamic of mission
as depicted in Acts.

God Calls Workers to Plant the Church

Church planters are called by God. This can be clearly seen not only with
Paul (Acts 13:2; 26:19–20; Gal. 1:11–12), but also with Barnabas, Peter, James,
and John (Gal. 2:7–9). The callings are expressed differently. In Paul's case it
came from a heavenly vision (Acts 26:19; Gal. 2:2) and was reaffirmed by the
Antioch church (Acts 13:1–3), but in Timothy's case it came through Paul's
invitation and the recommendation of his church in Lystra (Acts 16:1–3;
2 Tim.1:6). Although assurance of God's call comes in a variety of ways, it is
one of the pillars on which a lifetime of ministry must be built.[12]

The Holy Spirit Empowers and Guides Church Planting

A conscious dependence on the Holy Spirit permeates the accounts of
the early evangelists and apostles and constitutes part of the ethos of New
Testament church planting. Christ told the apostles to preach the gospel to
all creation, and then he added, "Do not leave Jerusalem, but wait for the gift
my Father promised" (Acts 1:4). The explanation is found in verse 8: "You
will receive power when the Holy Spirit comes on you." As James Cymbala
and James Merrill put it, "All merit is in the Son . . . and all power is of the
Spirit" (2001, 197).

While most Christians would affirm this, the apostolic church-planting teams
lived by it. The Holy Spirit is the Missionary Spirit, and church planting requires
his direct agency and the empowering of secondary human instruments. The
apostles depended on the Spirit's direction for their decisions about where to
go next, although the means by which that guidance was received varied from
case to case (Acts 8:26, 39; 10:9–16; 12:5–11; 16:6–7, 9–10; 18:9–11; 27:23–26).
When they arrived on location they preached in his power, and their proclamation was often accompanied by visible manifestations of his presence.

Luke intriguingly describes believers as "filled with the Holy Spirit" in a
special sense on particular occasions (Acts 4:8, 31; 9:17; 13:9). The recurring
expression seems to underline the special action of the Holy Spirit in each of
these cases. As they proclaimed Jesus or suffered for him, God gave them the
spiritual power and grace they needed—special anointing for extraordinary
circumstances. Furthermore, "filling by the Holy Spirit" is used not only in
reference to the apostles but also in reference to the Jerusalem church (4:31);
and this filling is later commanded of the Ephesian believers (Eph. 5:18).

12. This assurance of God's call is one of the essential competencies commonly used in
church planter assessments. For a discussion of the missionary vocation and calling see Ott
and Strauss 2010, 225–30.

Church planting remains fundamentally a spiritual enterprise that requires spiritual means found only in the Holy Spirit. All the human effort, strategy, talent, resources, and creative genius that go into church planting are vain unless endowed with his life-giving power. This is not only a pervasive pattern in Acts but a theological principle: No church planter will be successful apart from the agency, leading, and filling of the Holy Spirit.

Churches Are Planted through Gospel Proclamation and the Conversion of Hearers

Nothing could be clearer from a reading of the book of Acts than its emphasis on gospel proclamation as the catalyst for church planting. As the gospel is preached in the power of the Holy Spirit, the same Spirit applies that message to the hearts of the hearers (e.g., Acts 2:37; 16:14). When they receive it through repentance and faith, they are saved and become Christians (8:14; 11:1; 17:11).

The gospel is preached in many venues,[13] sometimes to large groups in public settings and at other times through a more personal dialogue. The response to the message also differs: large numbers of conversions (Acts 2:41; 5:14), mockery and ridicule (2:13; 17:32), persecution (7:54 60), or further inquiry (17:32). Yet consistently the apostles present Jesus Christ, crucified and risen.

The manner of preaching is adapted to the hearers.[14] But the message always leads to the need for repentance and faith in response to this message, God's power for salvation (cf. Rom. 1:16). Luke speaks of the planting and growth of the church in terms of the Word of God growing, spreading, multiplying, and prevailing (Acts 6:7; 12:24; 13:49; 19:20). *Spirit-empowered proclamation* plays a pivotal role in the book of Acts, and it is the very source from which church planting flows. Thus workers must remember that church planting begins with evangelism and that there is no substitute for bold, Spirit-filled sharing of the gospel. This is the methodological foundation on which the churches described in Acts were built, and it is the model we are to follow today.

New Believers Are Congregated in Spiritual Communities

"Paul's primary mission was accomplished when the gospel was preached, men were converted, and churches were established" (Hesselgrave 1980, 29). The fulfillment of the Great Commission requires the ongoing establishment

---

13. For example, in the temple courts (Acts 3:1; 5:21, 25; etc.), synagogues (13:14; 14:1), marketplaces (17:17), public places (18:28), homes (5:42), prison (16:25–34), and before government officials (chaps. 24–26). See Schnabel 2008, 287–305 for a broader discussion.

14. Compare, for example, Paul's messages to the Jews (Acts 13:16–41), in Lystra (14:15–17), to the Philippian jailor (16:31–32), and in Athens (17:22–31).

of new congregations that group together those who respond to the gospel. As noted in chapter 2 (and in the discussion of the parables earlier in this chapter), Christ adds people to a local church as they are saved (Acts 2:41, 47; 5:14; 11:24). This process, described in Acts 2:38–47, includes at least three activities: (a) communication of the gospel (v. 38), (b) teaching and baptizing disciples (v. 41), and (c) gathering them in kingdom communities (vv. 42–46). This threefold pattern, foreshadowed in Jesus's parables, is repeated throughout Acts. The incorporation of believers is an integral part of disciplemaking. While not all ministries establish new churches, those that have discipleship as their goal are missing a key ingredient unless the new believers are gathered into spiritual communities.

The Apostolic Team Established Local Leaders and Traveled On to Other Regions

Paul and his companions established local elders and deacons consistently, although the circumstances are not recorded in some cases. This seems to have been a priority since Paul either established them on his first visit (in spite of having very little time to prepare them) or returned at great risk to establish them at a later date (Acts 14:23). Only when such local leaders had been appointed was the work considered completed (Acts 14:23, 26; Titus 1:5).[15] Then the founders traveled on to other unevangelized areas rather than becoming local pastors and elders. Suffice it to say here that the long-term success of cross-cultural church planting is largely determined by the establishment of local lay leaders, the turning over of church governance to them, and the continuation of a relationship through visits and correspondence.

Churches Were Planted by Teams

There is also a clear pattern of teamwork in church planting. Jesus worked with a team—investing his life in others and preparing them to carry on his mission. Paul began as an associate of Barnabas and later formed and led various teams, constantly bringing people together for the cause of the gospel. The use of teams is a clear pattern in Acts. It is rare indeed to find the early apostles engaged in ministry alone.

Traveling in a group was a common feature of the era, necessitated by the rigors and dangers of crossing a rugged terrain infested with marauding robbers. "Moving around was a team exercise. As the narrative unfolds, the focus is upon the journeys of Paul and his companions. But the principle of traveling together pertained to all the others, like Barnabas and Mark,

15. See fuller discussion in chapter 1.

Silas and Timothy, and Timothy and Erastus. Frequently, too, local brethren would join them (e.g., 21:15–16)" (Coleman 1963, 71). Paul progressively brought more and more people together for the cause of the gospel. He went from a bicultural team of two on his first missionary journey to a large and diverse multicultural group of ten coworkers from the various churches he had planted.

Several reasons have been offered for the increase in coworkers. Members of the apostolic teams served several fluid and functional roles.[16] They alternatively served as associates, representatives of churches, assistants, and apprentices. First of all, as the work grew, so did the need for *ministry associates* to aid in the teaching, act as envoys, and build fellowship between the churches. As the span of ministry grew, some traveled with Paul (Acts 16:6), and others stayed behind (Acts 17:15). And on at least one occasion, some went ahead (Acts 20:5).

Second, Paul selected *representatives* from the various regions to demonstrate the essential unity of the church[17] and combat the excessive nationalism of certain Judean churches (Acts 15:1–35; 21:17–26). This can be most clearly seen with the team that went with him from Ephesus to Jerusalem, carrying the gifts for the relief of the Judean church. When Paul reported in Jerusalem "what God had done among the Gentiles through his ministry" (Acts 21:19), the seven delegates from different regions served as living evidence that the wall of partition between Jew and Gentile had been broken down (see Eph. 2:14).

Third, Paul's coworkers also served as *personal assistants*, ministering to his own needs. He stayed with Aquila and Priscilla and joined them in their trade (Acts 18:1–3). Later they risked their lives for him in some way (Rom. 16:4). Luke, the doctor, attended to his needs (Col. 4:14; 2 Tim. 4:11). Tertius served Paul as an amanuensis (Rom. 16:22). John Mark, who had earlier abandoned Paul, later assisted him and went on a mission with Timothy for him (Col. 4:10; Philem. 24; 2 Tim. 4:11). Paul also greets others who received him in their homes and helped him in prison, singling out a woman who had been a mother to him (Rom. 16).

Finally, it appears that high on Paul's agenda for building teams was the training of leaders for the emerging local churches. Paul consistently repeated the rabbinical pattern that Barnabas had used with him: he took on ministry apprentices to travel with him and gain experience in evangelism and teaching. Schnabel (2008, 248–55) affirms that the biblical terminology used to describe Paul's coworkers indicates they were not mere helpers but fully engaged in the same missionary activities as Paul himself, and were in no

16. The gifts and complementary roles of church planters on teams will be addressed in chapters 15 and 16.

17. Wolf-Henning Ollrog (1979) has argued in his dissertation that this was Paul's primary criterion for recruiting coworkers from the various churches that he planted.

way inferior to him.[18] The New Testament names over twenty-five associates of Paul who participated at varying levels of partnership in his mission. It has been estimated that 18 percent of his coworkers were women (Schnabel 2008, 251). We will discuss issues related to women in church planting in chapter 15.

New Coworkers Recruited from the Church Plants Expand the Missionary Force

One of the most noteworthy features of Paul's mission was his recruitment of coworkers *from the various churches he planted*. He recruits from the harvest for the next harvest. "The majority of Paul's coworkers came from the new churches that he had established. . . . The 'home churches' of these workers acknowledge that they share in the responsibility for the expansion of the kingdom of God by providing missionary workers who help Paul" (Schnabel 2008, 255). Though Paul's initial church-planting teams were sent out from Syrian Antioch and were composed of Jewish-background believers, he did not look to Antioch alone for new missionary recruits. Rather he recruited them from the churches he had planted, and these coworkers were increasingly of Gentile, not Jewish, origin (Ollrog 1979, 62). For example, about three years after the estimated time of Timothy's conversion in Lystra on the first missionary journey (Acts 14) Paul took him on as a missionary apprentice (Acts 16:1–3). Soon after that Timothy began working semi-independently of Paul in Thessalonica (Acts 17:14; 1 Thess. 3:1–5), Macedonia (Acts 19:22), Corinth (1 Cor. 4:17), Philippi (Phil. 2:19), and Ephesus (1 Tim. 3:14–15).

Apollos, a native of Alexandria who became a believer in Ephesus, was instructed by Priscilla and Aquila in Paul's absence and was sent as a relatively new believer to Achaia to refute the Jews and strengthen the church in Corinth (Acts 18:18–19:1). It is worth noting that Apollos is a third-generation missionary: Paul instructed Priscilla and Aquila, who in turn helped Apollos. Table 3.1 lists Paul's coworkers whose church of origin is explicitly known. Nearly every church Paul planted is listed! There were no doubt more coworkers from other churches he planted that are not explicitly mentioned.[19]

---

18. Robert Coleman (1963, 71) sees Paul's on-the-job training as a natural extension of Jesus's master plan of discipleship to prepare movement leaders: "No less than seven disciples were with Paul on his trip through Macedonia, making it a mobile school (Acts 20:4)." See also Ollrog 1979.

19. For example Titus, one of Paul's most important coworkers, was a Gentile (Gal. 2:3), but we do not know his church of origin. Eckhard Schnabel (2008, 252) speculates that he may have been converted during Paul's missionary work in Syria and Cilicia.

Table 3.1
Churches That Paul Planted and the Coworkers These Churches Produced

Church*	Coworker	Text
Lystra	Timothy	Acts 16:1
Derbe	Gaius	Acts 20:4
Thessalonica	Aristarchus, Secundus	Acts 20:4; 27:2
Berea	Sopater	Acts 20:4
Corinth	Priscilla and Aquila, Stephanas, Erastus, Achaicus,† Fortunatus†	Acts 18:2; Romans 16:23; 1 Corinthians 16:15–17
Ephesus	Apollos, Trophimus, Tychicus	Acts 18:24; 20:4; 21:29
Colossae	Epaphras, Archippus†	Colossians 4:12, 17
Philippi	Epaphroditus	Philippians 2:25; 4:18
Cenchrea	Phoebe	Romans 16:1

*The city named here is the place where the coworker either became a Christian or joined Paul's missionary band (e.g., Priscilla and Aquila were originally from Rome, Acts 18:2, but joined Paul in Corinth).
†The association of these coworkers with the city indicated is probable but less certain.

Thus many of the churches that Paul and his coworkers planted had spiritually participated in the vision to prepare and send workers for the larger mission (Ollrog 1979, 129). They trained missionaries who in turn trained others. The training was successful in most cases. We have seen that this was the case for Timothy, Apollos, Epaphras, and Aquila and Priscilla. In addition, after Paul was imprisoned Erastus stayed on at Corinth (2 Tim. 4:20), and Titus went to Dalmatia and later to Crete (2 Tim. 4:10; Titus 1:5). Recruiting workers *from* the harvest and *for* the harvest was clearly a key to the reproduction of churches and the expansion of mission. In this way training and multiplication were integrated into the church-planting approach.

Paul and His Associates Took Strategic Considerations into Account

The question of the nature and degree of Paul's strategic planning has been addressed by qualified authors (Allen 1962a; Hesselgrave 1980; Riesner 1998; Schnabel 2008; and others), and a full study is beyond the scope of this chapter. However the consensus is that Paul and his companions made strategic plans but held them lightly and adjusted them according to God's leading. In the words of J. Herbert Kane, "If by strategy is meant a deliberate, well-informed, duly executed plan of action based upon human observation and experience, then Paul had little or no strategy; but if we take the word to mean a flexible modus operandi developed under the guidance of the Holy Spirit and subject to His direction and control, then Paul did have a strategy"

(1976, 73). We will look at some strategic considerations that Paul appears to have taken into account to see how church planters today can benefit from his example.

First, Paul clearly had an *overall direction* in sight. He sought to share the gospel from Jerusalem to Rome, intending afterward to evangelize beyond Rome in the direction of Spain (Acts 19:21; Rom. 1:14–15; 15:19–24). Rome was the center of the empire and the metropolis that eminently represented the Gentile world to which Paul was called. This explains why he writes to the Romans: "I am so eager to preach the gospel also to you who are at Rome" (Rom. 1:15).

Second, it would seem that Paul did not rely excessively on long-term strategic plans. To those who postulate that Paul had an overarching plan concerning what nations and cities he would evangelize,[20] Schnabel responds, "Paul does not seem to have followed a 'grand strategy' with regard to his geographical movements. The available evidence indicates that Paul moved to geographically adjacent areas that were open for missionary work" (2008, 224). Indeed, at times Paul bypassed larger cites while focusing on smaller ones, or avoided routes that would have led more directly to provincial capitals (ibid., 281–82). This perspective echoes Kane's comments (1976, 73) just cited.

However, particularly in his later missionary work, Paul does seem to have used broad *strategic priorities*. He focused his efforts on cities with commercial, religious, or regional importance, and he did not work in villages. He sought out Jewish communities in key cities of Roman provinces along the Jerusalem-Rome axis (Allen 1962a, 13; Bruce 1977, 267; Bosch 1991, 129–30).[21] It seems that Paul followed this general plan—one province after the next, one metropolis after the next—though he may have chosen the sites progressively rather than from the outset.

Paul began in Tarsus and Cilicia (Acts 9:30), two of the Roman provinces closest to Judea. Then he and Barnabas established a base for their mission to the Gentiles in Syrian Antioch, the fourth Roman city in importance.[22] After preaching in Cyprus, the team went north to the nearest Roman province,

20. Rainer Riesner (1998, 253–55) suggests that the prophecy in Isaiah 66:18–21 about the conversion of certain nations and their inclusion in the messianic fold influenced Paul. He also (1998, 253) refers to J. M. Scott's theory (1995) that Paul may have used the table of Japhethite nations in Genesis 10:2–4. However, Schnabel rejects this theory (2008, 221). Indeed Luke never refers to Isaiah 66 or Genesis 10 in Acts, and Paul does not appear to follow a biblical road map.

21. However, Schnabel cautions, "it becomes obvious that it is a significant overstatement to say that Paul's passion was the planting of churches in metropolitan centers or in the 'strategic cities' of the Roman Empire" (2008, 281).

22. Antioch follows Rome, Alexandria, and Seleucia (Riesner 1998). Some have argued that this is not true of cities in Cyprus; but Barnabas, a native of the island, must have been aware of the strength of Judaism and its influence on the Roman populace, evidenced in the personal interest of the governor Sergius Paulus.

Galatia, which had sizable Jewish communities and a large Roman highway from Perga to the Black Sea coast.[23]

During the second and third missionary journeys, the pattern of selecting centers of Roman penetration with Jewish communities (Pisidian Antioch, Corinth, Ephesus) seems to emerge. As we have noted in chapter 2, Paul surprisingly claims that he has fully proclaimed the gospel from Jerusalem to Illyricum, so that no place remained for him to work in these regions (Rom. 15:19, 23), although many communities had not yet heard or received the message. This can be explained if Paul's strategy was to establish *strategic regional bases* that could later lead to the evangelization of entire provinces. Paul confirms this principle in the case of the Corinthians: "Our hope is that, as your faith continues to grow, our area of activity among you will greatly expand, so that we can preach the gospel in the regions beyond you. For we do not want to boast about work already done in another man's territory" (2 Cor. 10:15–16).

Paul also began by reaching out to *prepared people groups*. He went first to Jewish populations that respected the Old Testament writings and then to God-fearers associated with the synagogues. Paul apparently hoped that the latter could serve as a bridge-group to the Gentile populace at large (Bruce 1969, 277). Often a few Jews and God-fearers would come to Christ first, creating a new, mixed community that could serve as a base for Gentile evangelism. This was the pattern in Pisidian Antioch and Iconium; but in Lystra and Derbe Paul preached directly to the pagan idol worshipers. E. Stange (cited in Riesner 1998, 225–56) summarizes the factors influencing Paul's strategy:

- beginning in the Jewish synagogue (2 Cor. 11:24ff; Rom. 1:16), including the "God fearers"
- favorable or unfavorable travel circumstances (1 Cor. 16:5–6)
- focus on Roman provinces and centers (1 Cor. 16:1–16; Rom. 15:19)
- reception of or opposition to the gospel (1 Thess. 2:18)
- work in previously unevangelized areas (2 Cor. 10:16; Rom. 15:20–23)
- development and care of viable churches (1 Thess. 3:10; 2 Cor. 1:15; 2:10–13)
- leading of the Holy Spirit (Gal. 2:2; 2 Cor. 2:12)

Supernatural Guidance Took Precedence over Strategic Plans

It is apparent that Paul and his companions did not trust in their strategic plans but submitted them to God and were open to his redirection. This oc-

---

23. Riesner (1998, 276n66) argues for the strategic importance of Pisidian Antioch. Schnabel (2008, 264–66) similarly argues that both Pisidian Antioch and Perga were significant cities.

curred in several instances. They believed that God used favorable or unfavorable travel conditions (1 Cor. 16:4–9), specific revelations (Acts 16:9; Gal. 2:2), adverse circumstances (Acts 16:6), inner compulsions (Acts 16:7), and open doors (1 Cor. 16:5–9; 2 Cor. 2:12–13) to direct them. At times they were convinced that Satan was standing in their way (1 Thess. 2:18).

Paul used expressions such as "if the Lord is willing" or "if the Lord permits" (Rom. 1:10; 1 Cor. 4:19; 16:7; Phil. 2:24). Thus as he progressed God's will became clearer and clearer to him. At times, after sharing his intentions with a church, he had to change his plans, to the dismay of those he had planned to visit. After canceling a visit to Corinth he appears very human in the defense of his sincerity and integrity while he contrasts his vacillation to the certainty there is in Christ (2 Cor. 1:12–19).

Paul also took into consideration unique opportunities related to *key people and relationships*. This is true of his unplanned encounters with Lydia in Philippi (Acts 16:14–15), Priscilla and Aquila in Corinth (18:1–4, 18) and Apollos in Ephesus (18:24–19:2). More will be said in chapter 10 about taking advantage of open doors. But suffice it to say that the journeys of Paul and his companions were based on relational as well as strategic considerations and that although his team had a broad modus operandi, they were open to being redirected by God. This should serve as an encouragement to modern-day church planters to make their strategic plans humbly while always subjecting them to divine confirmation or redirection.

New Churches Were Interrelated

The churches described in Acts stood in a mutual relationship with each other. The churches were not independent but interdependent. This was demonstrated in several ways. First, the spiritual authority of the Jerusalem church and its leaders was recognized by other churches, as seen in the Jerusalem Council's decision regarding the place of the Old Testament law in the church (Acts 15). Second, churches contributed to the material needs of sister churches, such as famine relief for the Jerusalem church (Acts 11:28; 1 Cor. 16:1; 2 Cor. 8). Third, Paul recruited workers from nearly every church he planted to serve in various capacities on mission teams and in other churches. This created personal bonds between the churches. Fourth, the repeated sending of greetings between churches at the close of Paul's epistles demonstrates that a web of personal relationships had grown among them. Fifth, apostolic letters were circulated among the churches (Col. 4:16).

These examples of interdependence did not stifle the initiative or local leadership of the individual churches but reminded them that they were part of a larger body of Christ with ties of mutual responsibility and accountability. This reminds us that church planters, whether denominationally affiliated or independent, do well to help the churches they plant realize that they are part of the larger body of Christ. New Testament examples of interrelatedness should serve as an encouragement that no church stands alone, raise awareness of churches' mutual responsibility, and encourage them to work in common missionary efforts.

These principles (and the ones summarized at the end of the chapter in table 3.2) are only representative. Others could be cited. Attention to the principles found in the New Testament helps guard against the tendency to adopt methods or impose strategies that are based mostly on cultural assumptions or ecclesial traditions. New Testament principles have, throughout the history of missions, been the surest guide to avoiding many pitfalls and correcting unhealthy missiological practices.[24]

Pauline Reflections

We presented Paul's understanding and practice of mission as an argument for the importance of church planting in chapter 2. Here we look at his practice, reflected in his letters, to identify principles and emphases that will be helpful to church planters in the establishing and structuring phases.[25] We recommend the reading of Schnabel 2008, Riesner 1998, and Little 2005 for biblical studies of Paul and his mission. For a briefer but excellent summary, see Longenecker 1971.

Paul's primary mission, as he describes it to the Corinthians (1 Cor. 3) and Roman believers (Rom. 15:20), was the pioneering role of planting the initial church in a new region and moving on to new unevangelized regions. His statement about his call and priorities in the epistles is consistent with the pattern he set in Acts: "Here [in Acts 13:44–49] the typical pattern of the Pauline mission was established: an initial proclamation to Jews and Gentile adherents to Judaism, whether full proselytes or more loosely associated, and then, being refused further audience in the synagogue, a direct ministry among the Gentiles" (Longenecker 1971, 44).

Notwithstanding this singular focus for his own ministry, he demonstrated an obvious concern for the *entire process* of planting—in the sense of laying a foundation of new kingdom communities led by local leaders *and* guiding those leaders and communities so that they might have a broad and powerful impact for years to come. Even when he had to leave young congregations prematurely, he continued to strengthen them through follow-up visits, letters, and the ministry of coworkers.

24. For example, Roland Allen (1962b [1927]) and John Nevius (1958) appealed to the New Testament pattern to correct the practice of financial dependency of national workers and to establish principles of indigenous church planting.
25. Defined and described in figure 8.1.

Most of Paul's letters were written soon after the planting phase and thus give church planters valuable insights into the establishing stage of ministry.[26] They address church-planting problems that could impede the successful completion of the mission. From the epistles we discuss five aspects of the church-planting mission that are often bypassed. Many more could be explored.

Defend the Pure Gospel

The letter to the Colossians deals with influences of Judaism and local folk religions that had led to syncretism in the church. Paul confronts the issue by, on the one hand, taking the concerns and fears of the believers seriously while, on the other hand, asserting the supremacy of Christ over all powers and the adequacy of Christ to satisfy all spiritual needs (see Arnold 1996). Similarly church planters must be alert to the tendency toward religious syncretism and be able to discern how to communicate Christ effectively, addressing the worldview and personal needs of the believers in their context.

Paul passionately defends the pure gospel, writing to the Galatians: "I am astonished that you are so quickly deserting the one who called you by the grace of Christ and are turning to a different gospel—which is really no gospel at all" (1:6–7). He battles for the purity of the message of salvation with their eternal destiny in mind. He warns them that they betray the cross if they add to the gospel.[27] Paul also calls the Corinthians to be faithful to the gospel lest they believe in vain and reiterates it simply and clearly as something of utmost importance, reminding them that he did not come with clever words but preached Christ crucified (1 Cor. 15:1, 3; 1:18–31). Later he defends his apostolic call using strong rhetoric, even irony, not out of concern for his prestige or standing but because his call authenticates his message (2 Cor. 10–11).

In chapter 11 we will discuss worldview distortions of the message that lead to syncretism. Pioneer church planters must, like Paul, give careful attention to the purity of the gospel and to sound doctrine, especially when they are reaching people from a different worldview. There will invariably be those who attempt to water down, condition, expand, distort, or pervert the gospel message in some way. This is a battle that must be won at all costs. New disciples must learn to communicate the gospel to their peers faithfully so that its transforming power affects others as it has their own lives. Next they should learn to affirm and defend it using indigenous language and illustrations.

26. A discussion of the dating of Paul's journeys and letters is complex, sometimes controversial, and beyond the scope of our purposes. For guidance on dating, see works such as Ramsay 1982 (1895), Bruce 1969, Riesner 1998, and Schnabel 2004 and 2008.

27. In Galatians he retraces God's direct revelation, the apostles' hand of fellowship, and the confrontation with Peter in order to make the same point: any attack on his apostleship is an attack on the gospel of grace (Gal. 1:11–2:21).

Give Attention to Church Ethics and Discipline

More important to Paul than the welfare of his individual spiritual children is the welfare of church of Christ as a whole. He sees beyond these fledging churches to a world in need of Christ and will not allow one person's immorality to tarnish the name of Christ or cast disrepute on his body (1 Cor. 5). He calls on coworkers to solve their disputes for Christ's sake (Phil. 4:2–3) and on all believers to live and speak in such a way that Christ is honored. Although he commends the Thessalonians for their world-renowned testimony (1 Thess. 1:6–10), he also warns them about the danger of moral compromises (4:3–8). The Corinthian church wins the top prize not only for its spiritual displays of gifts and power but also for its divisiveness and impurity (1 Cor. 1 and 6). Paul is aghast at the theological drift regarding the person and work of Christ in the Galatian churches (Gal. 1–3) and he is also concerned over their backbiting and carnal behavior (Gal. 5:15, 26).

The church planter must be ready to guard the purity of the church. It is the church-planting team's responsibility in the early stage, and they need a plan for church discipline and the courage to implement it when the initial case arises (Acts 5; 1 Cor. 5). If a region's first churches cast disrepute on Jesus's name, it can hurt missionary work for generations to come. In the structuring phase patterns of church discipline should be well established, and the responsibility to exercise it should lie within the local leadership team.

Teach and Model Suffering for Christ

The danger of "rice Christians" still exists today and must be addressed by the teaching of sacrificial obedience to Christ as Lord.[28] The church faced opposition and ostracism from the beginning (Acts 4:1–17; 5:17–42; 6:8–8:3), as did Paul and his missionary teams on each of their journeys (Acts 13–21). The epistles illustrate how church planters can support those who face similar conditions. Paul encourages believers to stand firm and press on for the gospel, reminding them of his sufferings and those of their Lord. He calls them to share without wavering in the reproach and suffering attached to Jesus's name, because their reward is in heaven and their persecutors will answer for their abuses (2 Cor. 4:8–12; Phil 1:29–30; 1 Thess. 1:6; 2:2, 14–16).

Any self-serving motive for presenting the message is bound to be counter-productive. Rather, church planters must prepare converts for suffering and stand with them through it. This begins when the gospel is presented as an invitation to die as well as to live and continues as believers are reminded of their heavenly citizenship and of the temporal nature of their earthly pilgrimage. Finally, like Paul (and Peter in 1 Pet. 1–3), church planters should model

28. Expression used in China for people who professed to be Christians for personal benefit.

how to minister to a suffering church and a hurting world in the hope of a returning King (1 Thess. 4:13–18; 2 Thess. 2:8–12).

Worship in Love and Unity

Church planters are to be concerned about the spirit of worship as well as the patterns of worship. The churches Paul planted were less than stellar examples of orderly spiritual worship. The Corinthian church was particularly chaotic because of disruptive women, competing groups, unrestrained prophecies, and cacophonic sessions of glossalalia. He was most alarmed over the divisions and self-centeredness in the body, citing them as evidence of worldliness and immaturity (1 Cor. 1:10–17; 3:1–4). His severest criticism was reserved for those who participated in the Lord's Supper in an unworthy manner (1 Cor. 11:17–34).

Yet Paul did not appeal to order for order's sake, and all in all he was more concerned with the spiritual nature of worship than with the modalities involved. His goals were that the body of Christ be edified (1 Cor. 14:5, 12), the Lord's Table be honored (11:23–32), a good testimony be given (14:24), and unity be preserved (11:18–22). Following his example, church planters can find a balance between neglecting problems in community life and overreacting to them in a controlling way. Paul did not establish a detailed order of worship but called for orderliness in church meetings (1 Cor. 11 and 14) and allowed the Holy Spirit to guide believers along cultural lines. His central concern is that all be done in love and unity (1 Cor. 12–13). At one point Paul writes to the Corinthians: "And when I come I will give further directions" (11:34). Church planters can learn from Paul's extraordinary patience when dealing with problems and disorder in worship. They should take a pastoral rather than bureaucratic approach to church structure and customs of worship. In cross-cultural church planting this will avoid many cultural impositions and faux pas.

Equip Workers for Church Growth and Reproduction

In the letter to the Ephesians Paul unfolds the doctrine of the church as he does in no other letter. The Father builds the church on the foundation of the apostles and prophets, with Christ as the cornerstone (2:19–22). The equipping function of apostles, prophets, evangelists, and pastor-teachers (4:11–16) is needed to prepare believers for service (v. 12), maturity (v. 13), stability (v. 14), and mutual edification (v. 16). Investing in the lives of promising disciples pays great kingdom dividends and is essential for healthy church growth and development. The value of equipping servant-leaders can be seen in the fruit of Paul's traveling companions of earlier years: they carried on the work while he was under house arrest. Some, like Epaphras, took the gospel to new unevangelized cities while others, like Timothy and Titus, developed the churches and consolidated the work.

Paul instructs these associates about the standards for elders and deacons in more mature churches. Titus is urged to "straighten out what was left unfinished and appoint elders in every town" (Titus 1:5). The emphasis on teaching is geared not only toward purity of doctrine and of living but also toward equipping others who will also serve God faithfully (2 Tim. 2:2). This dual concern—for the health of the churches and the development of new workers—should be at the heart of every church planter's long-term vision. In church planting, the quality of ministry is dependent on the quality of leaders, and the sphere of ministry cannot grow beyond the ability to apprentice new leaders. Thus leadership development constitutes the sine qua non of church growth and church-planting movements.

Conclusion

Church planters will never exhaust the lessons found in the New Testament. Rather than pursuing the latest conference or methodological trend, why not study the Scriptures afresh to discover principles for each successive church-planting stage? While this is certainly neither the simplest nor the most popular approach, we have found that church planters who prepare well through a careful study of Scripture, and who acquire a deep understanding of the local people and their culture, have greater ministry longevity and are more likely to serve as mentors to other church planters in the future. The following twelve principles from this chapter can serve as a starting point for further studies.

Table 3.2
New Testament Principles for Church Planting

Principle	Explanation	Supporting Biblical Passages
1. *The call and guidance to plant the church*: Church planters start new churches where God sends them out of obedience to him.	The principle of calling to ministry can be clearly seen not only with Paul but also with Barnabas, Peter, James, and John. The means God uses to show his will vary.	Acts 13:2; 26:19–20; Galatians 1:11–12; 2:7–9
2. *The establishment of the church in places that are strategic for later expansion*: Church planters seek to establish churches in locations favorable to later church multiplication.	Paul established churches in urban centers of influence from which the gospel spread to the entire region.	The majority of Paul's preaching points (see principles in Acts for details)

Principle	Explanation	Supporting Biblical Passages
3. *The preaching of the Word of God for conversion*: Church planters are evangelists who share the gospel as much as possible and as effectively as possible.	The proclaiming of the Word is the primary means of kingdom advance and necessary to fulfill the Lord's Great Commission.	Acts 2:41; 4:4; 6:7; 12:24; 13:17–48; 16:31; 19:20; 28:31, cf. Matthew 28:18–20
4. *The adaptation of the message to the audience*: Church planters contextualize the message without changing its meaning.	Paul consistently tailored the message to the audience—a practice motivated by his desire to win as many as possible to the gospel.	Compare: to the Jews (Acts 13:16–41), the Lycaonians (14:15–17), the Philippian jailor (16:31–32), and the Athenians (17:22–31)
5. *The dependence on the Holy Spirit for guidance*: Church planters rely on the Holy Spirit above everything else. Spiritual guidance supersedes human strategy.	The Holy Spirit is the Missionary Spirit. The apostles depended on the direction of the Holy Spirit for their decisions although the means of guidance varied.	Acts 8:26, 39; 10:9–16; 13:2; 16:6–7, 9–10; 18:9–11; 27:23–26
6. *The use of teamwork in church planting*: Church planters work in teams and develop local ministry teams.	Jesus worked with a team of apostles and sent them out in pairs. Later Paul formed and led various teams and was constantly bringing people together to advance the gospel.	Acts 13:1–4; 15:36–41; 17:14–15; 18:1–5, 18–20; 19:21–22; 20:4–6
7. *The gathering of new believers in congregations*: Church planters help new believers form kingdom communities and grow in them.	The apostles consistently established new congregations of believers to group together those who respond to the preaching of the gospel.	Acts 2:42–47; 14:23; 18:7–8; 20:20
8. *The grounding of all new believers in their faith through teaching*: Church planters work toward the maturity and ministry of all believers.	Paul and his teammates devoted themselves to strengthening the believers through teaching, visits, and letters. They later returned to strengthen them further.	Acts 14:21–22; 16:4–5; 18:18, 26–28; 19:9–10; 20:7, 20
9. *The establishment of church discipline*: Church planters model, teach, and set up a healthy biblical practice of church discipline.	Paul followed the pattern Jesus taught and corrected churches that had neglected it. His concern was for the church's purity, its testimony, and the reflection of its conduct on the name of Christ.	1 Corinthians 3:16; 5:1–5; 6:1–20 (cf. Matt. 18:15–17); 2 Corinthians 13:1–4; Galatians 5:13–15; 6:1–5

Principle	Explanation	Supporting Biblical Passages
10. *The preparing and establishing of deacons and elders*: Church planters develop, empower, and establish local deacons and elders.	Paul established spiritual leaders initially or returned to do it. He urged his associates to establish them as well.	Acts 14:23; 15:41; 18:26–28; 19:9–10; 1 Timothy 3:1–13; Titus 1:5–9
11. *The responsibility of the local church and its leaders*: Church planters build the church along indigenous lines and turn it over to local leaders.	The apostles did not seek to maintain control over churches but turned leadership over to local leaders recognized by the people, and then moved on.	Acts 13:1; 15:4, 22; 20:17–38; 1 Timothy 5:1, 17–19; 1 Peter 5:1–4
12. *The defense of the purity of the gospel*: Church planters guard the gospel from any distortions or misrepresentations and train others to do so.	Paul fought against any compromise of the gospel. He was a servant of the cross and would not allow any watering down or distortion of the message.	1 Corinthians 15:1–3; 2 Corinthians 10–11; Galatians 1:6–7

Part II

STRATEGIC CONSIDERATIONS

4

Church Multiplication and Indigenous Church-Planting Movements

One of the emphases of this book is the expansion of kingdom communities throughout the world. The truth is that churches give birth to other churches. Living things that are healthy reproduce naturally as part of their life cycle. Churches often do not. They can grow to maturity, become numerically impressive, but remain sterile. Reproduction must be intentional if the local church is to accomplish the full purpose to which it has been called and created.

For this reason, we emphasize the need to plant churches that have multiplication potential in their DNA, that stress organic rather than organizational values, that favor centrifugal rather than centripetal growth (outward sending rather than inward retaining), and that use reproducible structures and ministries. The fulfillment of the Great Commission requires a Pauline type of commitment to taking the gospel and planting the church in outward concentric movements, always extending forward to regions it has not penetrated. In this chapter we will examine biblical and historic patterns and principles that support this outward movement of church multiplication.

Indigeneity and church-planting movements are both critical to multiplication. These two concepts go together, as we believe that only indigenous churches will truly reproduce and multiply. In the words of John Mark Terry, "The missionary effort to establish indigenous churches is an effort to plant churches that fit naturally into their environment and to avoid planting churches that replicate Western patterns" (2000, 483). Indigeneity is a necessary but not sufficient condition for church multiplication. Many other factors are at play in church-planting movements, some of which we will examine in the following pages. We also still have much to learn.

After a brief overview of church-planting movements and indigeneity in the New Testament, we will consider how these two critical factors developed in missiological thinking and practice. We then conclude with what we believe are principles and practices that contribute to church multiplication.

Church-Planting Movements and Indigeneity in the New Testament

Although the term *church-planting movement* is not found in the Scriptures, the phenomenon is. The early church did not grow in a systematic, graded fashion but through successive waves of expansion, penetrating new regions and people groups in its path.

The Judean movement that came from Pentecost (Acts 2–7) gave birth to the next wave as the believers were dispersed by persecution (Acts 8). New believers returned to their homes in Samaria, Galilee, Syria, Phoenicia, Cyprus, and Cyrene (Acts 8–10; 11:19).[1] The Syrian Antioch church came from the dispersion of believers rather than apostolic ministry (Acts 8). It became the center of a growing movement to the Gentiles (Acts 11:25–26), and from there successive waves of missionary activity extended the church through new geographic, linguistic, and ethnic frontiers (Acts 13–18).

Then Paul and his colleagues established new indigenous churches in centers of influence of the Jewish Diaspora and prepared the believers as best they could—in spite of the opposition—to spread the gospel to neighboring cities and villages. Movements also emerged from Thessalonica and Ephesus. Even Pisidian Antioch, the scene of fierce opposition to the gospel, became a missionary base such that "the word of the Lord spread through the whole region" (Acts 13:49).

Ephesus deserves special attention. As we have noted in chapter 2, it became a center for evangelism and training for the Lycos Valley and much of Asia Minor (Acts 19:26). The seven churches addressed in Revelation 2–3 and the churches in Colossae and Hierapolis were most likely extension works, and commentators surmise that the churches in Revelation were probably representative of many other churches that emerged from this movement.[2]

1. They had gathered in Jerusalem for the Feast of Tabernacles and extended their stay there to be founded in "the Way." Jesus had told them to go out with the gospel, and the persecution accelerated that movement.

2. James Moffat (1961) and Martin Kiddle (1940) suggest that there were even more churches in Asia Minor and that these were in some way representative of larger groups. William M. Ramsay (1963, 177) implies a strong movement when he writes: "There are seven groups of

Here we see an example of training local workers to start new churches. The exponential, lay-driven, evangelistic character of this growth may be observed in the highlighted phrases in the passages listed below.

- Acts 9:31. "Then the church throughout Judea, Galilee and Samaria enjoyed a time of peace. It was strengthened; and encouraged by the Holy Spirit, it *grew in numbers*, living in the fear of the Lord."
- Acts 11:20–21. "Some of them, however, men from Cyprus and Cyrene, went to Antioch and began to speak to Greeks also, telling them the good news about the Lord Jesus. The Lord's hand was with them, and *a great number of people believed* and turned to the Lord."
- Acts 12:24. James was killed, "but the Word of God *continued to increase and spread.*"
- Acts 13:49. "The word of the Lord *spread through the whole region*" (Pisidian Antioch).
- Acts 19:10. "This went on for two years, so that *all the Jews and Greeks* who lived in the province of Asia heard the word of the Lord" (Ephesus).
- 1 Thessalonians 1:8. "The Lord's message rang out from you not only in Macedonia and Achaia—your faith in *God has become known everywhere*" (Thessalonica).

In summary, the Holy Spirit led the apostles and lay witnesses to spread the Word always onward and outward, and in less than four decades the gospel had penetrated all the pagan centers of the Roman Empire. Figure 4.1 illustrates this outward movement of church multiplication.

Michael Green (1970) observes that although the apostles and evangelists had a role to play, the outward expansion of the church came primarily through the witness of lay believers as they moved to other regions. Historically, church multiplication has almost always been primarily from "Jesus movements" (lay driven and evangelistic). "So at the heart of all great movements is a recovery of a simple Christology (essential conceptions of who Jesus is and what he does), one that accurately reflects the Jesus of the New Testament faith—they are in a very literal sense *Jesus* movements" (Hirsch 2006, 85–86). The term *indigenous* is not found in the New Testament. However, New Testament studies have increasingly examined the way in which churches of the New Testament era engaged culture in ways that were both contextually appropriate and counterculturally biblical (Flemming 2005; Banks 1994; Longenecker 2002). The landmark decision of the Jerusalem Council in Acts 15 resolved the question

Churches in Asia; each group represented by one outstanding and conspicuous member: These representatives are the Seven Churches."

Figure 4.1
New Testament Church-Planting Movements

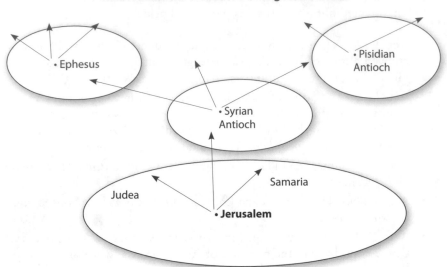

of the role of the law of Moses in the Christian church theologically. But the issue also had cultural implications inasmuch as it freed the church from its Jewish cultural confines and allowed Gentile churches to express themselves in culturally appropriate ways that did not violate biblical moral standards. Thus this decision, which has been called the "emancipation proclamation" of the church, has allowed churches to become acculturated and indigenous wherever they are planted (Flemming 2005, 43–55; Hilary 1995).

Perhaps more important, churches of the Pauline mission in the New Testament were quickly placed under the guidance and leadership of local (i.e., indigenous) elders, who were commended to the Lord (Acts 14:23; 20:32). Paul's missionary band never stayed in a long-term leadership role over the churches that were planted. Rather they itinerated, moving on to pioneer new regions with only infrequent contact with the established churches. These congregations were indigenous in that they were entirely rooted in the local culture, led by local leaders, and supported by local means. For the most part, they were led by unpaid elders and met in private homes.

Indigenous Principles

Although some of the terminology has changed, the study of church multiplication is far from new. Rufus Anderson (1796–1880) of the American Board of Commissioners for Foreign Missions and Henry Venn (1796–1873) of the English Church Missionary Society framed the Protestant understanding of indigeneity with their famous three-self formula: self-propagating, self-governing, and self-supporting (Anderson 1869). Though the three-self formula had its limitations and has been expanded upon (see discussions in Kraft and Wisley 1979), it became, at least in theory, the goal of most Protestant church planting until the midtwentieth century. But two others would critically reexamine missionary practice and shape mission thinking for decades in terms of practical ways that such indigenous churches could be planted and reproduce: John L. Nevius and Roland Allen.

John L. Nevius

John L. Nevius (1829–93), a Presbyterian missionary to China, experimented with new approaches to evangelism and church planting. He developed what came to be known as the Nevius Plan, which included three key elements: First, churches should be entirely self-supporting and led by unpaid national lay workers. He found the practice of hiring young Chinese believers as evangelists counterproductive, as such workers lost credibility, often became mercenary, and created financial dependencies in the emerging churches. Second, only church methods and means for which local believers could take responsibility should be used. He insisted that places of worship should be built in native style with local resources. Local believers should select and support their own leaders. The third element of the Nevius plan was that believers were to be carefully instructed in Bible classes. The Bible was to be central to the entire work. Converts should be tested and trained simultaneously in their natural environment (Nevius 1958).

The initial church planting in Korea serves as an example of a lay, indigenous church-multiplication movement. The response to Nevius in the missionary community was by no means unanimously affirmative. But in 1890 he received an invitation to speak to a group of seven young Presbyterian missionaries who were beginning their work in Korea. They wholeheartedly adopted his approach as mission policy. From the start the work was self-propagating, self-supporting, and self-governing, growing in four years from one church with 93 members to 153 churches with a total of 8,500 members and adherents (Glover 1960; Rhodes and Campbell 1964).

Some argue that the church's multiplication in Korea was simply due to a special work of God and the receptivity of the Koreans. However, Alfred Wasson (1934) compared the growth of the Methodist Church in Korea, which did not use the Nevius plan, with that of the Presbyterian Church, which did. He found that although these works followed parallel tracks for the first decade, the Methodist work leveled off in the next two decades while the Presbyterian work continued growing. He concluded that the main difference between the two movements was not the conversion rate but the higher rate of attrition in the Methodist Church, which he attributed to its failure to consistently follow indigenous principles (see also Brown 1994).

Roland Allen

Roland Allen (1869–1947), missionary to China and Africa and mission consultant, released in 1912 his revolutionary *Missionary Methods: St. Paul's or Ours?* and then in 1927 a sequel, *The Spontaneous Expansion of the Church and the Causes Which Hinder It*. Frustrated by the slow progress of missionary work, Allen argued for a return to methods similar to those that Paul employed to plant numerous churches over a short period of time. Observing that new church movements overseas suffered under missionary control, Allen took aim at mission leadership, contending, "If the church is to be indigenous it must spring up in the soil from the very first seeds planted" (1962b, 2). He urged missionaries to entrust local believers to the guidance of the Holy Spirit to manage their own affairs, free of missionary dominance, as Paul did, with a "profound belief and trust in the Holy Spirit indwelling his converts and the church of which they are members" (1962a, vii). Western forms of the church, foreign institutions, efforts at "civilizing the natives," outside financial support, and condescending attitudes must all be abandoned to release the spiritual dynamic evident in the mission of the early church.

The missionary church planter "then stands by as counseling elder brother while the Holy Spirit leads the new church, self-governing and self-supporting, to develop its own form of polity, ministry, worship, and life. Such a church is spontaneously missionary" (Beaver 1981, B–71). A movement that does not have these three self-characteristics will remain dependent and never become a missionary movement. Unfortunately, Allen's call to a spontaneous expansion under indigenous leadership, though widely praised, was not generally adopted in practice by most mission agencies until after World War II.

Research on Church-Planting Movements

If the nineteenth century was, to use Kenneth Scott Latourette's term, the "great century" of launching Protestant missions, then the twentieth century was the "growth century" of the churches in Africa, Asia, and Latin America. Those churches experienced exponential growth and by the 1980s came to constitute over half of all Christians in the world. By the midtwentieth century missiologists began empirically examining factors that contributed to rapidly growing movements, in an attempt to discern principles that could guide mission and church-planting practice.

The Church Growth Movement

Few have studied the dynamics of church growth and large Christian conversion movements as did Donald A. McGavran (1897–1990) and the Church Growth Movement (CGM) he launched. The CGM sought to utilize the social and behavioral sciences to research the causes of church growth and, in the process, produced hundreds of empirical studies of church growth and church-planting movements. Beginning with his landmark *The Bridges of God* (1955) and culminating in his classic *Understanding Church Growth* (1980), McGavran formulated several church growth principles that were at times controversial.

First was the principle of *people movements*—new believers should not be extracted from their natural sphere of relationships, but they should become "God's bridges" to reaching others in their society. A movement ensues when groups of people (not just individuals) decide to become followers of Christ and in turn lead others in their network of relationships to Christ. In this way believers are not socially dislocated when becoming Christians. McGavran claimed that up to 90 percent of church growth in the "younger churches" was a result of people movements.

Second, McGavran advocated the *harvest principle*, calling for missionary efforts to be concentrated on populations most responsive to the gospel. Mission outreach should focus on peoples God has ripened for spiritual harvest, much in the way that a farmer harvests only when and where the fruit is ripe. No people group should be without a witness for Christ, but the majority of missionary personnel and resources should be devoted to receptive people so as not to miss the opportunity and to maximize conversion and church growth.

By far the most controversial concept was the *homogeneous unit principle*. McGavran famously claimed, "Men like to become Christians without crossing racial, linguistic, or class barriers" (1980, 223). He argued for the planting of culturally, socially, or ethnically homogeneous churches, that is, churches composed primarily of people who are alike. In this way social barriers to reception of the gospel could be removed. People should not have to surrender their cultural identity to become Christians. The only obstacle to a person's becoming a Christian, McGavran claimed, should be the gospel itself, not culture, language, or race.

There are many parallels between McGavran's principles and concepts of indigeneity that preceded him. But the CGM came under heavy criticism for being overly pragmatic, theologically shallow, and methodologically reductionistic. Nevertheless, many observations made by McGavran and others are helpful if seen in the broader light that churches must be indigenous in form and leadership, Spirit directed, and self-supporting if they are to multiply and become a missionary force.

Sidebar 4.1

Garrison's Ten Common Elements of Church-Planting Movements

1. Extraordinary prayer
2. Abundant evangelism
3. Intentional planting of reproducing churches
4. The authority of God's Word
5. Local leadership
6. Lay leadership
7. House churches
8. Churches planting churches
9. Rapid reproduction
10. Healthy churches

Source: Garrison 2004a, 172.

David Garrison's Common Elements of Church-Planting Movements

As the twenty-first century dawned there was a renewed interest in rapid indigenous church multiplication, or church-planting movements (CPMs). Exponential church multiplication has been documented by several people, but David Garrison (2000 and 2004a), more than any other missiologist, has stirred broad interest in it through his qualitative study of CPMs in diverse settings.[3] His research focused more on the internal qualities of these movements and of the churches that reproduce to form them. He defined a CPM as "a rapid and exponential increase of indigenous churches planting churches within a given people group or population segment" (2000, 8). Although his studies of CPMs are very recent and are more descriptive than prescriptive, we want to explore the dynamics and DNA of CPMs, as well as church-planting practices that contribute to multiplication and those that deter it.

Garrison compiled breathtaking accounts of what God is doing through CPMs and identified some of their common elements. Though the accuracy of some of Garrison's case studies has been questioned, his findings are nevertheless instructive. Garrison and his research group have identified ten such common elements listed in sidebar 4.1.[4]

The suggestion is that these ten elements are indicators of the vitality and viability of the movement which enable it to transcend the lifespan of the founder(s), hurdle generational and cultural barriers, and have a broad and lasting impact. Church planters can also use them as leading indicators or benchmarks to assess their church planting, strengthen movement synergy, minimize movement deterrents, and move toward healthy practices for their context.

Without a doubt all these CPM common elements are desirable. While we find the common elements to be helpful benchmarks, reproduction cannot be expected to follow a similar path in all societies, nor will churches repro-

---

3. At the time of his study Garrison was a Southern Baptist church planter and former associate vice president for global strategy for the Southern Baptist International Mission Board.

4. Garrison also identifies factors that are often, but not universally, found and hindrances to the emergence of CPMs.

duce at the same rate or be shaped and associated together in the same way. It should also be noted that external factors such as the spiritual landscape, attitudes toward outsiders and their beliefs, and the social-political climate also play a role.

Church-Planting Movement Principles

What can we conclude from all the research and common elements discussed thus far? What are the principles and practices that will advance church multiplication and give birth to indigenous church-planting movements? It is essential that we wrestle with how to contribute to church-planting movements by identifying positive culturally adaptable practices rather than by building a global methodology or strategy. Sidebar 4.2 summarizes broad guiding principles that should serve the development of healthy culturally appropriate practices.

Church-Planting Movements Are Works of the Holy Spirit

The most commonly attested belief among people who are involved directly with CPMs is that these amazing movements are God-ordained special interventions. This is why they are sometimes described as *spontaneous* expansion or spontaneous combustion (Allen 1962b; Berg and Pretiz 1996). Humans can cooperate with God or get in the way, but God produces the growth (Mark 4:26–29; 1 Cor. 3:5–7). If there is anything that stands out in the spread of the gospel and growth of the church in the book of Acts, it is the dynamic working of the Holy Spirit. The Spirit empowers (1:8), emboldens (4:31), bears witness (5:32), gives wisdom (6:10), guides (8:29; 16:6–7), encourages (9:31), performs miracles (10:38), calls and sends workers (13:1–4; 20:28), and gives joy (13:52). CPMs are empowered by the Holy Spirit as he works through Spirit-filled church planters and believers.

Of vital concern should be the spiritual health and fervor of the initial disciples, leaders and churches. Fervent prayer and wide sowing of the gospel pave the way for church multiplication but cannot totally explain it, because similar efforts among other people groups do not always yield a church-planting movement. However, churches in CPMs display passionate spirituality, fervent prayer, strong spiritual disciplines of fasting and spiritual battle,

Sidebar 4.2

Church-Planting Movement Principles

- CPMs are works of the Holy Spirit
- CPMs are gospel centered
- CPMs are lay grassroots movements
- CPMs have a multiplication DNA
- CPMs are influenced by external factors

contagious worship, abundant evangelism, and wholesome loving relationships. Spirit empowerment and spiritual dynamics are more significant than
methodology and practices in CPMs.

Church-Planting Movements Are Gospel Centered

Church planters proclaim a gospel message that is presented in the language
of the people and touches some of their deepest aspirations. Again the book of
Acts unequivocally describes the spread of Christianity in terms of the Word
of God being proclaimed, changing lives, and giving birth to the church. The
gospel was the center of the apostolic message (4:31; 6:2; 8:14, 25, 40; 11:1;
13:5, 7, 44, 46, 48; 15:7, 35, 36; 16:10, 32; 17:13; 19:10; 20:24)—and the Word
of God itself, not the preacher or church planter, was called the primary active agent (6:7; 12:24; 13:49; 19:20). So it has been ever since: church-planting
movements are gospel driven. They uncompromisingly, boldly, and clearly
proclaim Christ, calling for faith, repentance, and obedient discipleship.

In order for the gospel to be the driving force, it must be expressed in a
language that conveys its full, powerful meaning. When the message is placed
into the hands of local people who communicate it accurately and relevantly,
it will provide the foundation for truly indigenous churches. Thus true "indigenization consists essentially in the full employment of local indigenous
forms of communication, methods of transmission, and communicators, as
these means can be prepared and trained" (Nida 1960, 185). Lamin Sanneh
(1989; 1995; 2008) has pointed out that the translation of the gospel into local
vernaculars releases the power of the gospel in the local culture and empowers
local people to self-theologize and apply that Word in fresh and relevant ways.
To become an indigenous expression of faith, a people group must go deep
into the Word for itself in order to demonstrate how the gospel addresses the
critical life issues and questions of its culture. This process of shaping life and
ministry around the Scriptures by engaging the culture through theological
reflection is self-theologizing at its best.

Church-Planting Movements Are Lay Grassroots Movements

Movement impact is directly proportionate to the degree of determined and
enthusiastic grassroots[5] participation and lay involvement. Church-planting
movements are disciple-making movements that empower ordinary people to
make a kingdom difference in the world as they rely on the power and gifts of
the Holy Spirit. This occurs when these people not only profess but also live
out the priesthood of all believers.

5. *Grassroots* evokes the sense of organic, native, rooted in the fundamental and base elements of the people group. CPMs are for the people and from the people (proletariat in the best
sense of the word) and thus are lay movements.

One of the most evident features of CPMs is that although they may be launched by missionaries, they become movements only when the local people have embraced the gospel and caught the vision to reach their people, towns, cities, and beyond. It is not a missionary, a strategic plan, or a cold sense of duty that drives the movement. Rather the Spirit of God instills new believers with a passion for Jesus Christ, a love for the lost, and a willingness to sacrifice whatever it takes to bring that message to others. Church planters can only pray for this and model it in their own lives. In this sense the "coming of age" of the movement can be jeopardized if local leaders are not Spirit empowered and sufficiently set free to set the course of the movement in the launching and establishing phases of a pioneer work.

Church-Planting Movements Have a Multiplication DNA

Church-planting movements are special works of God in which disciples, leaders, cells, and churches reproduce on an ongoing basis. Note the difference between reproduction and multiplication. If a very powerful church reproduces once every year for ten years and all the daughter churches survive, there will be a cluster of eleven churches in a decade. On the other hand, if both mother *and* daughter churches reproduce every year and all the churches survive, in the tenth year there will be 512 churches! Multiplication is multigenerational reproduction that is passed on from one generation to another as an organic part of the church DNA. Some churches will not survive birth, but those that do will be spiritually fertile. The goal is not multiplication for its own sake or even exponential growth in and of itself. The ultimate goal is the knowledge and glory of the true God over the whole earth. This will happen as more and more people groups are saturated with healthy, interdependent, indigenous kingdom communities that in turn send missionaries to the remaining unreached people groups until the Great Commission is fulfilled (see sidebar 4.3). The way this will take place is described in the healthy practices discussed later in this chapter.

....

Sidebar 4.3

Church Multiplication Terminology

- Planting: starting a new church
- Addition: starting another new church
- Reproduction: a church plants a new church
- Multiplication: churches reproduce over several generations
- Church-planting movement: the result of church multiplication; church reproduction becomes the norm and is built into the DNA of churches and church planting
- Saturation: when church-planting movements fill a geographic area with viable, reproducing churches among all its people groups

....

Church-Planting Movements Are Influenced by External Factors

The limited record indicates that all contexts are not equally suited to CPMs and that external factors are also at play.[6] Some who analyze CPMs have tended to be reductionistic, examining a limited range of influences and factors in attempt to find the golden key or silver bullet for church growth and multiplication. A more comprehensive approach, one that takes into consideration a wide range of factors and combines the various insights, will give the fullest and most realistic picture. Paul Hiebert and Eloise Hiebert Meneses (1995, 9–19) speak of various interpretive maps by which to interpret a phenomenon; each useful for its own purposes, but none gives the complete picture by itself. The church planter will, in fact, have little control over many of the important factors influencing CPMs.

For example, rapidly growing movements are found more frequently in col-lectivistic societies than in places where individualism and secularism have taken hold. McGavran's (1980, 269–94) study of people movements turning to Christ revealed that "the masses not the classes" tend to be most responsive to the gospel. It is among the poor and the working class, not the elite or upper classes, that most large movements to Christ occur. It would appear that CPMs most often emerge in times of change and upheaval, during abnormal disruptions in society, and in the midst of persecution, rather than in times of peace and stability. These seasons of change are hard to predict and impossible to control.

Often CPMs occur where folk religion or loosely structured religion pre-dominates (Grady and Kendall 1992). Clayton Berg and Paul Pretiz (1996) draw sociological parallels between grassroots Protestant churches and popular folk religions in Latin America. When the structures and expressions emerge from the local culture, like indigenous plants from their natural soil, the movement has a *natural feel* from the start. Congruent forms and functions serve like railroad tracks on which the movement can readily advance.

The relationship to the traditional establishment is also significant. If there is a mood for change, the movement should be poised to offer an alternative, but if the traditional belief system is still widely accepted, the movement should build on similarities (Allen 1962b; Peters 1970). This is perhaps why some marginalized people groups, ostracized by the majority, have embraced the Christian message more readily than the group in power (Garrison 2004a, 42, 109, 124, 221–24).

Therefore when the response is slow, church planters should pray patiently, sow the gospel, and make strong disciples using indigenous principles. There will be pressure to shift to another approach, to assume the pastoral role, or to become the primary "doers" of the ministry. But this is counterproductive in the long run. Expatriate workers who do this may plant a church—even a

6. Garrison 2004a does not list any true CPM for Europe or the United States. The closest thing to CPMs he finds are cell church networks and church-planting networks.

large church—but will not launch a CPM, and they may in the process set a negative precedent that hurts multiplication for another generation.

The following example illustrates the interplay of external factors and movement qualities. Between 1975 and 1985 in Quebec, a very traditional Catholic society, the number of evangelical local churches more than tripled, growing from fewer than 100 to 324 (Smith 1997). That period was called the Quiet Revolution because Quebec took a quantum leap toward secularization and modernity. The liberal government took over control of the public sphere from the conservative political and religious forces that had dominated society. Yet even in the wake of the Quiet Revolution the people of Quebec maintained a Christian worldview and looked for religious alternatives. This tension created a door of opportunity for the gospel. "The greatest growth took place in rural areas where disillusionment with Catholicism's grip on society left the greatest spiritual vacuum" (Wilson 1998, 28). Those who had faithfully and patiently sowed the gospel witnessed a great ingathering of believers.[7] This church growth movement waned in the twenty-first century as secularism and materialism set in, but by that time the religious landscape of the province had been changed.

Best Practices for Church Multiplication

Having examined these general truths about CPMs, the remainder of this book is devoted primarily to the church-planting "best practices"[8] that will most likely lead to church reproduction and multiplication.[9] Based on his research, Garrison has summarized "Ten Commandments for Church Planting Movements" (2004a, 257; 2005):

1. Immerse your community in prayer.
2. Saturate your community with the gospel.
3. Cling to God's Word.
4. Fight against foreign dependency.
5. Eliminate all non-reproducible elements.
6. Live the vision that you wish to fulfil.
7. Build reproduction into every believer and church.
8. Train all believers to evangelize, disciple and plant churches

7. Evangelistic efforts during the Expo 67 World Fair and the 1976 Olympics in Montreal exposed over one million to the gospel and contributed to the growth of the Catholic charismatic movement (Smith 1997).

8. The phrase is not used in the technical sense that would require controlled comparative studies but in the sense that these are presented as generally preferred practices that contribute to healthy church multiplication when adequately adapted to the culture and context.

9. Multiplication is when mother, daughter, and granddaughter churches all reproduce, producing exponential growth.

9. Model, assist, watch, leave
10. Discover what *God* is doing and join him

These practices are consistent with principles of indigeneity and church-planting movements; yet they must be applied in different ways according to the context. They are not a formula for success, and implementing them does not guarantee church multiplication. However, our observations, along with others', confirm that multiplication will rarely occur when these practices are neglected.

Unlike Garrison, we are concerned less with *rapid* multiplication than with *healthy* multiplication. He writes, "Most church planters involved in these movements contend that rapid reproduction is vital to the movement itself . . . and that when reproduction rates slow down, the Church Planting Movement falters" (2000, 36). It is desirable that churches have a short gestation period so that they do not become inward focused and fail to reproduce; and of course we rejoice when God grants rapid growth (as in the early church). Furthermore, an emphasis on rapid reproduction communicates the urgency of evangelism, the necessity of lay leadership, and the need to avoid encumbering elements such as salaries, buildings, and degrees.

However, although rapid multiplication produces more churches, it does not necessarily produce healthier churches or fruit that remains. There must be a balance between evangelistic urgency and healthy maturational growth. Forcing rapid church multiplication can sometimes backfire. Sometimes seemingly slower methods in the beginning can lay stronger foundations for not only healthier but indeed often faster-growing movements in the long run.

Interestingly, the Bible has a lot to say about church growth but not much about the rate of reproduction, and Jesus puts the emphasis on *abundant* fruit rather than rapid yield (John 15). He speaks about the mysterious (Mark 4:26–29), expansive (Matt. 13:31–32), and penetrating power of the kingdom (Matt. 13:33). But he never seems to emphasize rapidity of growth. On the contrary, he warns that *good* soil will yield different degrees of fruit (Matt. 13:23). Orlando Costas summarizes the biblical concept of balanced, healthy, and holistic growth:

> God wants and expects his church to grow—but not lopsidedly, not abnormally. He wants his church to grow in *breadth*, numerically, as an apostolic community. He wants his church to grow in *depth*, experientially, organically and conceptually, as a worshipping and nurturing community. He wants his church to grow in *height*, as a visible model, a sign of the new order of life introduced by Jesus Christ which is challenging this world's powers and principalities. (1979, 37–38)

Our responsibility is to plant churches according to biblical principles and ~~counsel~~. We strive to understand and apply best practices of indigenous ~~multi~~plication and then entrust the results, and the speed of those ~~results, to Go~~d.

Adopt an Apostolic Approach to Church Planting

Apostolic church planters (to be described fully in the next chapter) lay the foundation for reproducing kingdom communities. They equip and empower local believers and leaders using methods that can easily be replicated by these new church leaders as the planters move on to other areas to start new congregations. Then they return periodically to encourage and strengthen the leaders of established churches and may, in the process, raise up and coach another generation of church planters. The adoption of apostolic church-planting methods entails a radical rethinking of the commonly accepted role of the church planter in the Western church, away from that of a pastor-caregiver toward that of a pioneer entrepreneur who establishes new churches led by local disciples and leaders.

In areas of higher population density, such as growing multicultural cities, apostolic church planters may be involved in several church-planting projects at once, each having arrived at a different stage of maturity. In one neighborhood they may be sowing the gospel, in another establishing the leaders of a new church, and in a third helping an existing church to reproduce.

Develop, Empower, and Release Local Workers, Recruiting from the Harvest

Effective apostolic church planters identify potential local workers and pour themselves into their lives. These may be "men of peace"[10] (Luke 10:5–6; cf. Matt. 10:11–13) who welcome the gospel and grow rapidly into obedient disciples and effective lay evangelists. Many of these serve as bridge people to the community and become the most effective church planters.[11] The cross-cultural team is like the scaffolding, and the emerging national leaders are the pillars around which the church is built. A good rule of thumb is not to start a ministry or church group without local apprentices who can lead the church in the not-too-distant future.

One of the keys to the Pauline mission was the way in which Paul not only equipped and empowered local leaders to care for churches after his departure but also recruited members of his missionary team from the churches he had planted—coworkers like Timothy from Lystra (Acts 16:1) and Apollos from Ephesus (Acts 18:24–26). We shall return to the developing, empowering, and releasing of workers in chapter 17.

10. When Jesus sent out his disciples, he instructed them to seek out a "man of peace" who would welcome them and offer them hospitality. In chapter 11 we see how strategic such people of goodwill are in the early phases of church planting.

11. This was illustrated by David Garrison in a presentation to the Evangelical Free Church International Mission, February 6–7, 2006, Trinity Evangelical Divinity School, Deerfield, IL, and we have observed it repeatedly ourselves.

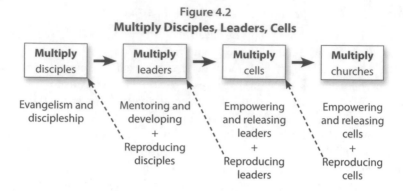

Figure 4.2
Multiply Disciples, Leaders, Cells

Maintain an Ongoing Emphasis on Evangelism and Discipleship

Since the basic building block of the church is the disciple, the focus of apostolic church planting must remain disciplemaking: Leading people *to* Christ, and instructing them to live *with* Christ, in the fellowship of Christ's community (the church). This was emphasized in Jesus's initial call, when he promised to make his followers *fishers of men*, and was his final commission, when he sent them out to *disciple the nations*. Although the need for evangelism and discipling appears obvious, it is often overlooked because the pastoral approach to church planting prioritizes plans, programs, and pastoral care. We suggest, though, that success or failure in church planting is directly related to fruitfulness in making new disciples (see figure 4.2). CPMs plateau and die when church planters move from an outward evangelistic focus to an inward-looking maintenance mode.

Build Multiplication into Every Level of Church Life and Ministry

The principles of multiplication delineated thus far apply to all phases of development of a church plant and to everything that can be reproduced: disciples, leaders or workers, cells, and churches. Thus evangelism must be done in a way that new believers can easily imitate, and those new believers must be taught to become the next evangelists. Similarly, as the first believers are discipled, they should be discipled in ways that they can in turn use to disciple others. As the first cell groups are formed, they should be led in such a way that new cell group leaders can be apprenticed to take over the leadership and then train others to do the same (2 Tim. 2:2). As cell groups divide and multiply, church multiplication is not far away because an ethos of multiplication has been built into the church from the very start. Bob Roberts (2008, 58–60) and others have argued that merely "hiving off" church members to start new churches will not in itself lead to multiplication (see figure 4.3). Multiplication must take place at every level.

Figure 4.3
Contrast between "Hiving Off" and Multiplication

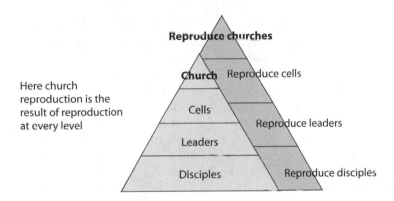

Model Ministry That Can Be Reproduced by Local People Using Local Resources

If multiplication is the goal, then the watchword in virtually everything the church planter does is *reproducibility*. Reproducibility goes beyond mere equipping in several ways. If local believers merely do what the pioneer church planters did, this will lead only to church addition. But when local believers, in turn, mobilize other local believers to serve and plant churches, multiplication begins to occur.

This can happen only when the methods modeled by the church planter are easily replicated by local believers using resources readily available to them in their context. If methods used to pioneer the church plant are not easily reproduced by local believers given their educational, financial, or other limitations, then the movement normally falters. Multiplication will be impossible. Nonreproducible methods such as short-term teams, English second-language camps, or large expensive campaigns may be employed initially to jump-start a movement. But much like jumper cables, such nonreproducible methods should be removed without delay in favor of more grassroots forms of witness and disciplemaking. Reproducible methods are characterized by the following qualities.

They Depend on Local Resources

Garrison (2000; 2004a) has demonstrated that CPMs do not normally depend on outside resources and can arise even among the poorest people group that is facing persecution. To avoid a *reproduction gap*, missionaries must begin with the resources locally available. Computers, projectors, vehicles, and large budgets may all be beyond the means of the local people. Occasional gifts of this sort may be appreciated, but if entire ministries are built on them, they will not be locally reproducible. We will come back to this below when addressing "deterrents to multiplication."

They Build on the Skills and Abilities of Local Believers

If local believers are illiterate or functionally illiterate, oral methods will need to be employed. Typically, such oral cultures are marked by exceptional storytelling traditions and skills. These can become wonderful and effective indigenous methods for evangelism and teaching. Expatriate workers are trained in ministry skills and leadership styles often not available to nationals. The expatriates may see the shape of a ministry as an issue of quality rather than culture and expect the nationals to rise to *their* standards and expectations.[12] Even if such standards were within reach of the locals, applying them would be counterproductive to the development of a CPM. Leadership skill levels should be determined by local standards and follow local patterns. For the church planter, this means maintaining spiritual requirements while intentionally keeping skill requirements to a minimum. The same principle applies to leadership style, teaching methods, standards of performance, and lifestyle expectations.

They Are Easily Taught, Caught, and Passed On

The multiplication of churches and church leaders will require methods that are not only based upon the resources, skills, and abilities of local people but also easily learned and employed by another generation of disciples. Apostolic church planters must learn to ask, "Could national workers work in this way? Would they naturally choose to do so and train others to do the same?" And they should answer these questions by progressively stepping aside and allowing local believers to adapt the pattern or develop their own.

12. Sometimes Christians from non-Western societies aspire to Western standards and "professional" quality. This may help them rise above the masses, but it diminishes their ability to reproduce their ministry patterns.

A rule of thumb is, if you can't teach local leaders to do it, and they couldn't teach others to do it, you probably shouldn't do it either. True multiplication has been achieved when local believers themselves are able to train the next generation of leaders. Whereas it may be advantageous for the long-term development of a movement that a few receive Bible school or seminary training (typically lasting years), the majority should be trained using methods that can be readily reproduced. Because such an approach is contrary to much common mission practice and may require more time initially, it is essential that everyone involved understand the importance of employing reproducible and sustainable methods that use only local resources.

Choose Contextually Appropriate Church Structures for Multiplication

When foreign church structures and traditions are imposed on a people, the church becomes, like David in Saul's armor, unnecessarily encumbered for battle. Church multiplication will rarely occur. The explosion of indigenous movements today is testimony to the importance of indigenous forms.[13] Just as a cactus would not survive long in Alaska, nor a pine tree in the Sahara, so too indigenous church structures must be developed that allow the church to thrive and multiply in its own environment. In chapter 6 we will discuss the various shapes that churches might take and how these affect the potential for multiplication in different contexts. One size and shape does not fit all. The Bible allows for great flexibility in the forms and expressions a local church might take, so long as these serve biblical purposes and are consistent with biblical values. In chapter 12 we will offer further help for discovering contextually appropriate forms of evangelism, discipleship, church meetings, worship, decision making, leadership development, and a host of other aspects of church life that are critical to church multiplication (see Hiebert and Meneses 1995). Such discoveries need to be made by local believers themselves under the guidance of the Holy Spirit and the authority of God's Word. Missionaries and outsiders may offer helpful counsel, but their role is to assist, not to dictate.

Deterrents to Church Multiplication

Movement expansion depends on the degree to which Spirit-led local believers are permitted to operate unshackled by traditional or imported structures and controls. What are some of the worst stumbling blocks on the road to church multiplication? By common consensus, the three expectations of the Western

---

13. Some of these grassroots churches are heterodox or syncretistic in their doctrine and practice. Yet their indigenous form enables them to multiply. Fortunately, with good Bible instruction and ongoing care, churches can be healthy, sound, and indigenous at once.

church that have done the most damage to indigenous church-planting movements are expensive meeting places, formally educated, paid church planters, and overdependence on outside resources. None of these were expectations of the New Testament church, and none of them survive periods of persecution. Buildings, degrees, and outside funds can occasionally be used to leverage growth, as long as they do not become part of the DNA of multiplying leaders and churches. "When, in the name of Christ's commission, we do for indigenous believers what they can and should do for themselves, we undermine the very church that God has called us to plant" (Saint 2001, 54). The following deterrents should be carefully considered.

Deterrent 1: Expensive Church Meeting Places

Garrison (2000; 2004a) observes that in CPMs the fellowships meet in homes or small storefronts. Obviously the Bible does not prescribe church size or church structure. In some contexts a movement of house churches may be the best vehicle for healthy, strong, indigenous reproduction. If a church plant decides that a more public meeting place is desirable, it is essential that the location be affordable and, in the early stages, flexible. Church plants burdened with heavy rents or mortgages will be reluctant to give away members to launch new churches. Expensive construction projects often sap the energy of the believers and can become prestige objects, distracting from more central ministries of evangelism and discipleship.

Flexibility is also essential to emerging movements. Long-term leases, contracts, or purchases can prevent a church from responding as new opportunities arise or needs change. A good alternative may be renting a public building on an hourly basis. Community centers, schools, hotel conference rooms, cinemas, concert halls, and recreational centers may be options. In rural areas, simple church buildings can often be constructed with local materials that are inexpensive and easily replaceable, but in urban centers that is seldom the case. Whenever the impression is given that to be a true church a congregation must have its own building, church multiplication will advance no faster than funds for property can be raised—and that is usually very slow.

Deterrent 2: Making Church Planting Dependent on Formally Educated, Paid Church Planters

This deterrent may come as a surprise, but it is perhaps the greatest obstacle to multiplication. There is simply never enough money to pay the increasing number of workers needed once a movement begins. Formal education of church planters, which typically takes several years at a Bible school or seminary, is not in and of itself bad. But it will take too long, and there will never be enough graduates to become church planters for a growing movement. It can also create the impression that an untrained layperson cannot or should not lead a church plant. The Western churches' clerical history and attachment to traditions are reasons that few organic movements are emerging in the West (Payne 2003). Church-planting movements normally rely on bivocational lay, local church planters and on informal (modeling and mentoring) and nonformal (church-based training and workshops) training methods rather than formal institutional education. They emphasize biblical understanding, character building, and practical ministry skills over theoretical knowledge. This is the kind of training that Nevius implemented in China and that was later adopted in Korea (Nevius 1958).

Church planting as a layperson or "tentmaker" is no easy task. Often lay-led churches remain small, but if they continually reproduce, then overall the movement will continue to grow. Lay workers who are less educated need continual encouragement and must receive ongoing training and biblical instruction, especially if they are relatively new believers. Otherwise the movement will be weak and eventually plateau or wither. As it grows, there will be increasing need for educated leaders who can provide theological guidance and depth. But making the expansion of the movement dependent on such persons creates false expectations and slows the momentum.

The Asociación Cristiana Colombiana calls its church planters *missionaries*. They have little theological education but serve with the hearts of lions. They sustain themselves through whatever employment they can find or raise minimal financial support in order to work as evangelists and disciplers but receive no outside subsidies. When a fellowship of about thirty adults and young people is formed, the search for a pastor begins, and the missionary moves on. This pattern can be repeated time and time again. Another example comes from Ethiopia. "Between 1993 and 1996 the Ethiopian Evangelical Church Mekane Yesus (EEC-MY) grew by 80%, and such phenomenal growth is due mainly to the commitment and witness of her voluntary ministries" (Gobena 1997, 15). These churches are what Iteffa Gobena calls "lay ministry churches."

One of Garrison's ten common factors of CPMs is that they are lay led, and one of his Ten Commandments for CPMs is to train *all believers* to evangelize, disciple, and start churches. "There are no passengers in Church Planting Movements; everyone is crew and expected to work" (2004a, 86).

Deterrent 3: Dependence on Outside Resources

Outside resources such as funding, financial support of church workers, equipment donations, or building projects can be a great boost to a church plant. But great caution must also be exercised to prevent the establishment of a precedent that is not reproducible and sustainable locally. This point is illustrated in the experience of Steve Saint, son of missionary martyr Nate Saint. He documents some striking examples of multiplication stumbling blocks among the Waodani. They had stopped building new bamboo "God houses" with thatched roofs. They explained that after a team came in to construct a better God house using a cement block foundation, "they concluded that only foreigners are able to build proper God houses, so foreigners should build all of them" (Saint 2001, 55).

Unwise use of resourses can inhibit church multiplication in several ways. First, outside resources are limited, and sooner or later they will end. If church planting is dependent on them, then church planting will also end. If multiplication is the goal, church planting must eventually proceed on the basis of local resources.

Second, the impression can easily be given that it is impossible to plant a church without outside sponsors and funding. Believers can end up excusing themselves from launching new church plants because they lack the sponsors that they suppose are necessary. They have no alternative models of how to do it apart from outside resourcing.

Third, when outside resources are used indiscriminately to launch a church plant, it is not unusual for the congregation to assume that outside resources should also sustain the church, according to the motto "The mission built it; the mission needs to maintain it." Stories abound of well-intentioned building projects sponsored by a mission or partner church, where the local congregation could not even afford to pay the utilities, much less multiply such churches! The patron-client relationship can quickly become the pattern for the church and mission (or sponsor), and this rarely leads to multiplication. In chapter 18 we will return to the question of resources in church planting and suggest some positive uses of outside resources.

Church Multiplication: From Generation to Generation

In the first generation of church multiplication (starting the first church), apostolic church planters must, out of necessity, model church-planting practices for local apprentices. In the second generation they work alongside the local leaders, who, having participated in the first plant, are able take the lead. In the third generation, new leaders are learning from their peers, using contextualized approaches, while the missionaries observe and intervene only when called on. If the multiplication takes place successfully, by the fourth generation the missionaries will have released the local leaders to continue the multiplication. They can advise, as needed, through coaching visits. When reproduction has taken place over three generations without the outside agency or its resources, then the DNA is set and reproduction is built into it. Furthermore, since the reproduction comes from leaders and systems that are home grown, the fourth generation can be considered truly indigenous.

The final word has not been written on indigenous principles and church multiplication. The few high-quality studies we have are often neglected. It is hard to go from descriptions of movements to best practices, especially when the contexts vary so greatly. Yet if these principles and best practices are applied in context, with much care and prayer, they can contribute to church multiplication in many more areas of the world until Christ returns.

5

Apostolic Church Planters

If launching a locally sustainable, reproducing church-planting movement is the goal, as laid out thus far, very different approaches must be adopted.[1] Perhaps most central will be a new understanding of the role of church planters. They will need to take an approach much closer to that of Paul's band of missionaries in the New Testament, what we call *apostolic church planting*. The term *apostle* is used in various ways in the New Testament, most prominently in reference to the twelve apostles who were personally called and commissioned by Jesus and to the apostle Paul, who also occupied a unique authoritative role in the first-century church. But the term is also used more generally in reference to some of Paul's coworkers who were part of his itinerant missionary band, including Barnabas (Acts 14:3, 14), Apollos (1 Cor. 4:6, 9), Epaphroditus (Phil. 2:25), Titus (2 Cor. 8:23), Silvanus (Silas), and Timothy (1 Thess. 2:6; cf. 1:1).[2] Moreover, apostleship is referred to as an ongoing spiritual gift, to be desired in the church (1 Cor. 12:28–31). Thus the term *apostle* can be considered a rough equivalent to *missionary* (see discussion in Ott and Strauss 2010, 230–36). By "apostolic church planting," then, we mean church planting that follows the apostolic model of developing, empowering, and releasing local believers for ministry and mission from the very beginning. The planters' role in the local church plant is temporary. They resist the temptation to plant the church in a way that makes it dependent on their gifts and resources.

1. Much of this chapter is adapted and expanded from Ott 2001.
2. Some Bible translations read "messenger" or "representative," but the Greek text uses the term that is normally translated "apostle."

Three Types of Church Planters

Essentially three types of church planters, corresponding to three broad approaches to church planting, can be identified: the pastoral church planter, the catalytic church planter, and the apostolic church planter.[3] Each has a different understanding of the church planter's role, will invest his or her time and energies differently, is faced with particular opportunities and challenges, is suited for a particular situation, and will have an effect on the likelihood that the church plant becomes a reproducing church (an overview is given in table 5.1).

Though the apostolic approach to church planting is not necessarily the best approach in every setting, it is the approach that has been most often blessed by God in launching locally sustainable and reproducing church-planting movements. Unfortunately most Western church planters have never observed it, were not trained in it, and thus hardly consider it as an alternative to the way they have seen churches planted in their home context. Even cross-cultural church planters tend to assume that apart from a few cultural adjustments they should plant churches as they have been planted in their home culture. But this will seldom lead to indigenous church multiplication.

The Pastoral Church Planter

The goal of the pastoral church planter is quite simply to begin a new church and pastor it. In the case of missionary church planters, normally the hope is that the church will soon be able to call and pay its own national pastor and the missionary can move on to plant another church. The method is straightforward: Initially evangelistic efforts are necessary to gather a congregation of new believers. But once a core of believers has been gathered, often quite small, the pastoral church planter tends to shift into the pastoral care–giving mode, focusing energy on preaching, teaching, counseling, and various other pastoral duties. If a church-planting team is involved, the team members assume roles similar to those in a multistaff church. Often the church planter simply stays indefinitely as pastor of the church. If the church planter is a cross-cultural missionary, the church is considered "planted" when it can call and pay a national pastor to replace the missionary.

In many parts of the world this is the most familiar and common variety of church planter. Most church planters, including missionaries, simply aren't aware of any other approach. Most seminaries train pastors, not evangelists or church planters; thus most seminary-trained church planters feel comfort-

---

3. The use of the terms *apostolic church planter* and *catalytic church planter* is by no means fixed or consistent in church-planting literature. For example, Fred Herron uses the terms in reverse manner from our use, calling the apostle Paul catalytic and using *apostolic* to characterize what we call *catalytic* (2003, 69–72, 75–76).

Table 5.1
Three Types of Church Planters

	Pastoral Church Planter	Catalytic Church Planter	Apostolic Church Planter
Goal	To plant the church and pastor it until it is large enough to call and pay its own pastor	To plant a church that will become the catalyst for mothering many other churches and launching a movement	To multiply churches that are not dependent on the church planter or outside resources
Method	The church planter serves as pastor; missionary church planters usually move on after the church has called a national pastor	The church planter plants a large, strong church and then remains as pastor or resource person to facilitate the planting of multiple daughter churches	• The church planter serves as equipper rather than as pastor, training and delegating ministry to nationals • The church planter moves on quickly, leaving ministry in the hands of local leaders
Assumptions	A church is established only when it can call and pay its own pastor	Under the right leadership a strategically located church can multiply daughter churches	Local lay believers can be equipped to provide their own pastoral leadership and multiply churches
Application	Suited for areas of moderate church growth, relative affluence, and available trained pastors	Suited for moderately responsive urban areas with potential for multiple daughter churches	Suited for most localities, especially areas with rapid church growth and rural settings
Strengths	• High quality of ministry by well-trained leaders • Long-term relationships in church and community	• Facilitates church reproduction • Networking among the new churches • Long-term relationships in the region	• Facilitates church multiplication • Promotes lay ownership and ministry • Free from dependency on outside resources
Weaknesses	• Rarely leads to church multiplication • The church planter stays too long at one location • Failure to mobilize the laity and dependency on professionals and outside resources • Rapid church-planting movements can be hampered	• Church planter must be exceptionally gifted • Not all church plants will grow or become strong enough to mother many churches • Dependent on the gifts of the church planter; reproduction may cease with the departure of the church planter • The church reproduces but seldom multiplies	• Progress is initially slower • Local believers are not always willing or capable to lead • Lay leadership may be weak or poorly trained • Most church planters are not trained in this method • Church planter may need to change location often
Examples	Most Western church planters	Rick Warren, Bob Roberts	Tom Steffen, George Patterson

able with this role. Western books on church planting assume this method. It is the model of ministry adopted in many, if not most, denominations internationally.

The members of the church plant often expect this of the church planter: "Be our pastor! That's what you are trained and paid for." Because church planters usually have more training and more time than lay church members, it is only natural that the planter bears the load of pastoral ministry. This problem is all the more aggravated if several full-time planters are serving in the same church plant on a team. The strengths of this approach are that the church plant has strong and expert pastoral care, that the local leaders can be developed over an extended period, and that the teaching is solid.

This approach to church planting works well under three conditions: (1) high potential for church growth, either because the people are responsive to evangelism or through the transfer of those who are already believers; (2) affluence, where the new church can finance its own pastor with relatively few members; and (3) the presence of trained national believers available to be called as pastor to replace the church planter. These conditions are present in much of North America; thus the pastoral approach has been generally successful there.

Unfortunately, these conditions are absent from most places where cross-cultural or pioneer church planting among unreached people is done. If church growth is slow and local resources are limited, the new church will have difficulty calling and paying a replacement for the missionary church planter. The longer the church planter remains in this role, the more the church becomes dependent on him. Sometimes a missionary church planter remains faithfully at the location for ten or even twenty years, hoping that one day a national pastor can be called to replace him or her. Usually frustration sets in sooner. The only solution appears to be for the mission to financially subsidize the calling of a national pastor—if one can be found—so that the missionary can finally move on. This only continues the dependency, which is increasingly difficult to break. Multiplication of such churches is very difficult and rare.

George Patterson warns that when the focus is on quickly starting church services with a Sunday sermon led by a missionary, the danger is establishing "preaching points" rather than New Testament churches. He writes, "Perhaps as many as 90% of church planting missionaries start preaching points with the hope that they will somehow evolve into a church. It does not happen except by the grace of God, if He's merciful. Preaching points tend to perpetuate themselves" (1981, 603). Our observations confirm this.

Furthermore, church plants that are planted and pastored by an expatriate often feel foreign to nationals, at least at first. Later, the transition from missionary pastor to national pastor can be difficult because the church has become accustomed to the foreign leadership style of the missionary. The transition will be all the more aggravated if the church planter is more educated than the national pastor.

One key conviction that underlies the pastoral church planter's self-understanding is that a church must have a fully paid, expertly trained pastor to be considered a legitimate, planted church. For sure, such a paid pastor is desirable in many situations, but a paid pastor is certainly not a biblical *requirement* for being considered an established church. The churches that Paul planted were virtually all lay led and had multiple elders. Indeed mission history up to our own day has demonstrated time and again that the most dynamic church-planting movements were lay led and not encumbered by the "how can we pay a pastor" dilemma. David Garrison (2000, 35) identifies local lay leadership, usually bivocational pastors, as one of the ten elements that rapidly growing church-planting movements around the world have in common. Only as the movement matures do paid clergy emerge.

Because the pastoral church planter assumes that one day a professionally trained pastor will replace him or her, minimal effort is invested in training and empowering the laity for genuine pastoral ministry. Furthermore, believers in the church plant can become "spoiled" by having a full-time pastor or even a whole team of fully paid workers on a church-planting team. The church planter-pastor has set a professional standard that is difficult to follow. Nationals may feel inferior because they believe that they cannot minister as well as the planter, and they fear that the church cannot survive without a highly trained, paid pastor. This thinking is perhaps the single most *unnecessary* hindrance to church planting and multiplication in most parts of the world today. Not only are missionary resources tied up at one location for many years, but a professional attitude toward ministry is instilled, which inhibits full mobilization of local lay believers and ultimately church reproduction.

The Catalytic Church Planter

A second church planter role is the catalytic church planter. A catalyst creates or effects a chemical reaction among other elements. The potential for reaction was latently present, but the catalyst sets it in motion. The catalytic church planter plants a church and remains as pastor in that church or serves as a resource person in the region to become a catalyst or facilitator for church reproduction. Considerable energy and resources are usually invested in establishing and strengthening the initial church plant with the goal that it will become a launching base for numerous additional church plants in the region. Like pastoral church planters, the catalytic planter may remain in a pastoral role in the initial church plant. But catalytic church planters differ from pastoral church planters in that they have not only the vision for church reproduction but also the ability and a strategy to realize that vision. Rather than focusing their energy on pastoral care and growth of the congregation, their energy is devoted largely to equipping, motivating, and releasing workers for church multiplication. They are not satisfied with planting one church and perhaps moving on to plant another—that is, church addition. They are committed to launching an entire movement out of the initial church plant, mobilizing multiple church-planting teams.

As we will describe in chapter 7, the mother-daughter or hiving-off approach is among the most effective methods for rapid church reproduction, and in North America multisite churches have become a way to reproduce churches. Such movements, however, rarely develop apart from catalytic leadership—leaders who not only have the vision but also are able to motivate and mobilize others for church reproduction. Once most church plants become established, energy shifts to caregiving and maintenance. Catalytic church planters provide the visionary leadership necessary to move the church out of its comfort zone so it can take steps of faith toward reproduction. Ideally a national pastor or laypersons should provide such leadership, but there can be a place for an exceptionally gifted cross-cultural church planter to play this catalytic role.

Catalytic church planters often work in urban areas, where the potential for planting daughter churches is great. For example, Rick Warren pioneered the planting of the Saddleback Valley Community Church. Though Warren did not leave his church to plant or pastor any of the daughter churches, under his leadership Saddleback went on to plant twenty-six new churches during the first twenty years. He was a significant catalyst used by God to ignite that reproduction of churches. Ron Sylvia planted the Church @ The Springs in Ocala, Florida, in 1995, and by 2006 it had planted ten new churches while itself growing from twenty-one to three thousand people (Sylvia 2006). Northwood Church, near Fort Worth, Texas, led by catalytic church planter Bob Roberts Jr., claims to have been instrumental in planting one hundred new churches! Roberts has discovered that a key to achieving church reproduction is to recruit and train up an army of new church planters. Like several other reproducing churches, Northwood has established its own church planter training program based in the mother church to raise up well-prepared church planters (see Roberts 2008). For an example of a catalytic church planter in Venezuela, see case study 5.1.

Such catalytic church planters are rare among nationals and even rarer among cross-cultural church planters because exceptional gifts are necessary to mobilize and sustain such a movement. Perhaps the greatest weakness of this model is the likelihood that a church planter would overestimate his or her ability to provide this kind of leadership, investing much time and energy in a single church plant while failing to actually reproduce churches. Furthermore, the church-planting movement may become very dependent on the ministry of the catalytic leader, which often ceases when that person departs. The catalytic church planter will rely on the recruiting and training of other church planters to lead the new churches. Finally, because catalytic movements are usually dependent on the gifted and visionary leadership of a planter in the mother

Catalytic Church Planting in Venezuela

Francisco Liévano, pastor of the Dios Admirable Church in Caracas, Venezuela, is a catalytic church planter. He explains the vision he had when he came to the church after being a seminary professor: "I came with the idea of planting churches. What was I going to do? Just preach and run programs for the church? Yes, I preach and run the programs but I also plant churches!" (quoted in Neumann 1999, 13).

And indeed he has. Within five years, five churches were planted, while at the same time the mother church grew from two hundred to four hundred people! Though the mother church was by no means a megachurch, catalytic pastoral leadership led to *both* the launching of daughter churches *and* the continued growth of the mother church simultaneously.

church, the church reproduces but fails to truly multiply: the church plants numerous daughter churches (reproduction), but the daughter churches do not plant their own daughter churches (multiplication). To reach multiplication, a movement cannot be dependent on just a few gifted and visionary leaders but must learn how to mobilize more ordinary leaders for further church planting initiated by the daughter churches.

A catalytic church planter needn't have the dramatic gifts or success of a Rick Warren or Bob Roberts to be effective. There is much to be said for remaining with a church plant until it has successfully launched its first daughter church and thus setting a pattern of reproduction that can be continued after the church planter's departure. Nor is it necessary that the mother church have thousands of members before it can launch a movement. Even in the moderately resistant cities of Germany, modest church-planting movements have emerged largely through visionary, catalytic leadership in churches with fewer than two hundred members.

An alternate form of the catalytic church planter is when the planter does not remain as the pastor of a reproducing church but becomes the trainer and coach of numerous other church planters. We will explain in chapter 17 how whole movements have been launched by the establishment of church planter training centers. Like the catalytic pastor, the catalytic trainer reproduces himself or herself by developing, encouraging, and mobilizing numerous other church planters who in turn plant numerous churches.

The Apostolic Church Planter

The approach of the apostolic church planter is radically different from that of pastoral or catalytic church planters. This church planter seeks to follow the model of the apostle Paul, who as far as we know never became the pastor of a church he planted. Instead, after initial evangelism, he focused on empowering the local believers, primarily laypersons, to carry on and expand the work after his departure. His ministry was more itinerate, seeking to plant reproducing churches with local leaders so that he could move on to pioneer work among new unreached peoples. Sometimes local believers would be recruited into Paul's itinerant missionary team, thus instilling vision for global multiplication and mission at the very inception of the young churches. Dependencies were avoided from the outset. With this model, the question "Who will replace the church planter-pastor?" never arises, because the planter never becomes the pastor. Rather he or she has from the start prepared local believers for pastoral leadership, convinced that they are able if provided with adequate teaching and models. This is a key to church multiplication and church planter phase-out.

If people are responsive to the gospel and a church-planting movement begins to develop, the planter may withdraw from directly planting churches altogether, allowing local believers to take initiative. The planter then assumes more the role of trainer, facilitator, and consultant to the movement. If responsiveness is slower, the church planter may phase out of the initial church plant and begin a pioneer work in the region. In this case, he should seek to recruit one or more local believers from the initial church plant to join him as apprentice church planters in the next church plant, as did Paul.

This approach has been advocated by numerous cross-cultural church-planting practitioners and writers. As early as 1851 Henry Venn, one of the first advocates of the "three-self" (self-propagating, self-governing, self-supporting) definition of church autonomy, argued that "missionaries should be very careful not to become pastors because it would divert them from their real task and would give the native pastors inappropriate European models" (Williams 1990, 6). Roland Allen's 1927 classic *Missionary Methods: St. Paul's or Ours?* drew attention to the itinerant nature of Paul's apostolic ministry and his bold empowering and entrusting of local believers to the Holy Spirit as a model for contemporary missionaries.

Glenn Kendall, who was a missionary in Rwanda and part of a rapidly growing church-planting movement, illustrates the difference between pastoral church planters and apostolic church planters in an article provocatively titled "Missionaries Should Not Plant Churches" (1988). He describes a missionary, Bob, who after fifteen years as a church planter in a large city had a small group of about sixty people meeting in a borrowed building. Another missionary, Jeff, had worked only four years in the same city but had already planted two churches and was working on a third church plant.

> Bob set out to plant a church and he succeeded, albeit slowly. Because none of his people had training or experience, Bob did almost all of the preaching and teaching. His people generously affirmed his ministry. They weren't ready to

assume his role and he wasn't eager to give it up. He has invested 15 years in this church and he didn't want to release control too soon and risk a failure.

Jeff, on the other hand, facilitated the starting of churches. He motivated and trained people to do it. He wasn't up front every Sunday. He encouraged new Christians and developed leaders from the beginning. He would not start church services unless he had nationals to lead them.

Jeff's ministry expanded as he drew out leaders to take over. Bob's ministry dragged on. He thought it would take another 10 years before he had responsible leaders. (1988, 218–19)

We would call Bob a pastoral church planter and Jeff an apostolic church planter. Kendall goes on to advocate that missionaries aim to be *facilitators* of new churches instead of leaders of them. He attributes multiplication of churches less to the responsiveness of the people per se than to a philosophy of ministry and methods that can promote church multiplication, even among peoples deemed unresponsive.

Kendall even suggests that the church planter work in two or three areas simultaneously, thus reducing dependency and forcing local laypersons to develop their churches and ministries: "Work in two or three areas or ministries at the same time. This really helps to get new churches started, because you will be the advisor, not the king pin. Working two or three places at the same time forces you to be away from them and gives room for national leaders to grow. You will strangle the new leaders unless you build into your plans time to be away" (1988, 221). Tentmaking church planters have an advantage in this regard. Because they are not able to serve the church full time, the church tends to become less dependent on them.

Garrison similarly advocates a facilitating role for the missionary church planter, saying, "Missionaries involved in Church Planting Movements often speak of the self-discipline required to mentor church planters rather than do the job of church planting themselves" (2000, 34). He observes that rapidly growing church-planting movements place a high priority on training local lay leaders who provide the pastoral care for the movement churches. One of the ten common factors of rapidly growing church-planting movements is outsiders' keeping a low profile. The church planter focuses on mentoring new believers behind the scenes. "This crisis of transferring responsibility can be minimized when the missionary shares responsibility from the beginning with those he is leading. A church-planting pattern of modelling new church planting and worship, then assisting the church members in the process of doing the same themselves, helps to pass on the missionary's expertise to the next generation of local church planters" (Garrison 2000, 44). Training such local leaders on the job (not in seminaries) is also a key to the rapid reproduction of churches. Garrison suggests a "MAWL" approach to training local leaders: "Model, Assist, Watch, and Leave." To do this the apostolic planter must model various aspects of pastoral ministry, but this is always with a view to equipping others

Case Study 5.2

> ## The Rashtiya Susmachar Parishad Church-Planting Movement in Uttar Pradesh, India

In 1992 an indigenous Indian mission began missionary efforts in Uttar Pradesh, India's most populous state. The original approach was the "old missionary model": the church planter lived in a town and held services in his home and conducted other meetings. After ten years the effort produced about seven hundred believers in ten fields.

However, in 2002 the strategy was changed and a more apostolic model was adopted. "In the first year the church planter will plant fellowships in ten villages, train a leader for every village fellowship and hand over that fellowship to him. The missionary moves to another ten villages in the following year." Equipping local lay leaders was central to the strategy.

The result was that within one year the number of fellowships grew from 65 to 130 and the number of believers grew to fifteen hundred. Thus, through adoption of the new approach, the accomplishments of ten previous years were more than doubled in twelve months (LOP 43, 2005, 26).

Discussion Questions
1. Why do you think the new strategy was so much more effective?
2. Might similar results also be achieved by such a strategy in other contexts? Why or why not?

simultaneously and not taking primary or long-term pastoral responsibility. Expatriate church planters will thus still need to learn the local language and culture to be effective. For an example of apostolic church planting in India, see case study 5.2.

George Patterson, another advocate of the apostolic model, was involved in a church-planting movement in Honduras that planted about one hundred house churches in twenty years. The approach relied heavily on theological education by extension and the in-service training of local leaders (Patterson 1981). Together with Richard Scoggins he has produced the *Church Multiplication Guide* (1993), and with Galen Currah he has developed "Train and Multiply" as a tool to train leaders and plant churches.[4]

Paul Gupta, who trained workers and launched a multiplying church-planting movement in India (see chapter 17), advocated an apostolic approach, which he describes in this way:

Sometimes candidates think that the mission is to start and pastor a church. We make it very clear that a missionary should never become the pastor of a

4. See www.trainandmultiply.info.

new church plant among an unreached people group. Following the vision of the mission, the team will serve as a catalyst to get the movement started. From the beginning the missionaries must understand that they need to identify gifts in new believers and equip them to do the ministry of the church. (Gupta and Lingenfelter 2006, 64)

From the outset nationals must be trained to do all essential ministries: evangelism, preaching, teaching, counseling, administration. The church planter must surrender the desire to have "up front" ministry. His or her primary role is behind the scenes, equipping others. The church planter who loves to preach must learn to focus on equipping others to preach; the church planter who is gifted in counseling will need to shift emphasis to empowering others to counsel. The lay sermons will probably not be as homiletically polished or theologically astute as those the missionary could preach. But the reward will be the development of truly empowered local leaders who will serve the church well after the church planter has departed (see case study 5.3). The missionary is constantly working himself or herself out of a job, performing a ministry only so long as necessary to train a national. Indeed, apart from evangelism and initial follow-up, if a national is not available and willing to be trained, the ministry should probably not be initiated. This may make for a slower start but will result, we believe, in a more solid finish for the church plant.

The apostolic church-planting model has several inherent challenges. The apostolic church planter may need to change location frequently, which is difficult for families and inhibits long-term relationships. Few church planters are trained in such an approach, and few are really willing to restrain their ministry or slow the advancement of the church for the sake of developing lay

Case Study 5.3

Who will preach Sundays?

While on a consulting trip, Craig sat in on a meeting of the leaders of a small new church plant in an Eastern European city. They were discussing how they might move from semiweekly to weekly church services. The main obstacle was the lack of a preacher for the additional services. The language skills and background of the missionary made it impossible for him to preach on more than two Sundays a month. The initial response of the group was to request from the mission agency another missionary or to look for other outside resources to meet the need. As they began to brainstorm the alternatives, it became apparent that several of the lay leaders would preach if the missionary were to assist them in their preparation. This solution guarded against increased dependency while at the same time promoting mobilization of the laity and their ownership of the ministry.

ministers and ownership. There are situations, especially in resistant areas, where local believers just aren't suitable for leadership or are unwilling to bear responsibility. Where new believers are illiterate or nomadic or come from a radically non-Christian worldview, the process of developing leaders and churches may be long and tedious. The early departure of the missionary may contribute to major problems in the new church, as the apostle Paul experienced with the church in Corinth. Nevertheless, this is the approach that Paul used and that has been used in most rapidly expanding church-planting movements in responsive parts of the world. Our concern is not so much for speed as for locally reproducible methods that in the long run can launch a self-sustaining movement.

Which Type of Church Planter Is Best?

Each of these methods can be used by God to fulfill biblical purposes. Those contemplating a church plant can determine the appropriate model by examining the compatibility of each with broader biblical principles and each model's ability to reach biblical goals of church planting such as spiritual health, multiplication, indigenization, and stewardship of resources. Judged in this way, any of the three models might be the best model depending on the church planter, the setting, and God's sovereign working.

As indicated above, the pastoral model works best in moderate to highly responsive settings and among relatively affluent populations where trained pastors can be called, local resources are available to pay the salary, and prospects for church growth are high. It also requires that qualified pastors, usually formally trained, be locally available. In the case of cross-cultural church planting, the difficulty in transition from church planter-pastor to national pastor can be alleviated when the planter completes an internship under a national pastor as part of his or her preparation. In this way the church planter learns to adapt the style of ministry to local culture and expectations.

The catalytic model is best suited for urban areas with potential for multiple church plants in the region. A larger church often has regional attraction through high visibility and specialized ministries. That church can then, with catalytic leadership, launch daughter churches through those who were attracted from the surrounding communities and outlying areas. A larger church also has a larger pool of believers from which to recruit, train, and support church planters. However the church planter must be exceptionally gifted and able to make a long-term commitment. It requires tremendous vision and effort to keep a larger church outwardly focused and committed to reproduction.

Though not without its challenges, the apostolic model is the one that we believe will best facilitate church multiplication, especially in cross-cultural ministry settings. It is most versatile, being suited for both rural and urban settings, affluent and poor populations, and seems to be the approach that God has most greatly blessed to facilitate rapidly growing church-planting movements throughout the world. But this approach demands far-sighted patience as well as significant rethinking and retraining of most church planters. Due to heavy dependence on local lay leaders, short-term growth and progress may seem at first very slow. On the other hand, the apostolic approach has the long-term promise of more rapid reproduction and multiplication because it is less dependent on missionaries or professional church planters and outside resources. Tom Steffen explains the importance of the apostolic approach in terms of preparing for the church planter's departure:

> *The more church planters become involved in the day-to-day activities of evangelism, church development, and church multiplication, the less delegation will take place.* Indeed, such an approach to ministry usually impedes the spiritual development of nationals, and ultimately slows or halts the phase-out process.
>
> The sooner the expatriates learn to delegate ministry opportunities and provide immediate feedback, the less the above axiom will apply. (1997, 174; italics in original)

This model may face difficulty where the focus population is highly professional or educated and has the same expectations of pastoral leaders. In such settings lay leaders may receive little respect or have little time to be able to lead the church effectively. Finally, using the apostolic model, attention must be given to adequately teach and prepare local leaders. Poor or even false teaching is often a problem in rapidly growing movements where churches are led by young, untrained believers. Overcoming deeply rooted patterns of sin and societal evil and growing in worldview transformation is a process that can demand years of discipleship and wise leadership. In situations where the church planter quickly moves on, as the apostle Paul did, equal attention must be given to itinerant equipping and teaching ministries, such as that of Paul's coworker Apollos.

The church planter and each member of the team needs to be aware of the various options, be unified in their choice of the appropriate model, and consistently implement the model, being aware of its strengths and weaknesses. These considerations will often need to be made in consultation with the national church or local believers in order to avoid misunderstanding and ensure realistic expectations. In many if not most cases this will demand a reassessment of the church planter's role and self-understanding. The effectiveness of any church-planting model will largely depend on the church planter's willingness and ability to adapt his or her role to fit and facilitate the model.

Apostles and Missionaries versus Pastors and Elders

In the Bible we find several helpful distinctions between ministries that are more pioneering and itinerant and those that are more strengthening and permanent. Recognizing these differences is important for understanding the role of an apostolic church planter. In 1 Corinthians 3:6 Paul writes, "I planted the seed, Apollos watered it, but God made it grow." Here we see a distinction between the pioneering work of a planter versus the strengthening work of a waterer. Both Paul and Apollos were itinerant, and both were important to the planting of healthy churches. Though the church of Corinth has already been planted by Paul, who had departed for other pioneer work, Apollos later visited Corinth to further teach and encourage the believers there (Acts 18:27; 19:1).

In Acts 14:23 we read of how Paul and Barnabas appointed elders in the churches they had planted and commended them to the Lord, thus fully entrusting them with the ongoing spiritual leadership of the churches. Similarly, when Paul departed from Ephesus he committed the Ephesian elders to God and entrusted the church to their care (Acts 20:32). These elders remained in the churches, whereas the missionary team moved on to pioneer new locations. Until elders were appointed in a church, the work of church planting was considered unfinished (Titus 1:5).

The role of elders is described in terms of being shepherds or overseers of the church of God, providing spiritual care, teaching, and leadership (Acts 20:28–31; 1 Pet. 5:2–3). Ephesians 4:11 speaks of how God "gave some to be apostles, some to be prophets, some to be evangelists, and some to be pastors and teachers." Though there is no doubt some overlap among the functions of these offices, there are still differences in emphasis. The Greek term translated as "apostle" derives from the concept of being sent, thus underlining the missionary and more itinerant nature of the ministry. The office of pastor and teacher is more or less equivalent to that of church elder. Table 5.2 summarizes our findings.

Table 5.2

Planters versus Waterers

Apostles, Missionaries, Planters	Pastors, Elders, Waterers
Itinerant	Remain
Pioneer	Strengthen
Initiate	Grow
Evangelize and disciple	Teach and counsel
Equip and appoint elders	Care for believers

These distinctions are not hard and fast. For example, although Paul was primarily an apostolic church planter, he also nurtured and taught the believers (e.g., Acts 20:20; 1 Thess. 2:8–12). But the apostolic planter always has an eye to his or her departure, the equipping of local believers who will remain behind, and the recruiting of additional church planters. The passion of the apostolic church planter is to move on to pioneer new regions (Rom. 15:20), not to remain as a pastor. Thus, after initial evangelism, the apostolic church planter will make the developing, empowering, and releasing of local believers a priority, will be ever cognizant of the temporary nature of her or his ministry, and will have a view to multiplication. This leads us to the evolving role of the apostolic church planter.

The Evolving Role of Apostolic Church Planters

Apostolic church planters have the goal of equipping local believers to lead the church and to become the next generation of church planters. In chapter 17 we will discuss specific methods for equipping local believers for ministry. But here we note that the role of the apostolic church planter must intentionally evolve during the process, moving from the pioneering phase to the establishing, strengthening, and reproducing phases of the church plant.

As a pioneer missionary church planter among the Ifugao in the Philippines, Tom Steffen developed a practical "phase-out" approach to church planting. This model is explained in his book *Passing the Baton: Church Planting That Empowers* (1997) and represents the apostolic model we are describing. From the outset the church planter intentionally seeks to phase himself or herself out of the work by continually empowering nationals for ministry and multiplication.

Steffen became aware of how his mission agency was failing to plant reproducing churches and had neglected phase-out-oriented role changes as a part of church planter selection and preparation: "As a result, a number of church planters perceived their roles to be long-term pastors. Moreover, local believers were trained to assist the expatriates in fulfilling their objectives rather than [being trained] to take over for them. Too frequently, expatriates assumed that many years of training and ministry experience were necessary in order for nationals to lead their churches effectively, let alone plant new churches" (1997, 40). Steffen developed a five-stage phase-out approach to church planting which led not only to the effective disengagement of the missionary but to modest church multiplication. "If church planting is to become a way of life within and without a particular people, national believers must own this vision and be trained to accomplish it. To facilitate this objective, church planters must be prepared for a series of changing roles that will swiftly propel national leaders into ministry roles, hence allowing them to become proficient" (Steffen 1997, 21). He describes these roles as moving from learner to evangelist, to teacher, to resident adviser, to itinerant adviser, and finally to absent adviser (see figure 5.1). The entire church-planting team must view its church-planting task as a temporary one: they exist to accomplish certain goals of equipping local believers and then moving on, what Steffen calls "phase-out." He claims that it takes a certain type of individual to adopt such a selfless role, to genuinely place the development of nationals as leaders above the church planter's own desires to serve and lead.

Figure 5.1
Tom Steffen's Phase-Out Oriented Role Changes
in Missionary Church Planting

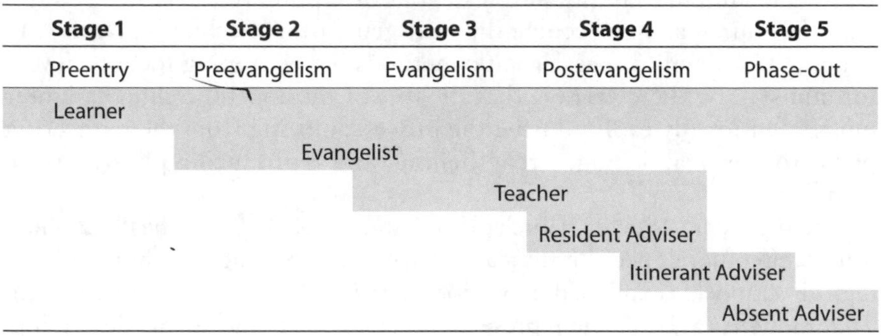

Stage 1	Stage 2	Stage 3	Stage 4	Stage 5
Preentry	Preevangelism	Evangelism	Postevangelism	Phase-out

Learner

Evangelist

Teacher

Resident Adviser

Itinerant Adviser

Absent Adviser

We suggest a "6-M" approach to the changing role of the apostolic church planter, progressing from motor to model, mobilizer, mentor, multiplier, and finally memory (see figure 5.2). In a pioneer church-planting situation the planter begins as the *motor* because there are few if any other believers present who can be mobilized. But as soon as people become believers, the missionary begins to become more of a *model*, doing ministry in a manner that is easily copied by the new believers. He or she *mobilizes* them to take ownership of the ministry and *mentors* them in developing their ministry skills. The church planter *mentors* young believers and trains them to train others, at which point true *multiplication* of workers, and ultimately of churches, is being achieved. At this point the church planter can fully disengage from the church plant and thus become a *memory*—either moving on to pioneer a new church plant (ideally taking members from the first church plant as trainees) or continuing as a regional church-planting coach to help nurture the movement and advise local church planters.

Figure 5.2
The 6-M Roles of Apostolic Church Planters

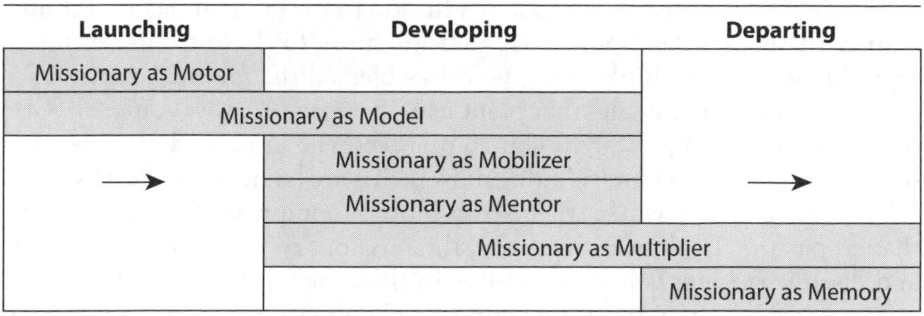

Launching	Developing	Departing
Missionary as Motor		
Missionary as Model		
→	Missionary as Mobilizer	
	Missionary as Mentor	→
	Missionary as Multiplier	
		Missionary as Memory

Missionary as Motor—In the pioneer situation there are no other believers present. Thus the missionary or missionary team must be the motor to get the work started. Primary focus will be evangelism.
Danger: Remaining a motor too long.

Missionary as Model—The missionary models ministry demonstrating evangelism, teaching, leading, etc. New believers will tend to follow the example of the missionary.
Danger: Modeling ministry in a way that is not reproducible.

Missionary as Mobilizer—As local people are won for Christ, the missionary motivates them for discipleship, service, and ownership of the ministry. They must come to sense God's calling in their lives. *They* will be the ones ultimately responsible for outreach and ministry, not the missionary or mission.
Dangers: The missionary doing too much too long, or pushing ministry ahead before there is real ownership.

Missionary as Mentor—The missionary equips local believers for all essential ministries *as* those ministries are initiated. From the start they are responsible. The missionary increasingly plays a background role as mentor, advisor, coach. On-the-job equipping is central.
Dangers: Overuse of the school approach to equipping (abstract learning separated from actual praxis). Setting standards for ministry too high.

Missionary as Multiplier—The missionary equips local believers to become equippers of others and coaches the planting of the first daughter church. The missionary no longer performs "front line" ministry.
Danger: Missionary remains the real leader behind the scenes.

Missionary as Memory—The missionary having reproduced him/herself in local believers departs, either moving to another location (perhaps taking a national along as apprentice missionary), or becoming a regional church-planting coach.
Danger: Staying too long.

While many church planters will agree with this approach in principle, difficulties arise when local believers seem to lag in their willingness or ability to bear the responsibility of ministry. Often the church planter becomes impatient and presses forward, initiating new programs and taking on more ministry responsibility, hoping that the nationals will catch up with a little time and maturity. But the opposite often happens: The local believers become increasingly dependent on the church planter, feeling inadequate to minister and convinced that the planter has no confidence in their abilities. Worst of all, they learn that if they just wait long enough, the missionary will plant the church and run the program without them! The church is viewed as the missionary's project apart from their contribution.

In this chapter we have seen that in addition to the familiar pastoral church planter there are other approaches that are more likely to facilitate church reproduction and multiplication. God has blessed the familiar pastoral approach, though the churches they plant usually reproduce slowly, if at all. God occasionally raises up catalytic church planters who impact whole cities. But the most remarkable church planting movements are launched and led by apostolic church planters who see themselves more as equippers of church planters than as pastors. In pioneer situations, the missionary will need to evangelize and disciple the first believers. But it is in those new believers that seeds for movement expansion and leadership lay. The greatest movement potential will be achieved by developing, empowering, and releasing local believers to evangelize, disciple, and plant churches in the power of the Holy Spirit.

6

The Shape of the Church

God himself, the creator of the church, gives its life and form. He transforms people, adds them to the community, gives them gifts, and calls servant-leaders. His primary focus in the Scriptures is on believers and their collective fellowship.

In chapter 1 we defined the church's essence and identified its key purposes. But when we speak in this chapter of *shape* we are referring to a church's chosen pattern of gathering and operating together—whether public or private, in small groups or as a large all-inclusive group, in one repeated type of gathering (such as a Sunday worship service) or according to a rhythm combining various types of gatherings. One might be tempted to think that shape is inconsequential. On the contrary, God has created the church as a living organism that adapts, penetrates, and transforms like yeast in dough (Matt. 13:33). The purpose of this chapter is to help church planters select a basic church shape and work with local believers to contextualize church structures and ministries. Many excellent works have been written on contextualization, and we encourage further study in this area.[1]

1. Paul Hiebert has summarized the historical approaches and laid out important parameters in his article "Critical Contextualization" (1987). For an overview of the topic of contextualization past and present see Flemming 2005, Shorter 1988, and Kraft 2005. Also consider Hesselgrave and Rommen 1989, Hiebert 1994, and Hiebert and Meneses 1995.

Diversity in Shape

Those who have visited church fellowships in different lands can attest to the great variety of manners in which the church meets for worship, edification, and service. Today larger celebrations flourish in some societies while in others, like sparsely populated tribal or nomadic regions, small family-based groupings are the norm. In densely populated cities you might find prison churches, street churches, school-based churches, company-based churches, churches in pubs, and other affinity-group churches.[2] Persecution or freedom, poverty or affluence, traditional or progressive societies—these factors were, and remain, significant in the formation of churches. And with Christianity's center of gravity having moved south and east, new forms of the church continue to emerge. As Andrew Walls observes, "This is likely to mean the appearance of new themes and priorities undreamt of by ourselves or by earlier Christian ages; for it is the mark of Christian faith that it must bring Christ to the big issues which are closest to men's hearts; and it does so through the structures by which people perceive and recognize their world; and these are not the same for all men" (1985, 223).

The Task of Shaping the Church

The Scriptures give broad guidelines regarding certain aspects of church organization, but few details are normative. Some might therefore neglect giving thoughtful consideration to structures and patterns of assembly. This would be a mistake.

> While there is no one right or final way to shape the church, this does not mean that shape is incidental or irrelevant. Form and content are intimately bound together—the medium is the message. The structure of the church is a visible and tangible expression of its faith and witness. As God's redeeming love is "enfleshed" or incarnated in Jesus Christ, so the proclamation of the gospel is incarnated (faithfully or unfaithfully) within the organizational life and practice of the church—the body of Christ within the world. (Dietterich 2004, 1)

Choices made by planters will have a significant impact on church establishment, growth, health, and reproduction; and the patterns that are set early in the life of the church become very difficult to change later. Just as patterns of common meals, family prayer, family discussions, education, and recreation determine the nature and health of the family unit, church patterns give the local church its character and health.

---

2. For contemporary examples see LOP 43, 2004, available at www.lausanne.org/documents/2004forum/LOP43_IG14.pdf.

Critical Reflection Needed

Neglecting critical reflection regarding the shape of the church would be a mistake for two additional reasons. On the one hand, when faced with the unavoidable decisions about church structure, planters will fall back intuitively on their default position—the model they are most familiar with or favor for personal reasons. On the other hand, experienced church planters often bring important elements to the table: biblical understanding, a broad transcultural point of view, and the spiritual maturity to handle difficult deliberations. The outsider, following the example of Paul,[3] is also in a position to biblically challenge certain aspects of social structure or values that may be blind spots for local believers. Thus in the conceptual phase it is important that the church-planting team engage in careful research, reflection, and dialogue.

One Size Does Not Fit All

Even as a laissez-faire approach would be a mistake, the attempt to make one prototype universal also falls short. Some advocate a purely *congregational design* based on the synagogue pattern. Yet although there are many similarities between the synagogue and early Christian assemblies, there are also notable differences.[4] Others appeal to the New Testament practice of meeting in homes to argue that the *house church design* should be the norm. Still, the question remains to what extent this approach can be attributed to necessity—because of persecution or lack of alternative meeting places. Furthermore, when the church was able to meet publicly, it apparently did so (Acts 20:20; 1 Cor. 14:23–24).[5] A third group defends *the large attractional church* based on the Jerusalem temple assemblies of believers and unbelievers (Acts 2:46; 5:12). But the large public gatherings of the Jerusalem church

3. Banks writes regarding local social structure and attitudes, "On some occasions [Paul] calls these into question and contradicts them by his own statements or behavior (1 Cor. 6:1–6); on others he insists they be carefully noted and followed (11:14–15). . . . In some measure the activities of Christians in his communities were conditioned by the values and patterns of the society around them and cannot be rightly understood unless considered in relation to them" (1994, 5).

4. The only time the New Testament uses the term *synagogue* to refer to a Christian gathering is James 2:2. This is a likely indication that Gentile or mixed assemblies of believers were distinguished from the Jewish synagogue. The influence of synagogue patterns is unclear since the synagogues themselves were based on voluntary associations and home meetings and not enough is known about them (Meeks 1986, 80–81). The evidence of the New Testament suggests that synagogue members who were believers left and formed a distinct local group of believers that crossed gender and ethnic lines. Their activities were based more on needs and the use of gifts than on rituals and traditions (Banks 1994, 88, 108).

5. "*The church* (as we usually translate *ekklesia*) in each city thus typically consisted of a number of small cells meeting in various private houses. Where the Christians were lucky enough to find a convert or sympathizer who could afford a more spacious house, all the cells in a city might come together on occasion for worship and instruction" (Meeks 1986, 110).

were very hard to replicate once persecution arose and after the temple was destroyed in 70 AD. Also, the source of the attraction seems to have been the supernatural works of the Holy Spirit (Acts 2:43; 3:1–8; 5:12; 9:32–42) and the convicting power of the preaching (4:13) rather than any deliberate attempt to attract people through publicity and programmatic choices.

Any of these prototypes might be appropriate depending on the context. The problem arises when a biblical precedent is applied universally and uncritically. Jesus told his followers that fresh wine requires new wineskins (Matt. 9:16–17), and he and his apostles ministered both in public venues and in homes. Furthermore, those who have studied New Testament communities in their historical context come to the conclusion that the *ekklesia* was something new rather than a carry-over of one particular social structure (Meeks 1986; Banks 1994). They also recognize diversity, functional fluidity, and evolution in the shape of early assemblies: "several customs and forms were taken over from Judaism, often with modifications: others were of purely Christian origin" (Latourette 2003, 203).

Multiple Influences in Shape

The term *shaping* should not give the impression that church planters, like potters, can imagine a final product, put their hands to the wheel, and fashion the church as they would a vase. Many influences come to bear in decisions regarding church structure: God's leading, the influence of other churches (especially the mother, sponsor, or national partner churches), the ideas of church planters, uncontrollable outside factors (persecution, resources), and the aspirations of the new community itself. The goal is to select the most strategic influences and structures so that the church is healthy, indigenous, and reproducible. Church planters would do well to understand and embrace God's creative diversity of design as they seek—along with local believers—the most culturally appropriate ways to fulfill his intended purposes for the life and mission of new congregations.

Relevant Principles

Freedom under the Holy Spirit to Shape the Church

Relatively few details regarding church structure are biblically prescribed; rather, the focus is primarily on purposes and values. From this, along with the decision of the Jerusalem Council (Acts 15), we deduce that congregations were given considerable freedom in the specifics of how church life should be structured. New Testament churches *had* to be very flexible and resilient, because in most cases they emerged in hostile territory and had to adapt to changing circumstances. It could be argued that this very ambiguity in regard to form gave the early fellowships the adaptability they needed to take root, prosper, and multiply wherever the gospel went.

The same openness and flexibility in the choice of a design is needed in our multicultural world, especially in urban centers. Relevant Scriptures should be applied to specific questions about church structure under the Spirit's guidance: "This work of the Spirit is our key resource for shaping the ongoing development of the church. As the church is taught and led by the Spirit, it develops new approaches to ministry and finds new ways to organize its life" (Van Gelder 2000, 43).

Understand the Culture before Determining a Church Design

Craig Van Gelder reminds us, "All ecclesiologies must be seen as functioning relative to their context. There is no other way to be the church except within a concrete, historical setting. . . . New contexts require new expressions for understanding the church" (2000, 40–41). Fulfillment of biblical purposes in congruence with culture, audience relevance, and missional effectiveness should be the major consideration when determining a design—not personal preference. "Though churches are all connected organically, each church has to design itself based on its local context" (Roberts 2008, 77). Planters should approach the shaping of the church humbly partnering with cultural insiders under the Word of God, and then travel together on an exciting road of discovery.

> We live in times of great social and ecclesial change. Our world is marked . . . with a radical plurality and ambiguity. These are turbulent times that affect us all as we witness the old breaking down and the new breaking through. This is not a time to foreclose experimentation, risk, alternative possibilities. Rather, we need to allow community to evoke a wide range of ecclesial expressions. I have a hope that the commitment, skill, and art required for people to create new beginnings and new communal bonds will release significant social energy and imagination. (Terry Veling, quoted in Dietterich 2004, 1)

Agents of Church Design

Contextualization is a process of prayer, reflection, and determination that the community of faith undertakes in order to become what God wants them to become. Lesslie Newbigin describes this journey: "True contextualization happens when there is a community which lives faithfully by the gospel and in the same costly identification with the people in their real situations as we see in the earthly ministry of Jesus. Where these conditions are met, the sovereign Spirit of God does his own surprising work" (1989, 154).

The community of faith must also be a hermeneutical community, interpreting both Scripture and context to make decisions about how the church will function (Hiebert 1987; 1994). The best *human agents* to guide the application of Scripture are biblically informed cultural insiders. Local people free from outside control and imported designs can, under the Spirit's direction, become the natural contextualizing community.

This hermeneutical community should be composed of church planters who are growing in their understanding of the culture and local believers who are growing in their understanding of the Scriptures. Expatriates should hold their ideas about design loosely and patiently until biblically informed cultural insiders join them in the shaping of the church.[6] They can then empower and advise these local believers in the formation of structures that they can embrace together. They should avoid excessive influence for three reasons:

1. The local church and its ministry ultimately belong to local believers under Christ. The role of foundation-layers is to organize a basic kingdom community that gathers for biblical purposes and fulfills the Great Commission.
2. Apostolic planters will move on, and if they impose *their* preferred model without the voice of the emerging community, they should not be surprised when that community sheds their idea to adopt a design that seems more natural or promising.
3. If the design is "owned" by the local leadership team, it is more likely to follow indigenous lines, draw local people, grow, and reproduce.

The hermeneutical community reflects on church shape, structures, and ministries as it studies the Word, lives out biblical purposes, and discovers what it means to be a kingdom community in its context. Then contextualization becomes the ongoing collaborative effort of this reflective leadership community.

Selecting a Basic Church Shape

Just as the church-planting team must decide which basic church-planting approach (pastoral, apostolic, or catalytic) best fits the context and mission, the hermeneutical community should select the basic shape of the church that best fits their context and mission. Every kingdom community has a unique calling and form, but understanding certain basic designs can serve as a useful starting point for contextualizing church forms and functions. That

6. Those who serve as part of the hermeneutical community should be selected carefully. Sometimes local believers become a Christian subculture out of touch with the contemporary culture. Local contextualizing agents should be believers who understand their neighbors and are able to be relevant while remaining biblical.

determination will make subsequent decisions about church structure easier. That is one of the functions of models or prototypes.

Two cautions are in order when using this approach. First, occasionally a context may require a starting point other than the three basic shapes in table 6.1;[7] second, this is only the beginning, and shaping the church contextually takes ongoing reflection and dialogue. We will begin by describing these prototypes. Table 6.1 gives a comparative overview of the designs, their strengths and weaknesses, and the context in which they tend to be most effective for God's kingdom.

House Churches

Robert Banks (1994, 26–66) lists three characteristics of the early house church.[8] Such a congregation resembled a household gathering, a loving family, and a functional body. Today house churches are built around edifying relationships using spiritual gifts, interactive study of the Word, and an incarnational approach to evangelism. They typically consist of twelve to fifty persons who meet regularly in a private home or other nonreligious venue and are led by a team of lay shepherds; however, the dominant characteristic is participatory, every-member ministry. Lay people lead worship, share in teaching responsibilities, and encourage or admonish each other during Bible discussions and prayer times. House churches are prevalent in much of the non-Western world and dominant in places like China and India. One house church movement in Cuba grew from 100 to 1,475 churches and another from 129 to 2,600 within a decade (Garrison 2004a, 134–35).

A modest house church movement emerged in the United States in the last quarter of the twentieth century.[9] Often these house churches form clusters that are loosely associated through the relationships of their leaders. The clusters are linked in church networks, a more fluid form of church association than denominations, which connect churches with similar values. Between 1998 and 2006 the largest of these, the Church Multiplication Associates (CMA), grew to over seven hundred churches. One of the catalysts was Neil Cole, pastor of

7. For example, shaping the church among nomadic peoples continues to challenge church planters. Malcolm Hunter (2000, 19) points to the tabernacle and wilderness community in Mosaic times as an alternative starting point to the temple or synagogue. One might also mention so-called new monastic communities (see for example Wilson-Hartgrove 2008) as a different model, although they generally do not see themselves as churches but rather as movements within or alongside of established churches.

8. The most authoritative biblical study is Gehring 2004. Gehring argues that the household was the most fundamental social and economic form of the ancient world: "scarcely anything determined daily life more than the *oikos* with its network of relationships" (2004, 17).

9. See for example Simson 2001, Zadero 2004, Payne 2007, and Kreider and McClung 2007.

Table 6.1
Simple Prototypes for the Initial Kingdom Community

	House Church	Voluntary Gathered Congregation*	Cell-Celebration Church
Description	• One basic Christian community • Focus on relationships and mission • Meets in home, store front, or neutral location • Often led by lay pastor • Often networked	• One congregational unit with affinity groupings • Often uses a program-based design • Meets in public building • Volunteer society • Led by ordained paid pastor	• Basic christian communities (cells) that work together for joint celebration, training, and mission • Meets in homes and periodically in a public setting • Grows by training leaders and multiplying cells
Metaphor	Church as family	Church as institution	Church as network
Examples and literature	• House churches in China • Rethinking Authentic Christianity Network, Japan • Church Multiplication Associates (Cole 2005) • Simson 2001 • Payne 2007	• Most North American congregations • Dietterich 2004 • Warner 1994	• Yohido Full Gospel Church, Seoul, Korea (Cho 1981) • "Two-winged church" (Beckham 1995) • "Metachurch" (George 1991) • Comiskey 1999
Strengths	• High accountability • Small group setting for discipleship • Able to survive persecution • Can penetrate urban settings • Does not require buildings or professional staff • Potential for rapid multiplication	• Visibility in community • Professional resources and ministry • Strong teaching and pastoral care • Time tested, familiar, stable • Can offer specialized ministries such as counseling, children/youth, recovery, etc.	• Benefits of both large church and small group • Church can grow, yet remain familiar • Decentralization of ministry into cells • Empowers lay ministry
Possible weaknesses	• Spirit of independence • Danger of controlling leaders and false doctrine • Relationships can become ingrown • Viewed with suspicion, lacking credibility • Often short-lived	• Vulnerable under persecution and demographic change • Expects professional pastor and building—expensive • Not easily adaptable to changing neighborhoods • Slow to reproduce	• Rogue cell groups • Same dangers as house church • Celebration can overshadow the cells • Demands great energy to do both cell and celebration well
Contextual fit	• Rural settings and where persecution exists • Where poverty or zone restrictions makes public building inaccessible • Rarely successful in traditional Western contexts	• Well suited for rural and face-to-face communities • Where land and buildings are accessible • In traditionally Christian areas	• Well suited for urban settings • Societies where both small and large gatherings are valued • Where voluntary associations in small groups are common

*We borrow this term from Dietterich 2004, 1.

Awakening Chapel in Long Beach, California.[10] CMA identifies itself as a network that groups several church multiplication movements around "(1) simple, decentralized, reproducible, organic systems and (2) disciplemaking" (Hirsch 2006, 80). Some North American house churches have proved remarkably effective in evangelism and reproduction.[11] Tim Chester, a British house-church leader, cites the following advantages of household-sized churches: "Household determines a *size* in which mutual discipleship and care can realistically take place. It creates a *simplicity* that militates against the maintenance mentality: there are no expensive buildings to maintain or complex programmes to run. It determines a *style* that is participatory and inclusive, mirroring the discipleship model and table fellowship of Jesus himself" (2000, 41).

House churches can multiply rapidly, but they can also be taken over by unhealthy leaders or false teachers and may have a shorter life span than traditional churches. They are normally unable to offer specialized ministries such as youth work or recovery groups. The lack of oversight can lead to instability, making it difficult to make disciples and develop leaders. Those that are connected within an association or network tend to be healthier in that their leaders can receive training, care, and oversight from theologically trained leaders.

Voluntary Gathered Congregations

In the United States the majority of Protestant churches fall into this category. They are simple congregations of fewer than two hundred people.[12] This structure has been shaped by American values and corresponds to an understanding of *ekklesia* as a voluntary gathered assembly rather than a community with diverse types of gatherings.

> Research indicates that this shape of the church has been determined more by the particularities of the North American religious landscape than by any distinctive theological stance. The legal separation of church and state, the development of a participatory democracy, the emphasis upon the religious freedom of the individual, the proliferation of denominational choices, the desire for religious association and nurture in a society of immigrants, and the shape of the modern bureaucratic organization have all contributed to the advancement of this particular model of the church. (Dietterich 2004, 2)

10. For a history of this movement and the work of CMA, see www.cmaresources.org (accessed September 16, 2009)

11. J. D. Payne studied responses to a web-based survey of 225 house church leaders in the United States. "Of these, 146 churches experienced at least one baptism in the previous year, and 123 planted at least one church within the past three years . . . 91 churches baptized at least one person in the previous year *and* planted at least one other church within the previous three years" (Payne 2007, 58–59). He calls this latter group "missional house churches."

12. See chapter 2n14.

In Europe, by contrast, national or state churches (*Volkskirchen*) had been created with the wedding of church and state in the Christendom model. Today there are few European churches that are strictly speaking state churches, though the established churches' relationship to the state remains strong as evidenced in church taxes and government sanction of specific confessions. Many people are considered "born into the church." Nevertheless, congregational life at the local parish level is more or less characterized by the features of the voluntary gathered congregation. Though the strict parish system had mitigated against church planting, in recent years church planting is being increasingly advocated by such national churches as a way to seek renewal and reach new generations (e.g., Hopkins 1988; Hempelmann 1996).

This congregational shape, though diverse in local expression, has some common features. "As the local branch of the people of God, it [the congregation] is the organizer of worship, religious instruction, community service, stewardship, and fellowship" (Stephen Warner, quoted in Dietterich 2004, 2). These typically have a professional pastor, employed either full time or part time, and volunteers who do secretarial, maintenance, administrative, educational, and youth work. Many are involved in committees, programs, and service projects. Most revolve around central programming and tend to be relatively stable and highly structured.

As Van Gelder (2000, 69) comments: "The social-contract theory of voluntary associations became deeply imbedded in North American ecclesiology. This has produced an ecclesiology with a strong bias toward treating the church primarily as an organization." These churches tend to produce workers and facilitate fellowship but may also foster static traditionalism and may deter gift-based mutual ministry because of the emphasis on clergy and a highly program-oriented approach to ministry. Decision making can become rather bureaucratic, occurring in committees, reflecting secular corporate structures.

In spite of these possible disadvantages, this type of church actually functions quite well in smaller, face-to-face communities in rural areas or ethnic neighborhoods. Though still the most common congregational form in North America, it has proved less effective in large urban settings. One key to combating the weaknesses of this design is to organize home groups and train lay leaders to lead them and facilitate mutual ministry based on spiritual gifts.

Cell-Celebration Churches

This church is also called the "two-winged church" (Beckham 1995) because it maintains a balance between the cell (small gathering) and celebration (large gathering). It combines strategies of attraction/gathering (regional public celebration) and dispersion/sending (neighborhood cells). Personal discipleship, spiritual nurture, Bible study, and evangelism are decentralized into the home groups—the church as family. Corporate worship, teaching, and attractional events occur in the celebrations or large meetings—the church as the people of God. Cell churches are different from churches *with* small groups in that the cell groups are basic communities with the entire DNA that a church should have. Even the ordinances and church discipline may be practiced at the cell level.

The challenge, however, is mustering the leadership, energy, and resources to do both wings well. In some cell church movements leaders and cells are reproduced through cloning. Each cell has an apprentice, and when the group reaches a certain number of people it multiplies by dividing the group in two and commissioning the apprentice to lead one of the groups. In cultures where individualism is not as strong a value, a cloning approach and centralized control are more acceptable. However, in many places today, forced multiplication (*grupos de doce*)[13] goes against the cultural grain and would be considered abusive. Another approach is to make the first task of a leader, whether in the cell or celebration wing, that of finding an apprentice with the right gift-mix, mentoring him or her so that reproduction can take place. Cells can have all the problems of house churches. The ongoing development of strong cell leaders is the key to healthy, yeastlike cell churches that can transform cities. For a comparative study of how cell churches function in a diversity of cultural contexts, see Mikel Neumann's *Home Groups for Urban Cultures* (1999).

Other more complex church structures also exist, such as multicongregations, where several ethnic congregations or subcongregations are part of a larger church, and multisite churches, which conduct services and ministries at multiple locations. These are, strictly speaking, not forms that a pioneer church plant would adopt, but from that could develop such a form as the church grows. Thus we forgo a discussion of them here but will briefly describe them in the next chapter, where we discuss models for church reproduction.

Examples of Determining the Most Appropriate Church Shape

Later we will discuss the process of contextualization in more detail (see table 6.2). Here we use a few examples to show how the same biblical values and purposes can be expressed through the different basic church shapes, depending on existing patterns of social gatherings.

In Tegucigalpa, Honduras, a bicultural church-planting team functioned as the hermeneutical community. As a result of a process of Bible study, reflection, and discussion (described earlier), the team members identified *core values* that they believed should shape the church. "Core values are consistent, passionate, biblical, distinctive convictions that determine our priorities, influence our deci-

---

13. The International Charismatic Mission of Bogotá (Colombia) was founded and led by Pastor César Castellanos. See Comiskey 1999 for more information on this and other cell-celebration churches in Latin America.

sions, drive our ministries and are demonstrated by our behavior" (Klippenes 2003, 95). These included both descriptions of what the church is *created to be* and the *fundamental purposes* that are part of its mission. Holding these values in one hand and key social patterns (discussed later) in the other, they looked for points of convergence. Those areas of congruence provided clues to the basic church shape that would correspond most naturally and function most effectively in their context. The result is found in case study 6.1.

In a rural, predominantly Muslim tribal society in central Asia, churches were formed in the home of seekers or "men of peace" who began studying the Scriptures. They met in large movable tents called *gers* or *yurts* (Russian term), and their structure and composition paralleled those of the extended family. Because of the importance of relationships, the gatherings included

- -

Case Study 6.1

From Core Values to Church Structure among the Poor in Tegucigalpa, Honduras

A pastoral couple that helped with relief work in the wake of the devastation left by Hurricane Mitch in Tegucigalpa, Honduras, sensed God's call to return full time to follow up their compassion ministry with disciplemaking and church planting. They were joined in the effort by a Honduran doctor and church-planting assistants from the United States. At the time some mission organizations were leaving the country, considering it evangelized. However, the team found that the poor in the barrios were largely ignored by the established, socially ascendant evangelical churches. Guided by their experience in relief work and their Honduran doctor, they chose the following core values to shape their church movement (our wording):

- compassionate ministry among the neglected
- intentional evangelism and disciplemaking
- joyful service
- loving communities of believers
- indigenous leadership multiplication

A breakthrough occurred when the expatriates and Hondurans in this reflective leadership team agreed on these values. The team then developed a vision to cover the capital and the country with disciplemaking house churches. They very deliberately developed a prototype house church led by the expatriate church-planting team with a couple of Honduran apprentices. As a result of the evaluation of the prototype group, they discovered that the new church felt too North American for Hondurans. For a house church to be truly Honduran, it had to be led by local believers. They discontinued the prototype group and established Honduran house church leaders, and the missionaries participated as church members. Some missionaries struggled with changes that followed but the movement became Honduran and continued to joyfully make disciples.

- -

both new believers and curious family members who w
teaching. Church planters found that to have any h
gatherings, they needed to include clan leaders whene
and to honor them in culturally appropriate ways.

However, in urban settings within those same coun
dislocated and are looking for friendships, often in ciub, p
societies. The level of education is higher, and social control is diminisned
diversity is much greater. In the capital of one such central Asian country, the
local believers, advised by missionary church planters, helped them to implement the cell-celebration pattern. The cell groups formed along relational
rather than geographic lines.

Contextualizing Structures and Ministries

How to determine the more specific church structures and ministries is really
part of the larger question of how to appropriately contextualize the church
in a particular cultural setting. Contextualization was the process used for
selecting the basic church shape in the examples above. Darrell Whiteman
defines contextualization in this way:

> Contextualization attempts to communicate the Gospel in word and deed and to
> establish the church in ways that make sense to people within their local cultural
> context, presenting Christianity in such a way that it meets people's deepest
> needs and penetrates their worldview, thus allowing them to follow Christ and
> remain within their own culture. (1997, 2)

We offer the following three-step process:

1. Define the nature and primary biblical purposes and functions of the
   church.
2. Study the culture to discover social forms and patterns that can serve
   the purposes of the church.
3. Implement existing, adapted, or new structures and forms to fulfill the
   biblical purposes.

In the words of C. Kirk Hadaway, Francis DuBose, and Stuart Wright, "We
can expect the church to assume certain functions growing out of its nature,
and we can expect these functions to be translated into structures as the church
takes root and grows in its cultural, social-economic, and political context"
(1987, 56). Examples of the purposes and relevant cultural forms pertaining
to this process of contextualization are provided in table 6.2. In later chapters
we will address many of these points in further detail. Here we simply give
an overview to illustrate the process.

Table 6.2

Contextualization of Church Shape, Structures, and Ministries

Define Biblical Purposes	Study Cultural Forms	Implement Contextualized Structures and Practices
Worship	• Formal worship in local religions • Structures, locations used for public worship • Forms of expression: art, music, ritual, etc.	• Those forms and expressions that are consistent with Christian worship may be adopted or adapted, many forms will be rejected
Evangelism and missions	• Channels of communication • Factors determining credibility • Individual and collective decision-making processes	• Approaches with maximum credibility, integrity and clarity will be of most importance • Accommodation of local decision-making processes
Teaching and edification	• Formal, non-formal, informal educational structures • Literacy levels • Use of story-telling and logic • Teacher-learner roles and expectations	• Initially familiar forms instruction may be adopted, but these may need to be expanded, e.g. move from rote learning to reflective learning
Service and community impact	• Ways the community meets personal and societal needs • Crisis support • Problem solving strategies	• Identify pressing needs that the church can address • Christians may come alongside existing structures or create new ones to meet needs
Fellowship	• How people informally gather for mutual support, work, and leisure • Community celebrations of important life events and transitions	• Christian gatherings may use similar venues, times, and number of participants or can be adapted consistent with biblical values and worldview • Events must counter-culturally overcome prejudices and social stratification
Governance and leadership	• Decision-making processes in families and communities • Manner of leader selection • Exercise of leadership • Change agents and processes	• Adapt existing leadership structures that exemplify servant leadership and plurality of leaders • Develop new empowering approaches such as mentoring and coaching if needed

Defining Biblical Purposes

The primary purposes as found in table 6.2 should be the starting point. The Scriptures allow much discretion as to forms, but the biblical values and functions of the church should be clearly identified and understood by the local believers. This will require much corporate Bible study and discussion. In cross-cultural church planting it is especially important that the believers come to their own biblical understandings and convictions about the church so that it is clear to them that the church is not merely an imported idea of the church planter. This will position local believers to discern how those biblical purposes can be fulfilled in culturally appropriate ways.

Studying Cultural Forms

As the church plant considers the appropriate forms and structures for fulfilling biblical purposes, they will look to structures that already exist in the culture. The list of potential forms and structures in table 6.2 is only suggestive, and many other aspects of the culture could be considered. In general one observes how people socialize, exercise leadership, make decisions, manage corporate life, and deal with change and challenges.

The entire social and cultural fabric can be compared to the streets of a city, which facilitate transportation and allow people to reach their intended destination. When contextualizing the church, the Bible determines the direction and destination, and the culture will provide most of the roads. The church will often travel in different directions with different goals from those of the general culture, but will use many of the same streets. Some lead to places the church will not want to go.

Implementing Contextualized Structures and Practices

The church may need to rename or resurface some streets. The church may also need to pave new streets to reach destinations that the general culture is unaware of. Only when one knows the cultural road map well is one in a position to plot the best route to arrive at the desired destination and identify what new roads may need to be paved. Some forms may be adopted as they stand in the church. For example, if people frequently gather in homes in the evening to share a meal and stories from the day, a similar form of meeting for mutual edification and fellowship in homes can be used. Some forms, such as the use of animal sacrifices in worship or ritual prostitution, will be outright rejected. Still other forms will be used but adapted to conform to biblical values. For example, harvest celebrations, common in agrarian societies, are often closely associated with non-Christian worship or fertility rites. Certain rituals closely associated with those idolatrous goals would be replaced even though the harvest celebration is maintained as a special time of thanksgiving.

Only the local believers can confirm that a new contextualized practice adequately fulfills a biblical purpose of the church. Such confirmation should be adduced from the response of the people as a whole (Hiebert 1987, 110). As members of the new church body implement these structures, they will be able to discern as cultural insiders that the form fits and will want to invite their neighbors. The initial core of believers may consider visiting other congregations with a diversity of structures and forms, and then reflect on those that are most appropriate in their setting (see case study 6.2).

As Hiebert (1989) has pointed out, the relationship of form and meaning is complex, and one cannot always adopt an outward form without also importing non-Christian meanings. Also, for some biblical purposes one may find few available cultural structures to serve the purpose appropriately. In such cases new Christian practices may be introduced (see case study 6.3).

Other Considerations and Cautions

The Need for Ongoing Innovation and Reform

Shaping the church is not a once-for-all task. The ongoing challenge is to facilitate internal changes so the church will remain relevant and effective as it grows and reproduces. The following considerations and cautions should help church planters grow as wise facilitators of ongoing church contextualization. Those who have traveled on this journey of shaping the church may become entrenched in their devotion to one particular shape. This would be a mistake, since social change is taking place ever more rapidly and the church must also change to remain relevant and effective in each passing generation. Churches that resist change are in danger of becoming irrelevant to a new generation around them and missing their unique calling and destiny. "It seems to me that any church which spends more on buildings than on outreach, holds all its gatherings only in 'the church,' puts its construction before missions and

. . . .

Case Study 6.2

Comparing Church Structures in Preparation for Public Worship

A church planter in a Western city decided to take the entire embryonic community (of about twenty new believers) to visit other more established churches. They had been meeting as two small groups but wanted to come together for public gatherings. The purpose was to experience various forms of worship firsthand before adopting their own. For several weeks they participated in the worship and small group meetings of other church groups. Afterward they met to discuss what practices they found most biblical, edifying, and culturally appropriate. They also identified elements that they would certainly avoid! In the process they discovered that they were part of an extended family of followers of Jesus, diverse but equally committed to the Word and the Lord. They decided to start a third cell group and then to meet together for initial worship services. They did this monthly at first and later moved to weekly public meetings.

. . . .

The Church among Nomads

Malcolm Hunter, a veteran worker in eastern Africa, discusses the challenge of finding appropriate structures for gatherings of public worship among nomads:

> To be relevant to nomads the church must . . . extricate itself from the usual sedentary model of a building. This is the greatest obstacle to overcome in countries where Protestant and Catholic missionaries have competed to build the biggest churches. The best commentary on this misguided model comes from a Somali camel herder who said, 'When you can put your church on the back of a camel, then I will think that Christianity is meant for us Somalis. I am a Muslim because we can pray anywhere, five times a day, every day. We only see you Christians praying once a week, inside a special building, when one man stands in front of and talks to God while everybody else hangs their heads and looks to be falling asleep.' Such is a nomad Muslim's view of Christianity.
>
> The church is also most relevant to nomadic societies where relationships are more important than real estate. Whatever else nomadic people may lack, they are usually socially rich, with strong family and clan ties. Abandoned or abused children are rarely seen and old people are respected and cared for within their families. Unless other influences have been introduced, such as Islamic practices, women can have a relatively high social position, as many nomadic societies are quite egalitarian. The question arises: Whose society is primitive?
>
> This social strength within nomadic societies needs to become the foundation of the church for nomads. Missionaries ought not to press for individual conversions, but to pray for transformed families which can begin to form the new redeemed society within that society. The church for nomads should not introduce unnecessary foreign religious practices, which will only alienate the new believers from their normal communities. It may even be wise to discourage the first individuals who respond to the gospel from calling themselves a church until there is a sufficient number of people, preferably whole families, that will allow the replication of all the normal social functions of the pre-Christian society. It is advisable therefore to determine early what is this minimum number that will be most conducive for healthy church growth and to work and pray towards that goal (Hunter 2000, 16).

Discussion Questions

1. What issues would you have to address because of the nomadic lifestyle? Which of the basic purposes would be most difficult to accomplish?
2. What nomadic social structures might be preserved in the Christian community?
3. What structures might be used for worship? Are there any lessons to be learned from the Israelites' wilderness experience and worship around the tabernacle?
4. What might a basic kingdom community among Somali nomads look like?

evangelism, refuses to use its building for anything other than 'sacred' functions, measures spirituality by the number of human bodies present within the four walls, has an edifice complex and is almost totally ignorant of what the Bible means by the church" (Snyder 1975, 77–78). Church planters must continually hold the things they hold dearly up to the light of the Scriptures to avoid passing on traditions. Likewise they must be willing to graciously confront "Christian" traditions in the cultures they serve, so that the churches planted truly become reproducing kingdom communities.

This does not mitigate healthy traditions, nor does it rule out the need for organization and structure. While retaining its essential nature, the church always exists in a historical form; there is no such thing as a "cultureless" church (Küng 1967, 3–5). In the words of Paul Sankey, "Incarnation requires that the gospel take expression in and through culture. There is no non-cultural or supra-cultural expression of Christianity. . . . If Christianity is not inculturated in one culture it comes in the appearance of another" (1994, 446). Because cultures are always changing, the church must continually reinvent itself while remaining faithful to its divine calling.

Thus reformers and innovators are constantly reengineering the church to come up with new types (see Towns, Stetzer, and Bird 2007). We value innovation and believe church forms should evolve—as long as the result is a healthier, more missionally effective, indigenous church that reproduces. Throughout church history God has raised up renewal movements that not only brought fresh spiritual vitality but also pioneered new expressions of Christian community.[14] These movements have often been controversial or prone to extremes, but they are nevertheless witness to God's desire to continually re-create and renew his church. There is something fresh and invigorating about a church that adapts to its context and embodies Paul's maxim "All things to all men so that by all possible means I might save some" (1 Cor. 9:22).[15]

The Dangers of Syncretism and Fragmentation

Syncretism occurs when the purity of the gospel message or the essential functions of the church are sacrificed at the altar of relevance. This can be a compromise with elements of another religion or with secular gods such as materialism, consumerism, and *me*-ism. The gospel needs to be *expressed* in contemporary forms but not at the expense of its transforming power, prophetic voice, or convicting penetration. There will always be a tension between what Walls (1982) calls the pilgrim principle and the indigenous principle. Even though the church will take new forms and expressions as

14. These include various monastic movements, Spener's *collegia pietatis* (pious groups), Methodism's "class meetings," the Pentecostal and charismatic renewals, Willow Creek's seeker-sensitive church, David Yonggi Cho's cell church, Chinese house churches, and other contemporary expressions of the church, to name but a few.

15. Indeed, we can expect that as the church is continually contextualized (or recontextualized), in the words of Whiteman, there will be new expressions of the gospel, "so that the Gospel itself will be understood in ways the universal church has neither experienced nor understood before, thus expanding our understanding of the kingdom of God" (1997, 4).

it moves into new cultural contexts (indigenous principle), it will always remain foreign as the gospel challenges and transforms culture (pilgrim principle).[16]

Another danger is overspecialization and fragmentation. Most urban centers today are characterized by a diversity of subcultures, immigrant groups, special interests, and religious affiliations.[17] Does each need a church of its own? Part of the gospel witness in New Testament times was its power to break down the walls of division in society (Gal. 3:26–29; Eph. 2:14–18). We dare not return to the excesses of the "homogeneous unit principle" to shape communities according to diverse microcultures. "The church's task is neither to destroy nor to maintain ethnic identities but to replace them with a new identity in Christ that is more foundational than earthly identities. . . . The purpose of maintaining the multiethnic church is to establish a church that is committed to seeing Christ reign among his people and to establishing a people of God who are united in their diversity" (Ortiz 1996, 130).

Finally, although shaping the church for relevance and penetration is desirable, we should not overestimate the power of contextualization nor put too much hope in our human designs. It is *the gospel* that transforms lives; and the point of contact is generally found in the marketplaces of life, not in the assembled church—whatever its shape. In fact no amount of engineering and creative contextualizing will capture the attention of the secular mind or draw the postmodern skeptic. The living Christ and the power of his message, demonstrated in transformed lives and lived out in authentic, loving communities, are the only hope of our modern pluralistic societies throughout the world.

Conclusion

The Lord did not prescribe church forms but rather allowed the apostles to follow the Holy Spirit's leading in establishing indigenous churches. Church

16. "Along with the indigenous principle which makes his faith a place to feel at home, the Christian inherits the pilgrim principle, which whispers to him that he has no abiding city and warns him that to be faithful to Christ will put him out of step with his society; . . . Jesus within Jewish culture, Paul within Hellenistic culture, take it for granted that there will be rubs and friction—not from the adoption of a new culture, but from the transformation of the mind towards that of Christ" (Walls 1982, 98–99).

17. The question is raised whether contextualization is still relevant in a "glocalizing" or "flat" world (see Andrews 2009). However, even in urban pluralistic contexts it is important to define and study the ministry focus people, though its boundaries may be in a state of flux and its values more diverse (see chapter 9). In these settings the church shape must facilitate unity around biblical essentials while allowing freedom for diversity in function. For a helpful discussion of the church in a pluralistic context, read Lesslie Newbigin's *The Gospel in a Pluralistic World* (1989).

planters today should not assume a preconceived church design that they
have experienced or seen at home. This has been done with the sad result
that often the missionary church planters are about the only ones who feel
at home in the church they establish. Rather, church planters can contribute
by helping local believers understand God's plan for the church, distinguish
between form and function, and make sure the nature and mission of the
church drive its ministries and organization. When structures are not suited
to a given context, it can lead to

- a foreign church that is never at home in the culture
- a sterile church that will never reproduce
- a syncretistic church that spreads false teachings or practices

Thus church planters must remain open to change, hold their preferred
models lightly, and serve as advisers while local believers who are cultural
insiders give shape to the church. The church is always a church *in the making*. Therefore even though the church planters' role is most important in the
conception and launch stages, they continue to exercise an influence through
their example, teaching, and spiritual guidance. Mature planters trust in God
to work in and through emerging local leaders, because the ministry and mission ultimately belong to them.

7

Pioneer, Reproduction, and Regional Approaches to Church Planting

Until recently there were relatively few well-developed models and methods for planting churches. Now so many strategies and methods abound that it can be difficult to assess which might be the most appropriate for any given situation. In this chapter we will survey a variety of approaches to church planting, beginning with pioneer church planting, where few if any churches already exist in the area and there is no nearby partner church in the effort. Then we will examine approaches to reproducing existing churches. Tim Chester (2000, 38) points out that these two broad categories, pioneering and reproducing, roughly correspond to what we find in the New Testament. Paul was primarily a pioneer church planter when he entered a new city to preach the gospel. But the churches he planted reproduced by forming numerous house churches in the same city.[1] In conclusion we will describe strategies for multiple church plants in a region.

Approaches to Pioneer Church Planting

By "pioneer church planting" we mean planting churches in locations where there are very few Christians and, apart from the church planting team, there

---

1. For example, Romans 1:7; 16:3, 5, 10–11; 1 Corinthians 1:11, 16; 16:15; Philippians 4:22; Colossians 4:15 -16; Philemon 1:2.

are few if any local Christians who will assist in the launch. The work will grow almost exclusively through evangelism. The possible approaches are summarized in table 7.1.

Table 7.1

Approaches to Pioneer Church Planting
Where Few or No Churches Exist in the Immediate Area or among the Focus People

Approach	Features
Solo pioneer *or* paratrooper church planter	A solo church planter moves to the target area and begins from scratch
Church-planting team	A church-planting team is formed and prepared; team members have diverse gifts but the same vision and calling
Colonization	A large number of persons (often from the same church) relocate to the target area, forming the new church
Nonresident *or* short-term church planting	A church planter or mission team seeks to plant a church or churches through short visits and efforts apart from a resident church planter or team
International church plant	When an international church is planted, nationals are also reached who might not otherwise be reached (usually in a context of persecution)
Indirect church planting	A church is planted as a by-product of development work, student ministry, Bible translation, or other ministries that do not normally intentionally plant churches

The Solo Church Planter

The solo church planter might be compared to a lone paratrooper who drops into a location. This has been perhaps the most common model of church planting and is the typical image many people have of the pioneer church planter. A "Rambo" ideal of a church planter comes to mind who single-handedly does the work of evangelism and discipleship, gathering the new believers to form a church. Indeed many churches have been planted this way by gifted and determined church planters.

Yet this approach is very difficult and has a high rate of failure. It may work well when the church planter is planting a church in his or her native culture and is exceptionally gifted; it may also succeed where people are highly responsive or where mature local Christians can be recruited to form a church-planting team. But it is rarely effective when crossing cultures or among populations resistant to the gospel. Most church planters are simply not gifted enough to go it alone in such settings. Even the very gifted church planter can quickly reach his or her limits, and then discouragement or fatigue sets in.

The Church-Planting Team

A second approach is the church-planting team. In this case a team of workers with a common vision and various gifts join together in the effort. Today, in cross-cultural mission, the team approach has become the norm for pioneer church planting. Often team members are all vocational missionaries, but this is not always the case; some may be bivocational. Team building and strategizing is an important part of preparing the church plant. Increasingly these teams are international or multiethnic. For example a team may be composed of an American, a Korean, a German, and a Filipino.

Clearly the team approach overcomes many of the difficulties of solo pioneer church planting, but it is not without challenges. Team building and maintenance demand much energy.[2] The potential for conflict is especially high in an international team, where culturally different understandings of leadership, decision making, and values collide. Teams, especially expatriate teams, must also be cautious that they do not become a clique. During the early days of the church plant, team members may rely too heavily on one another for support and friendship and thus fail to build relationships with local people. Too many expatriates in one small church plant can make locals feel like outsiders. One pioneer church-planting team in southern Germany consisted of several American families, and in the early years there were more Americans than Germans in the fledging church. Occasionally German visitors would enter and then turn around to leave, thinking that they had mistakenly entered the American military chapel!

Another challenge for the church-planting team can arise when the team members are full-time vocational ministers. Local laypersons may see a large number of "professionals" and feel excused from volunteering their time and energy. "Why should I sacrifice my precious time when there are so many professionals in a small church with nothing else to do? They are trained to do a much better job than I could ever do." Such teams might consider planting multiple churches at once to overcome some of these difficulties.

Church Planting by Colonization

Church planting by colonization is seldom practiced because of the high level of commitment it demands, yet it can be one of the most successful methods. A number of persons, often including whole families from the same home church or recruited from several churches, relocate into the target city or region. Like a "colony" of settlers, they form the core of the new church. This offers most of the same advantages as the team approach, except that the group relocating consists of more people and most are usually laypersons. Thus a church is virtually transplanted into the new location.

2. See chapter 16 for a discussion of church-planting teams.

This approach resembles mother-daughter church multiplication (to be discussed below). The difference is that the members relocate to an entirely new city or region, finding new homes and jobs, which presents a great hurdle. Not only is it difficult to persuade members of one community to relocate to another, but it may be difficult for them to find housing and employment there. This approach is normally possible only when the colony moves to a location of the same or similar culture. Large numbers of people are rarely willing to learn a new language and adopt the lifestyle of a new culture. Furthermore, their large foreign presence in the new church would overwhelm new believers from the local culture, giving the new church a foreign feel.

Pointing to Abbott Loop Christian Center in Anchorage, Alaska, C. Peter Wagner (1990, 63–64) notes that it planted forty churches over a twenty-year period using primarily the colonization method. Members who had relocated to start ten of the new churches numbered 137. These ten churches grew to a combined membership of 2,068. Community Christian Church of Naperville, Illinois, sent some twenty-five members with a staff pastor to relocate in Kansas City and form the core of a pioneer church plant in that city. Later thirty-five members sold their homes, quit their jobs, and moved to Denver to do the same.

Nonresident or Short-Term Church Planting

Nonresident or short-term church planting occurs when the church planter or church-planting team does not take up permanent residence at the launch location. They either make repeated short visits to the location or remain on site for just a few months. The idea is to quickly evangelize and gather a core of local believers, equip them with the basics of understanding the Bible and church life, and then move on. The planters then continue to strengthen the congregation through occasional short visits. The approach is well suited to locations where traditional resident missionary work is not possible, but it has been attempted in other contexts as well.

Efforts have been made by some mission organizations to fully plant churches using only short-term teams, such as with summer mission trips, or by showing evangelistic films and forming follow-up Bible studies with inquirers. However, such efforts rarely bear long-term fruit where there is no local, indigenous church or missionary familiar with the language and culture to provide ongoing guidance to the fledging work.

In his book *The Nonresidential Missionary* (1990) V. David Garrison describes this approach. Here the missionary operates from a nonresidential base but still seeks to learn the language and culture of the focus people. He or she networks with various Christian organizations and coordinates their efforts in order to evangelize and plant a church among a specific people group. A variety of people and projects may be combined in the overall effort: short-term teams, "tourist evangelists," medium-term exchange students, development workers, itinerant evangelists, or long-term immigrants or tentmakers. Garrison highlights the example of a Filipino nonresident missionary, Lena Rabang, who worked in the Sarawak Highlands of Indonesia to reach Muslims. She was already a seasoned church planter in the Philippines when God led her to minister among a people group where resident missionaries were not allowed. She established a steady witness for Christ and the beginning of a church by working on a six-month visa and with the assistance of rotating coworkers. "After ten years, she had seen 47 churches planted among the Visayan Negritos and an equal number of lay pastors trained to lead the churches in continued growth and witness" (Garrison 1990, 33).

In another example, churches were planted among the Xiao people, who live in a remote and restricted part of Asia. After research and mobilizing prayer, a nonresidential missionary coordinated the establishment of a Christian hospital, a Bible translation project, and Christian radio broadcasting, and placed twenty to thirty English teachers among the Xiao. After only two years an estimated three thousand persons were baptized and received into newly established churches (Garrison 1990, 65–68).

The International Church Plant

The international church plant may employ any of the above methods, the unique feature being that the church plant does not initially seek to be an indigenous church but rather is intentionally international in character. English is typically the language of ministry, and the church is, at least initially, composed of expatriates living in the target location: native English speakers from the international business community, diplomatic corps, students, refugees, or guest workers. By beginning with outreach to the international community, the church can often grow in numbers more rapidly. In addition to serving the spiritual needs of the expatriate community, it is hoped that the international church plant will attract local residents who either wish to improve their English language abilities or are curious about the Christian faith (Bowers 2005). Similar to the international church is the expatriate or immigrant church, which may not use the lingua franca but another language, such as Mandarin or Korean in the United States, and have a specific ethnic or cultural character. Such churches seek to serve the needs of recent immigrants or refugees, who often are not comfortable with the predominant host country language or do not feel accepted in other churches (Prill 2009). In predominantly Muslim countries, planting indigenous churches that reach Muslims is usually forbidden; however, churches for the expatriate community are allowed to exist and have relative freedom.

Some international churches, after establishing themselves and having reached a significant number of local citizens, have transitioned from using

English as primary ministry language to using the local vernacular. Sometimes a children's program is offered in both English and the local vernacular. Preaching may also be translated into the vernacular to ease the transition. This has been done in cities such as Moscow and Budapest. The church may also choose to remain international in character but serve as a base for further outreach and church planting among the indigenous people.

Mission organizations such as Christian Associates International have promoted this strategy in Europe, planting successful international churches in cities such as Amsterdam and Geneva. An additional advantage to international church plants is that they can be laboratories of innovation. Even in contexts where indigenous local churches are already present, international churches are generally less hindered by traditional forms of church life and can model alternative or creative approaches to ministry and outreach, stimulating such thinking among more traditional churches.

The international church strategy is, however, not without significant drawbacks if the goal is to reach beyond the expatriate community to the local residents. It is an option only where the target city is cosmopolitan with a sizable international community. Where English is not the heart language of the local people, the use of English as the language of ministry will appeal to only a small minority of the local population. At the same time, attempts to transition away from English to the vernacular are not always easy if one of the church's main attractions is use of the English language.

Another pressing challenge is that in an international church Christianity maintains a largely foreign face. The broader population may perceive Christianity as the faith of outsiders, of expatriates, but not a genuine option for nationals. This foreign image relates not only to language but to worship style, forms of leadership and decision making, and other culturally conditioned aspects of church life. Indeed, the church *is* foreign, not contextualized, and faces all the challenges of noncontextualized churches.

Indirect Church Planting

Often churches are planted by Christian organizations and ministries whose primary intention is not to plant churches. For example, Wycliffe Bible Translators / Summer Institute of Linguistics has the primary goal of translating the Bible into indigenous languages. Sometimes, due to contractual obligations with local governments, translators must depart after the translation work is completed. However, it is not unusual for a church to be established during the process of Bible translation. Similarly, churches may be planted by Christian staff at a local hospital, by relief and development workers, or by Christians on international business assignments.

Christian development workers in Curtea de Arges, one of the oldest cities in Romania, led several persons to faith in Christ and started a church there, though church planting was not the primary purpose of the organization. The leader of the developmental work was not trained as a pastor or church planter but ended up planting a church! In the mid-1990s Campus Crusade for Christ (CCC) staff in Budapest began meeting on Sundays with students and others who had come to personal faith in Christ. Though it is generally CCC's policy not to plant new churches, a church grew out of these meetings. The leaders then approached another mission agency for assistance with the church plant.

Though the persons planting such churches are seldom trained as church planters and rarely have a long-term plan for the development (much less for multiplication) of the church, there are advantages to the approach. Local laypersons are normally forced to take greater initiative in leading the church because the Christian worker remains busy with other responsibilities and cannot devote his or her full efforts to pastoring the new church. In the case of compassion or development ministries, the church plant is positively associated with the contributions of Christians to the community. In countries closed to traditional missionary activity, it is often possible for Christian relief, development, or educational workers to enter and then become indirectly involved in planting churches. The workers make a contribution to the well-being of the local people, and they are not perceived as a threat to established religions.

Approaches to Church Reproduction

We now turn to describing various methods by which existing churches reproduce by mobilizing their members to become directly involved in planting a new church in the same city or a nearby location. Such approaches move church planting from addition, planting one church at a time, to multiplication, churches planting churches that plant churches. An overview of these approaches is given in table 7.2.

Mother-Daughter Church Planting or Hiving off

The most common approach to church multiplication is "mother-daughter" church planting, sometimes called "hiving off." Planting churches by this method is comparable with the biological process of multiplication through cell division. What could be more natural than having a baby! The mother church births a daughter church by sending off some of its members to form the core of the new church. The number of members sent can vary from just a few to hundreds, depending on the size of the mother church, the location of the new church, and other factors. Staff members of the mother church may be sent out to help start the daughter church.

Typically the members forming the new church already live in the target area or belong to the focus population for the new church. Thus they do not

Table 7.2
Approaches to Church Reproduction
Where Churches Already Exist and Want to Reproduce

Approach	Features
Mother-daughter church plant *or* hiving off	Members of an established (mother) church separate to build the nucleus of a new (daughter) church
Multisite *or* satellite church plant	Mother church starts additional worship or ministry venues (often with video sermons); staff and organization remain largely centralized
Adopted daughter church plant *or* church replant	An independent fellowship decides to form a church by requesting assistance of an established church; or a small, struggling church is revitalized or "replanted"
Multi-mother *or* partnership church plant	Several established churches give members to start a common daughter church
Focus people church plant *or* multicongregation	A church establishes a new congregation among a particular ethnic or social group, often using the same building; the congregations are organizationally linked
House church network	House churches multiply by cell division, with minimal structure and usually lay led; the church planter is not a pastor but an equipper-coach of lay house-church planters

need to find new housing or employment as would be the case with church planting by colonization. Often one or more home groups affiliated with the mother church already meet in a particular community. The vision is cast to plant a church in that community, and the members of these groups prepare to become the core of the church plant.

For example, the Central Munich Evangelical Free Church (membership of two hundred adults) desired to start a daughter church in one of its suburbs. A home group had already begun meeting in the community of Ottobrunn, which was identified as an area in need of an evangelical church. Over many months the vision was cast and members were prepared to launch the new work. Eventually thirty-four adult members were commissioned to begin. The pastor of the mother church served both churches until the daughter church was able to call its own pastor. The mother church provided not only members but also financial support, pastoral care, and counsel as well as practical support in evangelism, music, remodeling, and a host of other services that extended beyond the resources of the daughter church. Thousands of such examples could be given.

There are many other ways to start a daughter church, such as intentionally recruiting from the mother congregation those who would launch the daughter church or hiring a church planter to lead the new work. Some reproducing churches avoid using the language and mindset of hiving off and speak rather of recruiting a missional team or core group to launch the daughter church. For example, Hill Country Bible Church in Austin, Texas, planted fifteen daughter churches between its founding, in 1986, and 2010 (figure 7.1). It shifted its approach away from merely assembling a critical mass of believers from the mother church to form the launch team and began to intentionally recruit families who possessed a mission mindset and calling. Hill Country speaks of a fourfold shift in strategy for planting daughter churches:

- from gathering from the church to gathering from the community
- from transplanting to transforming
- from critical mass to missional core
- from financial dependency to creative funding (Herrington 2009)

Figure 7.1
Hill Country Bible Church—Church Plants

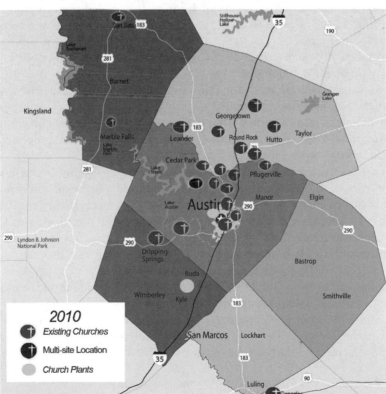

The launch team may be smaller in number, but it is more missional in outlook, with evangelism, sacrificial service, and community connectedness determining the DNA of the daughter church.

Numerous practical resources are available to aid the planning and planting of daughter churches. Most of these are geared to the context of Western cultures and must be adapted for use in other contexts;[3] nevertheless, they provide a good starting point for mapping out the process.

There are many advantages to the mother-daughter approach to church multiplication. The survival and growth rates of such daughter churches are higher than those of pioneer church plants because the launch groups are usually larger, more workers are present, immediate support and resources are available through the nearby mother church, and the launch can be carefully prepared and planned over time. Since the members originate from the same mother church, they tend to share a common vision, ethos, and philosophy of ministry. As a result, more time and energy can be devoted to evangelism and discipleship. Generally, the core launch group will include members who are experienced in ministry and mature in their faith, and this provides leadership and stability that are often lacking in pioneer works. Furthermore, the process of hiving off is easily reproducible. The daughter church is more likely to one day become a mother and birth its own daughter church.

An indirect benefit comes to the mother church. Not only does it have the joy of birthing a daughter, but it realizes that it too must mobilize for evangelism and recruit and train new workers in order to fill the void left by members who were commissioned for the daughter church. This keeps the mother church from becoming complacent, comfortable, and passive. In fact, it is not unusual for the mother church to experience a season of accelerated growth as God honors its vision and commitment.

Though effective, this approach also has pitfalls to avoid. If the mother church is small, starting a daughter church could potentially weaken the mother church enough to threaten its continued existence. Further, the daughter church should be cautious about duplicating in detail the ministry methods of the mother church. It needs to develop new approaches to ministry by adapting to the particular needs of its community. Much as in the relationship between real mothers and daughters, the mother church can overly dominate the daughter, and the daughter can remain overly dependent on the mother by being "tied to her apron strings." Unhealthy competition can also develop between the mother and daughter. These cautions notwithstanding, once a pioneer church plant has been established, the mother-daughter approach remains the method that God has most richly blessed in multiplying churches

3. See for example Logan and Ogne 1995 and Harrison, Cheyney and Overstreet 2008. These include worksheets and step-by-step guidelines.

around the globe. Most other methods of church reproduction are a variation of this approach.

Multisite or Satellite Church Planting

One of the most popular trends in church planting today among larger churches is the multisite concept (see Ferguson 2003; Surratt, Ligon, and Bird 2006; McConnell 2009). Much as in hiving off, new church venues are usually started by sending off members from the mother church. The difference is that here the daughter church remains closely tied to the mother church, without becoming autonomous; it normally remains fully integrated into the larger ministry of the mother church. A common multisite slogan is, "one church, many locations." On these grounds some do not consider the multisite approach real church planting. "A multi-site church is one church meeting in multiple locations—different rooms on the same campus, different locations in the same region, and in some instances in different cities, states, or nations. A multi site church shares a common vision, budget, leadership, and board" (Surratt, Ligon, and Bird 2006, 18).

The approach is comparable to a planet with satellites that orbit and remain within its gravitational pull, with the central or main church venue being the planet and the satellites being the various "campuses" or smaller venues. Sometimes dual campuses are started, with the additional site having equal status and size as the original site.

This model has been developed with many variations. Often all the venues share the same pastoral staff, though a venue may have a few of its own local staff. Budgets for the venues are usually centralized. The decision-making and leadership structure may be highly centralized, with a joint governing board, or the venues may be granted considerable autonomy in decision making while remaining legally under the umbrella of the central church. Some have only worship services at the various locations; others offer a full range of ministries at each location.

Today it is also common for attendees at the various sites to view the same Sunday sermon by the senior preaching pastor via video recording or live feed. This maximizes the listening and viewing audience for exceptionally gifted speakers but is possible only where the necessary technology is available and affordable. The strong preaching and leadership of the senior pastor often serve as the magnet that "keeps the satellites in orbit" and drives the launch of new venues. However, in some cases a team approach to preaching at different sites has been adopted, so that dependency on a single gifted speaker is reduced.

The multisite approach has the advantage that an effective ministry of the mother church can be consistently reproduced in the daughter churches. This is much like the concept of franchising a McDonald's or Pizza Hut, whereby the quality of the product is closely monitored and reproduced. On the other hand, some churches make an intentional effort to plant new sites that are quite different in ministry style, able to meet the diverse needs of various subcultures and communities. The multisite method has also been used for church "restarts" (discussed below).

Because most of the churches starting multisite venues are large, the plants are usually launched with a relatively large number of members. The venue builds on the strong reputation of the mother church in the community. By sharing staff, resources, and expertise with the mother, the site church can immediately offer a high-quality and wide range of ministries not possible in more typical daughter church plants.

There are also drawbacks to consider with this approach. Highly centralized ministry and staff may lack the flexibility to adapt to the needs of new locations. Decision making can be cumbersome for the off-site venue. It can also promote an overly professionalized concept of ministry that depends heavily on paid staff and technology. Start-up costs for staff and equipment can be high.[4] Because the multisite approach usually relies on the initiative of a strong mother church, the satellites seldom reproduce themselves. Thus the approach is effective for church addition but rarely leads to the multiplication of churches planting churches (or venues planting new venues).

One should not think that the multisite approach is a strictly North American phenomenon. Numerous examples exist on every continent. For example, the Works and Mission Baptist Church in Abidjan, Ivory Coast, has 150,000 congregants meeting at hundreds of satellite locations (Surratt, Ligon, and Bird 2006, 203). Such a church virtually takes on the character of a denomination!

Adopted Daughter Church Planting[5]

Occasionally a group of Christians has formed in a locality apart from the direct assistance of an established church. The group may be a home Bible study or a follow-up group from an evangelistic effort. When its members decide that they want to become a more formal church, they seek assistance from an established church that can provide guidance and possibly resources or pastoral care. When that established church decides to support the new church plant, in a sense it adopts the new work—the new church is not the result of "natural birth," growing out of a nucleus sent from the mother church. Though the members of the new church were not formerly members of the mother church, the adoptive mother church treats the new church as if it were its daughter.

4. In the United States net start up costs for larger churches can range from $75,000 to $110,000 for the first year (Surratt, Ligon, and Bird 2006, 104), though others estimate the net cost at closer to $140,000 (Ciesniewski 2006).

5. Here we are not speaking of international partnerships between congregations in different countries. Those will be discussed in chapter 18.

Shortly after the fall of communism in Hungary, for example, a group of believers formed in a small town as the result of an evangelistic concert. There was no local evangelical church in that town, and so no one conducted a formal follow-up to the effort. When these new believers came into contact with an evangelical church in Budapest, they requested assistance in their efforts to plant a church in their town. The church in Budapest became an adoptive mother, not providing members but providing resources, counsel, and occasional teaching and encouragement to the emerging church.

A variation on the adoption approach may be observed when a struggling or dying church approaches a larger healthy church and requests that it be adopted in order to, in effect, "replant" the church. Often the adopted church has failed to adapt to its changing community. But this approach is successful only when ownership of the facilities, decision making, and style of ministry is ceded to the mother church and an entirely fresh approach to ministry is launched. Sometimes members from the adopting church are commissioned to join the adopted daughter. Strictly speaking, this is not church planting but rather a form of church revitalization. First Baptist Church of Houston has partnered with twenty-four dying churches to revitalize them (Roberts 2008, 116–17). Sometimes the adopted church becomes an additional venue of a multisite church (see also case study 7.1).

The adoption approach shares most of the advantages of mother-daughter church planting. Furthermore, the group of Christians being adopted is usually highly motivated to start the new church and probably already has the

....

Case Study 7.1

Church Planting by Church Replanting

New Life Community Church of Chicago was founded in 1986 with eighteen people. In 1996 a second worship campus was launched. By 2009 New Life had become a multisite, multiethnic church with 14 locations, 170 home groups, and total weekend attendance of 4,200 in 25 weekend services. Of the 14 campuses, 7 were begun as restarts. New Life's church-planting strategy includes the restarting or replanting of struggling churches, often in older, changing communities, that request their assistance. In one instance they acquired a 125-year-old historic church building and revitalized it offering two services; a morning service made up of young adults and families and an alternative service in the evening for young adults and students from nearby DePaul University. In March 2009 New Life restarted a 115-year-old church with two services, one in English and one in Spanish. If the older church has failed to adapt to the changing community, the adoptive restart reinvents the church, designing it to more effectively connect and minister to the people and needs that surround it. You can view a ten-minute video explaining New Life's restart story at www.newliferestart.org.

....

kind of significant leadership and vision that would move them to seek to plant a church. The new congregation can gain credibility by associating with a church with an established reputation in the region. However, in order for the adoption to be successful, both the daughter and the mother must become well acquainted before the partnership is made official. Expectations of the two groups may differ widely. Doctrinal, philosophical, and financial arrangements should be clearly spelled out. Most of all, trust must develop between the two groups, and this takes both patience and open conversation. Sometimes such struggling groups do not seek genuine partnerships but merely aid to provide a building or to pay a pastor. In other cases the adoptive mother church may overly dominate the new church, and the transition can be difficult. Nevertheless, if these pitfalls can be avoided, adoptive church planting can be a wonderful way that established churches can partner with emerging churches for greater synergy.

Multi-mother or Partnership Church Planting

In much the same way that mother-daughter church planting occurs—by a mother church hiving off members—in this approach, two or more mother churches hive off members who combine to form one new church. This makes the core launch team for the new church larger, as members are recruited from two or more mother churches. But the plant is less demanding on the mother churches, because they share the responsibility. In this way smaller churches can become involved in church planting even when each lacks the resources to mother a church alone. For this approach, the mother churches typically originate from the same denominational background.

One example is the planting of the Free Evangelical Church of Markt Indersdorf, Germany, a small community just outside Munich. Two mother churches in Munich each had a cell group meeting in the region, which was about an hour's drive from the city. The groups were combined to make a total of ten families who became the launch team for the church plant. Both of the Munich churches contributed members and provided resources. The Markt Indersdorf church was lay led and relied on the Munich churches to provide counsel and regular preaching.

Iteffa Gobena, of the Ethiopian Evangelical Church Mekane Yesus, calls this the "bridging the gap" model. Rural churches team up "to close the unreached gap between two or more congregations or parishes. . . . They assign lay preachers who voluntarily take the responsibility to preach the gospel to close up the gap" (Gobena 1997, 15).

In order for the multi-mother approach to succeed, the various groups that form the new church must grow together and develop a common vision. Even if the mother churches are from the same denomination, it cannot be assumed that the groups will automatically harmonize. In the case of Markt

Indersdorf, the two groups prayed, played, and planned together for a year while developing a common vision and strategy, before publicly launching the church plant. The roles and responsibilities of the mother churches must be clarified so that the daughter has clear expectations and does not end up being orphaned, because neither mother church asumes responsibility.

Focus People Church Plant or Multicongregation

Many churches reach out to particular ethnic, linguistic, or social groups in their communities by starting an additional congregation that exists to meet the unique needs of one of these groups (see Prill 2009). Typically such a new congregation meets in the rooms of the mother church, often on Sunday afternoons, and remains to some degree under the authority of the host church. This has proven an especially effective way to reach first-generation immigrants who desire to worship in their mother language and to preserve many of their cultural values and traditions. In urban settings undergoing dramatic ethnic change, starting an ethnic congregation can be a means of helping a church transition and adapt to community change. It may even be a strategy for church survival (see case study 7.2).[6]

Particularly in large urban settings, there are dozens of ethnic groups unreached by the gospel who are unlikely to be reached by existing mainstream churches. Rodney Harrison, Tom Cheyney, and Don Overstreet describe the advantages of the multicongregational approach, which they call "nesting": "Start-up costs are minimal. Generally the new church starts under the legal and administrative umbrella of the sponsoring church. Church materials and staff salaries, if required, are the primary expenses. The host or sponsoring church should anticipate incidental costs, however, including the higher water, gas, electric, and phone bills, along with the higher cost of supplies and office machine wear-and-tear" (2008, 98).

Groups of people in need of specialized ministries are not limited to those of minority languages or ethnicities. Other focus people might include persons in the arts, street people, migrant workers, or shift and weekend workers. In Nuremberg, Germany, a special ministry was developed for bakers, whose early-morning working hours made attendance at typical Bible studies and worship difficult. They even started a bakers' brass ensemble!

The results of such efforts are multiple congregations that meet under the roof of one church. This demands considerable commitment and flexibility on the part of the mother church, and the challenges should not be underestimated. An additional congregation not only will impose new demands on facilities and resources but also will require an open and missional mindset

6. See Dudley 1979, Dudley and Ammerman 2002, Carle and Decaro 1999, and Eiesland 1999 for examples of how churches adapt to community change.

Case Study 7.2

Multicongregational Church Planting in Changing Communities

First Baptist Church of Flushing (FBCF), New York, has three congregations, with services in three languages: English, Chinese, and Spanish. In the 1960s the community began to shift from its predominantly white blue-collar and partially African American base toward a composition of largely Asian and Hispanic immigrants. After over one hundred years of ministry, in 1965 Hispanic and in 1968 Chinese ministries were launched, and this resulted in growth and community impact that would have otherwise been impossible. Though there were painful setbacks, eventually it became a model church of multicongregational ministry. In 1980 the three congregations were elevated to equal status under a common church board. FBCF was no longer a white church with subordinate ethnic congregations, and eventually the church called an Asian to the position of senior pastor. Each congregation can minister in ways appropriate to its focus people. FBCF has various community-service ministries and has even expanded to become a training ground for cross-cultural missionaries (Travis 1997; Ortiz 1996, 78–85; Wang 2007).

from the sponsoring congregation. People of different cultures and subcultures often have different sensibilities regarding scheduling, time, noise levels, child rearing, cleanliness, and a host of other potential points of conflict with the mother congregation. Members of ethnic minorities typically enjoy sharing meals together before or after services, and exotic aromas may fill the church for days! In many if not most cases, someone who possesses particular linguistic and cross-cultural relational skills will need to be trained or recruited to launch and help sustain the ministry.

House Church Network

In recent years a growing body of literature promotes and describes house churches.[7] Virtually all of David Garrison's (2004a) examples of rapidly growing church-planting movements consist of house church movements; thus many mission organizations are promoting this approach. The house church network reproduces through cell division in a way similar to mother-daughter church planting. In both models, members of an existing congregation are sent to begin a new congregation, but here the process occurs on a smaller, house church scale.

A house church typically has fewer than fifty persons and basically functions as a lay led, single-cell congregation. Thus with each cell division a new

7. Of the many works on house churches, the most practical with respect to planting house churches are Garrison 2004a, Kreider and McClung 2007, Payne 2007, and Simson 2001. See also the discussion of house churches in chapter 6.

house church is born. Because house churches do not require expensive meeting places, have minimal structure, and are lay led, they have potential for rapid multiplication. This is especially the case in societies that are highly relational, those in which the gospel can spread easily through kinship, occupational, and community networks.

One variation of house church reproduction is when two nuclei within one existing house church are formed. The two may meet in different rooms in the same house for a time, but eventually they meet separately and come together only periodically, perhaps once a month. Over time apprentice leaders from the two groups form leadership teams; then the two cells separate and are launched as autonomous house churches. The original house church becomes two new house churches, and the original one ceases to exist. The church planter coaches the new cells but is free to start another house church in a new area (see figure 7.2).

The key to house church multiplication lies in training enough house church leaders to keep pace with the multiplication of cells. The house churches typically maintain some form of networking by means of common leadership teams, consultation, worker training, and occasional joint celebrations. Because of their low visibility and simple, lay-led structure, house churches are more "persecution proof" than are traditionally structured churches. But because the lay leaders are often poorly trained, they can be susceptible to weak or false teaching, weak or inappropriate leadership, and unhealthy dominance by individuals. House churches also lack the kind of programs geared to special needs that are typically offered by larger churches (such as youth ministry); thus they often lose members to larger churches that offer higher-quality teaching and broader ministry opportunities.

Church Split or Unplanned Parenthood

A church split is a form of church reproduction that no one desires or plans for, but in reality it is the source of many new churches throughout the world. Splits resulting in plants have been called "splats" (Harrison, Cheyney, and Overstreet 2008, 102). They may be a result of leadership conflicts, power struggles, doctrinal differences, or simply interpersonal tensions. Whatever the cause, the result is that a faction of the church splits off and begins a new church under new leadership.[8]

These splits are seldom evangelistically motivated but are usually driven by the particular cause or personality that precipitated the split. They are

8. In some cultural contexts, pastors are so authoritarian that they feel threatened by emerging gifted leaders. The younger leaders thus see no opportunity to develop their ministry potential apart from starting a new church. This creates a vicious cycle in which leaders always feel threatened by the next generation of emerging leaders, who they expect will—and who often do—in turn create more splits (see Thornton 1984).

Figure 7.2
House Church Sub-Division

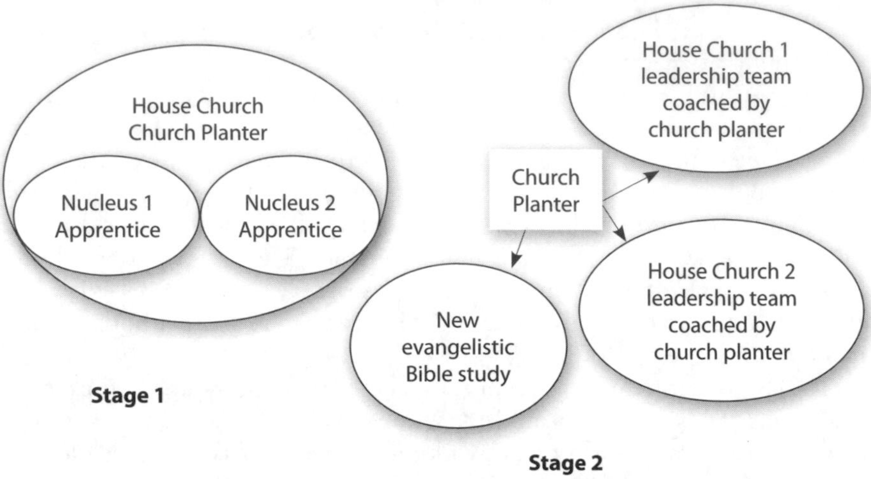

a poor public testimony to the gospel and a direct contradiction of Jesus's prayer "that all of them may be one, Father, just as you are in me and I am in you. May they also be in us *so that the world may believe* that you have sent me" (John 17:21, emphasis added). Needless to say, we do not recommend this approach to church reproduction! Nevertheless, in much the same way that the conflict between Paul and Barnabas resulted in two mission teams instead of one (Acts 15:39–40), God has used even church splits it to create new churches that will in turn reach new people.

Regional Strategies for Church Planting

We now consider strategies for planting several churches in a geographic region. The focus here is less on methods for planting a single church or reproducing existing churches than on determining the best long-term strategy for reaching a metropolitan area, county, or state. This will take into consideration the location of church plants, deployment of church-planting resources, and how the movement will expand from its beginnings. These approaches are summarized in table 7.3.

Harvest Priority Church Planting

As church planters enter a new region, the question is, where to begin? In the early years of Protestant pioneer mission work, missionaries often evangelized from village to village and then focused church-planting efforts on those locations where people were most receptive to the gospel. This approach is in

Table 7.3
Regional Strategies for Church Planting

Approach	Features
Harvest priority church planting	Evangelistic efforts are conducted in various locations and a church is planted in the location of greatest responsiveness
Strategic beachhead church planting	Seeks to establish at least one church in every un-evangelized city or town, usually separated by geographical distance
Cluster church planting	Seeks to establish a cluster of related churches in a limited geographical area
Spreading vine church planting	Churches are planted in consecutive cities or towns, often along major transportation routes
Dandelion, spontaneous, or diaspora church planting	(House) churches are planted spontaneously as local believers (who may be diaspora Christians) naturally spread the gospel

keeping with the harvest priority principle discussed in chapter 4: one should reap the spiritual harvest where the harvest is ripe.

All things being equal, this approach makes sense. When planters begin with a responsive location, churches are be planted that can later evangelize the less responsive areas. If one starts with a less responsive area, it may be a very long time before the first churches are planted, during which time resources are bound up and other more responsive areas remain without the gospel. The harvest priority approach seems to be the best way to deploy limited resources and manpower.

But usually all things are *not* equal. For example, one must ask how the receptivity of a locality is determined. A people may initially respond very positively to the *Jesus* film or an evangelistic "blitz" but then be uninterested in more serious, long-term discipleship and spiritual change. On the other hand, a group that is initially resistant, or takes more time to consider the claims of the gospel, might eventually make a deeper commitment to Christ and become a stronger church, able to reproduce. Most non-Christians need time to fully understand the meaning of the gospel in order to make an informed decision.

Furthermore, the gospel most often spreads from urban centers to outlying villages, but it spreads very slowly from villages to urban centers. Though an urban setting may initially be more resistant to the gospel, it can potentially have a greater long-term impact on the region. Thus focusing exclusively on immediate receptivity may be a less strategic approach in the long run.

Strategic Beachhead Church Planting

The strategic beachhead approach seeks to establish a spiritual foothold in several political, commercial, or educational centers. From those influential cities, churches can be planted in outlying suburbs, towns, or villages. This reflects the apostle Paul's focus on planting churches in centers such as Corinth and Ephesus, from which the gospel would emanate to the surrounding environs. In the early 1990s, as the Iron Curtain fell in Europe, many mission agencies sought to send church-planting teams to each major city of a formerly closed country; some attempted to send one team to the capital city of each former Warsaw Pact country. Sometimes various locations were sought out where no churches existed whatsoever, though these locations were quite a distance from each other. The advantage to this approach is that the gospel is spread over a broad region and less concentrated in a limited area. If entirely unreached locations are chosen, then church-planting energies are focused on the most spiritually needy.

The drawback to the strategic beachhead approach is that resources can be spread too thin over a large area. The church-planting teams and churches planted may thus be separated by hours of travel with little possibility for mutual encouragement, sharing of resources, or developing synergy to have a significant impact in any one region. It can end up being a shotgun approach, with the danger that isolated and weak churches are planted. Both the church planters and the churches themselves can become easily discouraged if progress is slow.

Cluster Church Planting

Cluster church planting is opposite to the strategic beachhead approach: the initial goal is to plant several churches in a *more limited* geographical area, such as a single major metropolitan region. Rather than church-planting teams being spread far and wide, they are clustered in one area. The strength of this approach is that the church planters and the emerging churches are in reasonable proximity to one another so that they can meet for mutual encouragement, have periodic common celebrations, offer joint training of workers, and assist one another in evangelistic and other efforts. If the movement is being driven by lay leaders, churches in the cluster can share lay preachers, further reducing the load on any one church. The church-planting team is spread over several churches, which heightens local lay leaders' responsibility for the individual church plants.

A sense of movement can develop when churches are planted in clusters. For example, Nairobi Chapel in Kenya has planted twenty-five Nairobi churches, many of which are in the slums, and has a vision to plant three hundred additional churches, at least half of them in Nairobi itself, by 2020 (Muriu 2007). In clusters, churches don't feel so isolated. They can learn from one another in the process, and synergy and a sense of movement ensue. Ed Stetzer and Phillip Connor's 2007 study of 2,080 church plants from twelve denominations in North America demonstrates the importance of church-planter peer support for church survivability. Such support is more readily available in the cluster approach.[9]

Church reproduction using the multi-mother approach is better facilitated by clustering. The region eventually becomes more saturated with the gospel, with a higher church per resident ratio, and the movement will have higher visibility. A study by Daniel Olson of Indiana University–South Bend that examined the factors contributing to the growth of new Church of the Nazarene congregations confirms the advantage of cluster church planting. He summarizes: "The focal question is whether there is an advantage when such congregations are located nearby already existing congregations. The answer is yes. In fact, location in a county with more Nazarene churches and more Nazarene members is one of the single strongest predictors of greater average attendance in the fifth year" (Olson 2002).

One of the most impressive examples of urban cluster church planting is the Encuentro con Dios movement in Lima, Peru. From 1973 to 1997, a church with 117 members developed into a movement, planting thirty-eight churches with a total membership of nearly 16,000 and a weekly attendance of 25,000 (Turnidge 1999; Mangham 1987). Austria is considered one of the most difficult countries in Europe for Protestant church planting; yet in the greater Vienna area, a cluster of church plants was launched in 1972 and grew to twelve churches by 1995. Growing out of a home Bible study, the first church, known for its location on Tulpengasse, in Vienna, was planted in 1972. Not until six years later, in 1978, was the first daughter church planted in Floridsdorf. But then additional churches followed more rapidly: one in 1980, two in 1984, and then nearly one per year. A remarkable feature of this movement is that it was Plymouth Brethren in orientation, being largely lay led with relatively few salaried pastors or church planters—and this took place in one of the most professional and culturally sophisticated centers of Europe! Similarly the cluster approach was combined with mother-daughter church planting in metro Paris, France—another difficult place to plant churches. A group associated with TEAM missionaries planted six churches over a fifteen-year period. Another group led by the France-Mission planted five churches in eight years, and these churches in turn planted another daughter and two granddaughter churches in the following years (Vajko 1996, 56–68, 86–93).

Numerous other examples could be recounted of cluster church planting in urban areas around the globe. Glenn Kendall (1990) describes it in a more rural movement in Rwanda. Baptist churches grew in fifteen years from a regional group of one thousand members to a national movement with over seventeen

9. "The church planter meeting with a group of church planting peers at least monthly increases the odds of survivability by 135 percent. We found that out of those church planters who were part of a peer group, 83 percent of their churches survived whereas only 67 percent of church plants among those who did not have a peer group survived" (Stetzer and Connor 2007, 14).

thousand members and more than three hundred new churches. The key was mobilizing national leaders to plant clusters of up to twelve churches rather than individual ones. Large evangelistic efforts generated enthusiasm, and five to seven new churches would be started during each thrust.

In such cluster movements, planting daughter churches often becomes part of the ethos of the churches. Rather than a single central church planting all the daughter churches, resulting in church addition, it is expected that newly planted churches will also mother new churches, thus resulting in church multiplication. As church members move to other locations, they often affiliate with another church of the movement (thus conserving fruit), or they become the seed for a new church plant. The only disadvantage to this approach is that considerable resources are concentrated (at least initially) in one region while other regions remain unreached. If receptivity to the gospel is slow, long-term commitment will be necessary.

Spreading Vine Church Planting

Strawberry plants grow and spread by extending a runner that then sets roots and grows a daughter plant. This new plant in turn sends a runner to start another, and so on. Many vines spread similarly, by extending stems along the ground or another surface and then periodically anchoring themselves. Church-planting movements can also grow like strawberry plants or vines, by planting one church after another, from one town to the next, often following a major trade route or highway. Each church planted becomes the launching point for another daughter church in the next town or city down the road. A simple example of this approach is the church planting by the Evangelical Free Church in southern Romania led by American missionaries when communism collapsed (figure 7.3). This was not an especially rapidly spreading vine, but it illustrates the approach. Churches were planted beginning in Craiova (pop. 300,000), then following the highway northeastward to Slatina (pop. 85,000), to Pitești (pop. 180,000), and finally to Cîmpulung (pop. 44,000).[10] Instead of following a highway or road, the string of new churches might follow a canal or river. Figure 7.4 illustrates how churches were planted by the German Allianz Mission extending out from Bamako, the capital of Mali, following the Niger Canal.

The spreading vine approach has many of the same advantages as cluster planting and is especially well suited for more rural areas. Each most recently planted church is responsible to assist with the planting of the next church; thus church planting is instilled in the ethos of the movement. One possible drawback is that once a church has helped plant the next church down the

10. Populations are approximate at the time of the church plant, based on www.citypopula tion.de/Romania.html, accessed January 22, 2009.

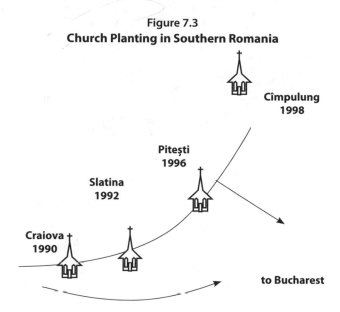

Figure 7.3
Church Planting in Southern Romania

Cîmpulung
1998

Piteşti
1996

Slatina
1992

Craiova
1990

to Bucharest

road, it may feel that its obligation for church planting is fulfilled. Also, if vocational church planters are assisting the movement, they may need to relocate frequently to keep moving with the spreading vine.

Dandelion, Spontaneous, or Diaspora Church Planting

The seeds of a dandelion float on their fluffy parachutes, blown by the wind, and randomly land wherever they find a foothold to sprout, sink roots, and become another plant. So too churches may be planted at almost random locations as Christians move about. As a result of employment, affordable housing, family needs, war, famine, migration, study, or any other number of crises or opportunities, believers move to new locations. Wherever they find themselves, they share their faith and form new fellowships that grow into churches. This spread of the gospel is more spontaneous and less planned. But this is nonetheless an effective means of planting new churches, maximizing natural personal relationships, mobilizing laypersons, and often pioneering otherwise unreached areas.

This is indeed the manner by which the gospel spread in the first century. As persecution of the church broke out in Jerusalem, we read in Acts, "those who had been scattered preached the word wherever they went" (8:4). Luke later continues, "Now those who had been scattered by the persecution in connection with Stephen traveled as far as Phoenicia, Cyprus and Antioch" (11:19); this resulted in the planting of the first predominantly Gentile church, in Antioch (11:20–21). Since then God has continued to use the most unlikely

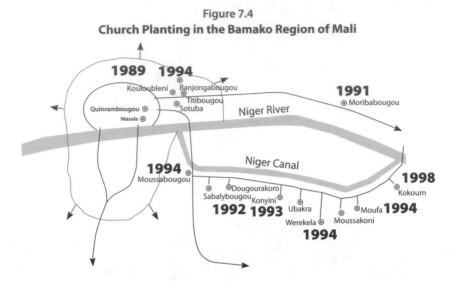

Figure 7.4
Church Planting in the Bamako Region of Mali

means to move his people about, bring the gospel to new places, and plant new churches.

In Ethiopia, Gobena calls one variety of this "the go home . . . AND TELL THEM . . . model." "This is a natural model where a Christian young man or woman who received the Lord Jesus Christ makes a conscious decision prayerfully to go to his or her village or locality (where in most cases the parents live) to witness to his or her relatives. Many times this leads to the conversion of the whole family, relatives and neighbors, and then the church planting takes place in the village" (Gobena 1997, 15). Kinship relations are often the most natural and effective ways for the gospel to spread, as whole families or clans respond to the gospel and build the core of a new church. In similar fashion a businessperson might move to a new location where he or she witnesses, leads others to Christ, and begins a small fellowship out of which a church grows. The diaspora of Christians can be either relatively local or quite international. For example, an entire mission strategy has been forged to mobilize the thousands of Filipino emigrant workers to share the gospel wherever they go (Pantoja, Tira, and Wan 2004). In an age of globalization, the possibilities for such international witness resulting in church planting are limitless.

For this approach to be effective, the believers who have relocated will need to be well prepared. In the Philippines a training program has been designed precisely to better equip Christian international workers for such ministry. Furthermore, ongoing equipping will be necessary because often the churches that are planted are small and lay led. The more spontaneous and rather random manner in which the churches are planted can make the coordination of equipping and the development of movement synergy a challenge.

Tokyo Horizon Chapel

Japan is known as one of the most difficult countries for evangelism and church planting. Tokyo Horizon Chapel is, however, a stand-out example of mother-daughter church planting. The church, established in 1991 by Pastor Koichi Hirano, had by 2007 planted sixteen daughter churches, though the mother church had a regular attendance of only about 150. The daughter churches are quite diverse, ranging in size from ten to seventy in attendance.

Unlike many Japanese pastors, Hirano is willing to experiment and take steps of faith. He and his team avoid investing time with many small matters, programs, and details of ministry, but focus rather on larger plans and vision.

Daughter churches are typically started when members relocate to another community and begin meetings in their homes. As the group grows, a public meeting place may be rented. Pastor Hirano may meet weekly with the group on a weeknight to get them started and then reduce his presence to monthly. Sometimes video recordings of the Sunday sermons are used at the new church.

Eventually a church-planting pastor will be sent from the mother church. These pastors are usually trained in the Bible school operated by the mother church. They are often bivocational, even taking menial jobs, until the church grows large enough to support them. Their bivocational status does not hurt their credibility; rather it is often seen positively as evidence of a deep level of sacrifice and commitment to the church and ministry. Hirano meets every two weeks on a weeknight with the younger pastors. All the pastors meet quarterly (every three months) for a "huddle," for which some travel up to four hours. They spend twenty-four hours together for a program that includes play, devotions, prayer, and encouragement.

Clearly, key factors in Tokyo Horizon's effectiveness lie in the encouragement of laypersons who relocate to become the catalyst for a new church, and in the training and mobilization of the bivocational pastors who give leadership to the new churches. The senior pastor has made the training and mentoring of the church-planting pastors a high priority in his ministry.

In this chapter we have surveyed a wide variety of approaches to pioneer church planting, church reproduction, and regional strategies. Each of these approaches can be appropriate and effective under the right circumstances. Often they can be combined, as in the example of Tokyo Chapel (case study 7.3). Church planters and movement strategists will need to carefully consider not only the local circumstances but also the gifts of the church planters and resources available to them in order to make the wisest decision in selecting a strategy. Ultimately one must seek the guidance of the Holy Spirit as the various options and factors are prayerfully weighed.

Part III

DEVELOPMENTAL PHASES

8

The Developmental Phases
of a Church Plant

An Overview

Much like human life and the life of nearly every organism or institution, church plants progress through reasonably predictable developmental phases. These phases reflect a fluid process rather than being clearly defined separate steps. Yet understanding the developmental phases and their characteristics is important to identifying the particular needs, challenges, and opportunities that face a church plant. Failure to give attention to the changing needs of a church plant as it develops can lead to unnecessary difficulties or stagnation.

Developmental Models of Church Planting

Numerous models for describing the development of a church plant have been proposed. Each tends to focus on a particular aspect of a church plant's development, and each has its own particular strengths and weaknesses. For example, David Hesselgrave (1980, 58–63) formulated the "Pauline Cycle," a framework based on the church-planting ministry of the apostle Paul as described in the book of Acts. Hesselgrave's model focuses more on the tasks of a missionary church planter and less on the development of the church itself. This model has the strength of drawing from a biblical example and of being well suited for pioneer missionary church planting. However, it gives little attention to church development and multiplication.

One of the most common ways of delineating the development of a church plant uses the analogy of a biological life cycle, popularized by Robert Logan[1] and expanded upon by many others.[2] The church plant progresses from conception to prenatal development, birth, growth (childhood and adulthood), and reproduction. This approach focuses mainly on the church plant itself and the planning process, with particular attention given to the prenatal phase leading up to the birth of the church, that is, the first public worship services. The organic imagery of this model is easy to communicate and conceptualize. Logan has produced very practical step-by-step materials and workbooks to implement the concept.

The limitation of this approach lies in its emphasis on the birth of the church in terms of the first public worship services. In many cultures public worship services are not possible or are not as central to the life of the church as in Western cultures. House churches rarely have a public launch. Also, from a biblical point of view the real birth of a church has little to do with the commencement of public worship. Nevertheless, as long as the metaphor is not pressed too far this model is very helpful, especially in Western cultures, where planting conventional churches usually emphasizes well-planned and attractive public worship services.

Tom Steffen describes yet another approach in his book *Passing the Baton* (1997). As the title suggests, his concern is that the church planter should seek from the very outset to intentionally work himself or herself out of a job—increasingly equipping and entrusting leadership to local believers. As discussed in chapter 5, Steffen maps out a process of phase-out, whereby the role of the church planter progressively changes from learner to evangelist, to teacher, to resident adviser, to itinerant adviser, and finally to absent adviser (see figure 5.1). Though his model was developed for tribal church planting, it has much to commend it to church planters anywhere.

The developmental model that we propose focuses on the goal of church reproduction and multiplication in the context of pioneer cross-cultural church planting. We affirm Steffen's emphasis on the need for church planters (or the church-planting team) to adapt their role with the objective of phase-out and leaving behind a multiplying movement. Attention must also be given to planning and structural matters, as emphasized in Logan and Malphur's approach. But in contrast to them, we describe church planting in various cultural settings, with various forms of the church (such as house churches), and

---

1. See Logan 1988 and Logan and Ogne 1991a. Logan attributes the life-cycle analogy to Don Stewart (Logan 1988, 1).

2. For example Malphurs 1992, 231–357; McNamara and Davis 2005; Harrison, Cheyney, and Overstreet 2008, 138–46.

Table 8.1
Comparison of Developmental Models of Church Planting

Hesselgrave The Pauline Cycle	Logan and others Church-Planting Life Cycle	Steffen Church Planter Phase-Out

Missionaries
  commissioned
Audience contacted
Gospel communicated
Hearers converted
Believers congregated
Faith confirmed
Leadership consecrated
Believers commended
Relationships continued
Sending churches convened
	Conception
	Prenatal
	Birth
	Childhood
	Adulthood
	Reproduction
		Preentry:
		  Learner (the church planter
		  remains a learner in all
		  phases)
		Preevangelism:
		  Evangelist
		Evangelism: Evangelist/
		  Teacher
		Postevangelism:
		  Resident adviser/Itinerant
		  adviser
		Phase-out:
		  Absent adviser

where resources are usually more limited. We also develop the model with the goal of a lay-driven church reproduction that is less dependent on vocational church planters or pastors. The model suggested here is in keeping with the apostolic approach to church planting described in chapter 5.

Overview of the Phases

Table 8.2 gives an overview of the phases of a pioneer church plant with the goal of multiplication and church planter phase-out. The following chapters will explain these phases in detail and with specific examples. Note that the upper part of the diagram describes the broad features of the phases through which a church plant progresses: *preparing, launching, establishing, structuring,* and *reproducing.* In the middle section we unfold the various tasks important to healthy development during these phases. The lower part of the diagram reflects the changing roles of a cross-cultural or itinerant church-planting team from entrance to exit. After the preparatory roles of team building and learning, the church planters begin the "6-M" roles discussed in chapter 5: *motor, model, mobilizer, mentor, multiplier,* and *memory.*

The transition from one phase or role to the next is more fluid than the diagram indicates.

Preparing

Preparing is the time of great anticipation! The groundwork is laid so that when the church plant is actually launched, it will be built by a crew of

Figure 8.1
Developmental Phases of Pioneer Church Planting

	PREPARING		LAUNCHING	ESTABLISHING	STRUCTURING	REPRODUCING
Phase	Targeting and Commissioning	Understanding and Strategizing	Evangelizing and Discipling	Congregating and Maturing	Expanding and Empowering	Strengthening and Sending
Tasks	• Define vision and CP* model • Determine location and ministry focus people • Select leader and recruit team • Consult with others • Secure prayer and financial support • Commission team	• Language and culture learning (as necessary) • Research the demographic, social, religious, and cultural context • Determine evangelistic and CP strategy • Build relationships and consult with others • Strengthen team, clarify roles, obtain training • Draft a CP proposal	• Develop relationships and initiate evangelism • Combine diverse methods and compassion ministry • Baptize and teach obedience • Disciple new believers and train to do the same • Form a foundational community • Wisely assimilate transfer growth • Begin training servant leaders	• Grow and develop life as the family of God • Discover, develop spiritual gifts for edification of the church • Appoint a preliminary leadership team • Meet regularly for corporate worship • Multiply cell groups and cell leaders • Formulate values and long-term development plan and biblical philosophy of ministry • Teach stewardship	• Formally call leaders and fully entrust leadership to them • Initiate new ministries and structures to meet needs • Multiply workers by training leaders to train others • Assimilate newer believers and visitors • Evaluate church development and health • Organize church legally • Achieve full financial autonomy	• Sustain evangelistic thrust (avoid maintenance mode) • Prepare the church for reproduction • Determine the location and approach of possible daughter or pioneer church plants • Launch the daughter or pioneer church plant • Send cross-cultural missionaries • Participate in common efforts with other churches
Role of Apostolic Church Planter	Team Builder • Define the general vision • Develop a spiritual and financial support system • Recruit and build CP team based on calling, gifts and chemistry • Make prayer a priority	Learner • Gain insight for an effective and culturally appropriate ministry • Learn the local language • Develop love for and ability to work with focus people • Internship, if possible under a national worker	Motor and Model • Initiate & model ministry • Outside resources may be necessary to "jump start" the CP, but avoid creating long-term dependency • Involve local believers in basic ministry	Mobilizer and Mentor • Instill vision and biblical values • Advance ministry only to the extent that local believers are willing and prepared • Expect commitment • Shift emphasis from direct ministry to equipping laypersons for ministry at all levels • Avoid setting standards too high	Multiplier • Not only empower local believers to assume all major responsibilities, but equip them to become equippers of others • Missionary works only behind the scenes • Discontinue any dependency on outside resources	Memory • Move on to another location or ministry; serve as coach or adviser from a distance • Coach the church in planting its first daughter churches • Local believers are the CPers

* = church planting

artisans who possess both the necessary skills and an accurate understanding of the task. Or to switch metaphors, players are recruited, drilled, and honed into a team. Then a game plan is forged, so that on game day the team hits the field poised for victory. Necessary support systems and resources are also arranged.

Preparing for the church plant includes two subphases: *targeting and commissioning* and *understanding and strategizing*. Neither should be neglected. During the targeting phase the church planter determines the location and ministry focus people of the church plant. A team is formed and commissioned by a local church or sending agency. Prayer, financial, and other necessary support is sought. Essentially this involves defining the goal, assembling the players, and securing support systems. The primary focus of the church planters in this subphase is to be *team builders*. This team-building process includes not only relationships among church-planting team members but also the building of strategic alliances with other partners, such as sending churches, national fellowships of believers, and parachurch groups.

The second subphase, *understanding and strategizing*, involves careful and prayerful planning. The focus people and location are researched, and initial networking may begin. Normally the team visits the target location or lives among the focus people during this phase to obtain accurate information. On the basis of information gathered from a wide variety of sources, appropriate evangelistic and discipleship strategies are formulated. Various roles for the team members are determined, and specialized training or preparation may be acquired as necessary. This brings the team up to the point of actually launching the church-planting effort.

During this second subphase of preparation, the church planters' primary role is to be *learners*. Experienced church planters may be tempted to assume that they know more than they really do and to move forward too hastily. But contextually appropriate approaches to ministry must be reconsidered with each new church plant or focus people. Even within the same country or region, local differences can be significant. Most of all, a deep love and appreciation of the focus people should be growing as the church planters learn more about them and embrace them in prayer.

Launching

Launching is the most exciting phase. At last the church-planting effort lifts off. Ground is broken. The team runs onto the playing field! This phase consists primarily of the pioneering ministries of *evangelizing and discipling*. Relationships are developed with the focus people, and evangelistic efforts are initiated. Hopefully the first new believers will soon be ready for baptism. They are then discipled in small groups, usually meeting in homes. Even at this very early stage it is essential that the new believers are trained to minister in the most basic ways and are mobilized to share their faith and disciple others. Thus it is important for the church planters from the very outset to use methods that are easily imitated and reproduced by the local people. The church planter shares leadership with the local people even at this most basic level. For example, the first generation of cell group leaders is trained.

During this phase initial ministries of compassion and service may be developed to demonstrate the love of Christ, build relationships, and be signs of the kingdom of God. However, church planters must carefully apportion their energies and capabilities so as not to begin moving in too many directions at once, inviting burnout or initiating ministries that cannot be sustained over the long term.

In pioneering situations where there are few or no local believers in the church-planting team, the apostolic church planters function as *motors*. Because there are no local believers to train and mobilize, virtually everything in the launching phase is initially done by the missionary or itinerant team. As local people become believers the planter *models* ministry that is easily reproducible by local believers.

Establishing

During the establishing phase the first fruits of progress are experienced as the local believers are formed into a functioning congregation of worshipers increasingly living out kingdom purposes. This phase focuses on *congregating and maturing* the budding church. Small groups may combine for celebration meetings or public worship, perhaps initially on a quarterly or monthly basis and progressing to weekly services later. Ministry, however, advances only as local leaders demonstrate ownership and the ability to lead new ministries. Though budgets may be formed and a regular meeting place secured, buildings and budgets should not be the central focus of the budding church.

A preliminary local leadership team of the church or emerging movement of house churches may be formed. As ministries expand and as the local believers assume increasing responsibility for leading those ministries, their spiritual maturity and equipping for ministry become increasingly the focus of the church planters' ministry. Typically, at the point when regular public services begin, the congregation looks to the church planter or missionary to provide pastoral leadership. Under the apostolic model this must be resisted. Rather, church planters place emphasis on equipping the local believers for such leadership. New ministries are initiated only as local believers are able to at least share responsibility.

From this it is evident that the church planter has now moved from being a motor and model to being a *mobilizer and mentor*. The local believers are mobilized to take ownership of the ministry as the ministry that God has entrusted to *them*, not the church planter. They must be motivated to invest their time, talents, energy, and finances in advancing and expanding the work of the kingdom community. As mobilizer and mentor, the church planter finds that his or her most important work lies increasingly behind the scenes, equipping, counseling, and encouraging others who will have the more visible ministries and ultimately bear full leadership responsibility.

In some ways this is the most critical phase, because so many precedents are set in the life of the church. The DNA of the church is determined. Patterns for ministry are formed that will guide the church in its future and will be difficult to change later.

Structuring

As the church matures, the structuring phase becomes a time of great satisfaction as the hard labor begins to pay off. Whether the new body is a movement of informal house churches or a more traditional church, structure must be provided to sustain growth, meet expanding needs, and promote discipleship. The organization of the church takes shape with the formal calling of the first leaders, the legal incorporation of the church (where appropriate), and new ministries to take advantage of new opportunities. This phase is characterized by the *expanding* of ministry and *empowering* of local believers for full responsibility, autonomy in ministry, and leadership.

For additional ministries to be developed, several things must happen: First and foremost, new persons must be fully integrated into the life of the church, trained, and mobilized for service. Second, teaching on stewardship cannot be overlooked if the growing ministries are to be adequately resourced. A growing church must overcome the temptation to continue to act like a small family church, unless of course it chooses to multiply into additional small family–sized churches. Leadership structures can no longer function on the simple family-like basis but must be expanded and the workload borne on many shoulders. If the church plant has been receiving subsidies or other significant forms of outside assistance, these must be reduced at this time so the church avoids long-term dependencies.

By this point in the development, apostolic church planters prepare for full withdrawal, entering the last stages of phase-out. This is especially difficult as the church planters are enjoying the fruit of their labors and there is seemingly so much opportunity for ministry. But local believers should bear the major responsibility for the leadership and expanding ministries of the church in this phase.

The primary role of the mission team members at this point is to be *multipliers*, as they equip local leaders to become equippers of others. Not only are local believers bearing the responsibility for ministry, with the church planter increasingly behind the scenes, but these leaders must learn to become equippers of others if true multiplication of the church is to occur. New local leaders for the first daughter churches are now in view.

Reproducing

A church planter's joy, not unlike the joy of becoming a grandparent, comes when the church plant has reproduced itself by planting another church. In addition to equipping local believers with the ministry skills and vision for multiplication, the young church must reassess and evaluate its continued development: is it still faithful to biblical purposes for the church, or has it perhaps become comfortable with its more established existence? Its salt-and-light kingdom impact should be reaching new levels. This phase can be characterized by the dual tasks of *strengthening* and *sending*.

By reproduction we have in mind not only the multiplication of daughter churches planted locally but also the church's becoming a missionary sending agent, facilitating the planting of churches among more distant unreached peoples. The church is also committed to cooperation with others, be it through a denomination or other forms of networking. It knows that churches can accomplish more together in synergy for the kingdom than it can alone.

Apostolic church planters may remain for a time, continuing as multipliers, coaching the movement as it reproduces itself, or becoming regional equippers and facilitators. But ultimately the apostolic team should move on to pioneer new locations and unreached groups. They become in essence a *memory*.

Equipping and Shared Responsibility—the Method behind the Methods

With the apostolic approach presented in chapter 5, the goal is a church that will grow and reproduce itself apart from continued outside assistance. At every phase, apostolic church planters must equip local believers to assume responsibility for the emerging ministries of the church. They resist the temptation to move the ministries and programs of the church ahead of the local believers' willingness and readiness to participate in, support, and ultimately give leadership to the given ministry or program.

After the launching phases of the church plant, every ministry or program must from inception be led or co-led by a local believer who will be equipped and eventually bear responsibility for that ministry. In this way the challenge of handing off a ministry from the leadership of a church planter to the leadership of a local believer is not an issue. After an initial time of equipping, the church planters should be able to withdraw at any time without threatening the ministry's existence. Furthermore, because equipping is included at the inception of every new ministry, an ethos of equipping and multiplication is modeled and instilled in the new church. *This is a key to long-term mul-*

tiplication. The principles of indigenous reproduction and multiplication delineated in chapter 4 must be implemented and kept in mind at every step of the developmental process.

Critical Spiritual Gifts for Each Developmental Phase

Though all spiritual gifts are important to the healthy function of the body of Christ, at each of the various phases certain gifts are critically important to facilitate the developmental process (see figure 8.1). Many church plants stall and fail to move forward because the planter emphasizes ministry based on his or her gifts alone. For example, many church planters are high-energy "doers" with little patience for equipping others—they are good motors but poor mentors. Or they may be strong in evangelism but weak in administration. In such a case the church plant may plateau and never move much past the establishing phase. The best way to overcome this challenge is to identify local believers with the critical gifts and help them develop and employ those gifts. Even if the gift mix of the apostolic church-planting team has all the necessary gifts, the key will be mobilizing local believers.

During the launch phase of a pioneer church plant, the gift of evangelism is clearly essential to win the first believers. We think of Philip the evangelist in the New Testament, whose ministry in Samaria led to the conversion of the first Samaritan believers and the establishment of a church there (Acts 8:5–13). However, the gift of apostleship is also essential so as to give the church-planting effort adequate strategic leadership for the multiplication of churches through a whole region.[3] The apostle Paul is the clearest New Testament example of such a gifted person.

As the church moves into the establishing phase, the needs of new believers for strong biblical teaching, personal counsel, and spiritual nurture increase. They also must be equipped to take on greater ministry responsibility. Thus pastoral and teaching gifts are particularly important during this phase. Barnabas comes to mind as an encourager of new believers in Antioch (Acts 11:22–24). But Barnabas was also an outstanding mentor, as in the case of his relationship with Paul (Acts 9:27; 11:25–26; etc.). Apollos, a man with great biblical knowledge (Acts 18:24), instructed the church in Corinth in Paul's absence (Acts 19:1; 1 Cor. 3:4–6; 16:12). If these gifts are lacking, then the new believers will likely remain immature.

As the church enters the structuring phase, new structures are created. new ministry teams are organized, and the church grows in financial stewardship; thus administrative gifts are important. James, the brother of Jesus and elder in the Jerusalem church, is perhaps an example, as he played a leading role

---

3. We are using the term *apostle* here in the sense of an apostolic church planter as described in chapter 5.

Figure 8.1
Critical Spiritual Gifts for the Developmental Phases

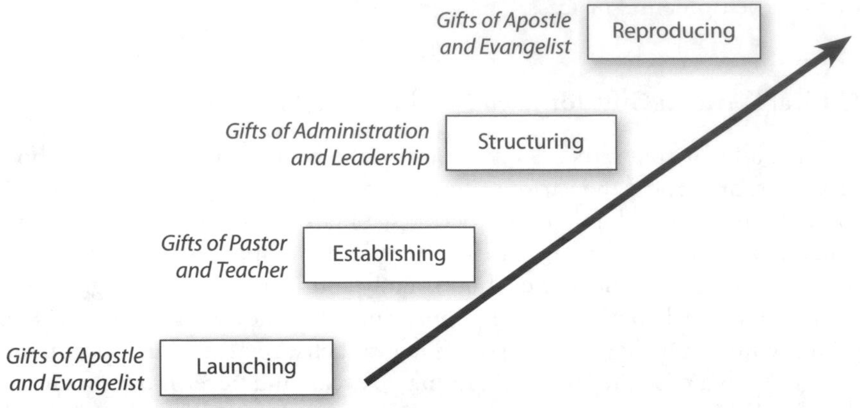

in the Jerusalem Council (Acts 15) and is frequently named as the key representative of the Jerusalem church elders (Acts 12:17; 21:18). The deacons who administered aid for the widows in the Jerusalem church most likely had administrative gifts (Acts 6:1–6). Often churches that have grown swiftly plateau simply because the church planter or congregation has not adapted methods and created new structures to deal with the changed situation and growth of the church.

Finally, as the church is poised to reproduce, once again apostolic and evangelistic gifts will be essential so as to launch the new church-planting effort. However, this time it should be local believers, recruited from the harvest for the harvest, who become the next generation of church planters. Epaphras was perhaps such a second-generation evangelist and church planter. He was originally from Colossae (Col. 4:12), probably became a believer in Ephesus under Paul's ministry, and then returned to Colossae to preach the gospel and plant the church there (Col. 1:7).

Wise church planters will be alert to their own limitations and realize that they tend to gravitate to their own place of giftedness and hold the church with them at that spot. In worst-case scenarios, painful conflict between the planter and the congregation can erupt. Thus it is essential that as the church grows and develops, all the spiritual gifts are valued and brought to bear at the critical time and occasion.

Avoiding Sequential Thinking

David Garrison and other advocates of church multiplication have warned against an overly sequential approach to church planting—that is, the view that a church cannot mature or reproduce without first passing through certain linear, step-by-step phases (Garrison 2004a, 243–45). Though the developmental phases of church planting may appear strictly sequential, in fact reproduction and multiplication should be built into each phase, as explained in chapter 4. As new believers are won, they are discipled and taught to evangelize others. As they grow in discipleship, they in turn learn to disciple others. As they participate in a cell group, they learn to lead cell groups and eventually train other new cell-group leaders. As a cell group is formed, the vision for multiplying new cells is born from the outset. In this way multiplication becomes part of the ethos of the church in *every* aspect of its ministry.

When the church progresses to the next phase, it does not cease to carry out the ministry functions of the previous phase. For example, even though the church plant may progress from launching to establishing, it should never cease to evangelize. As the church moves from congregating and maturing to expanding and empowering, it should not cease to multiply cell groups and cell leaders. In a sense ministry is cumulative, not sequential, with each phase continuing to reproduce ministries from the previous phase.

A church needn't be fully mature and operating a wide array of ministries before it can reproduce. Churches with that mindset rarely reproduce, because they never perceive themselves as quite mature enough! But if the ethos of multiplication is instilled in the life of the church from the beginning, multiplying evangelists, disciples, cells, and cell leaders, then reproduction will be experienced not as a monumental task but as a natural outgrowth of the multiplication process already under way.

9

Preparing, Part 1

Targeting and Commissioning

The worker who prepares for cross-cultural church planting can be compared to a runner who undergoes rigorous mental and physical conditioning for an upcoming marathon. Runners also prepare by designing a strategy that fits the terrain and climatic conditions. In chapter 15 we will discuss the *personal dimension* of preparation, including qualifications, education, family orientation, and emotional and spiritual preparation. In this chapter and the next we highlight important *strategic* preparations and *contextually appropriate* decisions. Church planting leaders estimate that between 60 and 80 percent of the problems encountered in church planting result from faulty strategic thinking in the preparing phase (Logan and Ogne 1991a; Klippenes 2003, 84).

In this phase the geography or ethnicity of the focus people[1] is chosen, a church-planting team is formed and commissioned, the central vision and core values are defined, and, finally, a financial and prayer support system is established. In summary, this preparation phase involves defining the goal, assembling the players, and securing the support systems.

Overview of Phase

Biblical Examples
Acts 13:3: The Antioch church sends the first missionaries
Acts 13:5: The team is expanded
Galatians 2:7–9: There is need for support and for a clear ministry focus people

---

1. We prefer the term *ministry focus people* to *target group*. Some are geographic, focused in a distinct neighborhood or town; others are ethnic, a people group segment that is distinguished by ethnicity or culture.

Key Steps
1. Define the church-planting vision and core values
2. Determine the ministry focus people
3. Recruit a capable team leader
4. Gather and organize the team
5. Secure prayer and financial support
6. Prepare and commission the team

Critical Issues
1. Agreeing on a clear vision, core values, and focus people
2. Having the right person to lead the effort
3. Building strategy on indigenous principles with the help of cultural advisers
4. Learning language and culture well
5. Assembling a healthy team

Define the Church-Planting Vision and Core Values

In twenty-first-century North America *vision* has become the cardinal virtue of effective entrepreneurial leadership. The word is popularly defined as the conceptualization of the preferred future toward which a group strives. Sometimes this vision is described in very specific quantifiable terms (such as a church of five hundred members that gives birth to ten daughter churches). At other times it takes a more nebulous form, more like a dream than a measurable outcome (a movement of organic churches in every neighborhood of the city that transforms families and communities). Henry and Richard Blackaby (2001) remind us that Christian mission must be rooted in the Great Commission and the Great Commandment. It must also come from God's purpose, not human ambition or imagination. The Holy Spirit communicates God's perspective and desires (vision) to those who seek him. Thus church planting is essentially a spiritual enterprise that grows out of an intimate walk with God and is further shaped by creative energy and imagination.

One danger to avoid is copying a church-planting vision from a different context. The Holy Spirit must guide in the shaping of a vision that fits the particular situation. The "broad strokes" can be outlined early, but determining specific evangelistic and disciplemaking efforts requires cultural understanding and cultural mentors.[2] The development of a church-planting vision should be approached as a process rather than a one-time decision. The church-planting leader resembles a navigator who charts a course for his ship on an ocean. He knows his final destination, but the wind and waves constantly seem to push him off course. He must consult his assistants, review his charts, and adjust his course on a regular basis. So it is with church planting. The vision is the

---

2. Sequence is important. Although God will give a vision that drives the launch of the team, the work-specific strategies flow from an understanding of the people. This falls in the next chapter, subtitled "Understanding and Strategizing."

final destination toward which the church is directed. This caution is not an argument against passion or entrepreneurial determination but an argument for humility, sincerity, flexibility, and openness in the journey.

Multiplication Movement Mindset

A movement of church multiplication must look down the road to indigenous churches that are reproducing with the manpower and resources available locally. Along with a plan to include local disciples and workers in the "control room" setting ministry direction, the apostolic team must have a phase-out strategy. In teams where some members come from the culture of the ministry focus people, there can be indigenous leadership from the start. This is ideal but cannot always be achieved in pioneer settings. In those settings the missionary team needs a progressive strategy of leadership development, empowerment, and role change before leaving local leaders in charge. "This is what David Bosch calls granting them a 'certificate of maturity.' It is responsible mentorship, the type of care Paul demonstrated to those to whom he ministered" (Steffen 1997, 9). Thus the future must shape the present and the apostolic team should function like temporary scaffolding (Saint 2001).

Church planting that empowers and multiplies flows from a compelling vision for healthy indigenous church multiplication and a firm belief that future gospel penetration and transformation of the ministry focus people belongs in the hands of the national church. The martyred archbishop Oscar Romero expressed the empowering power of those who accept the limitations and risks of laying seeds for future generations.

It helps now and then to step back and take a long view. The Kingdom is not only beyond our efforts; it is beyond our vision. We accomplish in our lifetime only a fraction of the magnificent enterprise that is God's work. Nothing we do is complete, which is another way of saying that the kingdom always lies beyond us. . . . This is what we are about. We plant the seeds that one day will grow. We water the seeds already planted knowing that they hold future promise. We lay foundations that will need further development. We provide yeast that produces effects far beyond our capabilities. We cannot do everything, and there is a sense of liberation in realizing this. This enables us to do something, and to do it very well. It may be incomplete, but it is a beginning, a step along the way, an opportunity for the Lord's grace to enter and do the rest. We may never see the end results, but that is the difference between the master builder and the worker. We are workers, not master builders, ministers, not messiahs. We are prophets of a future not our own.[3]

3. Oscar A. Romero, archbishop of San Salvador, was assassinated on March 24, 1980, while celebrating Mass in a small chapel in a cancer hospital where he lived. The citation attributed to Romero was composed by Bishop Ken Untener of Saginaw (Untener 2005).

Components of the Vision

In summary, vision for a church planter is the preconception of a preferred future, initiated by God himself but discerned progressively through prayer, consultation, and study. The vision should guide the church planter with the strategic choices discussed in chapters 5–7.

Chapter 5 outlined three types of church planters: pastoral, apostolic, and catalytic. The vision may include several of these types, such as an apostolic team working with local teams of laypeople led by a catalytic church planter. The leader of the church-planting team must understand his or her role as a foundation-layer and plan for transference of ministry responsibility to the local team of leaders. Thus leadership development is an important part of the vision.

Chapter 6 talked about indigenous principles and church-planting move-ments. The vision should lead to the reproduction of viable, healthy, indig-enous, self-supporting, and interdependent churches. In order for the church-planting team to build reproduction potential into the DNA of the first church, the initial vision must include the reproduction of disciples, small groups, and workers who, in turn, contribute to second- and third-generation churches.

Chapter 7 presented several church-planting models. Each one of them re-quires a distinct approach, a unique leadership team, and a different set of resources. When designing the initial vision statement, the church-planting team might discuss options like these: Will the new church be part of a cluster of house churches that grow like a spreading vine? Will it be a strong urban central church that will have satellites in outlying villages? Will it be a cell-church that covers the city, gathers together monthly for large, powerful celebration services, and carries out works of compassion in the neediest areas? The selection of a church-planting model will be an important part of the initial vision.

Church-Planting Core Values

As we noted in chapter 6, values are strongly held convictions that shape our decisions. If the vision is the final destination toward which the planter fixes the ship's bow, the values are the markers along the way that serve as points of reference. They are like the buoys that distinguish the navigable channel from the treacherous reefs in an estuary. One set of core values for a church-planting movement is given in sidebar 9.1.

Core values drive decisions, determine priorities, and facilitate evalua-tion. When held in common by the team, they foster cooperation and unity in ministry and allow for diversity in secondary things. Thus when common core values are identified, the team has an objective basis on which to build its unity and avoid unnecessary conflict. The core values are closely related to the ministry vision, functioning like pillars that hold it up. When shared effectively, they inspire people to action and help people embrace change. They influence team building, role clarification, financial management, and resource allocation. In Christian ministry they must be rooted in Scripture, particularly in the Great Commission and the Great Commandment.

In the Jerusalem church (Acts 6:1–7) there was a crisis over the care given to widows. Greek- and Hebrew-speaking widows were not being treated equally. The immediate action taken by the apostles indicates that care for the needy and equality were core values: spiritually mature and fervent leaders (another core value) were chosen to handle the growing pastoral and administrative needs. However, the apostles wanted to prioritize other core values: prayer and the ministry of the Word. In this situation there does not seem to have been a conflict of values, and in the end they preserved all the core values by finding competent people for a new, improved ministry. The final result was that the Word of God spread and the church grew.

Core values are especially helpful if they are expressed in term of priorities. Table 9.1 lists a few possible core values of an organic church-planting effort:

Determine the Ministry Focus People

Some resist choosing a ministry focus people, preferring to offer the gospel broadly to all. However, there are good reasons to select an initial primary focus people. First of all, having a strategic evangelistic focus has biblical precedents. The apostles agreed that Peter, James, and John would concentrate on the Jews while Paul and Barnabas would focus on the Gentiles (Gal. 2:7–9).

The focus can be part of a lifelong call, or it can be limited to a specific phase of the mission. Philip seemingly was led by God to reach the Samaritans without an apostolic mandate. Later the church in Jerusalem examined and affirmed his mission (Acts 8:4–17), and he continued for some time. While seeking God's direction, Paul received a vision of a Macedonian man, and Luke concluded: "After Paul had seen the vision, we got ready at once to leave

Table 9.1
Application of Core Values

Value Statement	Possible Applications
Small before large	Multiply cell groups before starting public meetings
Infrastructure before superstructure	Grow disciples and small groups before investing in a building
Proven before public	People are tested through service before receiving titles and responsibilities
Character before charisma	Focus on spiritual maturity over dynamic personality
Going more than staying	Meet people where they are instead of expecting them to come to you
Multiplying more than adding	Invest in people and ministries that are reproducible and don't make them depend on outside resources
The lost more than the found	Small groups and ministries should have an outward focus and make newcomers and seekers feel welcome
The lay more than the professional	Standards should be attainable by godly lay leaders. Do not use professional training in ways that are out of their reach

Source: Core values from Ferguson 2007, 2, were expanded with applications for ReachGlobal EFCA Cross-Cultural Church Planting School, May 2008, by Gene Wilson.

for Macedonia, concluding that God had called us to preach the gospel to them" (Acts 16:10). Following this pattern, church-planting missionaries have historically preached to all who would listen but concentrated their efforts on a primary ministry focus people at any given time.

A ministry focus people is the people group the new church will reach and serve. It can be defined by ethnicity, class, socioeconomics, geography, generation (boomer, buster, millennial), or by other criteria that set apart a segment of the population. Failure to define a focus people will usually mean that the church-planting team will tend to, by default, reach people most like themselves. The method of presenting the gospel, the language used, and the forms of communication are never culturally neutral. Defining a focus people does not mean that those outside that group are ignored, excluded, or overlooked, but only that a conscious decision is made to focus efforts on presenting the gospel in a way understandable and meaningful to a particular people. There are several factors to consider when selecting a specific demographic focus people:

Spiritual need. As an apostolic church planter Paul wrote, "It has always been my ambition to preach the gospel where Christ was not known, so that I would not be building on someone else's foundation" (Rom. 15:20). The reason for this was straightforward: people without Christ are lost: "for 'Everyone who calls on the name of the Lord will be saved.' How, then, can they call on the one they have not believed in? And how can they believe in the one of whom they have not heard? And how can they hear without someone preaching to them?" (Rom. 10:13–14).

Some people groups are unreached or less evangelized than others, and we know that God desires all peoples to have the opportunity to respond to the gospel (Matt. 28:18–20; cf. Matt. 24:14; 1 Tim. 2:4; Rev. 5:9).[4] A people group is usually considered "unreached" where there is no viable, indigenous local church that can communicate the gospel in a meaningful manner to that people. Another definition of *unreached* is that less than 2 percent of the population is evangelical, with minimal or no church planting among them (Holste and Haney 2006). Demographic studies may indicate that there is an unreached people group that needs the gospel. But need alone is not a sufficient basis for determining the focus people.

Greater receptivity. Though no people should be without a gospel witness, there is a scriptural and missiological argument for giving priority to receptive groups over unresponsive groups (Matt. 10:12–14; Luke 14:15–24; Acts 13:46–47). Studies and experience may show that a segment of the population is open to change and will listen to the gospel. Donald McGavran based his "harvest principle" on this receptivity factor.[5] Often the final decision is made when there is a convergence of several of these factors as a result of demographic study, prayer, and exploratory visits.

Strategic effectiveness. Since human and strategic resources are always limited, the church-planting team can make best use of them by prioritizing a specific group. The team increases its effectiveness by adjusting its efforts and ministries to the needs and worldview of this group. Contextually appropriate communication and action require the selection of a ministry focus people (Hesselgrave 1980 and 1991).

Geographic factors. Some of the wisest choices are made not in response to a situation on the ground but because of a strategic long-term plan to reach a city or region. In chapter 3 we noted that Paul's church planting concentrated on urban centers characterized by Roman administration, Greek civilization, Jewish influence, or commercial opportunity. Likewise, today's church planters may seek out strategic centers of influence, especially in pioneering efforts, and follow a natural progression along arteries of transportation such as highways, rivers, or subway lines. In areas where people

4. There is help available to find people groups that do not have a viable Christian church. For example, the Joshua Project (www.joshuaproject.org) identifies unreached people groups on all continents. The most current edition of Patrick Johnstone's *Operation World* (2005) is also a valuable resource in this regard.

5. Discussed in chapter 4.

Case Study 9.1

Selecting a Focus People as a Strategic Choice

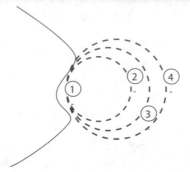

The work of the Evangelical Free Church of Peru began in the port district of Lima called Los Pilares. As the city grew in concentric circles away from the ocean, people from the original church moved to the suburbs. Bible studies were formed in those suburbs and some of those became new churches. Two of the suburban churches grew and began planting churches in developments that were less evangelized. Thus the church planting was driven primarily by the strategy of following demographic growth focusing on new emerging communities.

groups interact, information and influence flow more naturally in certain directions. Initially it may be preferable to reach a more influential group and later extend efforts to other groups. This can also apply to social classes (McGavran 1980; Nida 1974). When a team seeks a strategic place to work, it can ask questions like, What would be a good platform from which to reach other population segments? What is a natural extension of what God has been doing so far?

Preexisting core group or diaspora Christians. There may be a small group of believers who already live among an unreached people. Perhaps they became Christians elsewhere and later returned home; or they may be believers from elsewhere who have, as a result of war, famine, employment, or other reasons, relocated to the region. That displaced group of disciples can potentially become the core of the church and thus save the church-planting team the months, or even years, that it would otherwise take them to evangelize and gather an initial group. These persons may also have relationships in the community that can serve as pathways to communicate the gospel. We see something of this in the New Testament, when persecution broke out in Jerusalem: as a result, the believers scattered, the gospel was preached throughout the region, and the church of Antioch was planted (Acts 8:1–4; 11:19–21). In such cases the church-planting team must, of course, develop a relationship with the group of believers and determine whether there is sufficient compatibility to make a cooperative effort possible and desirable.

Exceptional opportunity. Sometimes an opportunity that does not necessarily fit the above criteria for determining a focus people presents itself unexpectedly (see case study 9.2). A "man of peace" (Luke 10:6; Matt. 10:11–14) from

Sidebar 9.2

Determining the Ministry Focus People

The Need Factor—Spiritual need

Romans 10:13–15; 15:20
- Communities, people groups, classes without an indigenous, evangelizing church
- Small percentage of evangelicals

The Responsiveness Factor—Receptiveness

Matthew 10:11–15; Acts 14:27
- The likelihood that people will be receptive to the gospel and the church will be able to grow and become reproducing within a reasonable period of time

The Strategic Effectiveness Factor—Potential for multiplication and influence

- Opinion leaders, high-credibility persons
- Social groups or subcultures that influence others
- People groups with extended family or relationships through the region
- People groups that are industrious or entrepreneurial

The Geographic Factor—Significant location

- Commercial, educational, political, or transportation centers
- Locations of population growth, movement
- Possibility of launching a regional movement from the location

The Diaspora Factor—Preexisting core group

Acts 8:1–4; 11:19–21
- A number of Christians living among the focus people to build the core of the church plant

The Open Door Factor—Exceptional opportunity

1 Corinthians 16:9; 2 Corinthians 2:12; Colossians 4:3
- Exceptional opportunities to preach the gospel and/or exceptional responsiveness to the gospel

The Supernatural Guidance Factor—Exceptional leading of the Spirit

Acts 16: the Macedonian call
- Direct guidance may at times override very well-reasoned plans

a certain social or ethnic group who is a strong witness among his people may ask for help establishing a church among his people. Or a strategic opening might arise. Paul postponed further pioneer work and remained in Ephesus longer than in most locations "because a great door for effective work has opened to me" (1 Cor. 16:9). He also reports, "I went to Troas to preach the gospel of Christ and found that the Lord had opened a door for me" (2 Cor. 2:12). Paul requested prayer that God would continue to open doors for his message (Col. 4:3). One of the most dramatic unexpected open doors of opportunity in recent times was the fall of the Iron Curtain in the early 1990s. Many Eastern European nations had been closed to missionary work but public preaching of the gospel suddenly became open and receptive. Mission organizations quickly reallocated personnel and resources to take advantage of the opportunity. Sometimes such a window of opportunity does not remain open for long, as government policies are revised or the spiritual atmosphere changes. Sadly, this is the case in much of Eastern Europe, where responsiveness has fallen since the 1990s.

Supernatural guidance by the Holy Spirit. On his second missionary journey, Paul and his team attempted to preach the gospel in Asia but were hindered by the Holy Spirit. They then attempted to enter Bithynia but were again not allowed by the Spirit (Acts 16:6–7). Only when Paul received a supernatural vision of a man from Macedonia calling him did God's guidance become clear (Acts 16:8–10). At a later time Paul would minister in Ephesus, in the province of Asia, where a church-planting movement would be launched. Sometimes our best plans, based on the most strategic and prayerful considerations, have to await God's timing. We must always remain open for the leading of the Holy Spirit, who may choose to redirect us to a more fruitful field of ministry that we had not identified or antici-

---

Case Study 9.2

Selecting a Focus People in Response to an Open Door

The building of a new church had been approved by the major local denomination, and two different neighborhoods in rural Quebec requested that the new place of worship be erected on their land. Residents of the neighborhood that lost were so upset that they locked the priest out of the old chapel and put an ad in the newspaper for a minister of another denomination to come and serve them. Missionaries who were seeking God's guidance about where to begin their work saw the ad and spoke to the people about the way of salvation. The people were ready for change, and eventually the chapel became an evangelical church. This was a unique opening in an otherwise difficult context (Duclos 1982).

pated. Sidebar 9.2 summarizes the key factors to consider when choosing a ministry focus people.

The church-planting team will have the ultimate responsibility of selecting the ministry focus people, in consultation with local advisers and collaborating churches. If after all these considerations two focus peoples seem equal in their church-planting potential, initial contacts can be made with people of both population segments to gauge their response. Finally a decision must be made. A tentative focus people, chosen prayerfully, is better than no focus people or several focus peoples. Many factors should be considered, but at the end of the day the church-planting team should be convinced that God has called them to reach a particular group of people.

Recruit a Capable Team Leader

One of the most common reasons church plants fail is that the wrong person is chosen to lead the effort. The wisest approach is to find a proven leader who fits the culturally appropriate church planter profile. Chapter 15 will provide an in-depth discussion of competencies. The leader casts the vision, keeps the team unified, and ensures that it stays on target with its mission. Preferably this leader will be a cultural insider or a person comfortable in the target culture. Church history records how God often used men and women who came to Christ outside their native people group to lead the efforts to reach their people and establish or expand the church among them.[6] This enables the church to have a more indigenous shape from the start (see case study 9.3). If no national leader can be recruited, then the leader should ideally be a person with experience in the culture of the focus people or in a similar context.

Although all three types of church planter have their place, as we have seen in chapter 5, cross-cultural missionaries who are apostolic planters work with and through emerging national leaders and move on. Those who have an apostolic mandate and gift, who are culturally adept spiritual entrepreneurs, who can lead a team, who prefer to see national leaders front and center, and who accept that theirs is a foundation-laying role make the best apostolic planters. On the other hand, those who have been pastors in their home country for many years before serving as cross-cultural church planters often find the role change difficult and slide back into a pastoral mode.

6. For example, Patrick returned to the Celts of Ireland, where he had been held as a slave as a young adult (Tucker 1983, 38–39). In the fourth century Ulfilas, the son of a Cappadocian Christian captured by the Goths, returned to his father's captors, evangelized successfully for forty years, and developed an alphabet so they could read the Bible (ibid., 35–37).

Case Study 9.3

The Importance of Leader Selection

Redeemer Church in New York City has been instrumental in planting 114 new churches throughout the world. It was listed by Lifeway researcher Ed Stetzer in *Outreach Magazine* (July 2007) as the number-one reproducing church in the United States. Twenty-nine of the plants are in postmodern European cities. Part of the strategy of the Redeemer Church Planting Center (RCPC) is to identify gifted leaders with a passion for church planting and come alongside them with resources and coaching to grow their church and plant others. Al Barth, European director of church planting, devotes much of his time to identifying and recruiting cultural insiders who are compatible with RCPC's distinctives and vision for church planting. This illustrates the importance of selecting a culturally astute and effective church-planting team leader.

Gather and Organize the Team

The primary focus of the lead church planter in this early phase is to be a *team builder*. Sometimes teams are put together haphazardly, using whoever is able or willing to join the effort. We will discuss church-planting teams in more depth in chapter 16, but the planter's primary role, rather than to be a pastor-teacher, is to lead the efforts, model church-planting best practices, and train others in evangelism and disciplemaking. The team is then built around the team leader, and he or she should have the greatest voice in assembling team members who can contribute significantly and be loyal to the vision and values (Exod. 18:21; 1 Chron. 11:10–25; Mark 3:13–14; Acts 15:39–40; 16:1–3). Of course, the leader will want to consult with others and may give team members a trial period to get to know them well.

The initial team should be kept "lean" and committed by the setting of high standards (Deut. 20:5–9; Judg. 7:4–8; Phil. 2:19–30; 1 Thess. 2:4–12). Those who lack maturity, loyalty, or commitment should not be accepted as full-fledged team members. One of the major causes of failure in church planting is the inability of team members to work together. The qualifications for participation on a church-planting team should be decided, made public, and used consistently. If a team is large it can be overbearing in its influence, both strategically and culturally. If it is "lean" there will be room for local believers to develop a greater role and voice on the local leadership team.

Chapter 16 discusses both foundational qualities that *all* team members should have, such as the ability to evangelize and disciple, and complementary qualities that should be found *somewhere* on the team. Generally speaking, members should be chosen because they complement the leader and because they have the gifts needed to develop, empower, and coach a local team of leaders. The team composition will also depend on the type of church planting adopted. Clarity on the type of church plant is needed so that a team with the appropriate skill and gift set can be assembled. For example, if an apostolic church-planting approach is chosen, the team profile will be very entrepreneurial and evangelistic with strong initiating, gathering, and developing skills. A pastoral church planter, on the other hand, may select team members according to their ability to lead the core ministries of the church. Whatever the approach, the process described below can be followed.

Once a team is assembled, its members should identify key roles and the constellation of gifts and competencies that corresponds to those roles. They will work together based on their gifts and abilities rather than affinity, personality, education, or experience. Teams composed of people with similar profiles tend to foster competition and conflict—and unfortunately, many implode. On the other hand, people with complementary profiles tend to work more productively together.

Some of the key roles that complement the leader may be (1) evangelist-gatherer, (2) teacher-trainer, (3) administrative assistant, (4) mentor-counselor, and (5) several helpers who can encourage and disciple new believers. The team leader will delegate responsibilities according to these roles and help members get the training they need. He or she will empower and facilitate ministry rather than micromanaging it.

Secure Prayer and Financial Support

Church planting is a cooperative effort that requires unity of vision and a pooling of resources from many sources. Once the focus people is adopted, it becomes much easier to raise a support team for the project. Building a financial and prayer support team is similar to erecting the support walls of a home. Support walls look like any other wall but must be strong and stable. They can never be removed, because the other walls and structures rest on them. When they are strong, almost any addition or renovation can be made. Church planters need to put up twin support walls of prayer and economic support. Nehemiah is a good example in this respect. He was a man of prayer, foresight, and planning who built the walls of Jerusalem before rebuilding the nation. He anticipated the physical resources needed for the project (Neh. 2:8) as well as the spiritual opposition he and his team were sure to face (4:9–16).

Prayer Support

Paul and Barnabas had a special relationship with the Syrian Antioch church that sent them out on their first missionary journey with prayer and fasting (Acts 13:3). Later they returned to share and celebrate the results (Acts 14:26–28) and remained in Antioch until their next assignment. This relationship was not exclusive. Paul also appealed to other churches and individuals to support him in prayer (e.g., 2 Cor. 1:10–11; Eph. 6:19–20).

The need to rely on God's power and intervention through corporate prayer is documented in the annals of church-planting history. God opens doors, removes obstacles, prepares hearers, and protects workers in response to prayer. The Moravians sent out more cross-cultural workers per capita than all other Protestant groups combined had sent in the two previous centuries (Tucker 1983, 71). What propelled this great missionary advance? There were undoubtedly many factors, but the turning point was a revival in Hernhutt that gave birth to a prayer movement with daily meetings and an around-the-clock prayer vigil that lasted one hundred years (ibid., 70). In North America, concerts of prayer for revival and missions accompanied the First Great Awakening. In 1748 Jonathan Edwards echoed a call from England to rally extraordinary prayer efforts in a pamphlet titled *An Humble Attempt to Promote Explicit Agreement and Visible Union of God's People in Extraordinary Prayer, for the Revival of Religion and the Advancement of Christ's Kingdom on Earth.*

Church-planting advance depends on both spiritual dynamics and human strategy. Prayer must infuse both for kingdom breakthroughs to take place. Paul associates prayer with the spiritual battle for the lost. Although no magical formula should be sought, nor guarantees given, the intentional use of prayer to break down spiritual opposition has been documented in a broad array of literature (Taylor 1959; Robb 1990; Piper 1993). All those involved in church planting should maintain a strong discipline of intercessory prayer, but even that is inadequate. They need others who will faithfully stand with them in prayer. A prayer team should be built so that strong, sustained prayer can easily be mobilized when decisions need to be made and spiritual battles take place. This involves asking for a specific commitment to pray regularly,

---

Case Study 9.4

Prayer and Revival

A godly Indian woman, Pandita Ramabai, became burdened by India's need for revival. In 1903 she became interested in the movement of prayer in Australia that preceded the Torrey-Alexander campaigns there. A year later, she learned of the revival in Wales. So Ramabai began special prayer circles at the beginning of 1905, and hundreds of her helpers, friends, and missionaries attended these sessions (Orr 1970, 62). While missionaries were heavily involved, the leaders were almost always Indian (Duewel 1995). The result was a great extension of the gospel. "The number of Christians in the Punjab quadrupled from 37,695 to 163,994. During the decade of revival in India, the Christian population increased by 69.9 percent, which was sixteen times the amount of increase in the Hindu community" (Duewel 1995, 227).

---

communicating key prayer requests on a regular basis, and returning to report in person (Acts 14). The principle of prayer as the driving and sustaining force behind church-planting ventures can be summarized by this axiom: *No church-planting movement will rise above the prayer ministry of those involved with it.*

Financial Support

Poor financial planning and practice destroy many homes. They also undermine many otherwise sound church-planting projects. Economic issues and financial support can be major factors in the success or failure of church planting. When asked, "Why do church planters fail most often in Latin America?" many church-planting leaders mentioned a lack of funds, financial support, or denominational backing as a primary cause (Wilson 2001, 229). Few things teach dependence on God as well as financial need. Ernesto Zavalla, then Latin America director for Scripture Union, said: "God's business is in the hand of failing men. . . . We need to come naked before God every day" (quoted in ibid.). On the other hand, several approaches to financial support have been used effectively, and the history of the church abounds with evidence that in spite of meager resources, God provides for every endeavor he directs and every person he calls.

No rules can be made concerning the mechanics of financial support, but in this preparation phase church planters should have a reasonable and viable plan for the financial support of their families (1 Cor. 16:1–4; 2 Cor. 8–9; Phil. 4:10–17). Some church planters use "faith" as a pretext for acting irresponsibly. Dependence on God's supply does not relieve church planters of their responsibility as providers (1 Tim. 5:8). There are three major options: (1) full-time secular work, (2) full-time church planting by raising full financial support beforehand, and (3) bivocational church planting requiring partial support raised beforehand.

Cross-cultural church planters typically raise all or most of their support at home in order to have a stable income that does not depend on the local church or community of their ministry focus people. Many have to show the authorities that they are not taking a job from a local worker. The apostle Paul's life is instructive at this point. He worked as a tentmaker, and God supplemented his revenue with gifts from at least one church. Paul wrote about his personal needs and the needs of established churches in distress (1 Cor. 16; 2 Cor. 8–9; Phil. 4). He also avoided depending on those he was discipling for his livelihood (Acts 20:34–35; Phil. 4:16; 1 Thess. 2:9). He argued that laborers in ministry are worthy of their wages and that he could have asked for support if expedient (1 Cor. 9:7–14). But he chose not to do that for several reasons: (1) he did not want to be a burden to new believers; (2) he wanted to

give his opponents no pretext for questioning his motives; and (3) he wanted
to set an example of hard work.

In Paul's day people were profiting from the gospel (2 Cor. 2:17), so he
needed to set himself apart from them by relying on his tentmaking work and
receiving only voluntary gifts from outside churches. There is a healthy pattern here for cross-cultural missionaries to follow. Not only should they not
depend financially on those they are discipling, but they should be willing to
support themselves if needed and should always give an example of hard work.
As a result, when it is time to leave they will not be financially dependent on
the new church for their income and will not open themselves to unnecessary
criticism in financial matters.

An increasing number of missionaries going into creative-access countries[7]
are starting businesses that provide part of their income and give them a platform for their ministry. In this case, they are self-supporting to some degree
and rely on the contributions of outside churches and friends to supplement
their business income. Handling two lines of work in a credible manner and
coping with the stress of managing both responsibly is not easy.[8] In some
cases the church planter's spouse and members of the team are able to find
some form of income and contribute financially to the project. The goal is
that, as soon as possible, the new local disciples learn Christian stewardship
and shoulder the financial responsibility for the work.

Besides the day-to-day expenses for oneself and one's family, there are usually initial costs involved in outgoing travel, setting up a home, and launching
new ministries. In some cases the sponsoring or supporting group helps with
seed money (Prov. 24:27; Luke 14:28–33) for such expenses. The expression
"seed money" comes from the agricultural world. The farmer counts on
the harvest to cover most expenses but needs to cover the cost of the seed
ahead of time. Seed money is a minimal provision that allows the farmer to
begin working the land. To use another analogy: just as parents who plan
for a new baby make some basic provisions ahead of the birth or adoption,
church leaders who plan for a new spiritual family gather some launching
funds before planting. Ongoing ministry expenses such as rents or salaries
should be borne by local believers as the ministry grows (see chapter 18 on
the use of resources).

Ultimately, God will supply for his work done in his way according to his
timetable (Phil. 4:18–19). Church planting is a venture of faith that depends on
God's supply in ways humans cannot anticipate. Church planters must teach
and exemplify both trust and sacrifice. If the team waits for all the needs to
be met, it may never begin; on the other hand, the team should not incur debt

7. Creative-access country: a country that will not admit expatriates under a religious
worker visa and that prohibits or restricts missionary work.

8. The challenges of bivocational church planting will be discussed in chapter 15.

or move far ahead of God's supply. God supplies in his time, and the church-planting team should wait on him, take one step of faith at a time, and model both confident faith and patient dependence on God.

Prepare and Commission the Team

While team members are making personal plans, growing their prayer and financial support teams, and gaining whatever knowledge they can about the ministry focus people and the mission at hand, the team should solidify into a cohesive unit following these three steps.

Devote a time to focused team building. It is wise to carefully select an appropriate venue and a strategic time for team building. This is when relationships, vision, and strategy are adopted. Teams go through a cycle that includes tension and conflict after the honeymoon stage (see chapter 16), and it is important to begin addressing differences before the pressures of church planting emerge. During this period the team members will make a covenant with each other and to the mission ahead of them. Those who cannot make those commitments should be released graciously. Although the team clarifies the goal and makes key decisions, it should not prematurely map out detailed strategies and specific ministry plans. Rather it should wait to be on location and get the indispensable insights of cultural insiders.

Address deficiencies in preparation. Paul had many years of gospel ministry in Tarsus, Cilicia, and Syria before he left on his first journey with Barnabas (Gal. 1:15–2:2). He was uniquely prepared by God with languages and cultural understanding from his youth. Some of his associates had less depth of preparation. For cross-cultural workers we would affirm the crucial importance of thorough language learning, growing cultural understanding, and a strong biblical foundation. This should be considered one's first ministry, and time must be set aside and plans made accordingly. In the case of those who are planting in their own home country, although less time needs to be devoted to it, some demographic and cultural study is still very important. We will talk more about that in the following chapter.

Commission the team. Team commissioning has great spiritual and practical value (Acts 13). The sending group pledges its prayer, financial, emotional, and logistic support. The team promises to be faithful to its Lord and its calling. The team covenant can be read at this time. Both the joy of following Christ and the somberness of difficulties ahead are felt. Church leaders lay their hands on those who are being sent (Acts 13:3) as a charge to service, a symbol of consecration, and an invocation of God's blessing and protection. This commissioning should not be seen as a ceremonial requirement as much as an intimate pledge of support and partnership in mission.

10

Preparing, Part 2

Understanding and Strategizing

The "preparing phase" involves the laying of foundations for church planting that empowers and multiplies. The steps laid out in the previous chapter occur for the most part before the church-planting team arrives on the ministry location. In this chapter the team is on location. The activities described in this chapter can be summarized with two words: *understanding* and *strategizing*. These tasks require that the team be on location.

Many ministries fail because they are built on inadequate cognitive, attitudinal, and relational foundations. Unless the team members live among the people they are called to reach, they will not go very far in the church-planting mission. This is when culture shock often occurs. It is a period of service and sacrifice that requires a commitment to incarnational presence, sacrificial service, and deep learning.

Overview of Phase

Biblical Examples

Acts 13–18: Differences in approach and preaching to Jews, proselytes, and Greeks

Acts 14–20: Those who respond become bridge-persons and hosts for gospel study groups

Acts 17:23–29: Paul demonstrates an understanding of Greek philosophy (quoting the Stoics and Epicureans)

The New Testament itself is contextualized, a process that demonstrates keen cultural awareness and ability to relate the gospel to various hearers and situations (Flemming 2005)

Key Steps

1. Language and culture learning (as necessary)
2. Research the demographic, social, religious, and cultural context
3. Determine evangelistic and church-planting strategy
4. Build relationships, consult with others
5. Strengthen team, clarify roles, obtain training
6. Draft a church-planting proposal

Critical Issues

1. Gaining understanding of the ministry focus people
2. Identifying complementary team roles
3. Putting research to good use by generating a profile of the ministry focus people and an entry strategy
4. Identifying receptive peoples, gatekeepers, and "people of peace"
5. Teaching and mentoring for disciplemaking in contextually appropriate ways
6. Planning for the emergence of a local core group and local apprentices

Language and Culture Learning

Most church planters work within their own culture, and consequently they speak the language and feel at home. Yet even when one is working within one's native culture, communicating the gospel still presents a challenge. The longer a person has been a Christian, the more he or she tends to grow apart from the general culture into a Christian subculture. It is thus easy to lose touch with the people one is trying to reach or have misconceptions of their needs, lifestyle, and worldview.[1] Today worldview change is occurring at an increasingly rapid pace. Different subcultures, classes, generations, and educational and socioeconomic groups within the same general culture may have distinct values, beliefs, and aspirations. For this reason all church planters should carefully study and become acquainted with the ministry focus people, even if it is not a cross-cultural work.

Some cross-cultural church planters work through translators initially. However, in most cases it is important that they become proficient in the language of the people. At least one year of full-time language study, done while immersed in the ministry focus people, is normally required to learn a new ministry language, and more difficult languages will require longer. During this time, mother tongue ministries (not in the new ministry language) should be kept to a minimum so that energy is not diverted from the primary task of language acquisition. Language will be the foundation of communication with the people not only for evangelism but also for teaching, leadership development, and coaching. In addition, language serves as a key to understanding people's worldview, thought patterns, customs, manners, and expressions.

---

1. *Worldview* has been defined as "the foundational cognitive, affective, and evaluative assumptions and frameworks a group of people makes about the nature of reality which they use to order their lives" (Hiebert 2008, 25–26).

Supervised Ministry Experience

Once a reasonable level of language proficiency has been attained, team members commonly complete an internship under a national pastor or work as an apprentice alongside another seasoned church planter.[2] They may be interns in different local churches that are in geographic proximity and come together to compare notes and make plans. Such internships allow the learner to improve her or his ability to minister in the new language, grow in appreciation of the host culture, build friendships with local people, and develop wise, culturally appropriate ministry and life skills.

Many cross-cultural church planters will have had experience as church or business leaders in their home country prior to leaving. They often want to lead, teach, and fix society's problems without first learning, understanding, and loving the people they come to serve. Oscar Muriu explains how factors that are considered strengths in one culture can be liabilities in another culture: "Americans always enter from the top. Because they're well resourced, they represent a majority culture. . . . Americans come to Africa, and they want to solve Africa. But you can't solve Africa. It's much too complex for that. And that really frustrates Americans. And the assertiveness you are taught in school becomes a curse on the field. I often say to American missionaries, 'When the American speaks, conversation is over'" (2007, 1).

Reading about History and Culture

Suggested reading should be provided to orient new church planters; the ideas that follow should help church planters design a reading plan. People are a product of their past and cannot be understood apart from their collective experiences. They are molded by events as well as their physical terrain. As they live through crises and triumphs together they develop a collective consciousness, collective memories, and common values. Contrast, for example, the shaping of Mexico and the United States: "The land that became the United States was, for the most part, rich, and for much of the nation's short history, seemingly endless. Thus anyone, the national myth had it, could make his way in this world. There was opportunity for all. . . . The Mexican story was different. The land had been populated for centuries by warring tribes numbering in the hundreds (even today about 150 different languages are still spoken in Mexico); there was no 'frontier'" (Condon 1997, 3). History can also open a window of understanding. For example, in several Latin American countries, particularly Mexico, there was a polarization between liberal reformers and

2. In pioneer situations where the first gospel church is being planted in a region and the guidance of local believers and experienced missionaries is not available, the new workers can still learn a great deal from local cultural insiders during this stage. Later, they will need to exercise patience and care to work with new believers in forming the first local Christian community.

Catholic conservatives in the nineteenth and early twentieth centuries. The liberals, wanting to break the hold of the Catholic Church, allowed Freemasonry and Protestantism to become established in certain areas, and to this day some of those regions are more open and receptive to the gospel.

Although the study of history and culture remains general at this point, it will prepare church planters to research the specific ministry focus people and design an evangelistic strategy. At least one serious work on the roots of the ministry people group should be read at this stage. Cultural information can also be found in government reports, letters, journals, oral and electronic questionnaires, newspapers, and archives. Paul Hiebert and Eloise Hiebert Meneses's *Incarnational Ministry: Planting Churches in Band, Tribal Peasant, and Urban Societies* (1995) is an especially valuable resource for understanding culture and social structure and their implications for church planting; it deserves a careful reading. It could serve to stimulate discussion as the church-planting team conducts its research and forges a strategy to effectively reach and minister among the focus people.

Research the Demographic, Social, Religious, and Cultural Context

Reasons to Study the Ministry Focus People

Some neglect the study of the ministry focus people because of a sense of urgency about the mission. Team members may feel that studying the people is impractical or a waste of time. Yet successful church planting always requires a basic understanding of the people that are being reached.

This may be obvious when the cultural gap is great, but church planters also need to understand their ministry focus people when they reach out to a similar culture, another generational group, or a different class. Figure 10.1 depicts three types of evangelism that are needed to complete the Great Commission: near neighbor evangelism within the same cultural group (E1), evangelism to a culturally similar but distinct group (E2), and evangelism to a culturally distant group (E3; Winter et al. 1999). Church planters should evaluate whether the cultural distance is great or small and develop their evangelistic approach accordingly. Here is a rule of thumb for cross-cultural church planters: The time you need to spend as a student of culture is directly proportionate to the cultural distance between your upbringing and that of the people you are trying to reach. And the greater that divide, the more Christ's humility, love, and patience will be required in your life and the lives of local believers.

There are several good reasons to engage in ethnographic and demographic study. First, understanding transforms the messenger. "Culture is the soul of the . . . nation" (Morin 1994, 579). A man seeks to understand his fiancée because he loves her, and real success in courtship comes when the one pursued unveils her soul and there is deep communication. Cultural study is not only

Figure 10.1
Cultural Distance as Barrier
to the Spread of the Gospel

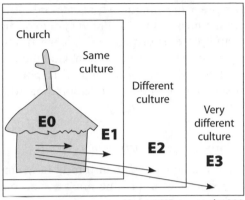

Source: Winter, et al. 1999

an intellectual exercise or a means to evangelism. It must move us, change us, and bring us to a deep level of appreciation of the people, making us insightful and caring bridge-people for the gospel.

Second, understanding is needed for effective communication and relationship building. Communications theory stresses the need of audience analysis. When church planters enter the world of another culture group as cross-cultural messengers, their actions and words will be understood in terms of *the hearers'* horizon of understanding. Of course messages can be crystal clear, and faithful to the meaning being transmitted, yet remain unheard because they are unwanted. They can be avoided entirely, misconstrued, or overlooked by the hearer. Church planters should become familiar with key concepts of effective cross-cultural communication and ministry.[3]

Duane Elmer (2002, 64–65) compares entering a new culture to playing a new game with new rules. Outward similarities between the two cultures can be deceiving. For example, baseball and cricket both use balls and bats, but a skilled baseball player will be a failure at cricket unless he learns the rules of the game and develops the skills needed to play it. So too people who enter a new culture cannot assume that the communication or relational skills that served them well in their mother culture will be effective in the new culture. They will need to learn the different rules, norms, and skills required to be effective in the new context.

Third, understanding is needed to inform communication of the gospel message and make biblical truth meaningful. It must be presented both verbally

3. See, for example, Elmer 1993, 2002, and 2006; Hesselgrave 1991; and Lingenfelter and Mayers 2003.

and nonverbally, in such a way that it is understood. Effective communication must take into account the worldview and potential misunderstandings and objections of the hearers (see Hiebert 2008). One of the tasks of contextualization is to make the message meaningful—that is, more easily understood, not more palatable. Culture incorporates a shared system of meanings including worldview, values, and patterns of perception learned, revised, maintained and defined in the context of human interaction. Communication is successful when hearers (1) understand the message and (2) respond to the truth about God and Jesus Christ based on adequate understanding, whether the response is positive or negative.

Approaches to Studying the Ministry Focus People

Juan grew up in a middle-class Cuban family in Miami, where vertical social ascent (the possibility of improving one's socioeconomic standing in society) is normal.[4] He now serves as a missionary assigned to start a church in a barrio on the outskirts of Tegucigalpa, Honduras. He already knows the language and is anxious to speak of God's love to a hurting people. His emphasis when sharing the gospel is on how God can give eternal life and give meaning to our present life in spite of difficult circumstances.

Ricardo, a Honduran laborer, is living from day to day in a fatalistic culture in which vertical ascent is near impossible. His primary aspiration is to have meat on his table, at least on the weekend, and shoes for his children so that they may be allowed to enter school. He has no doubt that God exists. His question is "What will God do to provide a decent supper for us?" How then does Juan begin the process of getting to know Ricardo and the others in the barrio? What should he do before he talks to them about his God? Juan would do well to look at life in the barrio using three lenses: the lens of lived experience, the lens of demographic research, and the lens of participant observation (see figure 10.2).

Once there is a sufficient grasp of language and general culture, all three lenses described in this chapter should be used concurrently (rather than one after the other). In other words, while Juan gets accustomed to living in Tegucigalpa (lived experience), he will also collect and analyze demographic data (demographic research). His general observations and findings will shape further questions and discussions with his neighbors (participant observation).

THE LENS OF LIVED EXPERIENCE

In the apostles' preaching there was no single methodology or strategy, nor was there any uniform presentation, because the Holy Spirit led the

---

4. This illustration is based on facts, but details have been changed.

Figure 10.2
Three Lenses of Understanding

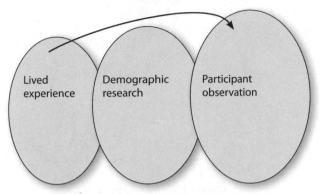

gospel messengers to formulate the message for the given situation. "True contextualization happens when there is a community which lives faithfully by the gospel and in that same costly identification with people in their real situation as we see in the earthly ministry of Jesus. When these conditions are met, the Sovereign Spirit of God does his own surprising work" (Bibby 1987, 154).

The early church lived out its gospel contextualization. Likewise, for Christ's ambassador in a pluralistic world, contextualization is not a communications theory, nor is it primarily an intellectual exercise: it is a lived experience. After working for decades among the lower classes of Honduras, David Harms, a medical doctor, commented, "When you can see the world through their eyes, then you will able to make Christ known to them."

Therefore there is no substitute for living with a people if the goal is to understand and appreciate them. One experiences firsthand their lifestyle and ways of interacting socially and discovers at a personal level their interests, worries, joys, fears, and beliefs. This is the way church planters, fueled by Spirit-given empathy and insight, can develop an insider's perspective over time. Juan and his family may choose to live in the barrio alongside the people they hope to reach. In some cases this is not advisable because it would be impractical, unsafe, or suspect. Either way, they will spend a considerable amount of time with Ricardo and his neighbors and develop the *confianza* (trust) that leads to long-standing friendships. Ricardo may even become Juan's cultural mentor and interpreter if he sees that Juan's motives are noble and his mission is born out of love.

The Lens of Demographic Study

Demographic information is used to describe the population of the target group *from the outside* and depends primarily on quantitative research and

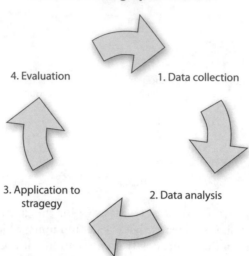

Figure 10.3
Process of Demographic Research

4. Evaluation   1. Data collection

3. Application to   2. Data analysis
   stragegy

data. Church planters examine many factors and use a variety of tools such as random sample surveys, questionnaires, or census data. In order to avoid rabbit trails, they start out with specific parameters and particular questions that need to be answered. A focus that is too narrow might exclude valuable information, but without focus, much time and energy would be wasted. Figure 10.3 outlines a process we recommend: (1) data collection, (2) data analysis, (3) application to strategy, and (4) evaluation.

These steps can be repeated cyclically, because demographic information should be reviewed and updated periodically. The evaluation and review can raise new questions that drive further research. In many countries census reports come out every four or five years, providing a natural cycle of demographic study and review. Table 10.1 gives an idea of the kinds of demographic data that can be helpful for church planters.

Table 10.1
Demographic Information Helpful to Church Planters

Population growth/decline	Biological: births/deaths Movement: people entering or leaving the community Gains or losses in housing Future development plans (new housing, industry, etc.)
Family	Percentage for various age groups (e.g., children, seniors) Size of family Number of persons per household Single, married, divorced

Economic	Average household income
	Standard of living (e.g., indoor plumbing, nutrition, automobiles)
	Commercial, industrial, agricultural activity in the community
	Primary forms of employment
	Unemployment rates
	Public or other assistance for poor or unemployed
	Transportation, commerce, tourism
Education	Educational levels of the population
	Literacy rate (including functional illiteracy)
	Schools and postsecondary educational institutions
	Availability of libraries, tutoring, adult continuing education
Social/political	Ethnic groups
	Language groups
	Subcultures
	Refugees, immigrants, undocumented aliens
	Political parties and affiliations, power changes
	Available social services
	Availability of medical care (e.g., hospitals, clinics, pharmacies)
Religious	Religious affiliation
	Active practice of religion
	Beliefs
	Religious institutions: churches, mosques, temples

Sometimes government agencies, chambers of commerce, universities, and nongovernmental organizations (such as UNESCO) conduct and publish useful demographic studies that can be consulted in libraries or online, or obtained at the given offices. Many reports are published soon after a new census is done. It may take persistence to find them, but they are worth tracking down. In the United States several professional services will, for a fee, provide information on specific communities. Mission organizations such as the Caleb Project conduct "research expeditions" to provide information about specific ethnic groups or locations and how they might best be approached with the gospel. Here is a summary of possible sources of information:

- government offices
- chambers of commerce
- libraries and universities
- nongovernmental organizations (NGOs)
- professional research services
- newspapers
- Internet databases
- local ecumenical, ministerial, or mission organizations
- interviews of community leaders

It is especially useful to compare census data from different years and make note of patterns. Those patterns often signal trends. For example, Kirk Hadaway studied church growth over time in five diverse cities in the United States. "Our findings indicate that a major part of the growth or decline of urban churches results from changes in and characteristics of the context. Population growth or decline is the most important factor, followed by racial transition, neighborhood social class, and the proportion of young children in the area" (Hadaway 1982, 548).

One should always consider the reliability or accuracy of the information provided by the various sources. There is generally a motive behind research that will shape the way the data are summarized and presented. Governments may skew data to make government performance appear favorable. Industry or commerce may try to make investment or potential for new business appear attractive, and NGOs may emphasize numbers that could help their fundraising efforts. Data on religious affiliation usually say little about actual belief or practice and can be intentionally falsified in favor of the official or dominant religion. For this reason it is wise, whenever possible, to use and compare several sources and supplement raw census information with surveys and interviews.

In some parts of the world demographic data are not available to the public. In such situations, the church-planting team may undertake its own limited demographic research using opinion surveys and interviews. The team must realize that good original demographic research is very difficult to conduct well.[5] We strongly advise against using opinion surveys as a hook for opening evangelistic talks. It is unethical to approach people under the guise of serious research when the only motive is evangelism and the collected data will not be used. There are many other creative ways to engage people in discussion about Christianity. In the process of conducting research one might ask whether the respondent is interested in receiving information, but that should not be the primary goal of the research.

Though it is very difficult to do opinion survey research for large populations, helpful information about communities of limited size can be obtained through informal surveys. For example, in Germany groups of seminary students engaged in door-to-door opinion surveying to discover felt needs of the community and how a church might address those needs. The following steps were undertaken:

1. *Survey design.* A brief questionnaire was formulated with a specific research goal in mind. It used only questions that would yield useful

---

5. Because such information is often extremely sensitive, the team should ensure that research methods will not violate the law or raise suspicions that would undermine its long-term efforts. Conducting telephone or door-to-door surveys without first learning how to do so will yield poor and misleading data. Fowler 2009 is a good starting point for best practices.

information. Open-ended questions like "What would you say the greatest need in this community is?" serve to open up long conversations and yield insights into community concerns, feelings, and experiences. Short answer questions like "Do you have a Bible in your home?" allow needed data to be gathered for later analysis.

2. *Survey strategy.* The neighborhood was mapped out and blocks were randomly selected for surveying. This gave some measure of representativeness to the responses. A plan was made for conducting the survey. The teams, orientation, and schedule were designed.

3. *Letter of introduction.* Letters on church letterhead were sent to residents of the selected streets, announcing that seminary students would be conducting an opinion survey lasting approximately ten minutes on certain dates. This served to reduce the potential for respondents' suspicions and increase participation. The letter stated that the information would be used to help a new church address local needs and concerns, that the surveyors would not attempt to sell or solicit anything, and that the privacy and anonymity of all respondents would be ensured.

4. *Orientation.* The students were carefully instructed how to introduce themselves and maintain the informant's anonymity, how to record the open-ended questions (one person asks the questions and the other writes down the exact wording of the answers), and how to conclude the interview (thanking respondents and recording the results).

5. *Survey execution.* A prayer team was mobilized before and during the survey. Then, on the predetermined days, seminary students went door to door in teams of two to carry it out. They went at different times of the day (so as to encounter people with diverse schedules), and where no one answered the door initially, they returned at a different time. Usually both genders were included on a team to put respondents at ease. The address and time of each interview were recorded on a separate sheet.

6. *Survey analysis and use.* After collecting and analyzing the data, the group drew out the research's implications for evangelism and church ministry. Respondents were not contacted a second time unless they requested it.

The data from such informal surveys cannot be broadly generalized to statistically describe a population, but it can reveal insights into people's thinking and perceptions that are very useful for ministry strategy. For example, in one such study it was discovered that a growing community had very few activities for children and youth. The church plant then proceeded to offer children's Bible clubs, which were well attended by mostly unchurched children, and later started Bible studies with some of the parents.

Case Study 10.1

Using Demographic Study to Choose a Target Community

As preparations for a church plant in the city of Munich were being made, demographic information revealed that half of all households were single-person households. Thus ministry to single, divorced, or widowed persons would have to figure largely in the overall ministry plan. Also, one in five residents of the city was a non-German citizen, so ministry to internationals would be an important potential focus to consider. Detailed information was gathered on the various city districts (population growth and movement, numbers of internationals, age structure, etc.), and this was compared with the number of evangelical churches (if there were any) located in those districts. On the basis of this information and other factors such as plans for city expansion to the north, a northern district of the city was chosen for the location of the church plant.

THE LENS OF PARTICIPANT OBSERVATION

Participant observation is a discipline used in ethnographic study. We have seen that reading about history and culture provides insight into general thought patterns and attitudes, while demographic research can help us construct a descriptive profile of the focus community or group. The purpose of ethnographic study is to gain deeper insight into the behaviors, values, and worldview of a people from an insider's perspective. "Ethnography is an exciting enterprise. It reveals what people think and shows us the cultural meaning they use daily. . . . Ethnography offers all of us the chance to step outside our socially inherited ethnocentrism, if only for a brief period, and to apprehend the world from the viewpoint of other human beings who live by different meaning systems" (Spradley 1980, vii–viii).

Ethnographic study allows the researcher to focus on a more specific ministry focus people. Most modern cultures are not homogeneous; rather, they are increasingly complex, like puzzles with many interlocking pieces. Urban societies, with great influxes of rural people, are increasingly pluralistic—they typically have multiple subcultures with different ethnicities, worldviews, value systems, and classes interacting and modifying each other. Rural traditional roots and modern education are intermeshed with postmodern thought on many university campuses. Often the higher, educated class is more optimistic and increasingly secular, whereas less educated, more traditional people are more fatalistic, religious, mystical, and tradition-bound. Thus an ethnographic study of the ministry focus people, who may represent only one piece of the puzzle, can reveal how they fit in the whole.

While demographic information is primarily *quantitative*—expressed in terms of statistics, numbers, or measurements that apply to large portions of a population—ethnographic findings are more *qualitative* in nature. Qualita-

tive information does not involve broad generalizations about whole populations or statistical data but, rather, is gathered for the purpose of gaining an
in-depth understanding of the meanings and reasons behind the behavior
or beliefs of a specific group of people. Qualitative research typically uses
observation, interviews, or focus groups[6] to obtain such information. Both
forms of research—quantitative and qualitative—are helpful, but in different
and complementary ways.

Most church planters should not try to be amateur ethnographers, because
ethnography is a well-defined discipline that requires training. However, by
using *observation and interviews* they can gain valuable understanding and
learn to interpret behavior within the conceptual framework of the respondent,
not their own. Church planters must get out "on the street" and investigate
by directly observing living conditions, social interactions, shopping, schools,
commercial establishments, construction projects, leisure activities, and religious institutions. This may not yield quantitative data, but it can reveal
valuable information.

Interviews may be conducted to gather deep-level information about people's understandings, motives, and perceptions. A church-planting couple in
Montreal, Quebec, designed a simple questionnaire and interviewed several
neighbors around Saturday afternoon coffee or an evening meal. Open-ended
questions were used, and the conversations flowed naturally. One of them
posed the questions while the other took notes. Later they met with other
members of their team to compare findings. An important discovery—that
could never have come from reading a book—was the ambivalence many
respondents felt regarding Catholicism, the dominant religion. Some older
people expressed strong feelings of hurt and abuse but continued to go to
church. Most younger Quebecois no longer attended church, but clearly the
church was still a part of their identity. A man commented: "Although as an
adult I have moved away from my mother [the Catholic Church], she is still
my mother and no one had better denigrate her. I may not practice my faith
but I am even less interested in someone else's." A young lady said: "I believe
in God but I don't know how to situate him in my life."

The attitude that the interviewer projects will influence the quality of the
information gathered. It helps to be genuinely curious and caring and approach people sincerely and humbly. This disposition usually creates trust.
Interviewees may disclose personal feelings and struggles. However, it would
unethical to use the pretext of an interview to share one's own religious
beliefs. That may come later, when a desire to know them is expressed by
the interviewee.

6. The term *focus group* is not to be confused with our term *ministry focus people*. A focus
group is a small group of individual persons selected for research proposes. *Ministry focus people*
denotes an ethnic group or subculture among whom a church is to be planted.

Caution must be exercised when one is interpreting respondents' statements. Church planters should record observations and the questions that flow from them in a journal. Later they can come back to them, compare them to attitudes or ideas expressed by other interviewees, and discuss them with a cultural mentor. Accuracy in interpretation requires that one lay aside assumptions, prejudices, and preconceived categories or explanations. Interviewers should avoid drawing hasty conclusions or making unsubstantiated judgments. Rather than risk reading into someone's statements, plan to return and ask follow-up questions at a later date as needed.

Sometimes a focus group can be interviewed as a whole. The focus group is a method used in qualitative research—often used for marketing purposes: a group of people are gathered and asked about their attitudes toward an idea, product, service, or concept. Questions are asked in an interactive group setting where participants are free to talk with other group members. This allows more freedom of expression, and "groupthink" can emerge through the cascading effect of commonly held opinions. The focus group method is more difficult to conduct and use than one-on-one interviews. Generally church planters will use this approach only if they have a trained moderator and a natural grouping of willing and qualified participants.

Determine the Evangelistic and Church-Planting Strategy

With their research findings in hand, church-planting teams are ready to craft a strategy for evangelism and church planting that is suited to the focus people, taking into consideration their needs, culture, social structure, and religious convictions, along with other factors. An entry strategy is a plan to engage in appropriate initial ministries that show God's love and share his message based on both the felt and real needs of the people. The strategy will take into account signs of opportunity, such as receptiveness to the gospel, and anticipate potential obstacles, such as suspicions about the motives of outsiders or religious leaders who oppose the entrance of Christianity.

The entry strategy might begin with the crafting of a *respondent profile*—a profile of the typical person and family and key entry points for the gospel. Bill Hybels popularized the idea by describing "unchurched Harry and unchurched Mary," and Rick Warren described "Saddleback Sam" (Warren 1995). Such a profile helps church planters personalize, visualize, and remember who God has called the team to reach. The focus should be on four main areas: (1) felt needs, (2) life aspirations, (3) decision-making patterns, and (4) responsive segments. However, it should be kept in mind that such a profile is a composite characterization. No person will fully reflect the profile, and every person must be related to and understood individually.

Felt Needs

People respond positively when they perceive that a message or service proposed corresponds to personal felt needs. Those needs can be in any realm of life that the gospel addresses. The gospel can transform character as well as family life, provide hope and meaning, and offer solutions to spiritual and social ills such alcoholism, demon worship, and domestic abuse. People become interested in spiritual truth to the extent that they see its relevance to their life and felt needs. In societies with a supernaturalistic worldview, one's felt needs may relate to spiritual questions and eternal destiny. In materialistic societies, felt needs often relate to people's emotional, physical, or social well-being.

When Jesus met people, he related to them as individuals with real questions, longings, and shortcomings. Yet in a sensitive and insightful manner he always brought the conversation to a deeper level than the surface felt need. Addressing felt needs may be a starting point that allows one to demonstrate the relevance of the gospel to every aspect of life. The gospel does not offer a cure for all of life's ills, nor does it guarantee employment and material success. Thus this approach must not become a manipulative trick of "bait and switch." Rather, we should demonstrate how knowing Christ addresses a particular felt need by meeting much deeper needs and addressing the underlying problem of human sin and separation from God. In this way the power of the gospel can begin its transforming work on several levels at once.

Case Study 10.2

Communicating the Gospel to Slum Dwellers

Oscar Muriu explains how Nairobi Chapel (described in chapter 7) adapted its entry strategy for church planting among slum dwellers: "They do not understand a reference to a movie; they've rarely seen a movie. So the language of the educated elite excludes them. What they understand, what persuades them, are real-life stories and parables like Jesus told. . . . So we find leaders who can speak the language of the poor, and we link the poorer churches with a richer, more educated church. I have the responsibility to resource and enable the churches in the slums, and develop ministries that will be a blessing to them, and to help my members have real presence in the slums as a result of our generosity. We recognize that we need one another and we are going to work together. It's not the same gathering, but there is a relationship there. . . . One of the first students who came along is now an associate pastor with us, and several other students who came are now pastoring congregations we planted" (Muriu 2007, 1).

Life Aspirations

Evangelism should not simply be corrective, addressing needs and ills. Christ satisfies the deepest longings of human beings created in his image. In individualistic societies these longings often have to do with forgiveness, purpose, and meaning in life. In collectivistic societies they may have more to do with a solution to shame or the procurement of harmony within the family, with God, and with one's community.

All people aspire to a better life, but they often have deeper, more specific longings as well. Those can be identified through conversation, reading, and interviews. Most religions or worldviews grapple with certain existential questions: Why are we here and where are we going? Who is God, and how can we know him personally and live with him eternally? How can we be freed of the deep pain caused by sin, sickness, and guilt? The entry strategy's respondent profile should describe how the God-shaped vacuum that Blaise Pascal speaks of is felt by the hearers.

Decision-Making Patterns

Decision-making processes vary greatly from culture to culture depending on what is considered important, persuasive, or credible. They are also influenced by the role of the group versus the individual, the use of logic, and the view of time. Are decisions made individually, as a family, or in a larger group? If they are made as a family or in a larger group, it will be wise to approach the leader of the group. Sometimes there are informal opinion leaders in a group other than the de facto leader. These persons should not be overlooked. Gender and age also affect decision-making patterns. Often a concentrated effort should be made to reach the head of household first. When more responsive women and children are baptized first, a social distance may be created within marriages, and it becomes more difficult to reach the husbands. Christianity can come to be viewed as a threat to family life. Although it may take longer for the husband to be baptized in *machista* cultures, once he does convert the entire family often comes to Christ together.

When community leaders of some tribal societies are first to accept the Christian message, often large numbers of others will follow their lead, and a people movement will ensue by means of what has been termed "multi-individual" group decisions (see case study 10.3). "A people movement results from the joint decision of a number of individuals—whether five or five hundred—all from the same people, which enables them to become Christians without social dislocation, while remaining in full contact with their non-Christian relatives, thus enabling other groups of that people, across the years, after suitable instruction, to come to similar decisions and form Christian churches" (McGavran 1980, 335).

Group Decision Making in Tribal Societies

An example of this is Lin Barney's experience among the Hmong of Vietnam. People of a remote region invited him to tell them about the "Jesus Way," so he presented the gospel to the men in their long house. The men then broke up into clan groups to discuss the new way. After arguments, pro and con, the leaders of the clans gathered as elders to decide for the village. In the end, they told Lin that they had all decided to become Christians! (Hiebert and Meneses 1995, 159)

"Western missionaries, reared in a culture that stresses individualism and personal choice, often misunderstand such decisions. Many of them ask people to go back and then come to Christ one by one. In so doing they say to people that this is an unimportant decision, for only minor decisions are made by individuals. Moreover, people often feel rejected by the missionary and return to their old religion" (Hiebert and Meneses 1995, 159). Furthermore, sometimes a group decision "to become Christians" is really a decision to further explore Christianity or experiment with the power of Christianity to overcome evil spirits, sickness, or achieve material gain. In the words of Hiebert and Meneses, "Decision making in a group society is often a multi-step process" (1995, 160). While we cannot unravel the mystery of how God accomplishes his sovereign will through human decisions, we can understand and work in harmony with the human element of the process and not unnecessarily hinder it.

Responsive Segments

Some people groups are more responsive to the gospel than others, and within a people group some individuals or segments of the population will be more responsive than others. Though everyone should have an opportunity to hear the gospel, evangelists and church planters will give priority to those who evidence interest and openness. In one of Jesus's parables, when the guests of honor were not ready to come to a banquet, the master sent his slaves out to bring in the poor of the town (Luke 14:15–23). Paul remained in Ephesus longer than most locations, postponing further pioneer work, because God had opened up exceptional receptivity to the gospel there (1 Cor. 16:8–9).

By *receptivity* we mean a person's ability or inclination to receive something different. It can include openness to new ideas, to change, and to spiritual truth from a new source. One of the great challenges when one is working among less responsive peoples is how to identify those who are open and whom God has prepared to receive the gospel. "Receptivity is measured, first of all, by questions focusing on satisfaction with life as it is and willingness to change. . . . A second dimension of receptivity is commitment to an alien religious belief. Receptivity varies inversely with the strength of this commitment" (Engel 1977, 49).

In collectivistic societies, the level of receptivity of the entire group should be assessed. In individualistic societies, receptivity will vary among smaller segments of the population, the family or group, or even the individual. This is the case with many urban dwellers who have left their families and roots. Here is a list of common groups in life circumstances that may indicate openness to change or receptiveness to a new spiritual message:

- those who experience a major personal crisis such as death of a close person, divorce, or unemployment
- those who are going through a major life transition such as marriage, childbearing, change of employment or career, or move from rural to urban life
- societies undergoing extreme social upheavals such as war, natural disasters, famine, or rapid change (such as industrialization) of which the former worldview cannot make sense
- persons who have changed residence and been separated from their former social network
- groups with religious structures that are only loosely organized, such as most folk religions
- people with defined concepts of sin, guilt, and a personal, Creator God
- people who have experienced great disappointment with their present religion
- marginalized groups and lower classes that have little to lose and much to gain through social or religious change
- young persons who are being exposed to new ideas, such as college students

The church planter should never underestimate God's ability to surprise and break though among people who do not fit into any of the above categories. However, to be good stewards of limited time and resources, generally we are wise to focus on those most likely to be responsive. Special efforts can be geared to building relationships with such persons and sharing the good news with them.

Build Relationships in the Community

Once the church-planting team members have identified one or two segments of the community or ministry focus people that appear to be more receptive, they should try to spend at least 50 percent of their time with people from

Case Study 10.4

Using Demographic Information in a Church-Planting Strategy

When initial plans were being made to plant a church in the city of Ingolstadt, Germany, demographic information gathered from the local city statistics office yielded helpful insights. For example, it was discovered that nearly every third person in the city was a member of a sporting club. The church planters decided that joining a sporting club could be a good way to enter the social networks of the community. Eventually an evangelistic Bible study was started among families of members of one of the clubs, and a planter was able to minister to club families who faced personal crises.

It was also determined that the population was growing in the western district of the city, where a new regional medical clinic had been built. There were long-term plans for a large housing development in that neighborhood. So an initial Bible study group was started there with hospital workers. Because most members of the initial core group worked at the regional clinic, they provided a natural entry point for evangelism among other hospital employees and nursing students. This effort bore fruit.

But in this regional center for government, transportation, education, and health care, the population was very diverse, and the focus turned to other segments. The largest employer of the city was the automobile manufacturer Audi, and the second largest was another manufacturing company. Thus efforts were also made to reach blue collar workers. For example, evangelistic campaigns using large tents located on the public folk festival grounds proved very effective (Germans enjoy visiting beer tents, so the venue was a familiar and inviting one!).

that group (see case study 10.4). They may begin by making courtesy calls to community leaders and community gatekeepers. In democratic societies, community leaders are civil servants and should be willing to answer questions and help people wanting to start a new church, as long as they are approached in a straightforward, sincere, and humble manner. They are easy to find because of their official roles. Whether they are elected officials, educational leaders, civil servants, village chiefs, or religious leaders, they will soon hear that a new religious group has arrived.

Community gatekeepers influence others in less formal ways. They are opinion shapers who hold moral authority in the community even if they do not have a formal position of authority. In rural settings people gather around them in the marketplace; in cities people listen to them on the radio or consult them in their offices. They are well connected and help with issues like immigration, housing, financing, and jobs. If the team gets their backing, the door will be open.

Acceptance by a gatekeeper usually allows a stranger or outsider to be accepted in the community. Some gatekeepers are also sincere seekers of God, like Sergius Paulus, the proconsul of Cyprus, who called for Paul and Barnabas so that he could hear the word of God (Acts 13:7). Jesus instructed his disciples as they were sent out on ministry tours to seek out and stay with a "man of peace" who would welcome them and offer hospitality (Luke 10:5–7). These are people of goodwill who can become bridge-people for the gospel. Church-planting teams should be spiritually alert and observant, engage in discussions, attend community service events, and ask questions of neighbors to identify those who might be bridge-people to the community. In the next chapter we will discuss such "people of peace" at greater length.

Deciding Team Roles and Strengthening Team Preparation

At this stage it is very important that the team leader provide good direction and facilitate role differentiation. He or she will lead members as they consider spiritual gifts, aspirations, and abilities and define their respective roles for the next phase of evangelizing and discipling. This phase is critical in team development because patterns of corporate prayer, mutual support, outreach, and decision making are being set. It is a period when team members spend a lot of time together and tensions invariably arise (see the Team Conflict Cycle in chapter 16).

Common struggles arise from the fact that team members have different learning styles and aptitudes. Some are ready to transition to productive ministry before others. Some may learn the local language and adapt faster than others. The members should be encouraged to prepare well; and those who are ready earlier should be allowed to begin without unnecessary delay. Depending on one's role on the team, special biblical or practical training might be called for. Healthy teams take a long-term view of preparation for ministry and empower each other as they begin to engage in church-planting activities.

Drafting a Church-Planting Proposal

The church-planting proposal is the initial comprehensive ministry plan or entry strategy. Not every church-planting venture will need to draft a formal proposal, but often such a proposal helps the team to clarify and focus its efforts, budget realistically, enlist prayer support, and communicate the vision to sponsors. Before entering the ministry focus area, the church planter and sponsoring churches may have developed a broad vision to recruit the team and gather resources for the mission. When a team begins to encounter an unreached or unfamiliar people group, it can take six months to a year to acquire an adequate understanding of the ministry focus people and be able to formulate the key elements of the proposal (vision, values, ministry focus people description, and evangelistic-discipleship plan).

The proposal is founded on biblical principles and precedents, crafted prayerfully and carefully with the help of wise counselors, and based on adequate understanding of the church-planting terrain, target, and team. It gives the team's vision, rallies team members as they write it, unifies them as they execute it, and later helps them evaluate the progress of the work. It is not set in concrete but constitutes a work in progress. Yet it clearly, concisely, and comprehensively gives direction to the work.

The proposal should identify the segments of the ministry focus people that are to be given priority. From the beginning the work should be built on indigenous principles and use reproducible patterns, as explained in chapter 4. It should include a plan for the discipling of new believers and their gathering in small groups (ideally hosted by the new believers themselves). If there is no plan, often small groups are formed around the team's gifts and training rather than around those of local believers. Intentional planning is required so that hosts and apprentice group facilitators are chosen and mentored by team members according to the pattern Model-Assist-Watch-Leave, outlined in chapter 17.

The apostle Peter wanted his readers to have the kind of knowledge that bears fruit. He writes: "For if you possess these qualities in increasing measure, they will keep you from being ineffective and unproductive in your knowledge of our Lord Jesus Christ" (2 Pet. 1:8). Two extremes are to be avoided. Evangelizing without understanding the people is foolish and often counterproductive. But a failure to put understanding into action is just as culpable.

Sidebar 10.1 can be used to generate research and interview questions. One should investigate not only the "what" but also the "why" behind the various values and behaviors. Answers or behaviors that are particularly baffling to the researcher can be especially fruitful avenues of investigation with potential to reveal deep differences between cultures. It should be evident by now that this study will continue for years, but early breakthroughs are possible as well. In time, church planters can develop bicultural lenses and be able to see events from the perspective of a cultural insider much like missionary children or second-generation immigrants.

Here is a summary of some concrete steps that can be taken based on the research during this phase:

- Read and interact with others about the culture.
- Ask honest questions.
- Continue to interact with people in the neighborhood, the marketplace, and other natural gathering venues.
- Meet with sympathetic cultural insiders with whom you can discuss your observations.

Sidebar 10.1

Twenty Questions to Understand a Ministry Focus People

1. What are the core values of this group evident in their choices, speech, and practices?
2. What are their convictions regarding the supernatural: God, spirits, demons, unseen powers? How do they talk about God? How do they feel about him?
3. What do they fear most? What do they value most: objects, ideals, goals, principles, standards? What are some of their deepest longings and aspirations?
4. What is their understanding of causality, that is, the role of blessings and curses, taboos, charms, prayer, natural laws, personal efficacy, fatalism, and the like?
5. What concept of time do they have? Is it linear or cyclical, more task oriented or event oriented? Are they most focused on events of the past, the present, or the future?
6. What is the social structure of the society? What is the most important social unit: the nuclear family, the extended family, the clan, the nation, or the tribe?
7. How is the larger society governed? Who are the key people of influence? What are the primary institutions?
8. How are decisions made? Is individual freedom valued over the wishes of the group, or are personal decisions subordinate to the wishes of the group?
9. What are the forms of socialization? How are children disciplined and educated? How does the society deal with social deviation and reward positive behavior?
10. What are the means of social control: police, courts, jails, peer pressure, or ostracism?
11. What are the means of transportation and communication? How is information passed on or disseminated? What or who is considered a credible source?
12. What are the key rites of passage (e.g., birth, entering adulthood, marriage, death), and how are they conducted or ritualized? What meanings are associated with them, and what larger role do they play in society?
13. What can you learn from their holy days and festivities?
14. Who are their heroes, past and present?
15. What do popular myths, legends, stories, and metaphors communicate about the culture and worldview?
16. What is their attitude toward social outsiders and people of other faiths?
17. How attached is the younger generation to the traditional way? What segments of the society are more tradition oriented? Which are open to change?
18. How is interpersonal and intergroup conflict resolved?
19. How do people understand and deal with guilt, suffering, and death?
20. What are the most offensive sins of the society? What are the highest virtues?

- Join community groups that are attempting to serve or improve the community.
- Keep track of real and felt needs that you observe.
- Build relationships with community gatekeepers, people of influence in the community, and "people of peace" (Luke 10:6; Matt. 10:11).
- Use your talents and abilities to serve people around you.
- Exercise hospitality in culturally appropriate ways.
- Work diligently on the language.
- Conduct a questionnaire, opinion poll, or survey. Discuss the results with many.
- Get specialized training as necessary.
- Pray fervently for open doors, open hearts, and prepared people.

We have stressed the challenges of engaging with a new people group and wrestling through the adjustments. There are also unique joys in this stage. One of them is seeing doors open that only God could crack. Another is the excitement of discovery. Church planters should take time to discuss their questions and theories as a team, enjoy new insights, and not feel guilty about the time they invest. Focused research will usually reveal entry points to the ministry focus people and allow you to avoid costly mistakes. As the team members learn about other cultures, they invariably learn more about themselves. This can be a period of deep inner growth.

11

Launching

....
....

Evangelism and Discipleship

Church planting is that ministry which, through evangelism and discipleship, establishes multiplying kingdom communities of believers in Jesus Christ who are committed to fulfilling biblical purposes under local spiritual leaders. This definition underlines the fact that evangelism and discipleship are the heart of church planting. At the same time, not all kinds of evangelism and discipleship contribute to the establishing of new kingdom communities. The expressions *church-planting evangelism* and *church-planting discipleship* will be used here for the types of efforts that contribute to the congregating of committed followers of Jesus Christ.

In our experience with consulting and coaching church planters around the globe, except among the most responsive people groups, evangelism and discipling are the greatest challenges for pioneer church planters. They require that spiritual strongholds be overcome to establish a beachhead in enemy territory, that the gospel be communicated through words and deeds in culturally meaningful and reproducible ways, and that new disciples be gathered and prepared in such a way that they will in turn make other disciples. Because this phase is so central to the task of church planting, and in many contexts the most difficult one, this chapter is longer than most in our book. Yet we have only scratched the surface of the subject; thus we encourage readers to explore the various other resources referred to in the discussion that follows.

Overview of Phase

Biblical Examples

Acts 2–5: Proclamation and disciplemaking in Jerusalem
Acts 10–12: Multiplication and expansion to other places and groups
Acts 18: Aquila and Priscilla and Apollos
Acts 18–19: Paul's Ephesian ministry

Key Steps

1. Develop relationships and initiate evangelism
2. Evangelize holistically, addressing felt and real needs
3. Baptize and teach obedience to Jesus
4. Disciple new believers and train them to do the same
5. Wisely assimilate transfer growth
6. Form a foundational community
7. Begin training servant leaders

Critical Issues

1. Adequate and sustained evangelistic thrust
2. Approach to evangelism and discipleship that deals with sin and worldview and builds spiritual disciplines
3. Believers are trained immediately to make disciples and to serve
4. Discipling so that the first kingdom community becomes truly indigenous and can multiply
5. A discipleship plan that addresses problems of worldview, spiritual strongholds, transfer growth, and defection

Develop Relationships and Initiate Evangelism

The launch phase should build on the insights gained during the preparation phase as described in chapters 9 and 10. No disconnect may be allowed between personal preparation, strategy development, and gospel proclamation. The emphasis on church planting as a spiritual endeavor must continue under the guidance of the Holy Spirit. Jesus is the one building his church, and he will direct his colaborers if they seek him. That spiritual discernment and direction comes both from hearing his voice and from observing and understanding those who are being reached. The gospel must be shared broadly, constantly, and powerfully. However, not all communication of the gospel has the same results. The following discussion presents principles that can be used to develop an effective evangelistic approach or to assess existing evangelistic efforts.

Building Relationships in the Community

As members of the church-planting team mobilize for evangelism, they begin by building personal relationships with people in the community. Already, during the preparation phase laid out in chapter 10, responsive segments of the society will have been identified and contacts will have been made with community leaders and gatekeepers. The methods of evangelism that seem to best suit the people should have been discussed. But now personal relationships must be built. One must get to know the people personally, and this takes time. Planters from Western cultures can tend to be very task oriented, and activities like socializing informally, drinking tea, and chatting can feel like a waste of time. But in most cultures relationships come before tasks. Evangelism is first and foremost about loving people the way God loves them and then sharing the message of God's redeeming love with them. People are not objects or targets. They want to be respected and understood. They are people worthy of love, respect, and *time*.

Building relationships can begin in one's neighborhood, by becoming acquainted with neighbors, shopkeepers, mail carriers, and those with whom one has natural contact on a regular basis. Visiting shops daily to buy bread or groceries is a way to get to know the shopkeepers or cashiers. One church planter never purchased more than a few dollars of gasoline for his automobile at one time, so that he would have more opportunities for conversation with the attendant. Using public transportation instead of a personal automobile also gives one a better sense of connectedness and feel for people's daily lives, and it often opens opportunities for conversation. Another place to begin is a community organization, such as a school-related parent-teacher association, Rotary club, renters' association, or friends of the library.

The team should discover the venues where people congregate, spend leisure time, and socialize. As noted in case study 10.4, in one German city sporting clubs proved to be one of the primary forms of social interaction for whole families, even for participants who were no longer active competitors. In other places coffee or tea shops, a local trading post, or a water well may be the place where much social networking occurs. The church-planting team should commit a sizable amount of time—this will vary depending on other responsibilities but should be 50 percent initially— to involvement outside the home with people from the community. One weekly evening may be devoted to a non-church-related community organization, where one can build relationships with non-Christians and make a contribution to the community.

Exercising hospitality is a good way to move relationships beyond casual acquaintance to a deeper level. But one should become familiar with local customs regarding the exercise of hospitality: there are many unwritten rules of etiquette, manners, protocol (who invites whom, for what purpose—a full meal or just tea—what type of food should be served, and how long the visit should last). When one is new to a culture or community, vulnerability and social ineptness can actually provide opportunities to meet people as you simply ask for help: "Forgive me, but I am new here and want to learn about the ways of your wonderful people. I am embarrassed at how ignorant I am about _____. Could you please help me?" Such moments can open up great insights into local customs and thinking as well as build relationships. Requests for this kind of help also contribute to building mutuality in what might otherwise be one-sided relationships.[1] Of course after a while locals will lose patience with one's incompetence, so this method must be used early and often.

If the church planter is from an affluent country and working in a poorer country, he or she will usually have little difficulty making friends! Also if the planter is a native English speaker, she or he may be sought out as an English conversation partner. Many have used English classes or cooking classes as a way to meet people and build relationships. Such activities need not be overtly evangelistic. But they do provide the church-planting team with occasions to move out beyond their comfortable circle of Christian friends and get to know the people they are seeking to reach. In casual conversation one learns about the joys and sorrows, the dreams and aspirations, the worries and fears of the average person. Many preconceived false impressions are corrected. One develops a genuine understanding and love for the people. Apart from this, neighbors will quickly sense that the church planter is more concerned about a project than about people.

A Strategy Tailored to the Ministry Focus People

Chapter 9 addressed the importance of selecting a ministry focus people, and chapter 10 provided guidelines to understand it through the lenses of lived experience, demographic research, and participant observation. It is essential that there be alignment between one's understanding of the ministry focus people and the evangelistic approach and tools of communication that are used. Those who neglect this conceptual preparation and jump straight into evangelism based on their preferred strategies or doctrinal emphases will usually live to regret it. One can be a personal witness in one's own culture, but it is quite another thing to develop a plan for church-planting evangelism that will penetrate a different cultural group and help members of that group carry the gospel to their own people!

The church planters should prayerfully review what has been gleaned so far about the ministry focus people, discuss their philosophy of evangelism, consider the categories of evangelistic methods (see sidebar 11.1), and then decide on those methods best suited to their philosophy, the focus people, and the gifts and interests of the team members. There are thousands of methods of

1. Especially when the newcomer has more education, more money, and more power than the local people, it can be very difficult for relationships to have true mutuality or reciprocity. Suspicion about motivations can be present on both sides of the relationship ("Do they only like me for what I can give them?" or "Why would that rich person come to our poor village? A normal person would never do that! He must want something"). Vulnerability on the part of the newcomer can reduce suspicion and build trust.

Methods of Evangelism

Personal evangelism
- Relational or friendship evangelism
- Personal testimony
- Hospitality, house parties
- Use of tracts such as "The Four Spiritual Laws"
- "Gossiping the gospel" in the neighborhood
- Internet blogs, chats, forums

Public proclamation evangelism
- "Crusade" evangelism
- Lectures
- Open-air preaching on streets or in parks
- Chalk talks, street theater, and the like
- Evangelistic or "seeker-oriented" church services
- Tent campaigns
- Book table or information stand in public places

Special event evangelism
- Concerts
- Celebrity speakers
- Sporting events
- Special interest groups
- Public debates
- Mimes or theater

Literature and video evangelism
- Bible and tract distribution

- Mailings and door hangers
- Evangelistic films and videos such as the Jesus film
- Newspaper, radio, television, internet
- Books
- Local lending libraries

Small group evangelism
- Evangelistic Bible studies
- Chronological Bible story telling
- Inviting guests to cell groups
- After school groups
- "Andrew suppers"—meals where a testimony is given

Visitation evangelism
- Visitation of inquirers or church visitors
- Hospital visitation
- Prison visitation
- Door-to-door visitation, community canvassing

Seminar and course evangelism
- Alpha courses
- Marriage enrichment
- Adult evening school courses
- Bible as literature
- School religion classes
- English language classes or retreats

- Cooking or other skill classes
- Spiritual retreats, Christian ashram

Servant evangelism
- Community service projects
- Medical, dental clinics
- Education and tutoring
- Food pantry or distribution
- Community health evangelism (CHE)
- Legal counsel
- Crisis counseling and hotlines
- Economic development
- Volunteering at community organizations

Focus people evangelism
- Student groups
- Children's Bible clubs, AWANA, Royal Rangers
- Mother-child groups
- Single parents, divorce, grief, special need groups
- Addiction and codependency recovery groups

Prayer evangelism
- Praying for the sick
- Praying for people in personal crisis
- Praying for deliverance from spiritual bondage
- Praying at public events

communicating the gospel. Approaches differ greatly depending on the varying convictions of the believers and the varying situations of the unbelievers
they are attempting to reach. Evangelistic methods can be categorized several
ways, including the following:

- more personal (building on relationships) versus less personal (allowing
  anonymity)
- individual versus groups or large meetings
- narrow appeal (to segments of the population) versus broad appeal (to
  anyone)
- program or event oriented versus informal or spontaneous
- attractional (invite people to an event) versus incarnational (go to the
  people with the message in word and deed)
- "decision" oriented (calling for an immediate response) versus process
  oriented (allow inquirers time to grow in understanding)
- instructional or confrontational versus conversational or dialogical

The exercise in table 11.1 uses slightly different categories to help team
members personally identify the evangelistic approaches that fit both the
church planter and the ministry context. Respondents indicate their evaluation of each approach on a scale of 1 to 5, 1 being "poor fit" and 5 being
"excellent fit." Then they answer the final questions and highlight the top
approaches for their situation, remembering that there is no one magic
bullet.

Prioritizing Receptive Persons or Groups

During the preparation phase, potentially receptive members of the focus
people were identified. As the church planters now initiate evangelistic efforts,
they will focus on these receptive persons. Ralph Neighbour's pyramid of
receptivity can be a helpful tool in the process (figure 11.1). It can be applied
in any culture and identifies different levels of receptivity. Christian witnesses
can use this pyramid of receptivity in two ways: First, they can adapt their
prayers and witness to the receptivity of the person and help them move to
the next stage. Second, they will want to seek out a certain type of people
and associate themselves with groups based on their current receptivity level.
For example, if young people are more receptive, student ministry will be
a good investment. In Quebec, Canada, church planters found that people
who respond to Christian witness move though several steps, needing to hear
the gospel several times in different ways, before making a real commitment
to Christ. Furthermore, prior to that commitment they made successive
incremental decisions *toward Christ* in response to a series of observations

Table 11.1
Evangelistic Methods Used in the Bible

Evangelistic approach	Biblical example	Natural fit for me? 1 to 5	Natural fit for context? 1 to 5	Total
1. Testimonial approach	• The Samaritan woman and townspeople, John 4:39–42 • The blind man, John 9:13–34 • Paul before Felix and Festus, Acts 24:1–25:12			
2. Intellectual (or apologetic) approach	• Paul in Athens, Acts 17:16–34			
3. Confrontational approach	• Peter in Jerusalem, Acts 2:14–40			
4. Service approach	• Dorcas, Acts 9:36–43			
5. Interpersonal approach	• Andrew to Peter and Philip to Nathaniel, John 1:40–46			
6. Invitational approach (meal, event, party)	• Matthew's party, Luke 5:29			
7. Teaching approach	• Paul in the synagogues and at the hall of Tyrannus, Acts 13:5, 14; 14:1.; 19:9			
8. Discovery approach (asking questions)	• Nicodemus, John 3:1–21 • Jesus and the Samaritan woman, John 4:1–26			
9. Bible study approach	• Paul and the Bereans, Acts 17:11			
10. Prayer approach (healing or power encounter)	• The Jerusalem apostles, Acts 5:12–16 • Paul and the demonized fortune-teller, Acts 16:18			

and insights (Smith 1995). The pyramid of receptivity for the Quebec team looked like this:

Level A—Open to a friendship with the messenger and to a discussion of the message: some youth, some spiritual seekers, and people in crisis.

Level B—Open to the messenger but not to a discussion of the message: youth, nonpracticing nominal Christians, friends, and family of believers.

Levels C and D—Not open to the messenger or to the message: antireligious or conservative religious people, people who have had bad experiences with Christians.

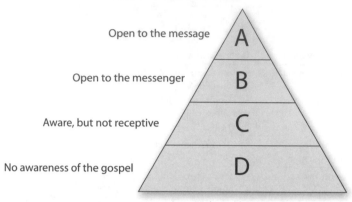

Figure 11.1
Pyramid of Receptivity

Open to the message   A

Open to the messenger   B

Aware, but not receptive   C

No awareness of the gospel   D

Source: adapted from Neighbour 1990, 245

One of the great challenges for church planting among resistant populations is how to find receptive people whom God seems to have prepared to
hear the gospel. Often church planters who have relied solely on personal
evangelism among friends and neighbors have an aversion to less personal
approaches, especially mass evangelism. Although personal evangelism may
be a good approach, in many cases it will not be adequate because the number
of one's personal contacts is simply too few and none of them are ready or yet
willing to hear the gospel. In such situations the church-planting team must
also "cast the nets widely" with methods that identify prepared persons and
seekers among the larger population. Otherwise progress will be painfully
slow and it may take years to gather a core of new believers. Dick Grady and
Glenn Kendall's (1992) study of effective missionary church planters revealed
that regardless of the receptivity of the region, more effective church planters
used broad-based and flexible evangelistic methods (sidebar 11.2). "The most
effective church planters had a greater tendency to use outreach methods that
provide a large number of contacts in a given community. Those who enter a
new cross-cultural situation, and devise a method for sharing the gospel with
a large number of people, may then identify from this large group those who
appear to be spiritually hungry. They invest productive time in discipling those
who are more interested" (Grady and Kendall 1992, 366). They also use a wide
variety of evangelistic approaches, because different methods appeal to different
people. One cannot always predict which method will be most effective.

Mass distribution of literature, radio evangelism, door-to-door visitation,
campaign evangelism, and other approaches that make contact with large
numbers of people are entirely appropriate as long as the follow-up is carefully
planned and personalized. The planters can then concentrate their energy on
those persons who have indicated spiritual interest. As a church was being

Sidebar 11.2

Keys to Effective Church Planting

Dick Grady and Glenn Kendall (1992) surveyed one hundred missionaries described as successful by their agencies and received responses from eighty-five. The following seven strategy principles were developed based on their responses.

1. More effective church planters spend more time in prayer.
2. More effective church planters use more broadly based evangelistic efforts.
3. More effective church planters are more flexible in their methods.
4. More effective church planters are more committed to a doctrinal position.
5. More effective church planters establish greater credibility.
6. More effective church planters have a greater ability to identify and then work with people who have a loosely structured religion.
7. More effective church planters have a greater ability to incorporate new converts into evangelistic outreach.

planted in Ingolstadt, Germany, thousands of mailers were distributed with a return postcard through which interested persons could request a Bible, literature, or a personal visit. Only three cards were returned, but two of the three persons who sent them eventually came to faith in Christ. For a church with fewer than twenty members, that was a major breakthrough!

Mass approaches to evangelism will always need to be complemented with personal follow-up and discipleship. This may happen in small groups or in one-on-one relationships. As is true with the people in Quebec, many, if not most, people will need to hear the gospel many times and in many ways to grow in their understanding of the message and experience its full transforming power. Ultimately there is no substitute for personalized teaching and spiritual nurture.

Evangelism as Both a Decision and a Process

When we read the book of Acts, we see that the earliest evangelists were bold to call both Jews (e.g., Acts 2:38–39; 3:19) and Gentiles (e.g., Acts 17:30; 26:20) to repentance and faith in Christ. Repentance involves turning from sin and idolatry to receive salvation in Christ and serve God (e.g., 1 Thess. 1:9). So too our ministry of evangelism must call hearers clearly to a decision for repentance and explicit faith in Christ, confessed with the lips and in the act of baptism. At this point a person is forgiven and born again into the family of God.

Yet evangelism must also be understood as a process. Though regeneration occurs at a particular time, there is a process leading up to that point and a process leading onward in Christian growth. Focusing too narrowly on a single decision for Christ often leads to superficial conversions that are rooted in misunderstanding or are wrongly motivated. In chapter 10 we discussed how the decision-making process differs in various cultures. Paul Hiebert tells the story of Papayya, an Indian peasant who gladly listens for hours to the gospel and is deeply moved by the message about God becoming man in Jesus Christ. Papayya prays to Christ but wonders whether Christ is just one more among millions of *avatara*—Hindu gods who have descended from higher spiritual realms. "As a Hindu he worships Vishnu, who incarnated himself many times as a human, animal, or fish to save mankind. Papayya also knows many of the other 330 million Hindu gods. But the stranger says there is only one God, and this God has appeared among humans only once. Moreover the stranger says that Jesus is the Son of God, but says nothing about God's wife. It's all confusing to him" (Hiebert 2008, 10). Hiebert asks whether Papayya can become a true Christian after just one hearing of the gospel, to which he answers yes. But the path of discipleship and true understanding will be a long one. The more the messenger can understand Papayya's world and beliefs, the better he can avoid misunderstandings and help Papayya to comprehend the gospel and become a faithful follower of Christ.

The story of Papayya illustrates that understanding of the gospel must grow in depth, which is often a long process.[2] Alan Tippett's (1992) studies of conversion led him to view conversion in terms of stages: people move from a period of awareness, to a period of decision making, then a period of incorporation, and period of maturity. He also found that rituals marking the transition from one stage to the next stage, such as an altar call, baptism, or destruction of fetishes, were critical to long-term conversion and discipleship among animists (Tippett 1967, 109; 1971, 169). An understanding of these processes will influence how the gospel is presented, expectations regarding responses, how to interpret people's responses, and how to help people come to a place of true saving faith in Christ and follow him.

Evangelism That Deals with Worldview

The life and work of Jesus have meaning only in the context of the biblical worldview of creation, sin, and redemption. Consequently church planters ministering to people of another worldview—including the Western postmodern worldview—must begin with God's nature, his creation, the fall and the nature of sin, the need for redemption through the atoning work of Jesus, and the final judgment or reward at his return. Hiebert warns, "Too often conversion takes place at the surface levels of behavior and beliefs; but if worldviews are

---

2. For discussions of the problems with a "one-step decisionism" approach to the conversion of Muslims, see Conn 1979 and Teeter 1990.

not transformed, the gospel is interpreted in terms of pagan worldviews and the result is Christo-paganism" (2008, 69). A host of other worldview issues such as the spirit world, ancestors, the nature of biblical revelation, or life after death may also need to be biblically addressed. Evangelism that addresses worldview is essential to building a solid foundation of faith and obedience by helping the listener receive God's truth, confront cultural distortions, and build a new and lasting conceptual framework.

In the example of Papayya we also see that evangelism that does not address cultural distortions of the biblical worldview may produce professions of faith but will not produce transformed disciples, families, and communities. Nineteenth- and twentieth-century missionaries to Africa brought Western patterns of thinking that, for example, separated the spiritual and physical realms and emphasized truth over power. African theologian Van der Poll describes this failure: "Because the Gospel was not brought to the people as a totally encompassing life view, which would take the place of an equally comprehensive traditional life view, the deepest core of the African culture remains untouched" (cited in Miller and Allen 2005, 42). Hiebert (1982) pointed out that most Western missionaries failed to construct a biblical worldview of the spirit world including angels, demons, unseen powers, blessings, and curses. African people believed such powers to be the ultimate cause behind most significant events, including illness and drought. The failure to give new believers a biblical cosmology and help them know how to respond to such events left many confused and feeling powerless. And many simply returned to the traditional shaman in times of crisis.

Evangelistic Methods Adapted to a People's Learning Style

Many popular evangelistic methods were developed in Western cultures and have proved effective in that context because they are well suited to the Western mentality, worldview, and learning style. For example, the well-known tract "The Four Spiritual Laws" has been very effective with certain groups; however, as shown in table 11.2, not all people groups share that Western thought-pattern.

Table 11.2
Four Spiritual Laws and Worldview

Some people . . .	But many people . . .
understand all of life in terms of fixed and predictable laws[*]	view life in terms of mystery or as being subject to capricious unseen powers, not law
think in abstract categories such as law and emphasize fact over faith and feeling	think in more concrete terms, use stories and proverbs, and intermingle facts, feelings, and faith

Some people . . .	But many people . . .
have a very linear logic—progressing from one law to the next	use nonlinear logic and think in terms of events or cycles rather than cause and effect
think of life in terms of a plan for the future	think of life fatalistically or more in terms of the past than in terms of "plans"
view "abundant life" as a primary goal	see survival or life after death as their greatest need
can make sense of abstract diagrams and representations such as circles, arrows, a cross	do not understand abstract diagrams but relate well to drawings of people or objects
prefer an ordered or structured life to a more spontaneous, disordered life	prefer a spontaneous life to a structured and ordered one
are accustomed to making personal individual decisions	normally make major decisions in consultation with family or peers

* The opening sentence of the "Four Spiritual Laws" is "Just as there are physical laws that govern the physical universe, so there are spiritual laws that govern your relationship with God" (Bright 2007).

Furthermore, many concepts in the "Four Spiritual Laws" can be easily misunderstood, such as "abundant life" (as material wealth), "new birth" (as reincarnation), and "sin" (as an especially wicked deed, or as getting caught violating a social norm). Even the image of Christ knocking at the door (Rev. 3:20) can be interpreted as aggressive. In some cultures, houses do not even have doors that can be knocked on! All this is to say that although the "Four Spiritual Laws" has been a wonderful tool to share the gospel with millions of people, it will not be equally effective everywhere.

In recent years excellent materials have become available to share the gospel in very different ways that emphasize the element of story, concrete thinking, and oral communication. For example, Trevor McIlwain developed a chronological approach to telling the story of salvation history from Genesis through the Gospels in *Building on Firm Foundations* (1987).[3] The use of this method was wonderfully illustrated in the film *EE-Taow*. One advantage to this approach is that nearly everyone can understand and relate to stories. Abstract concepts such as God, sin, and redemption are unfolded in the context of the concrete acts of God in history and his dealings in the lives of people. Thus truths are discovered in a context that brings their meaning to life. Another major advantage to this approach is that as the message is communicated beginning with the story of creation and progressing through the fall, the call of Abraham, the Old Testament sacrificial system, the promise of a redeemer, and so on, a biblical worldview is constructed. The message of the redeeming work of Christ on the cross can make sense only against this background. In the words of one seasoned church planter working in East Africa, "We

3. For another example see Slack, Terry, and Lovejoy 2003.

have found that those who come to Christ through hearing the chronological narrations have far less of a struggle with syncretism in their Christian walk because their understanding of the whole framework of God's plan is much more complete" (Lyons 2009, 2).

Authors such as Tom Steffen (1996; Steffen and Terry 2007) have pointed out that about 75 percent of the Bible is narrative and that story is the dominant form of communication in many cultures.[4] Martin Goldsmith (1980) argues for the effectiveness of parables in the context of Islam. Oral learners may be illiterate, functionally illiterate, or literate, but all oral learners are simply more comfortable with the oral communication of information. "Making disciples of oral learners means using communication forms that are familiar within the culture: stories, proverbs, drama, songs, chants, and poetry. Literate approaches rely on lists, outlines, word studies, apologetics and theological jargon. These literate methods are largely ineffective among two-thirds of the world's peoples. Of necessity, making disciples of oral learners depends on communicating God's word with varied cultures in relevant ways" (LOP 54, 2005). Such an approach is relevant not only in traditional societies but increasingly also in modern and postmodern settings where people do not have a biblical worldview and where story is more communicative and persuasive than abstract reasoning. "Making Disciples of Oral Learners," the Lausanne report quoted above, goes on to point out, "Oral strategies are also necessary in reaching people whose orality is tied to electronic media. They may be able to read well, but they get most of the important information in their lives through stories and music from the radio, television, film, Internet and other electronic means" (ibid.).

Storytelling approaches to evangelism and discipleship have the added advantage that new believers can easily continue to tell others the Bible stories they have learned, and as a result, the method is locally reproducible and can easily lead to multiplication. Thus when the skill is learned, narrating the plan of redemption can capture the attention of hearers, enable them to interact directly with God's revelation, deepen their understanding, and facilitate retention.

Locally Reproducible and Sustainable Methods

Storytelling illustrates a principle. Approaches and ministries used by the church-planting team should be ones that local believers can use and will want to use. In order to be reproducible, they must rely on natural and readily accessible local resources and means. Usually this involves working primarily through relationships and avoiding using technology and imported means. Simple, cost-

---

4. At the 2004 Forum for World Evangelization an issue group produced a report, "Making Disciples of Oral Learners," that is an excellent introduction to the topic. It includes an extensive list of other helpful resources. Lausanne Occasional Paper 54 is available online at www .lausanne.org/documents/2004forum/LOP54_IG25.pdf (accessed June 5, 2009).

Case Study 11.1

Storytelling and Church Planting

Pastor Dinanath of India tells his story of ministry among his people: "I was saved from a Hindu family in 1995 through a cross-cultural missionary. I had a desire to learn more about the word of God and I shared this with the missionary. The missionary sent me to Bible College in 1996. I finished my two years of theological study and came back to my village in 1998. I started sharing the good news in the way as I learnt in the Bible College. To my surprise my people were not able to understand my message. A few people accepted the Lord after much labour. I continued to preach the gospel, but there were little results. I was discouraged and confused and did not know what to do."

But then Pastor Dinanath's story takes a major turn: "In 1999 I attended a seminar where I learnt how to communicate the gospel using different oral methods. I understood the problem in my communication as I was mostly using a lecture method with printed books, which I learnt in the Bible school. After the seminar I went to the village but this time I changed my way of communication. I started using a storytelling method in my native language. I used gospel songs and the traditional music of my people. This time the people in the villages began to understand the gospel in a better way. As a result of it people began to come in large numbers. Many accepted Christ and took baptism. There was one church with few baptized members in 1999 when I attended the seminar. But now in 2004, in six years we have 75 churches with 1350 baptized members and 100 more people are ready for baptism" (LOP 54, 2005).

effective approaches are often the best. Tools such as literature and media are effective only when they lead to an exploration of Jesus's words and deeds in the context of the full biblical worldview, as illustrated in the above examples.

Priority should be placed not on strategies that require a high degree of education, specialized training, or exceptional gifts, but rather on methods that draw on ordinary Christians' natural means of communication and social intercourse. Another consideration in reproducibility is the ability to transfer such methods to young believers relatively easily using familiar learning styles and communication patterns. In oral cultures, narratives are readily transmitted from one generation of believers to another. The personal testimonies and transformed lives of local new believers are important elements of any evangelistic strategy. Working as a group in evangelism models Christian community in action and provides strength through cooperation.[5] Cooperative evangelistic methods can also demonstrate unity and love among believers (John 17:23), as is seen in case study 11.2.

5. This is especially true in collectivistic societies. Western individualism should not undermine cooperative evangelistic efforts. When Jesus told the disciples they would be fishers of people, his analogy involved fishing together as a group using boats and nets—not fishing alone with a pole.

Evangelism That Leads to Discipleship

In Latin America and in many other places, a common problem is that a lot of energy is spent on evangelistic efforts that produce many inquirers and "decisions" but few lasting converts. Some evangelistic strategies have a built-in *follow-up gap*, which occurs when the respondents have no prior relationship with those calling on them. It can also occur when it is assumed that respondents have understood the gospel and been truly born again. Assessment of understanding and response should be the first step in follow-up, though the depth of the conversion experience may not be evident for months to come as the person grows in understanding and evidences Spirit-empowered life change. Robert Priest (2003) studied thirty-four conversion narratives of the Aguaruna in Peru and found that initially converts lacked any sense of sin but such awareness grew over time as they heard the Word of God. In such situations it is especially important to consider evangelism as a process that flows into discipleship.

When the gospel is shared face to face or in a small group by neighbors, friends, or relatives, follow-up is much easier. Questions and obstacles can be addressed. While personal approaches take more time, they lessen the follow-up gap and yield most lasting fruit.[6] When, on the other hand, evangelism occurs in the form of large meetings, literature or media campaigns, concerts, open-air preaching, and formats that are less personal, extra effort must be given to following up on those who express interest. Personal information will need to be obtained from inquirers so that they can be contacted. Merely sending a letter or making a phone call is seldom adequate. Often follow-up is done through a personal home visit—though this can be difficult or impossible in large cities, where addresses are inaccurate, difficult to find, or located in inaccessible places (such as protected high-rise apartments or gated communities). Another approach is to offer a follow-up Bible study or other form of small group discipleship. One will need to consider the best venue for such meetings: the home of a believer, the home of an inquirer, a church building, or a more public, neutral location like a restaurant? It's best to pick the venue that inquirers are most likely to come to and feel comfortable in.

Common Mistakes in the Launching Phase

1. Church planting suffers when evangelism is only pursued during the first stage of the church plant.

   Often evangelism is the focus initially because there is no church and no other way to grow the church, but once a congregation has been

---

6. The problem of attrition is different. It presumes that inquirers are incorporated and then leave. However, the two are related, as some attrition is also due to inadequate follow-up. Attrition will be addressed at the end of this chapter.

Case Study 11.2

Evangelism through Cell Groups

The Dios Admirable Church in Caracas, Venezuela, began in 1965 as an evangelistic Bible study targeting college students. Pastor Francisco Liévano, its former pastor, led the church from two hundred to four hundred people by using discipling cell groups. By 1999 it had grown to twenty-five cell groups, and many others were used to start five new churches in Caracas. They are called Grupos Básicos de Discipulado Cristiano (Basic Christian Discipleship Groups).

This initiative was based on the convictions that (1) if believers are growing in the Lord, they will be bringing new people into the kingdom, and (2) evangelism is accomplished best along interpersonal networks, with people brought into neighborhood groups as they come to Christ. One of the men in the church stated that at least 75 percent of the new converts had come through the home group ministry. He also reported that 90 percent of the active ministry of the church was done through the home groups (Neumann 1999).

gathered, evangelism gets neglected as the focus shifts to working with Christians. However, evangelism is not a phase beyond which the church eventually moves but the missional heartbeat of the church. When church growth is slow, the first question to ask is "How are we doing in our evangelism?"

2. Church planting suffers when there is only one evangelistic approach.

The early church used a diversity of means and methods (Green 1970), and the Scriptures talk about making use of every opportunity (Col. 4:5). As noted above, Grady and Kendall (1992) found that effective church planters use broadly based evangelistic efforts, are flexible in their implementation, and combine them by integrating social activity (compassion ministry) and gospel witness. In so doing they establish credibility and build relationships. Those who focus on finding the one key to unlock the door often miss out—several keys are needed. Many different approaches are listed in sidebar 11.1 and table 11.1.

3. Church planting suffers when we rely only on the trained and the gifted for evangelism.

The Bible teaches that there are persons with the gift of evangelism (Acts 21:8; Eph. 4:11). But every Christian is to be a witness for Christ (Acts 1:8; 1 Pet. 3:15) and joyfully share the message of Jesus with others. New believers from the ministry focus people normally become the most effective evangelists. Therefore effective church-planting teams do not isolate new believers from relationships with unbelieving friends and relatives.

Evangelism and Discipleship in Montreal

Most people under fifty years old in Quebec have a Roman Catholic cultural heritage and believe in God but have little understanding of who he is or how he relates to them. Few have even considered the possibility of a daily relationship with him. In order to better communicate the gospel to this people group, Christian Direction, a service organization for the Quebec church, asked people in existing churches what had led them to a personal relationship with God. They found that respondents had heard the gospel –or parts of it—eight times on average before making a decision for Christ!* The greatest influence on their decision was the life change of a family member or friend (Smith 1995).

While this indicated the need for patient gospel sowing through relational networks and community involvement, other factors indicated that some would respond to larger group proclamation: (1) There was respect for the Bible as God's revelation. (2) Most respondents had wanted to see Christians in action in a group setting before making their decision. (3) Most had made their final decision in a group setting where a clear message and invitation were given.

As a result, the church-planting team adopted a three-pronged strategy: (1) Relational approach: They became members of community groups, built personal relationships with neighbors, and shared Christ as they had opportunity. (2) "Gospel net" approach: All team members met weekly to share progress and pray together for evangelism activities and appointments. They organized public community events in neutral places to draw seekers. (3) Multiplying witnesses: They immediately trained new believers to share their testimony and a simple gospel presentation.

The strength of the team's evangelism came from its broad strategy, teamwork, and perseverance. Several discipleship cell groups were formed. The greatest fruit came when Quebecois themselves shared their newfound love for Jesus with their peers.

*Study by Christian Direction in Montreal, Quebec, done in the late 1990s. Based on these findings, Glenn Smith (1995) suggests that in secularizing societies like Montreal, the goals should be to elicit progressive decisions in response to biblical truth, to maintain a strong emphasis on community, and to work on a decentralized network of small groups that meet for contextualized worship.

Grady and Kendall's 1992 study confirms that effective church planters are able to integrate new believers into evangelistic efforts. They become the "bridges of God"[7] to non-Christians because they have many natural relationships with unbelievers in the focus people. And because they have been converted recently, they still understand the thoughts and

7. A phrase coined by Donald McGavran in his landmark work *The Bridges of God* (1955), describing people movements that ensue when new believers are not extracted from their natural sphere of relationships but are encouraged to remain within them and share their faith naturally.

questions of unbelievers and can communicate with them compellingly. Kenneth Strachan of Latin America Mission found that movements grow in proportion to the church's ability to mobilize all members in the propagation of its beliefs. The impact of "every member mobilization" was demonstrated through Evangelism in Depth campaigns in many Latin American countries in the 1960s and 1970s (Strachan 1968; Roberts 1971).

4. Church planting suffers when evangelism is built on plans and programs alone.

It is commonly accepted that the greatest influence in a person's coming to Christ is the witness and life of a friend or family member (Gómez 1996; Smith 1995). If we equip Christians to live and share the gospel in their relational network, the evangelistic potential of the church is multiplied. Programs are great supplements to but poor substitutes for personal evangelism.

5. Church planting suffers when the basics of evangelism are neglected.

Prayer and use of the Scriptures are the biblical basics of effective evangelism. Grady and Kendall (1992) list prayer ministry as the number-one factor in fruitful church planting. The other basic is a clear gospel presentation. As the apostle Paul wrote, "I am not ashamed of the gospel, because it is the power of God for the salvation of everyone who believes" (Rom. 1:16).

Giving a personal testimony of what Christ has done for an individual is no substitute for explaining the offer of salvation in Christ as testified to in the Scriptures. We must remember that people from other religions also have their testimonies. A witness may begin with her personal story, but no one will be saved until they hear Jesus's message and story. The Word of God is powerful and active like a two-edged sword, and the gospel alone is the power of God that leads to salvation (Heb. 4:12; Isa. 55:10–11). It is ultimately the work of the Holy Spirit to convict the hearer of the truth of the gospel and open the hearts of the hearers (John 16:8–10; Acts 16:14). An Indian evangelist expressed it this way: "Jesus cannot be explained, He can only be revealed."[8] Prayer and the gospel are the basics. Many new ideas and strategies can be attempted; the question is, "How do they incorporate these fundamentals?"

Evangelize Holistically by Addressing Felt and Real Needs

During the preparation phase (chapter 10) the felt needs of the focus people were investigated. Felt needs are those needs that people recognize and are

---

8. Ajay Pillai of the Indian National Mission, speaking at Oakwood Community Church (Tampa, FL) on March 8, 2009.

motivated to resolve. They might include existential ones, such as food and water; personal ones such as love and significance; social ones such as transportation and security; spiritual ones for forgiveness or freedom from demonic forces; or any other host of needs that affect people's sense of well-being. Real needs are those that are needs *from God's perspective*. A felt need for food would be also be real need, but a felt need for material wealth would not. All felt needs must be taken seriously, but ultimately the church planter will seek to address real ones. Many people are unaware of their real needs for such things as forgiveness of sin and eternal life but are awakened to them by the Holy Spirit and the Word of God. Jesus not only preached the truth but healed the sick, gave sight to the blind, restored outcasts, and cared for people as whole people. By addressing people's needs, one demonstrates goodwill and compassion. As messengers of the gospel, we must not only tell people of the good news: we must also *be* good news when possible.

In chapter 19 we provide a detailed discussion of holistic ministries with kingdom impact. Suffice it to say here that as evangelism is launched, it must be accompanied by deeds of compassion and service. The church-planting team will need to assess local needs and realistically evaluate which of them can be addressed competently and adequately given the available personnel and resources. Ways to meet real needs might include hospital or prison visitation, tutoring programs, operating a food pantry, and digging fresh-water wells. In community health evangelism (CHE), an approach that has been thoughtfully developed and widely used, local people are taught how to analyze their community's needs and how to meet those needs using local resources. "CHE seamlessly integrates evangelism, discipleship, and church planting with community health and development."[9] In the early stages of the church plant, however, the team must carefully discern where to best invest its time, energy, and resources. Ministries of compassion and service can consume endless quantities of resources. Balance and a clear sense of priorities need to be maintained.

Rick Grover (2004) points out that in suburban churches Sunday mornings drive ministry, whereas in urban churches ministry drives Sunday morning. That is to say, in suburban settings the Sunday morning service is the primary focus of church life, and people are drawn to an attractive worship experience. Service ministries are an outgrowth of what happens on Sunday. In contrast, in urban churches the service ministries during the week (e.g., food pantry, job training, legal counsel) tend to be the primary focus of church life, which also draws people to Sunday services. This difference should not be missed when a team is planting urban churches. Grover continues, "I recommend that the new urban church begins prior to the first public worship service with one

9. From the CHE PowerPoint available at www.cheintl.org, where more information about the CHE Network can be found. See also www.lifewind.org.

need-meeting ministry in the community that can grow and be done with excellence" (2004, 49).

Local values (what is important, what needs are most significant) should be considered when the team is deciding about forms of evangelism, service, and development ministries. Many cultural values and customs are neither right nor wrong but matters of convention, tradition, or aesthetics. Christ does not destroy local cultures; he redeems them, purifying the good and irradiating the evil. Cross-cultural church planters must be sensitive not to impose their own cultural values—values that are not necessarily biblical—on others. This is one of the great challenges of contextualization.

David Britt studied local factors in urban multicultural church growth. He concludes that congruence—the quality of according or coinciding, the ability to come together in harmony—not homogeneity, is what church planters should seek.[10] Churches and church plants grow best when they address local cultural values and show how Christ fulfills the heart's deepest aspirations and greatest needs. How does this apply to ministries of service and evangelism? First of all, it underscores the need to study the community and understand their perception of Christians and Christianity. Second, it challenges the notion that to attract people we must be distinctive in every way. The church should stand out because of its message, love, and integrity—not because of the language, music, and other cultural values and symbols it uses. Finally, we should seek common spaces—both cultural and physical ones—with those we are reaching. Engaging the culture through involvement in community activities and services is one way of demonstrating the salt-and-light impact of the gospel on everyday life.

Baptize and Teach Obedience to Jesus

The Great Commission in Matthew 28:19–20 speaks of making disciples by baptizing in the name of the Father, the Son, and the Holy Spirit and teaching new believers to not merely know but *obey* all that Jesus commanded us. As we have noted above, a plan for evangelism must always include a plan for follow-up of new believers. Yet often such follow-up plans fail on precisely these two points: baptism and obedience. The follow-up often involves neophytes in a study that is primarily an intellectual exercise. They can quickly

10. "The presence of different or conflicting values is threatening. They make our own values seem arbitrary and, to use again Berger's word, precarious. Pluralism in urban life, by definition, quickly brings city dwellers into contact with different values and points of view. Though people in the city may assimilate many different or conflicting values, even city folks tend to gather around shared values. . . . Where the cultural symbols of a congregation are congruent with those of a local community, the gospel will receive an easier hearing. Church-community congruence forms the backdrop for church growth or decline" (Britt 1997, 143–44).

gain the impression that Christianity is first and foremost about knowing the Bible—that the measure of maturity is Bible knowledge. While the Christian faith is unquestionably grounded in God's truth as revealed in the Bible, the goal of Bible study is not knowledge in and of itself but rather Bible knowledge that leads to a closer relationship with God and a walk that is pleasing to God. James 1:22 exhorts, "Do not merely listen to the word, and so deceive yourselves. Do what it says."

We sometimes treat disciplemaking like a program or a class. A leader in Brazil once said, "When you speak of discipleship it sounds like a transfer of knowledge; for us it is the unfolding and outworking of the life of Christ in the believer." Neighbour observes, "We have spent all our training in the cognitive domain. We mistakenly think teaching and preaching change the values of Christians. . . . The curse of the traditional church is that there is no model, no leader who says, 'Pattern your life after me'" (1990, 2). This underlines the need for modeling and mentoring through a relationship of trust. Ranjit DeSilva defines spiritual formation as "the development of the inner life, so that a person experiences Christ as the source of life, reflects more Christ-like characteristics, and increasingly knows the power and presence of Christ in ministry" (DeSilva 1996, 50). God uses many means for life transformation. Robert Coleman (1987, 59–97) points out some of them:

- the importance of relationships— Mark 3:13–15; John 1:35–42
- meeting in homes—Acts 5:42; 20:20
- putting Scripture into practice—Matthew 28:20
- baptism—Matthew 28:19
- a new community—Acts 2:42–47
- loving obedience to a new Master—John 15
- the transforming of worldview and values—Romans 12:2
- a new source of life and power—Acts 1:8; Galatians 5:22–23

Thus a balanced follow-up plan will include Bible study that not only clarifies central Christian truths but also helps new believers apply those truths to their everyday life. It will include much prayer for new believers and practical instruction in Christian disciplines. A key will be helping them discern the will of Christ for their life and ordering their affairs under Christ's lordship. Often it is during the first days and weeks that new believers are most open to change and reordering of their personal affairs as they are particularly sensitive to the reality of God's fresh work in their life. This opportunity should not be missed.

One of the principal outward signs of becoming a disciple of Christ in the New Testament is baptism. Baptism has many levels of biblical meaning: public confession of repentance and faith (Acts 2:38), entry into the Christian community (1 Cor. 12:13), identification with the death and resurrection of Christ unto new life (Rom. 6:1–10), and cleansing from sin (Acts 22:16; 1 Pet. 3:21). In some contexts, such as the Muslim and Hindu world, it has been suggested that a substitute for baptism as a rite of passage should be practiced because of baptism's negative associations or false understandings.[11] However, three reasons argue in favor of the universal practice of water baptism: First, the theological meanings associated with it are reflected in the physical act (Rom. 6:1–10; 1 Pet. 3:21); second, Matthew 28:19 explicitly commands us to baptize "all nations"; and third, in Acts both Jewish and Gentile new believers were baptized—we have no example of any substitute. Indeed, Ephesians 4:5 speaks of *one* Lord, *one* faith, and *one* baptism. Westerners with a highly rationalistic bent tend to underestimate the spiritual, social, and psychological importance of rituals such as baptism. Ritual acts that mark the transition from one stage to the next stage (such as an altar call, baptism, or destruction of fetishes) can be essential elements in the process of conversion and critical to identification with the new faith and church (Tippett 1967, 109; 1971, 169; 1992).

Church planters will have several decisions to make about the practice of baptism within their context: the time of baptism, its form (immersion, pouring, or sprinkling), and whether it should be public or private. Many factors come into play, including the beliefs of the planter; thus we limit ourselves to a concise, but important, look at some of the issues.

The question of time concerns not only whether infants or only adults should be baptized but (especially in pioneer settings) also whether there should be a period of instruction and waiting or baptism should be administered without delay. In every example in the New Testament, baptism (even of pagan-background Gentile believers) was administered almost immediately after the person's conversion and simple confession of faith. This should warn against an overly cautious stance. On the other hand, many professions of faith are shallow and based on a very inadequate understanding of the gospel or on questionable motives. Baptizing a person who later turns out not to be genuinely converted can have many negative repercussions. Rather than establishing a mandatory waiting period, an emphasis should be placed on waiting to see clear evidences of commitment and change. Planters will want to consider the perspective of other local believers and the reaction of the new disciple's peers as they look for evidence of new life in Christ.

For those who come from Muslim, Hindu, and even Catholic or Orthodox backgrounds, water baptism (or "rebaptism" if they were baptized as infants) is

11. For the Muslim context see, for example, the discussion in Parshall 1979 and 1989; Woodberry 1989; Stricker and Ripken 2007. For a discussion in the context of India, see Singh 1985. For a substitute for water baptism even in Western contexts, see Kraft 1979, 257–60.

seen as the final threshold that marks conversion to a new faith and community. If that threshold is crossed willingly, publicly, and with clear understanding of its implications, new disciples are more likely to grow in their identification with the church and its practices. It will often have a significant impact on the disciple's relationship to his or her family, friends, and former community of faith. Thus church planters must not take the command to baptize lightly, overlooking the *theological and personal* significance of baptism for the new believer and for the healthy development of the church.

Disciple New Believers and Train Them to Do the Same

Evangelism must lead to discipleship, and discipleship must include baptism and learning obedience to Christ. The separation of evangelism and discipleship is an artificial one. The mandate for both comes from the same command to "make disciples" (Matt. 28:19). In the New Testament, discipling bridges the proclamation of the gospel and the establishment of believers in the faith. Multiplying biblical disciples is the sine qua non thrust of church planting.

Disciples and Discipling

Church planters should have a good understanding of what a disciple is biblically and what a disciple would look like where the church is being planted. Disciples are those who follow Christ and his teaching in order to become progressively more like him and accomplish his will for their lives. In the New Testament a disciple is not an "advanced" Christian: people are called disciples from the moment they begin to follow Jesus and as long as they continue in his way. The twelve apostles had a particular calling as apostles, but they continued to be called disciples (Mark 3:7, 13–15). In Acts 14 the term "the disciples" is used for those in Derbe who had just turned to Christ (vv. 20–21), for young believers who came to Christ during the first leg of Paul and Barnabas's journey (v. 22), and for the more mature believers in Antioch who had sent them out (v. 28). Thus a disciple of Jesus is a follower of Jesus regardless of maturity level. However, in this chapter we are primarily concerned with the first stages in the life of disciples.

We define *discipling* as helping new Christ-followers become established, grounded, stable, and secure in him and in their practice of obedience to him. If we are called to make disciples, we should have a clear idea of what Jesus expects of his disciples and what he promises them. Table 11.3, which compares the costs and rewards of following Jesus, was used by a church-planting team in its discipling efforts.

Table 11.3
The Biblical Profile and Reward of a Disciple

Profile of a Disciple		Reward of a Disciple	
Remains in Christ and in his Word	John 8:31; 15:4–6	Loved by Jesus and his Father	John 15:9, 15
Keeps his commandments	John 14:15; 15:10, 14	Receives answers to prayers	John 15:7, 16
Loves Jesus more than anyone else	Matthew 10:37	Bears much fruit	John 15:5, 8
Loves others with Jesus's love	John 13:35; 15:12, 17	Becomes more and more like Jesus	Luke 6:40
Gives witness of Jesus	John 15:27	Experiences deep joy	John 15:11
Denies self	Matthew 10:38; 16:24	Experiences extraordinary peace	John 20:19–20
Accepts opposition	John 15:20	Receives correction to bear more fruit	John 15:2
Exercises trust in Jesus	John 14:1	Is filled with the Holy Spirit	John 14:16; Acts 1:8

Jesus's description reminds us that being a disciple is a life transformation, not simply adopting a new set of doctrinal propositions and religious behaviors. It is a new way of life guided by the Word and the Spirit, motivated by a transformed mind, a grateful heart, and new affections. Thus the emphasis is not on becoming a bona fide church member but on becoming a faithful, obedient, and fruitful follower of Jesus—although belonging to a community of faith is an important outcome and outward sign.

Growth is the measure of progress in discipleship. Disciples grow in many ways, and these dimensions of growth cannot be isolated from each other; God expects them all. We can identify in the Scriptures at least seven ways he expects disciples to grow and produce fruit to his glory:

- in character and fruit of the Holy Spirit (John 15; Gal. 5:22–23), maturity in Christ (Eph. 4:15), faith and love (2 Thess. 1:3)
- in knowledge and truth from the Word (1 Pet. 2:2; 2 Pet. 3:18)
- in service and prayer (Acts 6:1–5; Eph. 6:10–20)
- in love and mutual edification (John 17:20–26; Eph. 4:1–6; Col. 3:12–17)
- in witness and missional impact (Acts 1:8; 1 Tim. 5:7–10; 1 Pet. 3:15)
- in social impact (Matt. 4:23–25), including healing (Acts 9:32–43), spirit deliverance (Acts 19:19), social justice (James 2:1–7), and care for the needy (Acts 4:34–37)
- in unity amid ethnic and other differences (John 17:20–23; Eph. 2:11–22; Rev. 5:9–10)

Why so many dimensions of growth? So that God's people will spread the knowledge of the Almighty, declare praises of his mercy to the world (Eph. 1:6–8; 1 Pet. 2:9–10), and draw people from all nations to faith in Christ and obedience to his Word (Matt. 28:18–20).

Corporate and Peer Discipling

Discipling takes place in both individual and corporate settings. Both individuals (Matt. 8:22; 9:9; 19:21; John 1:43) and groups (Matt. 4:19; 10:38; 16:24; John 10:27; 2 Thess. 3:7–9) are called to follow Jesus. Jesus called his disciples individually, indicating that he knew them particularly and had a plan for their individual lives (John 1:48; 15:16). This is accentuated by the fact that in Jesus's day most disciples chose their rabbi (Costas 1979).[12] He calls his disciples "friends" (15:15) and "his sheep" (John 10), going after the individual lamb in danger (Luke 15:1–6). Even in group settings Jesus addresses disciples individually and deals with their questions and doubts personally (John 14:5, 8). Correction must also be initially handled on an individual basis (Matt. 18:15–17). One-on-one relationships are an important but not exclusive means of discipling in church planting.

Jesus and Paul also often address disciples corporately. Their modus operandi was to use dialogical teaching in groups of various sizes. Like grapes, disciples are naturally found in clusters and grow together. Jesus alternately spent time with a group of three (Peter, James, and John), with the Twelve, and with larger groups. Meeting in small groups for discipleship can strengthen members' motivation as they develop group solidarity and hold each other accountable. Especially in more collectivistic societies, groups are a more natural and motivational setting than one-on-one meetings. Thus discipleship encompasses many types of intentional interpersonal and group relationships. When these are held in balance and centered on Jesus, they provide the broadest and most effective discipling.

Discipleship and Multiplication

The goal of discipling is the multiplication of Spirit-transformed witnesses for Christ who become agents of his kingdom.

> Probably the Christian community within three decades had multiplied four hundredfold which represents an annual increase of 22 percent for more than a generation, and the rate of growth continued remarkably high for 300 years. By

---

12. Although there were many similarities, Orlando Costas (1979, 15) lists seven core differences between rabbinical disciplemaking and Jesus's practice with his disciples from Juan Stam, "Bases bíblicas para el discipulado" [Biblical bases for discipleship], *Ensayos Ocasionales* 6, no. 3 (1976): 1–22.

the beginning of the fourth century, when Constantine was converted to Christianity, the number of disciples may have reached 10 or 12 million, or roughly a tenth of the total population of the Roman Empire. . . . The early church grew by evangelistic multiplication as witnesses of Christ reproduced their life-style in the lives of those about them. (Coleman 1987, 39–40)

Discipling that requires formal education or resources will stand in the way of total mobilization and multiplication; only discipling that is simple, organic, relational, and accessible to every believer will lead to multiplication. The pattern must be taught, modeled, and maintained. Effective multiplication approaches often include both personal mentoring and small group accountability. Neil Cole (2004; 2005) has modeled and taught the use of small disciplemaking groups as a means of multiplication. Disciples do not make others in isolation but in small groups Cole calls "life transformation groups" that use mutual discipling and do not require theologically trained leaders.

Discipling centers on Jesus's teaching. In the Gospels he is constantly giving the disciples lessons about the kingdom of God, using parables, and correcting their faulty patterns of thinking. He clearly expects them to make every facet of their lives conform to his teaching under the control of his Spirit ("obey" in Matt. 28:20). Paul also practiced life teaching for life change. He reminds the Ephesian elders: "You know that I have not hesitated to preach anything that would be helpful to you but have taught you publicly and from house to house . . . for I have not hesitated to proclaim to you the whole will of God" (see Acts 20:20, 27).

Discipling is costly and time consuming. While striving for multiplication, church planters must avoid shortcuts. Several authors have identified three stages in Jesus's plan of spiritual formation (Bruce 1971; Hull 1988). It is helpful to envision discipleship reproduction as a process, and what better pattern to follow than the one Jesus established with his disciples? In the first stage, the disciples observed Jesus's ministry of teaching, healing, and serving. Later they were called to leave their occupations to follow Jesus. In the third stage they received deeper teaching and were sent out on practical ministry tours.

Discipleship is also costly because it involves life-on-life mentoring in order to extend the lordship of Christ to a person's entire being: thought, belief, behavior, relationships, and character. This is the New Testament pattern. Jesus walked, talked, taught, corrected, demonstrated, fed, helped and received help from his disciples. His first discipling activity was hospitality. He asked two curious followers of John the Baptist, "What do you want?" and then invited them to share a day with him (John 1:38–39). Paul followed the Master's plan of discipling and compared his care for the Thessalonians to the nurturing of a mother (1 Thess. 2:7–9). Spiritual parenting can be painful as well: Paul addresses the Galatians as "my dear children, for whom I am again in the pains of childbirth until Christ is formed in you" (Gal. 4:19).

Responsible parents plan for the shelter, nourishment, protection, and exercise of their children. Yet every child is different, and individual care and interventions must be carried out. Likewise, a basic discipling plan will have a primary (preferable natural) mentoring relationship, a discipleship group in which the new believer learns to live in community, and a Bible study plan that establishes new biblical patterns of thinking and behavior in direct obedience to God's Word. The Grace Brethren have been among the strongest advocates of the centrality of disciplemaking to church planting. Sidebar 11.3 explains some basic principles they use in their "apostolic church-planting team strategy" (Julien 2000).

Special Issues in Discipling

Discernment is needed to help new disciples with personal problems that are deeply rooted conceptually or spiritually. Although all believers are new creatures in Christ, they can come with a significant history of destructive spiritual practices that may have created deep roots and chains of demonic bondage. Sinful habits, if not identified and abandoned, will invariably choke the seed of new life.

New Christians come into the Christian community with unresolved conflicts and unhealthy relational patterns. Like the Samaritan woman, some come with dysfunctional marriages and families. They also come with distortions from their former worldview and need a worldview transformation. In all these cases discipling must be corrective as well as developmental. It must deal with the realities that are present below the surface. Satan's lies and destructive patterns must be confronted in love. It is often helpful to have someone on the church-planting team with skills and gifts in counseling to help new believers work through such issues biblically, and someone who is studied in apologetics or the religion of the focus people to help answer questions and anticipate misunderstandings.

When a new Chinese believer committed suicide, the local church was shaken and the church planter was confused. The young man had been a faithful disciple and appeared to be a promising future leader. He had never shared his internal conflicts and struggles, though, and he chose to take his life over living in hypocrisy and failure. The church planter commented in a letter: "I think there is greater need for . . . awareness of the spiritual battle, where each one has had a chance to deal with the strongholds and footholds of evil they have allowed in their hearts before and after beginning their walk with Christ." Some form of discerning spiritual influences is needed. Sometimes this is done in the context of preparation for baptism. Assessment tools such as those used by Freedom in Christ Ministries can be helpful (Anderson 2001). However, much more is needed. Here are some recommendations:

- Anticipate these cultural/spiritual strongholds by studying the history, cultural sins, and worldview distortions of the ministry focus people.
- Continually foster an atmosphere of grace and trust in the community.
- Invest in personal relationships where honest and vulnerable communication of questions and struggles can take place.
- Seek the counsel of mature local believers who understand the cultural complexities of an issue and perhaps are even familiar with the personal and family roots of the new Christian.
- Exercise spiritual discernment through prayer and careful listening for patterns of conflict or struggle.
- Ask the new believer to tell about his or her religious and spiritual pilgrimage, and ask questions.

Wisely Assimilate Transfer Growth

Existing believers are often drawn to a new church plant. Church growth that comes from the addition of members who are already believers is called *transfer growth*. They come for a wide variety of reasons: because they have caught the vision for the new church, because they have moved to the locality and do not yet have a home church, or out of curiosity. But some may be running away from relational problems or conflict in another church. The worst-case scenario is when newcomers have ulterior motives, wishing to exercise power or influence in the church plant. Persons with different doctrines or traditions can become a source of conflict if the church plant does not align with their expectations. The key is to discern whether these transfer believers are workers coming to help and disciples willing to learn or disgruntled people who will sap energy. Worse yet, some may be wolves in sheep's clothing coming to exploit or divide. The goal is to identify those who come for the right reasons and selectively enroll and engage them in the church-planting vision. These guidelines can be used:

1. Someone on the church-planting team should meet with the newcomers, find out their history and the reasons for coming, and get permission to contact their former church.
2. Contact their former church and find out under what conditions they left. Cooperate with their former church when it is a case of church discipline.
3. Ask the would-be new members what they are looking for in a church and what their core beliefs and values are. Lay out the beliefs, values, and vision of your work and see if there is alignment.

Discipleship and the Apostolic Church-Planting Team Strategy

1. Discipleship is the major mandate of church planting.

The development of strong spiritual families, leadership, and churches are all based on making disciples who are faithful in obedience to all that Christ has commanded (Matt. 28:16–20). Healthy and growing disciples are the building blocks of healthy and growing churches. Both the book of Acts and church history demonstrate that churches are formed where there are faithful, reproducing disciples of Jesus Christ.

2. Center discipleship on the development of personal growth disciplines.

Many traditional forms of discipleship lead to dependency on teachers and discipleship materials—that is, passive discipleship. However, converts who develop the ability to build a deep relationship with God through the practice of Christian growth disciplines take responsibility for their spiritual lives (Heb. 5:14). The disciple's five basic disciplines are Bible study, prayer, worship, fellowship, and witnessing. Other discipleship activities must be secondary to the development of these disciplines, since they are central to a growing walk with God.

3. Use discipleship methods that foster personal discovery of God's truth.

Without diminishing the importance of the teaching ministry, the priority should be to help new believers understand God's Word and feed themselves. God will reveal himself to his children as they seek him through his Word. The mentor's goal is then to help new disciples make their own discoveries. When learning is based on personal study and discovery rather than on another person's ability to teach and motivate, disciples are able to nurture their own walk with God and help others do the same.

4. Establish patterns of mutual discipleship.

One of the best ways to avoid the dependency syndrome, foster personal discovery of Bible truth, and develop leadership qualities is to structure discipleship around the concept of mutual accountability. This style of discipleship places the responsibility for developing the Christian growth disciplines on the believers themselves. The church planter equips others to help each other and hold each other accountable for their spiritual disciplines. This promotes a high sense of ownership and personal responsibility for oneself and for the spiritual well-being of others.

5. Use the home as a central stage for discipling.

"Nowhere is this [reproduction through discipling] more evident than in Christians' homes. Here, where friendships are most natural and genuine, evangelism centered . . . witnessing was not a technique or a program, but a life-style" (Coleman 1987, 92–93). One of the most neglected virtues in Western societies is hospitality. Family life is highly instructive to new believers (adapted from Julien 2000).

4. Regardless of their experience and maturity, do not move them into places of influence or leadership rapidly. Rather invite them to work and serve in simple ways. Watch for a humble, cooperative, submissive spirit.
5. If their motives are good, make them feel welcome and help them make the transition into a small group and ministry. Make sure someone in the church, or on the team, builds a relationship of trust with them, encourages them, and helps them find their place in the family.

Form a Foundational Community and Begin Training Servant Leaders

During this launching phase the foundational community of the emerging church will be formed. New believers will be meeting in small groups for discipleship, prayer, simple worship, and planning. These new believers will become the nucleus of the church. Thus it is important to gradually instill in them the sense that they are the people of God, a distinct body of believers, brothers and sisters in Christ. This sense of identity will be developed further during the next phase. But even from the earliest gatherings, a sense of fellowship and spiritual bonding should be encouraged. The core values of the church-planting vision should be modeled and taught. Conflicts should be dealt with lovingly and biblically. The DNA of the church will take shape gradually during this phase.

The future leaders of the church are often already present among the first new disciples. In chapter 17 we will discuss at length how to identify and develop leaders in a church plant. But once again, even from the earliest days, responsibility should be increasingly borne by the local believers themselves. Their natural tendency will be to look to the church planters to do the work of the ministry, but they should be encouraged to give to others what they have received. New believers can share their testimony, begin discipling another new believer, and help others in practical ways. By creating an ethos of empowerment, planters will both mobilize local believers for ministry from the outset and combat the idea that one must be highly trained or have been a Christian for many years before one can serve. This ethos is essential to the entire process of reproduction and mobilization. The seeds of church reproduction are sown right here: a new believer evangelizing others, a new disciple discipling others.

The Problem of Attrition

Several studies indicate that the evangelical church has a serious "backdoor problem" in many parts of the world: visitors, members, and new believers may attend church for a time but then leave, never to return (Rainer 1999;

Stetzer 2001; King 2007).[13] Some have estimated that in the United States 50 percent or more of people added to the church drop out within a year (Klippenes 2001). Reasons for attrition are many and varied, but studies from various contexts reveal that recurrent themes emerge. In Costa Rica almost one-third of those who left their church took responsibility for their choice and said their conduct and lifestyle led to the choice (Gómez 1996). Another third were disillusioned by the management of finances or the conduct of leaders or members. The final third gave a variety of answers like the pressure of family and friends, the appeal of another religious group, or a lack of help in difficult times. Few respondents attributed their desertion to external factors such as persecution.

Many had never understood the implication of the gospel and of their decision to follow Jesus. "The results show that there must be a commitment by the leaders so that, within the first year after conversion, the implications, the content, the expectations and the privileges that go with the message of salvation are clearly understood. Forty-one percent of those interviewed with a year or less of conversion did not clearly understand the message of salvation that was presented to them" (Gómez 1996, 68). However, steps can be taken to reduce attrition. For example, according to Patrick Johnstone (2001, 206), addressing the problem directly in Costa Rica has helped to reduce the rate of attrition and spur on a new wave of growth.

We will not achieve 100 percent retention, nor should we try to. There are some people who *should* leave. On the positive side, we should be proactive and ask, "What helps to retain sincere believers?" A study of Pentecostal churches in Brazil revealed that while many were attracted to churches by healing and supernatural manifestations, it was close personal relationships and care that led to retention (Duck 2001, 230–32, 238–48, 331–44). An investigation into exceptionally high retention rates of over 80 percent of new believers among the 'Nso people of Cameroon found six significant factors: attending lessons on "counting the cost" before baptism, prebaptismal attendance at worship services, previous attendance at a church of another denomination, involvement in evangelistic activities, involvement in worship leadership, and contact and conversion by an evangelist (Kee 1991). In Taiwan it was discovered that new believers were more likely to remain in churches if they had a relatively long, intensive relationship with a Christian prior to their conversion, which could be understood as a warning against rushing people into hasty a decision for Christ (Swanson 1986). Case study 11.4 describes Costa Rican churches that are effective at retention.

In the North American setting, Thom Rainer wrote a book whose title underlines one key factor for retention, *High Expectations: The Remarkable*

13. For much of the material in this section we are indebted to the research of Gómez 1995 and Hibbert 2008.

Churches That Are More Successful at Closing the Back Door

Eleven factors found in Gómez 1996, 135–37

1. They use collective evangelism efforts as well as personal witness.
2. They put the emphasis on unchurched people.
3. Church members have a clearer understanding of the gospel, evangelism, works and grace, and the message of the cross.
4. They demonstrate a higher level of pastoral care.
5. They have more members who have been discipled and can help new Christians.
6. They are more sound doctrinally (less perfectionism, universalism, and prosperity gospel).
7. They prepare their members to mentor others.
8. They balance the needs of men and women in their pastoral care.
9. They have more accessible leaders who can give advice.
10. They have more efforts and programs to help new Christians.
11. They make a greater effort to seek out and reintegrate those who have been absent.

Secret of Keeping People in Your Church (1999). In essence, churches that expect more get more. Larry Osborne (2008), pastor of one of America's largest churches, emphasizes the importance of integrating newcomers into sermon-based small groups that "velcro members to the ministry."

In summary, reducing attrition and raising retention can be improved by addressing the following dimensions in the discipleship of new believers:

- *Spiritual*: clearly articulating the gospel and the cost of following Christ, and praying for new believers that they might be strengthened in their faith
- *Intellectual*: helping new believers understand the Bible, integrate their newfound faith with daily life, and develop a biblical worldview
- *Social*: helping new believers build close personal relationships with other believers so that they gain a new social network, support, and identity as well as a loving experience of the family of God
- *Ethical*: helping new believers learn how to overcome sin—on the one hand living by the grace of God and on the other hand taking seriously the importance of a life growing in holiness

If making disciples is the heart of church planting, and if disciples are obedient followers who become like their Master, it would seem legitimate to evaluate our success in church planting by the quantity and the quality of disciples. "Disciple-making is an indispensable criterion for evaluation missional faithfulness. One way to evaluate our missional program is to ask three questions: (1) Is it leading women and men to follow Jesus at each crossroad of life? (2) Is it enabling them to participate in Jesus' mission in the world? (3) Is it teaching them to obey him in all things? Following, participating and obeying—these are marks of authentic discipleship of a faithful Christian mission" (Costas 1979, 24).

12

Establishing

::

Congregating and Maturing

After the initial launch of the church plant, the first believers are growing into faithful disciples of Jesus Christ. During this phase the group will begin to fulfill all the functions of a biblical church, moving beyond initial evangelism and discipleship. Now an awareness of becoming a community, the body of Christ, should be cultivated, nurtured, and lived out. Evangelism and discipleship continue, but the sense of being the people of God, Christ's local church, begins to take shape. The gathered believers are his chosen people, called to the praise of his glory and sent on a collective mission. With this sense of calling and identity the believers become more than a random collection of individual Christians and begin to take on the life of a church.

Overview of Phase

Biblical Examples

Here we look more to the epistles that describe the life of the churches that Paul planted.
Romans 12:3–8 and 1 Corinthians 12: The exercise of spiritual gifts for edification of the body of Christ
Romans 12:9–10 and 1 Thessalonians 4:1–9: Growth in love and maturity
Ephesians 5:19–20 and Hebrews 10:24–25: Regular meetings for worship and encouragement
Galatians 6:1–2: Mutual correction and bearing of burdens

Key Steps

1. Grow and develop life as the family of God
2. Discover, develop, and employ spiritual gifts for edification of the body of Christ
3. Appoint a preliminary leadership team
4. Meet regularly for corporate worship
5. Multiply cell groups and cell leaders
6. Formulate values and a long-term strategic plan for ministry
7. Teach stewardship

Critical Issues

1. Understanding what it means to be the church
2. Growing in commitment to one another
3. Local believers taking responsibility for ministry

Grow and Develop Life as the Family of God

The fellowship of believers as the family of God is one of the most wonderful things that a new Christian experiences. But this sense of spiritual family does not always come automatically. Indeed, in contexts where believers face persecution, the response is sometimes suspicion or distrust of others who claim to be believers.

As a part of the discipleship process, church planters must begin teaching explicitly on the nature of the church, using biblical texts such as Acts or Ephesians. Such teaching must also be accompanied by *experiencing* the family of God, the church, in specific ways. In the early church the apostles' teaching, fellowship, breaking of bread, and prayer were central features of common life (Acts 2:42). Members of the Jerusalem church went so far as to sell their possessions to meet one another's material needs (Acts 2:44–45; 4:32–35). Common meals, hospitality, praying for one another, and meeting one another's needs are powerful signs of the work of the Spirit that grow a bond of fellowship. These need to be intentionally modeled and promoted by the church-planting team.

An understanding of the believer's new identity in Christ goes hand in hand with the sense of being the family of God. In many contexts, such as the Muslim world, this is a critical and controversial question. Here again, intentional biblical teaching is imperative. In Christ we are new creatures (2 Cor. 5:17); we are born again by the Spirit and the Word (John 3:3–8; 1 Pet. 1:23; 1 John 5:1); and we become children of God with a common Father in heaven (John 1:12; Gal. 3:26; 1 John 3:1–2). Our identification with Christ as Savior and God as Father trumps all other allegiances and bonds. Our citizenship is in heaven (Phil. 3:20) and is no longer based on nationality, ethnic background, economic status, gender, caste, education, or any other human feature. "You are all sons of God through faith in Christ Jesus, for all of you who were baptized into Christ have clothed yourselves with Christ. There is neither Jew nor Greek, slave nor free, male nor female, for you are all one in Christ Jesus. If you belong to Christ, then you are Abraham's seed, and heirs according to the promise" (Gal. 3:26–29).

This new identity transcends divisions that have contributed to war, ethnic rivalry, oppression, abuse, and hatred between peoples and individuals. Only by the cross of Christ and the transforming power of the Spirit can the walls of hostility between people be broken down. Nowhere was this more powerful than in the removal of divisions between Jews and Gentiles in the early church (Eph. 2:14–17). A negative example is found in the church of Corinth, where social distinction led to divisions and unfair treatment at, of all places, the celebration of the Lord's Supper. Upper-class Christians likely ate a "private meal" in the smaller dining room of a villa, while the lower classes ate in the larger atrium (or courtyard) with differing menus. Paul would have nothing of such discrimination and distinctions in the church (1 Cor. 11:17–22; cf. Fee 1987, 533–34). A similar situation arose in a caste-based society in Micronesia, where Christians from different castes ate at different tables with different foods at a church picnic. Ethnic and class tensions still plague the church around the globe.

Therefore the churches we plant are truly to be kingdom communities that reflect the lordship of Christ and model reconciled relationships. Our new identity in Christ and a sense of Christian community must be taught and experienced in the emerging church. Social barriers are deeply rooted and complex. They are overcome only with great patience, bold examples, and persistent teaching.

An additional question often arises in Islamic and similar contexts: should believers call themselves Christians, or are other terms such as *followers of Isa [Jesus]* appropriate?[1] The term *Christian* is often associated with Western culture and its unattractive excesses such as crime, violence, licentiousness, pornography, materialism, disrespectful youth, colonialism, and perceived wars of aggression against Islam. Many feel that avoiding use of the term *Christian* will help avoid such misunderstandings and may prevent new believers from being immediately ostracized from the community they hope to reach. How one answers such questions will depend much on the approach to contextualization that has been adopted. We cannot expand on these questions here, but this example highlights how important it is for the church-planting team to familiarize itself with contextual issues and alternatives so as to respond appropriately to such challenges. The local believers will need to be a part of that discussion and decision-making process.

---

1. For an excellent summary of the discussion on Christian identity and contextualization in Islamic contexts, see Tennent 2007, 193–220.

Discover, Develop, and Employ Spiritual Gifts for Edification of the Body of Christ

The ministries of evangelism and discipleship have been modeled during the previous stage. Now as the group matures, its members must begin to minister to and serve one another in additional ways. New Christians can easily get the impression that the church planters are there to serve them and that Christianity is mainly a matter of learning the Bible, praying, worshiping, and having their own needs met. But in order to mature in one's walk with Christ, one must follow his example of service, considering the needs of others higher than one's own (Mark 10:45; Phil. 2:3–8). As believers grow in maturity and in a desire to serve, they should also grow in awareness and use of their spiritual gifts. These gifts are for the purpose of building up the body of Christ (1 Cor. 1:7; 1 Pet. 4:10). Thus helping believers to develop their gifts and ministry skills will become an important task for the church planter during this phase. In chapter 17 we will describe in more detail methods of equipping believers for service.

During this phase more public corporate worship services or celebrations may be started and additional cell groups launched. Children's ministry, community service projects, and specialized outreach events may also be initiated. Such ministries will require additional workers, people able to take up the challenge and serve. Because the church at this point of development is usually still rather small, the number of workers will be limited. Enthusiasm may lead the church to want to attempt more than it can handle. The church planter will need to help the church understand its limitations and remain focused on the essential ministries. Ministry should be expanded only as adequate and gifted personnel are available and trained.

How can a person's spiritual gifts be identified? There are numerous questionnaires and surveys available that one can fill out. Such tools may be a good starting point to identify interests and stimulate discussion, but they have limitations. They are usually not available in many languages and tend to be very specific to churches in Western cultures. Because they are self-reports (i.e., the person assesses his or her own skills and interests), they are not always accurate. We all know the person who thinks that he or she is musical, but isn't! Furthermore, spiritual gift inventories can be frustrating when a person discovers that he or she has a spiritual gift but there doesn't seem to be a corresponding appropriate ministry in which to use it.

The better way to discover gifts is by actually serving. As people experiment with various ministry opportunities, they often discover a joy and fruitfulness that they had not anticipated. Each person's gifts can also be confirmed by others who have observed her or his ministry. Of course even the most gifted persons will need to hone and develop their gifts over time, but usually the potential is evident early in the faith journey. Cell group and ministry team leaders should be taught how to identify giftedness and how to help their group or team members develop and employ those gifts.

Appoint a Preliminary Leadership Team

As long as the church is very small and consists of just a few families, decision making and planning will be largely informal, with broad consensus and input from the group. But as the church grows, so too grows the need for a smaller leadership team. Initially this might be a planning committee composed of one representative from each family. However, once this group grows beyond about ten persons, effective planning again becomes difficult and a smaller decision-making group should be appointed.

The purpose and manner by which these initial leaders are appointed is critical. In some situations the church planter may hand-pick the leaders, who are appointed for a limited term of leadership. For example, if several cell groups exist, the cell group leaders might form the preliminary leadership team. In most situations, however, a more participative approach such as an election is recommended. Whatever approach is taken, several principles should be observed:

- All committed participants in the emerging church should have some say in the process of determining the leaders. Whether through a formal election process or informal discussions, their opinions must be sought and respected. It is essential even at this stage that leaders have the trust and confidence of those they are leading. Unfortunately cross-cultural church planters often choose leaders who appeal to their cultural standards and personality but who lack the respect of the local people within the culture. This must obviously be avoided.
- This leadership team should be clearly a provisional, temporary appointment. The reason for this is that in the early months of a church plant there are often too few mature believers qualified for the office of elder. Yet a decision-making team is needed. At a later time during the structuring phase mature believers who are better qualified for formal church leadership will emerge, and at that time a more formal calling of church elders can occur. Not all the provisional leaders will be among them. Thus at this point it is wise to avoid formal titles such as *elder* and thus preclude false expectations and any compromise of the biblical qualifications for leaders. Terms such as "provisional leadership team," "planning team," or "steering committee" will make clear the temporary nature of the decision-making group.
- The role of this preliminary leadership team should be clearly spelled out as primarily planning, prayer, and organizational leadership. The

spiritual oversight carried out by elders is not yet primarily in view. This temporary team will serve in some ways as a testing ground for the spiritual qualification and leadership abilities of those who might later be appointed to long-term leadership roles.

One of the key roles that must be fulfilled at this stage is treasurer. During this phase of the church plant, expenses will be incurred and financial collections from the congregation will become necessary. The congregation must take primary responsibility for the financial needs of the ministry, and thus one of its own should be responsible for the collecting, accounting, and administration of funds. To foster accountability, two persons should normally count the offerings and sign checks. It is generally unwise for the church planters to occupy this position. For obvious reasons this is a sensitive responsibility requiring the highest integrity, trust from the congregation, spiritual maturity, and basic accounting skills. Unfortunately many churches have experienced great heartache and setbacks because of appointing the wrong person to this office. The temptations are many, as one not only has access to financial resources (often in a context of poverty) but often also has knowledge of the personal giving patterns of members. A culturally appropriate form of financial accounting and accountability should be instituted early on. A high level of accountability is not a sign of mistrust but rather is wise protection for the treasurer and the congregation alike.

Meet Regularly for Corporate Worship

Regular gathering for teaching, singing, mutual encouragement, reading of Scripture, celebration of the Lord's Supper, and collection of offerings is a natural expression of being the people of God. This is what we mean when we speak of corporate worship. In the establishing phase these activities become a regular part of the emerging church's corporate life.

When such worship occurs primarily in homes or small groups, we can speak of a house church movement. However, in most settings the cell groups or house churches will want to gather together for larger combined meetings of celebration, even if irregularly. We have a hint of this in the church of Corinth: as in most of the early churches, the Corinthian believers gathered in several homes as house churches, but "the whole church" also came together for worship in one place, presumably in one larger home (1 Cor. 14:23; cf. 1 Cor. 11:20; Rom. 16:23; Gehring 2004, 139, 142).[2]

2. This supports the widely held scholarly view that the primitive church existed in two different church forms: individual and smaller house churches where most activities occurred, and a single larger assembly of combined house churches, "the whole church," which would have met less often (Gehring 2004, 157–59).

Some churches will either by choice or by compulsion[3] remain house church movements with only informal worship times in private homes. Most churches will, however, choose to eventually begin more public worship services. In many contexts public services are a good venue for inviting unbelievers, to evangelize them and introduce them to the Christian community. In some cultures the notion of entering a stranger's home under any circumstances is uncomfortable; thus to attend a church meeting in a private home would be considered bizarre, and the church might be viewed as a dangerous religious sect. More formal public worship services can give the church greater credibility and may be more inviting for outsiders. Public worship services can be advertised and are more accessible to those who have no personal contact with church members. In such contexts a decision may need to be made as to whether such corporate worship is conducted primarily with the needs of believers in view or more evangelistically or "seeker sensitive" so that unbelievers who attend can understand and relate to what is happening. In the New Testament church we see that both concerns, edification of believers (e.g., Eph. 5:19–20) and sensitivity to impressions on unbelievers (e.g., 1 Cor. 14:22–25), were to be kept in view.

The timing and preparations for the launch of regular corporate worship must be considered carefully and prayerfully. Because North American church planting often places great emphasis on the launching of public worship services, numerous resources are available to plan the event. We only summarize here a few key factors to consider as public worship is begun.

When to Start Public Worship

Starting too soon can make people feel that the church is too small, and workers can become overwhelmed with all the energy that must be invested in preparing and leading worship services. Advocates of launching large, with fifty to a hundred or more persons in the launch team, believe that this is important to be attractive to potential visitors and provide a quality worship experience (e.g., Gray 2007, 107–17). This approach involves gaining high public visibility, drawing a large "crowd," and then building a "congregation" and "core" from the crowd—working from a large group to form small ones (e.g., Sylvia 2006). In many settings launching large is not an option, however, because there simply aren't that many believers. This is one reason that we have advocated beginning at the small group level of disciplemaking, building the launch team through evangelism and discipleship, and then moving outward to more public worship. On the other hand, waiting too long to start public worship can sometimes lead to loss of motivation, stagnation, or departures

3. Many if not most rapidly growing house-church movements are in the context of persecution or under legal constraints that limit the freedom of Christians to exist publicly as a formal church.

from the emerging church in favor of an already established one. Usually the best time to start public worship is when the local believers sense a need to do so. However, the church planter may need to temper the enthusiasm of the group and carefully think through all the conditions for the start.

Some cell church advocates suggest that public worship services not begin until at least three healthy cell groups have been formed. The reason for this is that with commencement of weekly Sunday public worship, energy tends to shift to the worship service and away from the cell groups. The life of the cell groups can suffer as a result. Furthermore, if only one or two cell groups exist and one dissolves, then the cell life of the church will be overshadowed.

Particularly when planting a cell-based church, one should consider beginning with quarterly or monthly worship services. With time and as the group's numbers, resources, and abilities grow, the church can offer more frequent services. This has several advantages. First, the primary emphasis of church life remains at the cellular level. Church at the cell level is no less "church" than public worship services are church. Second, the strain on finances, energy, and talent is less if public worship is offered less often. Preparing music, sermons, decoration, a children's program, and so on demands a considerable investment of time and money that can be a great burden on a small church with mostly new believers. Third, a neutral meeting place can be rented on an hourly basis. It is much easier to find and finance a meeting place for quarterly or monthly services than for weekly services. Fourth, even though weekly services are not yet offered, periodic congregational meetings give believers a sense of anticipation and help them assess their ability to conduct weekly services.

For churches that intend to use the worship service as a high-visibility opportunity for evangelism, an attractive program for visitors, it is often recommended to begin with "preview" services. These are occasional services that are offered once or several times prior to the commencement of weekly services. They create a sense of anticipation in both the launch team and the community, and also give the church the opportunity to "practice" worship in a new location, develop skills, and work out logistical issues. Preview services can also be a way to build the core group of the church prior to launching weekly worship services.

Where to Start Public Worship

Determining and finding an appropriate meeting place for public worship is one of the greatest challenges faced at this phase. Especially in urban areas, real estate and rents are expensive. The location, space, and atmosphere of the locale will be of critical importance. When a church plant is first launching public worship, it is normally recommended to rent a meeting space on an

Meeting for Worship in the Gramin Pachin Mandal Church

Paul Pierson describes the contextualized worship of the rapidly growing Gramin Pachin Mandal Church among the Dalits of India.

"The people engage in corporate worship once a week. This can be on any day, since the pastors each cover twelve village congregations, leading worship twice a day. No congregation can be larger than forty families. When they arrive the pastors visit the believers house to house, inviting them to worship. They also do pastoral work and receive offerings at that time. Then the people come together and draw a circle, or mandal. The sanctuary, or worship center can be created in a few minutes. It is built around the Hindu concept of a shrine where God is honored and respected. Even though it is a temporary place set up with a rug thrown on the ground it is considered holy ground and no one stands on it without taking off his or her shoes. This reminds the people of Moses who took off his shoes in the presence of God" (Pierson 2004, 41).

Various symbols are used as didactic aids. Because 95 percent of the members are illiterate, various prayers are memorized. Pastors teach from a fixed curriculum that covers the entire Bible, articles of faith, and the Apostles' Creed. Many of the hymns are Bible texts put to music. Plays have been written that dramatize the Gospels.

hourly basis and avoid long-term rental agreements or purchase of property. A small church plant does not normally have the finances for expensive rents or mortgages, and it would be unwise for an outside agency to provide such funds. To grow commitment and avoid unhealthy dependencies, the offerings of the congregation should cover such ongoing expenses. Renting on an hourly basis allows maximum flexibility at minimum expense. Should the church outgrow the meeting place, or should the location turn out to be disadvantageous, another can be sought and the church is not contractually bound. Owning property may be advantageous later, but many a church has purchased property early along only to regret it when it has proved unsuitable but difficult to sell or enlarge.

There are many creative options when a church is seeking temporary or longer-term meeting places for worship. Typical venues include schools, conference rooms, hotels, community centers, museum or library lecture rooms, restaurants, the cafeteria of a factory or office, or even a pub! Some churches use open public spaces such as parks (see case study 12.1, the Gramin Pachin Mandal Church).

In addition to looking at issues of affordability, when the emerging church is considering the location of a meeting place its leaders should ask the following questions:[4]

4. See also Malphurs 1992, 295–302; Stetzer 2006, 239–50.

- Is there adequate space for the number of persons anticipated, and are there rooms available for children's ministry? Will there be adequate heating, ventilation, sanitary facilities? Will there be the possibility of cooking or meals at the location?

- Are the rooms inviting, attractive, and comfortable to the ministry focus people? Are they too elegant (perhaps uncomfortable for working-class or poor people)? Are they too simple (perhaps unattractive to members of upper classes)?

- Are utilities, furnishings, sound system, and other necessities provided, or must they be purchased and stored?

- Will renovations or structural changes be necessary? If so, how will they be done or paid for?

- Is the location easily accessible via public transportation, or where people own vehicles, is there adequate parking?

- Will usage permits be necessary, or is the venue already legally available for public meetings with the number of anticipated persons? Will neighbors be disturbed by singing, preaching, and traffic on Sunday mornings when they wish they could sleep?

- How important is high or low visibility? In some contexts high visibility can be a good means of advertising, but in other contexts a very public site may attract undue attention and opposition in the community.

- Is the environment potentially disturbing or distracting? Noise from traffic, railroads, or a neighboring factory or disco may make meetings impossible at certain times of day. One church rented space next to an apartment whose residents' television, stereo, flushing toilet, and other sounds were clearly discernible through the wall in the worship room!

- Is the location perceived as safe? High-crime neighborhoods, red-light districts, proximity to a cemetery or slum, and other factors may make the location unattractive. In one case, to enter the church rooms visitors had to pass by a yard where they were greeted by a large, frightening, barking German shepherd.

Clearly the focus people must be constantly kept in mind when these questions are being considered. A meeting place that is suitable for one group may be unacceptable to another. Again, local believers will be the best resource to answer such questions. The cross-cultural worker might miss many subtle nuances that are glaring obstacles to the local people.

Preparing for Public Worship

Beginning public worship usually involves formidable planning and preparation. Much will of course depend on what kinds of ministries will be featured as part of the worship experience. Even very informal worship requires careful preparation. Poorly prepared worship can communicate lack of reverence, give negative impressions, and create unnecessary frustration and stress. In many contexts there is an expectation of high quality and professionalism that should be reflected in the worship experience. The leadership team will need to clarify whether the worship service is to be primarily structured to meet the needs of believers or whether it is also to be attractive and speak to the needs of unbelievers who may attend as visitors. All these matters must be prayerfully taken into account in the planning process.

Typically the following specific matters must be organized: a meeting place must be found; materials such as chairs, pulpit, projector or songbooks, and children's and nursery furniture secured; advertising, publicity, and signage undertaken. Perhaps most importantly, workers must be prepared. These will typically include preachers, worship leaders, and musicians, children's and nursery workers, ushers and greeters, technical workers, and setup and teardown teams. Numerous workbooks, checklists, and literature are available for church planters in Western contexts.[5] Whatever approach one takes, the primary source of materials and finances should be the local believers, using local resources that are contextually appropriate and can be locally replicated when the church is ready to reproduce.

Contextualizing Worship

Few aspects of church life are so affected by culture, for good or for ill, as is worship. Language, music, dress, posture and body language, art and architecture, symbols and rituals, punctuality and length of service, preaching style, level of spontaneity and formality—there is hardly an element of worship that is not somehow culturally conditioned. Cross-cultural church planters must make extra effort to avoid inadvertently introducing unnecessarily foreign, uncomfortable, or even offensive cultural elements into worship. How worship forms can be an obstacle to the gospel is illustrated by this example from a letter written to J. Dudley Woodberry from a West African country (certain terms have been excised to protect local believers):

> Their customs are too different from ours. They keep their shoes on, sit on benches (and close to women at that), and they beat drums in church. We are used to worshipping God by taking our shoes off, sitting and kneeling on mats, and chanting prayers in the Arabic and _____ languages. Also we teach our women at home. If we go to the _____ church, we feel very uncomfortable. What's more, our Muslim friends will not join us. If we worship God the way we are used

5. See for example Logan and Ogne 1991a; Malphurs 1992, 288–309; Stetzer 2006, 251–59; Sylvia 2006, 107–19.

to, other Muslims will be interested. But we will pray in the name of Jesus and teach from the Arabic and _____ Bibles. (Woodberry 1989, 283)

In this context, removing shoes and kneeling on mats is not contrary to biblical teaching (recall Moses) and could be adopted as forms that demonstrate greater reverence. The seating custom could also be adapted to respect cultural norms of propriety so that especially women could feel at ease attending worship. Basic elements of worship can be easily misunderstood, as Darrell Whiteman describes in Melanesia: "Although villagers may not understand the content of the Prayer Book, Bible and Hymn Book, they nevertheless consider them to have *mana* and to be *tabu*. In many villages these are used only in the chapel and left there with the other 'holy paraphernalia' when people leave the chapel and return to their houses" (1983, 379). The Aziana of the Philippines confused celebration of the Lord's Supper with their ceremonial worship of the sun, whereby an animal was sacrificed and its blood and liver were consumed as a ritual of forgiveness (McIlwain 1987, 49).

Biblical contextualization faces the challenge of how to fulfill biblical purposes and values that are in many ways countercultural while at the same time employing culturally appropriate forms and expressions.[6] As the Lutheran World Federation statement on worship and culture notes, "The task of relating worship and culture is ultimately concerned with finding the balance between relevance and authenticity, between particularity and universality, while avoiding eclecticism and/or syncretism" (quoted in Stauffer 1996, 183). The early church adopted many elements of worship from the Jewish synagogue, but it remained subject to the creative leading of the Spirit and adapted to each local situation (cf. Longenecker 2002, 81–86).

In deciding such matters it is essential that local believers have the primary voice. As cultural insiders they are in the best position to discern the meanings of various practices and expressions. They may naturally look to a missionary or other churches for guidance, but walking (with the church planter's help) through the process of discerning biblical purposes and values and how their cultural norms and practices will advance or hinder them is a valuable learning experience that will serve them well long after the church planter has departed. We can comment briefly on just a few cultural factors that must be considered in public worship.

Language. Language is not merely a neutral means of communication but is closely tied to ethnic identity. If various dialects are spoken in a region, a national language or common trade language may be used so as to avoid giving preference to one ethnicity. However, this may exclude women or children who are not fluent in that language. If a Bible translation is not available in the local

6. For general discussions of contextualization in this regard, see Gilliland 1989; Hiebert 1994; Whiteman 1997; Kraft 2005; Moreau 2006.

vernacular, another version must be used and translated. Many languages have different grammatical forms for formal or informal address. Worship leaders and speakers must determine the appropriate level of familiarity.

Music. Whenever possible, indigenous musical styles and instruments should be adopted. However some styles, rhythms, or instruments may be closely associated with non-Christian worship or meanings (such as sensuality or drug usage). Those meanings may be lost to later generations of believers, but for the first generation they can awaken inappropriate responses (cf. Kraft 2005, 255–73). In many parts of the world believers want to adopt Western hymns or contemporary Western praise music. If such music speaks to their hearts and lyrics are translated, it is surely appropriate. However, more indigenous forms of music should also be explored and encouraged, and they can sometimes be blended with more modern musical styles. Ethnomusicology, a growing field of study devoted to the cultural and social aspects of indigenous music, has exciting applications for contextualization of Christian worship. Contextualized Christian music is important for proclamation, evangelism, theology, teaching, confession, and more (cf. King 2005; Neeley 1999).

Body language. Is respect demonstrated by standing, and humility by kneeling or prostrating? Is prayer expressed by folding hands, raising them, or washing them? The meanings of these expressions are not universal. In many cultures dance is an especially rich form of bodily expression and worship, often overlooked by Western missionaries. In the words of Ghanaian John Pobee, sacred dance should be a part of prayer because "Western-influenced prayer is very much an exercise of the mind, while the African . . . has to pray much more with his whole body" (1981, 49). Clothing also communicates in culturally specific ways: formal or informal, amount of exposed skin, head covering, wearing or removing shoes, and so on. The church of Corinth was exhorted to give attention to the cultural propriety of women's dress (1 Cor. 11:5–16).

Time. Ten or eleven o'clock on Sunday morning as a time for worship is not sacred; it was originally chosen as the time after which farmers had milked their cows! Another time might be more appropriate in a different setting. Cultures also have different understandings of punctuality. Regardless of stated time, in many places events begin only after everyone has arrived. The length of the sermon and of the service is also culturally conditioned. In some cultures services must end in time for wives of non-Christians to return home and promptly serve the family noon meal. In other cultures spending the entire day together, including meals, is entirely appropriate.

Art and furniture arrangement. Elements such as seating arrangement (as in the letter Woodberry quoted), decoration and art, a sense of what is an appropriate level of crowdedness or appropriate personal space, quality of furnishings, and meanings of various colors all vary greatly between cultures and are significant factors in what people perceive as appropriate, comfortable, or aesthetically pleasing. Yet their significance is easily overlooked by cross-cultural church planters. Even plants can have symbolic significance (Felde 1998, 46). Drama is familiar in most cultures and can provide a powerful means of communication to be explored in worship.

Symbols and rituals. Mathias Zahniser has argued in *Symbol and Ceremony: Making Disciples across Cultures* (1997) that Western evangelical missionaries have tended to view worship very rationally and underestimate the importance of visual and symbolic expressions in worship. Yet ceremonies and visual symbols are very powerful communicative tools in most cultures, and neglecting them can leave a sense of emptiness in worshipers. Often local customs such as harvest festivals (thanksgiving), marriage customs, and ritual washings can be easily adapted for Christian worship. For example, the famous early morning prayer meetings of Korean Christians, *sae byuk kido*, were adapted from pre-Christian Korean religious practice (Brown 1994). However, such practices can have non-Christian meanings that must be carefully discerned. Paul Hiebert's (1987) four-step process of critical contextualization can be used to contextualize such practices: (1) cultural exegesis of the custom from an insider perspective to discern meanings, (2) biblical exegesis of relevant Bible teachings, (3) critical evaluation of the custom in light of biblical teaching, and (4) creation of a contextualized practice. Some practices will be rejected outright, others will be adopted with little change, but most will require either significant change or the substitution of a new practice to convey Christian meanings and avoid false associations.

Multiply Cell Groups and Cell Leaders

As the church grows, new cell groups will be formed or existing cells will multiply. This presents the need to continually raise up new cell group leaders. This should be done with intentionality. Even if the cells grow numerically, they will not reproduce unless new cell leaders are equipped. After potential new cell leaders are selected, they might receive a basic orientation or initial training, serve as apprentice under an experienced cell leader, and attend a monthly or regular cell leader meeting. Steve Cordelle (2005, 91–93) describes training methods such as the encounter retreat, school of discipleship, and coaching group. Our discussion focuses on initial training, apprenticeship-mentoring, and cell leader meeting.

Identifying Potential Apprentice Cell Leaders

Finding and recruiting apprentice leaders is one of the greatest challenges to cell group multiplication. Several steps can be taken to enlist apprentice leaders. First, don't set the standard too high. On the one hand, participation in leader training and being a positive example are essential and nonnegotiable. On the other hand, every believer is a work in progress, and the perfect leader has yet to be born. If the church is growing rapidly by conversion, most potential leaders will be new believers. This only underscores the next point: provide adequate, practical equipping through mentoring and the leader meeting. If potential leaders understand that they won't be left ill equipped and alone at the task, they will be more likely to volunteer and step out in faith.

Important qualities of potential cell leaders include spiritual maturity, faithfulness, adequate Bible knowledge so as to correct false teaching, ability to inspire confidence in cell members, and some basic interpersonal skills in leading a group. Because cell groups, as the church's basic building blocks, are the primary locus of fellowship, discipleship, spiritual care, and evangelism in the life of the church, a cell group leader should have the goal of exhibiting qualities similar to those of a church elder (1 Tim. 3:1–6; Titus 1:5–9). Indeed gifted and effective cell leaders are often the best candidates for the office of elder. However, a growing church is often largely composed of new believers who are still in the early stages of the character development as Christians and will need to grow into the role under the guidance of a more mature believer.

Initial Training of Cell Leaders

Cell leaders learn mostly from the example of mentors and the practice they receive as apprentices. However, there are three good reasons to launch their training with a training event or retreat. First of all, cell leaders must understand and believe in the core values of a cell church. At the initial training they will also learn the responsibilities of a cell leader, commit to this ministry, and design a growth plan (character and skills) that will help in the mentoring process. An added benefit is that new cell leaders form a bond that will motivate them to work together, help each other, and pray for each other. This helps to launch or strengthen the leadership community.

This initial training might be offered annually in a growing cell church and can take the form of an intensive weekend retreat, a series of four to six workshops, or a combination of the two. At the close of the training the core commitments of a cell group leader should be explained and trainees can pray for each other (see sidebar 12.1).

Mentoring Apprentice Cell Leaders

The most basic approach to equipping new leaders of any kind is personal mentoring or coaching. The concept is simple: an experienced leader identifies a person who has demonstrated potential to be a future cell leader and invites that person to become an apprentice. Often that person will already be a member of the leader's group. As Cordelle reminds us, "The process of leadership development starts with the relational discipleship of a cell group" (2005, 89). One does not begin by making a leader; one begins by making a

Sidebar 12.1

Commitments of Cell Group Leaders

The basic commitments of cell group leaders need to be presented clearly during the training and reviewed periodically. Consider the following eight key commitments to be a fruitful cell group leader:

1. *Pray.* I commit myself to seek God for my life and my cell group daily and to intercede regularly for my cell group's members.
2. *Prepare.* I will prepare my mind and heart for the cell meeting, and I will involve my cell intern(s) in the preparation.
3. *Develop.* I will invest in cell apprentices and rising leaders, encourage them, give them ministry opportunities, and debrief them on their contributions.
4. *Win.* I will build relationships with nonbelievers, serve them, and share Jesus through word and deed. I will also encourage others to do this.
5. *Serve.* I will serve others with my gifts, my knowledge, my energy, my time, my possessions. I will visit and telephone others as God leads me.
6. *Lead.* I will lead the meetings so that the focus is on Jesus, mutual edification is the norm, and newcomers feel welcome.
7. *Edify.* I will encourage cell members to grow in their relationship with God and in service to the church and community.
8. *Stimulate.* With God's help I will lead the cell in outreach and service efforts according to the leading of the Holy Spirit (Wilson 1998, 230).

disciple, which is one of the primary functions of a cell. The leader models effective cell leadership and meets regularly with the apprentice to discuss the nature of leading the group and issues that have arisen, and to pray together. The apprentice is given opportunity to be a coleader of the group or leads the group in the absence of the leader. The leader gives the apprentice constructive feedback about his or her leadership. Over time, the ability of the apprentice to lead and serve the group can be assessed. The trust level of the group members and their response to the apprentice are important indicators of the apprentice's readiness to lead her or his own group. We shall discuss mentoring and coaching in greater detail later in chapter 17.

The Cell Group Leader Meeting

One of the most effective ways to equip apprentice cell leaders and provide ongoing equipping for cell group leaders is holding a regular leader meeting.[7]

7. For an excellent discussion of cell leader equipping, see Carl George's *Prepare Your Church for the Future* (1991, 119–49).

At least monthly the leaders and apprentices meet for approximately two hours for prayer, vision casting, organization, and teaching. The teaching segment should explore practical skills necessary to lead a cell group and take up issues that the groups are currently facing. Topics might include the following:

- methods of Bible study and interpretation
- formulating discussion questions and leading a Bible discussion
- visitation of sick or otherwise needy cell group members
- evangelism in the cell group
- prayer in the cell group
- conflict resolution
- dealing with dominant or difficult personalities
- balancing the personal life of the cell group leader
- stimulating the spiritual growth of cell group members
- helping cell group members identify and use their spiritual gifts
- assessing the quality and health of one's cell group
- reproducing and forming a new cell group

Apprentices attending the leader meeting will not only receive instruction but come to better understand what is entailed in cell group leadership.

Multiplying Cells

As a cell group grows and an apprentice matures to the point of being able to lead a new group, the time for reproducing a new cell is near. However, birthing a new group out of an existing one is not always easy. In a healthy cell group, friendships have grown and trust has been established. Understandably members will want to remain together and not divide to begin two groups. This is a universal challenge faced even in China, where house churches are multiplying at an unprecedented rate. This challenge can be overcome by emphasizing that first and foremost the ultimate goal is not that members of the cell be comfortable and happy together; the foremost goal is making disciples—more disciples and better disciples. This will entail growth through evangelism to the point that the group will eventually become too large to retain the intimacy and accountability necessary for discipleship.

Often it is better for a cell group not to divide half and half (half the group members departing to form a new group, the other half remaining) but rather to send or commission three or four group members as a missional team to establish a new group. The advantage is that the relationships of the existing group are not as severely severed and the new group has a greater missional-evangelistic thrust. Because the new group is smaller, its task will be more clearly evangelistic, and members will be more motivated to recruit, disciple, and integrate new persons into the group.

Formulate Values and a Long-Term Strategic Plan for Ministry

As the church begins to grow and expand ministries, determining the core values of the church, formulating a vision statement, and defining the church's distinctives and a long-term strategic plan will become important. Early in the preparing phase an initial strategy will have been formulated. But as the church plant progresses, that strategy will need to be refined and adapted to the realities experienced in the launching of the church plant. At this point local believers must have a voice in that process, to ensure that they own the vision, provide an insider perspective, understand the strategy, and are committed to its execution. The same can be said regarding the core values of the church. To facilitate this process, it can be helpful to lead a series of Bible studies on evangelism, mission, and the church. Often a retreat setting is ideal to bring the core group together for a time of concerted and undistracted prayer and planning to discern the course that the church should take.

A strategic ministry plan should address points such as these:

- effective and affordable evangelistic methods for reaching the focus people
- methods of discipleship and assimilation of new persons into the fellowship
- how to equip and mobilize workers for various ministries
- church structures such as cell/celebration or house church, leadership structures, and children's ministries
- style of worship
- a philosophy of cell multiplication
- potential locations for daughter churches or pioneer church plants

Several large North American churches have well-known strategic ministry plans:

- Willow Creek Community Church's seven-step philosophy: relationship, verbal witness, weekend service, New Community, small group, service involvement, and stewardship
- Saddleback Church's purpose-driven "CLASS Strategy": leading people from community to congregation to commitment to core through a series of seminars

- Community Christian Church in Naperville's "Followership": celebrate, connect, contribute

These ministry plans are well thought out, delineating a process of leading people to faith and moving them to greater levels of commitment and service. Specific programs, services, events, and benchmarks are usually spelled out and very intentionally designed to promote the growth process, as in a well-conceived business plan. Often diagrams help communicate the process. Most such plans are easy for the average congregant to grasp, seeing where he or she is in the process and how to contribute to help others grow. Those seeking guidance in the strategic planning process should consult works such as Aubrey Malphurs's *Advanced Strategic Planning: A New Model for Church and Ministry Leaders* (2005). But the process at this point needn't be overly complicated.

Such refined ministry plans may seem unnecessary for house churches or simple church structures. But every church should be clear about how it carries out the disciplemaking process in its context—be it a simple one-on-one approach or a highly programmed, professional approach. Table 12.1, "The Disciplemaking Church," lays out a strategic ministry planning aid that has been used in several church plants in Germany. Based on Matthew 28:19–20, the leadership team or core group can consider the various steps of conversion, discipleship, service, and spiritual growth, and the values inherent in each step. The first steps have as a primary goal leading people to know Christ; the following steps seek to help them glorify Christ as they live for him and become involved in spiritual growth and service. Then they ask what activities or programs can contribute to leading people to the next level of becoming a devoted follower of Jesus Christ. A church may be tempted to adopt a variety of programs or activities that leaders have observed in other churches. But the team should adopt only those ministries and activities that will contribute to the overall purposes of the church, in particular the making of disciples.

At this point in the church's development, many of the elements of such a strategic plan may not yet be realized. But it is important to have the big picture of the goal and how over the course of time that goal is to be attained. In the process of carrying out the plan there will be unexpected developments and changes will be necessary; thus plans must be held with an open hand and remain flexible.

Pitfalls during the Establishing Phase

There are several dangers to which planters should be alert during this phase. In a sense the DNA of the church is being set: habits established, patterns formed,

Table 12.1

The Disciplemaking Church

The Command	The Method	The Step	The Target	The Key Idea	The Goal	The Values	The Activities
Make disciples of all nations	Go . . .	Build relationships	Indifferent	Love	Knowing God	Relevance, relationships, meeting needs, trust, seeking the lost, credibility, service, "a Greek to the Greeks"	
		Communicate the gospel	Interested	Evangelism		Biblical proclamation, finding the lost, every Christian a witness	
	Baptizing them . . .	Lead to repentance and faith in Christ	Seekers			Necessity of a personal decision	
		Follow up in faith and obedience	New believers	Discipleship	Glorifying God	Following Christ, practical faith and obedience, truth, personal renewal, Christian disciplines	
	Teaching them to obey everything that I commanded you	Enfold into the church	Disciples	Fellowship		Commitment, faithfulness, unity, spiritual family	
		Train to serve	Members	Service		Spiritual gifts, responsibility, servanthood, stewardship of time, talent, and resources	
		Promote further spiritual growth	Servants	Edification		Sanctification, increasingly honoring God, Christlikeness	

and models of ministry launched that will become determinative for the future development of the church and increasingly difficult to change later.

Failure to Exercise Church Discipline

Exercising church discipline is never a happy task, but church planters can be particularly tempted to avoid it because the nascent church is small and the loss of even one individual can seemingly set back progress. But discipline will often be necessary if the health of the church is to be maintained. Of course new believers (as well as old) come into the church with an array of sinful attitudes, behaviors, and habits that won't be resolved overnight. One will need much wisdom in determining when discipline is called for. But those who after counsel and exhortation stubbornly persist in behavior dishonoring to God, discrediting to the church, and harmful to themselves and others will eventually need to be disciplined.

In the words of Ken Baker, "The entire realm of church discipline is generally a mine-strewn land where trespassers must beware" (2005, 339). This is especially so in cross-cultural ministry situations where the church planter is unfamiliar with the subtleties of cultural norms, values of honor and shame, and local strategies for conflict resolution. In collectivistic cultures, disciplining one member can result in the loss of entire extended families. Nevertheless, compromise here can have devastating consequences. Before situations of apparent entrenched sin arise, planters will need to study relevant biblical texts[8] with the local leaders and settle on a course of disciplinary action that is appropriate to the culture while maintaining biblical norms and goals. First Thessalonians 5:14 is perhaps the best summary: "We urge you, brothers, warn those who are idle, encourage the timid, help the weak, be patient with everyone."

Church Planters Adopting a Pastoral Rather Than Empowering Role

As the fellowship of believers takes on the life of a congregation, there will be a temptation for the church planters to move into a pastoral and nurturing role. There are many new believers with many personal needs. One must rightly be concerned with the continued growth and maturity of these believers, who will become core of the church, and some its leaders. Further, as many new ministries are launched, church planters will be tempted to provide all the preaching, teaching, and organizational leadership. Especially if the church-planting team is composed of theologically trained and experienced workers, new believers will naturally look to them to staff the various ministries.

But if the apostolic model is being adopted, rather than believers looking to the church planters for teaching, administration, and nurture, the focus

8. For example, Matthew 18:15–18; 1 Corinthians 5:1–5; 2 Corinthians 2:5–11; Galatians 6:1; 1 Timothy 5:19–20.

must be more on the equipping of local believers to meet those needs. Here is where the critical shift in church planter role from motor and model to *mobilizer* and *mentor* must take place. Gradually the church planters are less and less the doers of frontline ministry and increasingly the equippers behind the scenes, empowering local believers to be those doers. Ministry skills still need to be modeled, especially new skills needed for new ministries, but the planters should no longer be the primary motor of those ministries.

Loss of Evangelistic Thrust

An additional danger is a loss of evangelistic momentum as more energy is invested in bringing to maturity the believers already present. It is natural for a church to go through a period of evangelistic harvest followed by a period of slower growth during which new believers are discipled. But if the young congregation remains permanently in a maturing mode, growth will stagnate, and the congregation will begin to perceive itself not as a church on a mission but as an institution that exists to meet the needs of its members. This is one reason that after initial growth many church plants plateau with only a few dozen members.

Loss of Focus and Overcommitment

There is a temptation for the young emerging church to take on too many ministries and become overwhelmed. The expansion of ministries in new directions occurs more in the next phase of structuring. During this phase, as the church is only emerging, energies must be focused on those ministries that are essential. This is not to suggest that no works of compassion are initiated, but they must be reasonable and limited in scope so as not to diffuse the energies of the emerging church in too many different directions.

Unwise Use of Outside Resources

As we have argued throughout this book, a key to long-term church multiplication is the ability to plant churches using locally available resources and locally sustainable structures. When the church comes to the point of offering regular public worship services, there is often a great need for materials such as projectors, furniture, and room renovations, and need to increase the budget to cover ongoing expenses such as rent, utilities, printing, advertising, and children's curriculum. While outside resources may to a limited extent assist, the primary provision for ministry must originate with the local believers. In most cases this will be a test of faith. But church members have opportunity to demonstrate commitment to the effort, create ownership, exercise faith, and set a pattern of locally driven church planting that is not dependent on outside resources. In chapter 18 we will offer detailed guidelines for the wise use of outside resources in church planting. The current phase, however, is perhaps the most critical time to build the church ministry on the basis of *local* resources, because this is probably the first time that significant financial and other resources become critical to the advancement of the church plant.

During the establishing phase many exciting developments take place: the new community takes on its unique character and mission, local leaders emerge, the body of believers identifies more clearly with the culture, and the shift from external to insider direction takes a major leap forward. Members of the apostolic church-planting team will rejoice as they empower and release disciples and workers, remembering that this is why they were sent.

13

Structuring

Expanding and Empowering

During the establishment phase of the church plant, the group began to take shape as a congregation, functioning as the body of Christ with increasing mutual ministry, regular worship, a provisional leadership team, and equipped workers. As the church moves into the structuring phase—and this is a gradual transition—ministries are expanded and members are empowered for greater responsibility and service in the church and community. The church grows in its kingdom impact, calls and recognizes its spiritual leaders, and establishes formal legal status. As God blesses the church with growth, new structures will need to be created to adapt, deal with the challenges that growth brings, and continue to progress in effective ministry. At this time the traditional "three selves" of indigeneity should be attained: local believers are evangelizing and making disciples (self-propagating), local believers exercise full spiritual leadership (self-governing), and the church is sustained on the basis of local resources and giving (self-supporting). During the previous phase the church should have been well on the way toward reaching these goals, but now they are essential as the church positions itself to reproduce and the church-planting team begins to disengage.

In some regards house-church movements might seem to have no need for the structuring phase. Because by nature house churches remain small, they can more quickly reproduce and have less need for programming and structure that larger, more traditional churches need as they grow. However, even house church movements need structures to facilitate development and equipping of

267

leaders, networking between house churches, specialized ministries to people with special needs, and cooperative efforts in compassion and service ministries that are too involved for a single house church to undertake alone. As we shall see below, even the small house-sized congregations of the New Testament encountered growth pains that required new structures and ministries.

Overview of Phase

Biblical Examples

Acts 6:1–6: The office of deacon is created in the Jerusalem church to care for congregational needs

Acts 14:23: Paul and Barnabas appoint elders in the churches that they had planted, committing them to the Lord

Pastoral Epistles: Issues of church leadership and organization as these churches mature, including the appointment of elders and deacons and their qualifications (1 Tim. 3:1–13; Titus 1:5–9), honoring them and dealing with accusations against them (1 Tim. 5:17–20), and caring for widows and maintaining lists of those receiving church assistance (1 Tim. 5:3–16)

Revelation 2–3: Jesus examines and assesses the seven churches of Asia Minor

Key Steps

1. Formally call leaders and fully entrust responsibility to them
2. Initiate new ministries and structures to meet needs
3. Multiply workers by training leaders to train others
4. Assimilate new believers and visitors
5. Evaluate church development and health
6. Organize the church legally
7. Attain full financial autonomy

Critical Issues

1. Multiplication of workers
2. Need-oriented ministries
3. Preparing the congregation for growth

Formally Call Leaders and Fully Entrust Responsibility to Them

Though some today decry any established church leadership or offices as contrary to a spirit of egalitarianism, such an approach is both naive and unbiblical. Paul calls the church to "respect those who work hard among you, who are over you in the Lord and who admonish you" (1 Thess. 5:12). God appoints in the church "those able to help others, those with gifts of administration" (1 Cor. 12:28). The church in Philippi had overseers and deacons (Phil. 1:1). The author of Hebrews exhorts, "Obey your leaders and submit to their authority. They keep watch over you as men who must give an account. Obey them so that their work will be a joy, not a burden, for that would be of no advantage to you" (Heb. 13:17).

Formally appointing spiritually mature leaders is one of the most important signs that a church has matured and been "planted," which enables the church-planting team to disengage. Local elders are to become responsible for the ongoing spiritual care, teaching, and guidance of the church after the departure of the apostolic missionary (Acts 20:28–31; 1 Pet. 5:1–4). When on the first missionary journey Paul and Barnabas appointed elders in the churches of south Galatia, these churches were no more than two years old (Acts 14:23; Schnabel 2008, 77). Yet Barnabas and Paul committed the believers to the Lord and departed. The work there was then considered "completed" (Acts 14:26). Though Paul later wrote the letter of Galatians to these churches and strengthened them during another visit (Acts 16:1–5), they were clearly no longer under direct missionary care. Similarly, upon his departure from Ephesus after over two years of ministry, Paul commends the Ephesian elders to the Lord noting that he will not see them again (Acts 20:25–32). In contrast, the work in Crete was considered "unfinished" because elders had not yet been appointed (Titus 1:5). Thus the appointment of local elders is a significant milestone in the planting of a church, making the disengagement of the apostolic missionary possible.

This raises a crucial question: how mature and qualified must local leaders be before the church planter can depart? On the one hand we are struck by Paul's willingness to trust the work of the Spirit in these relatively new converts as they took responsibility for the spiritual care of the newly planted churches. Possibly these leaders were Jewish believers already well versed in the Old Testament, though this viewpoint is conjecture since most commentators believe that these churches were composed predominantly of Gentile believers (e.g., George 1994, 44; Guthrie 1973, 9). As noted above, elders had been appointed in the Ephesian church after Paul's ministry of just over two years. On the other hand, at least eight years later[1] Paul instructs Timothy that an elder in the church of Ephesus must not be "a recent convert, or he may become conceited and fall under the same judgment as the devil" (1 Tim. 3:6). *New* is thus a relative term. In the very young church, growth in character, faithfulness, obedience, and the ability to shepherd God's flock will be essential. As the church grows in both size and maturity, qualifications and standards for elders should also increase.

The decision of when and whom to appoint as leaders should not be made lightly but with much prayer and fasting (Acts 14:23). Richard Hibbert (2008) studied a church-planting movement among the Millet people[2] of Bulgaria that began in the late 1980s and by the early 1990s had grown to an estimated ten thousand believers. However, the movement stagnated by the end of the 1990s, with attendance in the nearly one hundred churches dropping to just over six thousand. Hibbert interviewed numerous defectors and discovered

1. The church in Ephesus was planted in AD 51 (Schnabel 2008, 107), and Paul wrote the Pastoral Epistles sometime after AD 60 (Kelley 1963, 78).
2. The Millet are Turkish-speaking Roma and self-identify as Muslims.

that apart from migration to Western Europe, the most often cited reason for leaving the church was not reversion to Islam but problems related to church leaders: conflict, misuse of power, poor pastoral care, and the like. The study underlines the importance of developing and selecting the right people for church leadership. Especially in rapidly growing movements with mostly new believers, the question of leadership cannot be ignored.

At the same time, we need to remember that historically missionaries have too often failed to entrust local believers with leadership because they have believed that the local believers are seemingly never mature enough to assume full responsibility. Ultimately this leads to unhealthy missionary dominance, and the church planter remains indefinitely in one location, unable to pioneer new locations or mobilize local believers for mission. Knowing whom, when, and how to empower is thus of critical importance and must be accompanied by much prayer and spiritual discernment. We shall return to the question of how leaders are prepared and selected below under "Assimilation," and further in chapter 17.

Initiate New Ministries and Structures to Meet Needs

Church growth brings not only joy but also new challenges and growth pains. A church that fails to adapt to changing circumstances and needs will eventually either stagnate or face crisis. As a church grows it moves from being a largely face-to-face, family-like community to a larger group with diverse needs and subcultures and attenders who are more peripheral to the life of the church. Many church plants fail to adapt to these needs, continuing ministry as it has always been. This leads to frustration and stagnation and ultimately blocks healthy reproduction.

One of the earliest instances of a growing church's need to structure to meet new needs is found in Acts 6 in the Jerusalem church, which had experienced explosive growth. Jews considered care for widows a high moral obligation, and the early church adopted this concern. However, a problem arose when Greek-speaking Hellenistic widows complained of being neglected at the distribution of food, feeling that Aramaic-speaking Hebraic widows were being given preference. This reflected long-standing tensions between Hebrew and Hellenistic Jews in the general Jewish community (Longenecker 1981, 329). How common it is that general societal conflicts are also present in the church. The challenge here involved both an ethnic conflict and the absence of a structure to ensure fair distribution. Furthermore, until this point the apostles had apparently been responsible for overseeing the food distribution in addition to all their other ministry responsibilities in the burgeoning church. The solution was found in creating a whole new ministry team (in modern parlance), the deacons. As Richard Longenecker summarizes, "Luke's narrative here suggests that to be fully biblical is to be constantly engaged in adapting traditional methods and structures to meet existing situations, both for the sake of the welfare of the whole church and for the outreach of the gospel" (1981, 331).

This solution resolved several challenges and is especially instructive for the church in all times and places. First, it took the problem seriously and resolved the immediate issue of fair food distribution among the widows. Church conflicts cannot be ignored or minimized but should be taken seriously and dealt with promptly. Second, ethnic tensions were addressed by the appointing of seven deacons who all had Greek names (Acts 6:5). Thus those who felt discriminated against were represented among the deacons. Minority parties or groups must not be marginalized—indeed extra effort may be called for to ensure their inclusion in the total life of the church. Third, new leaders (the deacons) were empowered and released for ministry; this expanded the base of workers and demonstrated that the apostles and elders were not the only ones qualified for service. Fourth, the manner of selection of the deacons, though not spelled out in detail, is instructive. It defined the qualifications, included the participation and the approval of the congregation, and involved a public laying on of hands (vv. 3–4, 6). In this way a precedent was established for including the congregation in resolving problems and appointing people to ministry in a publicly recognized and approved manner. Fifth, by delegating this responsibility, the Twelve were able to devote themselves to the ministry that was their primary calling and gifting: prayer and the Word of God (v. 4). Leaders can easily become overwhelmed with the needs of a growing church and must delegate ministry to guard their priorities. Sixth, the church demonstrated that spiritual, physical, and social needs are to be taken seriously within the total life and ministry of the church. New structures, identification of spiritual gifts, and the creation of an office were all necessary to adequately address these various needs. Finally, the church continued to grow rapidly (v. 7). It is no accident that Luke includes a statement regarding the spread of the Word and growth of the church at this point in the narrative. Unresolved conflict and overworked and distracted leaders in the church would surely have hindered growth. When churches deal with challenges and crises appropriately—which often includes the creation of new structures and delegation of ministry—God causes the church to prosper.

As a church grows, needs that were previously met on an individual case-by-case basis must be dealt with in a more systematic manner. We see this in the care of widows in the church of Ephesus (1 Tim. 5:3–16). Church resources were no doubt limited, and thus a need arose to determine who was genuinely worthy of receiving aid and who might be provided for in other ways. J. N. D. Kelley comments, "At Ephesus there is now an officially recognized order of widows, with definite conditions of entry which Paul, it appears, wants stringently observed, and definite duties for those on the roll to perform" (1963,

112). In other words, as the church grows, new ministries and structures must be created to fairly and adequately meet personal and corporate needs.

Church planters and leaders must stay attuned to needs in the community as the church grows. Much like in the church of the New Testament, in some contexts the care of widows and orphans, the hungry and unemployed, and others without the means to adequately provide for themselves and their families will constitute the most pressing need. Later, in chapter 19, we will discuss in detail the launching of ministries of compassion and social transformation. It is during the structuring phase of the church plant that such ministries are launched or significantly expanded.

Another need encountered in nearly every church plant is the personal nurture and counseling of new believers who enter the church with emotional wounds, broken relationships, addictions, and traumatic experiences. Creating counseling ministries and equipping for them may become a priority to strengthen and bring healing to such persons. Often special needs groups are launched to minister to them. Also, ministry geared to particular age or interest groups, youth, single parents, or senior adults, may be initiated.

Often during this phase a church may begin outreach to unreached or underserved ethnic groups or subcultures in the community, perhaps as God raises up a person in the church with a particular vision and concern to reach out to such a group. For example, a member of a small church in Monrovia, Liberia, became concerned about former child soldiers who, now grown, had become street criminals and drug addicts. He began visiting them and eventually started regular afternoon street worship services for them right in the public marketplace, which was closed on Sundays. If the special needs group speaks a foreign language, a person fluent in that language will normally be necessary to give leadership to the outreach. Such ministries can serve as a local introduction to cross-cultural mission, stimulating the church to take a larger role in raising up and sending missionaries. But new ministries should not be expanded beyond the availability of motivated workers to take up the responsibility. If the church planter has a vision for a new ministry, that vision must be compellingly communicated, the ministry should not be initiated until local persons are ready to take ownership, and the full burden must not lie solely on the shoulders of the church planter.

Sometimes local believers will recognize a need, such as for children's ministry, but assume that meeting the need is the responsibility of the church planter or a team member. They tend to assume that the church planter is in full-time ministry, has the time, and is trained for such tasks. If an apostolic approach has been adopted, however, the church planters must resist such assumptions. They should offer to train and assist local believers in launching ministries but should not become fully responsible. If the church planter becomes fully responsible, then she or he will face the challenge later of finding someone to assume that ministry. Also, if local believers discover that if they wait long enough the church planters will eventually take on the ministry, they have learned how to avoid ministry. Resisting the urge to just do the needed job will at times require great patience on the part of the church planters. But if all new ministries are required to be the responsibility of local believers, they will not become dependent on the planters, and the challenge of phase-out will be lessened. Leaders for ministries are raised up *with* the initiation of ministries, rather than at a later time when the ministry has grown and local believers feel inadequate to the task. The ministry does not need to be "handed over" to local believers, because they have been the primary leaders all along.

Multiply Workers by Training Leaders to Train Others

To achieve long-term church reproduction and ultimately multiplication, it is not enough that the church planters reproduce themselves in local believers through mentoring and equipping. Real multiplication occurs when workers trained by the planters in turn train others. Paul instructs Timothy, "And the things you have heard me say in the presence of many witnesses entrust to reliable men who will also be qualified to teach others" (2 Tim. 2:2). Four generations of leaders are mentioned in this verse: (1) Paul to (2) Timothy to (3) faithful people to (4) those they are able to teach. This means that the church planter increasingly transitions from motor and model to mobilizer and mentor, and here to *multiplier*. As a multiplier the planter is involved less and less in direct "frontline" ministry and more and more in training others how to train others.

During the establishing phase, cell group leaders should have been taught how to mentor new apprentice cell leaders (as described in chapter 12). The same principle must now be applied to all areas and at every level of ministry. For example, ministry team leaders must learn to recruit and train new team members and leaders. An apostolic approach to church planting seeks from the outset to equip local believers to provide leadership and pastoral care for the emerging church. This means that both the manner of ministry and the methods of equipping must be easily reproduced or imitated by local believers. If they are illiterate or semiliterate, the planter will need to use methods that are not dependent on books and written sources until their literacy level can be increased. If local believers are relatively uneducated, planters will need to preach and teach in simple terms that they will understand and are able to explain to others. Because church planters are often seminary trained, they may be tempted to unwittingly set such a high standard of ministry that local believers feel that they can never measure up. If believers have access to a Bible dictionary or concordance, they can be taught how to use such tools. Sermons should make transparent that sources of information are sources also available to local leaders. In this way ministry is modeled in a reproducible manner.

Assimilate New Believers and Visitors

At the end of chapter 11 we briefly discussed the problem of attrition and reasons for it. Here we will see how intentional and healthy integration of new believers can lead to a new generation of workers and leaders. When the church is small, newcomers are easily identified and assimilated, but as the church grows such assimilation becomes more difficult. A key to sustained growth is the ability of the church not only to reach new people for Christ but to disciple them and assimilate them into the life of the larger congregation. House churches may simply divide as the group becomes too large to meet in one home. But larger congregations may find it quite hard to adapt to growth. Ideally cell groups offer a continuing structure for intimate fellowship and nurture which the congregation can no longer offer in large meetings. Yet if newcomers do not enter the church via small groups, it cannot be assumed that they will easily find their way into small groups.

Here many churches fail to adapt to the changing situation, resulting in growth stagnation, shortage of workers to bear the increasing ministry load, and frustration and burnout among those who have been bearing that load and serving in the church plant from the start. This is one reason that many church plants plateau in growth or face a leadership crisis after about five years.

Growing congregations typically go through three developmental stages that can lead to this problem, as illustrated in figure 13.1. During the launch

Figure 13.1
Assimilation and Unhealthy Development

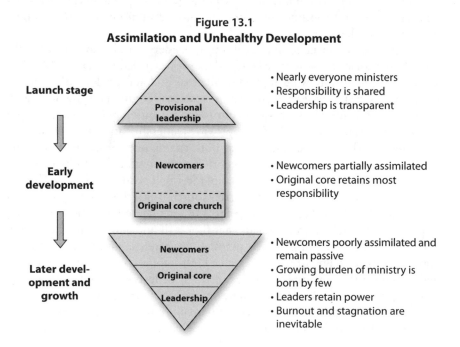

stage the church is small, interactions are face to face, decisions are shared, leadership is provisional and transparent, motivation and energy are high. When new persons enter the church, they are immediately noticed. Everyone is eager for the church to grow; thus members are generally quick to assimilate newcomers into existing relationships. Often the newcomers already have personal relationships with existing members. Because the church is small, responsibilities are shared, and there are few passive members. This makes for a broad base of service and a shared ministry load. There is plenty of energy and manpower to be outward focused, and minimal energy is required for the internal life of the church.

If the church continues to grow, the situation gradually changes. The workload of ministry increases with an increased number of people and needs. By this time the leadership has become more formalized. The original core group of the church continues to bear the weight of most ministries. The number of persons not serving, mostly newcomers, begins to grow. As people become busier, newcomers are only partially assimilated into the church.

If growth continues, the church moves into a critical stage. Newcomers are poorly assimilated and are slow to take responsibility; anonymity and passivity become problems. The original core group continues to carry a now unbearable weight of ministry, as needs have continued to grow but the number of workers has not. The leadership and service base is now too narrow to sustain the growth of the church. This leads to burnout on the part of the workers and leaders, and the leadership base becomes even narrower. Ironically, the original core tends to continue to retain power: church is "their" church, born from "their" vision and grown as a result of "their" hard labors. Why should newcomers have an equal voice?

A few telltale signs indicate that the church is approaching a crisis of assimilation. One hears older members say things like "Remember when we all knew each other by name? We were like a big family," or "I feel like a stranger in my own church." Whether these statements are made aloud or not, newcomers pick up the message that they are unwelcome and are disturbing a happy little family. Another sign is the resignation of workers and leaders from positions of responsibility as the weight of serving and the frustration become unbearable. Church growth is no longer quite so exciting. Leaders may begin to feel resentment that newer members are not serving as sacrificially as they should. This in turn sends another message to newcomers, that serving in this church lacks joy and may result in burnout. Newcomers begin to think, "If this is what serving in the church leads to, count me out!" Workers become harder to recruit, the dwindling number of workers become more stressed, and the vicious cycle continues. We have seen church plants come to a complete standstill when all the early leaders have left or resigned and no new leaders whatsoever are willing to serve.

This scenario is not inevitable. Alternatives exist, but they must be initiated before the crisis sets in. One way this problem can be avoided is illustrated in figure 13.2. As the church grows, new believers are assimilated via two routes. One is by becoming part of a cell group, where church is experienced as a small personal family. The other is by recruitment into ministry teams. Sometimes the cell group is responsible for a ministry and the two coincide. In both cases, assimilation is not a matter of programs but of *relationships*.[3] The existing members must intentionally welcome and build relationships with newcomers. Sometimes newcomers enter the church via an evangelistic cell group; in this case personal relationships already exist. But especially in attractional churches, newcomers may first attend a larger worship service or meeting where they have no personal relationships, and they must be intentionally contacted and assimilated. This means mobilizing cell groups to be open to receive new persons and actively inviting them. Cell group leaders need to be instructed in how to appropriately recruit new members from among newcomers. Not only are personal relationships formed in the cell group, leading to a bond with the larger church, but the cell group is the ideal venue in which to begin informally discovering and using one's spiritual gifts. Those with leadership gifts and skills will gradually emerge, and they in turn become potential leaders of cell groups or other ministries. Ministry teams are a similar way to assimilate newcomers and involve them in the life of the church. Newer attenders can become involved in helping roles of low responsibility, and as they demonstrate giftedness and faithfulness they can grow into leadership roles.

One of the challenges that growing churches face is how to select leaders at the highest level, such as elders. Part of the problem is that there are often few midlevel opportunities to develop leadership skills and evidence potential and suitability for higher levels of leadership. As new believers develop personal relationships in cell groups or in "entry-level" opportunities for serving, they can grow into leadership, confirm their gifts and faithfulness, and be entrusted with higher levels of responsibility. We have found that those who have demonstrated pastoral and teaching gifts at the level of leading a cell group, winning the love and trust of their group members, are usually the best candidates for the office of elder. If one can faithfully shepherd a small group or ministry team, one will likely be suitable for a shepherding role in the church as a whole. One of the biggest mistakes a church can make is to appoint unproven members to leadership.

3. Win Arn believes, on the basis of data on churches in North America, that "each new convert or new member should be able to identify at least seven friends in the church within the first six months. Friendships appear to be the strongest bond in cementing new converts or members to their congregation" (1986, 97). A figure like "seven friends within six months" is highly subjective and culturally conditioned but nevertheless points to the importance of significant and multiple relationships for assimilation.

Figure 13.2
Assimilation and Healthy Development

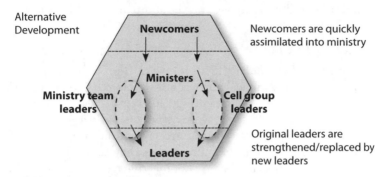

The path to leadership can be facilitated by making the leadership team accessible and their work transparent. For example, ministry cell group and team leaders can be invited to occasionally attend elder board meetings. Not only can they report on the progress and needs of their ministries, but they will see firsthand the ministry of the elders.

Finally, the congregation must continually be reminded of the vision of the church to make more and stronger disciples. Fostering a nostalgic attitude—"remember the good old days when the church was small"—is one of the best ways to keep the church small. Numerical growth is rather to be welcomed, and it will be if means are developed to retain the personal character of the church through small groups and through opening various avenues to service to newcomers. Burnout by workers can also be prevented by allowing them leave or sabbaticals, rotating workers, delegating and resisting controlling, and welcoming new ideas from newcomers.

Evaluate Church Development and Health

As a church grows, it experiences the excitement of seeing God touch lives and communities. But there can also be chaos! The church may find itself trying to catch up in developing new small groups and ministries to address the growing needs and opportunities. Evaluation should not be seen as a technique but as a life skill and a spiritual activity. The Bible speaks of using the Word as a mirror and making changes based on what God shows us (James 1:22–24) and of calculating before we start a task whether we can finish it (Luke 14:28–30). We are invited to turn to God for wisdom (James 1:4–6). The best evaluation has several characteristics:

- ongoing—conducted regularly with a spirit of always trying to improve
- corporate—conducted by a diverse group of qualified people

- specific—conducted in such a way that specific improvement can be made
- productive—followed up with prayer and plans to address key issues

Congregational Health

At this point it is particularly critical for the church, beginning with the leaders, to reexamine the biblical purposes of the church and discern whether the various activities are in alignment with these purposes, priorities are in place, and ministries are effective. More activity is not necessarily better activity. Too many programs can distract from essential programs. Thus the church must give direction to the ministries as they develop and must have courage to cut back ministries that are not meeting real needs, are ineffective, or are consuming so much time and resources that more essential ministries are suffering.

If the church has adopted "The Disciplemaking Church" plan for ministry (chapter 12), then that tool can be used to assess the church's overall development. This can be done by the leadership team, but it may also be helpful to include a wider circle of ministry team leaders in the process, going through each point and discerning how well the church is succeeding. Today many other assessment tools are available to aid churches in this process. Table 13.1 summarizes and compares indicators from five such sources. *Natural Church Development* (Schwarz 1996) is one of the most widely used tools and has been translated into many different languages. However, just as people living in different parts of the world face different health hazards (frostbite is not a problem in the tropics, and malaria is not a problem in the Arctic), so too churches in different parts of the world face different health hazards. These differences are related to the differing cultural, spiritual, and political environments. Churches can be encouraged to study for themselves Bible passages such as Acts 2, Ephesians 4, and Revelation 2–3 and then make their own list of church health indicators. They can prioritize these in light of the local spiritual health hazards.

The processes by which evaluation is undertaken will vary widely depending on the local culture, size of the church, and other factors. When the church is small, informal discussions of core values and goals may be adequate. As the church grows, initial evaluation may be undertaken by the leaders, and then the congregation may be included at meetings where open discussion can take place. Sometimes a retreat weekend allows for more a relaxed atmosphere where there is adequate time for prayer, Bible study, and discussion. One church plant in Munich conducted semiannual assessment retreats—initially including all members and then, as the church grew, including only the core workers and leaders. This became a time not only to evaluate the past development of the church but also to consider future goals. A church plant in Mexico City found

Table 13.1
Indicators of Church Health, Quality, and Effectiveness

Macchia 1999	EFCA n.d.	Dever 2000	NCD (Schwarz 1996)	Barna 1999
God-exalting worship	Spirit-filled worship		Inspiring worship	Genuine worship
Spiritual disciplines	Passionate spirituality		Passionate spirituality	
Learning and growing in community	Intentional disciplemaking	Concern for discipleship and growth	Holistic small groups	
Loving and caring relationships	Loving relationships		Loving relationships	Lasting, significant relationships
Servant-leadership development	Leadership multiplication	Biblical church leadership	Empowering leadership	Leader directed
Outward focus	Fruitful evangelism	Biblical understanding of evangelism	Need-oriented evangelism	Strategic evangelism
		Biblical understanding of conversion		
Stewardship and generosity	Stewardship of resources			Holistic stewardship
	Great Commission driven		Functional structures	Structure for impact
	Centrality of God's Word	The gospel		Systematic theological growth
		Biblical theology		
		Expositional preaching		
Networking with the body of Christ				
Wise administration and accountability				
	Church planting			
		Biblical understanding of church membership		
		Biblical church discipline		
			Gift-oriented ministry	
				Serving the community
				Equipping the family

that when decisions about important matters needed to be made, it was best to present the issues and take questions at one congregational meeting and delay decision making until a later congregational meeting. Although two meetings were required, more people participated, the meetings were less divisive, and there was a greater sense of ownership of the decisions.

Evaluation, tools, and checklists cannot produce church health any more than a thermometer can produce a healthy person. But they can be helpful in diagnosing health problems. The key to being a healthy church is having a healthy relationship with Jesus. As Jesus taught, "Remain in me, and I will remain in you. No branch can bear fruit by itself; it must remain in the vine. Neither can you bear fruit unless you remain in me. I am the vine; you are the branches. If a man remains in me and I in him, he will bear much fruit; apart from me you can do nothing" (John 15:4–5). The spiritual health of a church depends greatly on the spiritual health of its members, beginning with the leaders.

Leadership Health

Perhaps the most important thing that can be done to maintain the spiritual health of a church is to give attention to the spiritual health of the leaders. Jesus asked, "Can a blind man lead a blind man? Will they not both fall into a pit? A student is not above his teacher, but everyone who is fully trained will be like his teacher" (Luke 6:39–40). Paul exhorts Timothy as a leader in the church of Ephesus, "Don't let anyone look down on you because you are young, but set an example for the believers in speech, in life, in love, in faith and in purity" (1 Tim. 4:12). It is not the authority of his office or his standing as disciple of Paul that should win Timothy the respect of the church, but rather his example. A holy lifestyle will set the spiritual tone of the church. Similarly, if the church leaders are not living in unity and love, it can hardly be expected that the church be any better.

A church can be no healthier than its leaders. As Jesus's earthly ministry progressed, he spent more time with his disciples and less time with the masses. The apostolic church planter must also adopt such an approach. In the structuring phase the planter spends more time equipping leaders to minister to the broader needs of the church and less time directly meeting those needs.

There is a temptation for the church planter to be so consumed with ministering to especially needy persons that they neglect the spiritual care of church leaders. They may assume that leaders can take care of themselves. But we all need to be mutually encouraged and kept accountable, and this is especially true of leaders, who bear the weight of responsibility and come under spiritual attack. Leaders must challenge each other to continued spiritual health and growth, as iron sharpens iron. Regular meetings with leaders in mentoring relationships, in small accountability groups, or to personally share and pray for one another (discussion of church business forbidden) can be immensely significant in maintaining the spiritual health of church leaders and, in turn, of the church.

Evaluate the Kingdom Impact of the Church

Sometimes a church may seem to be doing everything right, with no obvious signs of dysfunction or conflict, but kingdom impact remains minimal. Only the work of the Holy Spirit can produce transformational change in the life of believers, who in turn bring change to the community. Yet Scripture warns believers not to grieve or quench the Spirit (Eph. 4:30; 1 Thess. 5:19). Of course these exhortations apply to all believers and the church at every phase. But the concern is critical as a church assesses its impact.

How easily the life of a church becomes routine and self-satisfied. If a church is going to reproduce, there must be vitality in the spiritual life of the believers that is overflowing into relationships. Families are healed, broken relationships are restored, bondage to sin is released, and the fruit of the Holy Spirit is increasingly evident. Nominal faith that fails to make a difference in daily life is one of the most common problems that churches face. Syncretism is another problem, as believers mix beliefs or practices of their former religion with their Christian faith. Occult practices, visiting a shaman in times of crisis, and materialistic lifestyles that foster greed and stifle compassion are all evidence that the beliefs of Christians are shallow and deep-level worldview transformation is not taking place (see Hiebert 2008). Such habits, values, and convictions die hard. Biblical teaching, modeling character, living out new values, prayer, and experiences of the sufficiency of Christ are all part of the long process of discipleship and sanctification that cannot be neglected for the sake of increasing numbers. Reproducing congregations of syncretistic, materialistic, or shallow believers will not honor Christ and will not provide the spiritual capital to launch a movement of multiplying kingdom communities.

The leadership team must further examine the extent to which the congregation is having an influence on the larger community. As churches grow, they tend to become more and more consumed with their internal needs and with programs that serve their members. This is necessary, but it cannot be allowed to overshadow the church's missional calling to be salt and light in its neighborhood and the broader society. True spiritual nurture will not lead to ingrown spirituality but rather to missional involvement. Often non-Christians have the impression that the church is something like a voluntary club or a hobby that occupies Christians on certain days of the week but is entirely irrelevant to concerns of anyone outside that club. The church must constantly be challenged to move beyond its comfort zone and engage the needs of the community in the name of Christ. In chapter 19 we will consider how a church plant can have kingdom impact.

Organize the Church Legally

In the New Testament local churches did not legally organize, though initially, as members of a Jewish sect, Christians fell under the legal status of Jews. This does not mean that the early churches were without formal structure. As we have seen in the Pastoral Epistles, the churches were to have clearly defined qualifications for appointing, honoring, and dealing with accusations against leaders (1 Tim. 3:1–13; 5:17–20; Titus 1:5–9). Lists were also kept of widows qualified to receive assistance (1 Tim. 5:9, 11). These are indications of increasing formalization of church structure and polity. Most churches today have a constitution and bylaws that define the purpose, practices, and procedures of the church as an organization. Usually a statement of faith is included. In most contexts the church will acquire some form of incorporation and legal status, with the local government allowing the church to rent or own property, receive tax-deductible donations, obtain exemption from taxes, protect individual members from legal liability, and give the church a public identity. Governments often have requirements regarding the use of funds, accounting, membership, and other matters. Usually churches can work within these parameters. Sometimes this is not possible, or the church leaders may feel that such official registration might compromise their convictions or security.

Many church planters have little patience with the technicalities of creating a church constitution and bylaws or legal registration. Nevertheless, it is wise practice to give attention to this as the church grows. Clear polity and doctrinal statements can help clarify purpose and avoid conflict. Fortunately most denominations provide sample documents that can be adopted or adapted to local needs. Cross-cultural church planters should, however, avoid importing a foreign constitution and bylaws. Even statements of faith may need to be contextualized.[4] The goal is not conformity to an outside standard but faithfulness to biblical truths and principles. As local believers participate in the formulation of such documents, they will both understand them and have a greater sense of ownership. But in a church of predominantly new believers, the church planters will need to give considerable guidance to the process.

Formal membership clarifies who is fully committed to the church and is a means of public identification with the church, of formal submission to the spiritual care and leadership of the church, and for congregants to declare, "This is my spiritual home." It also clearly defines what persons may have a formal voice or vote in the important decisions of the church and who might be entitled to services provided by the church (such as aid for widows in the New Testament). Experience teaches that neglecting to formalize membership can have the high price of conflict later when important decisions involving the congregation must be made. Peripheral persons can attempt to influence

4. For a discussion of the challenges of translating creeds, see Strauss 2006.

decisions and even rally extended family or others who have even less of a relationship to the church to support their cause.

We offer several recommendations regarding the process of formally organizing the church. First, keep the constitution and bylaws as simple and flexible as possible, while at the same time defining the essential aspects of church organization and authority. The most essential issues should be defined in the constitution. Ed Stetzer recommends, "The constitution should be simple. Long constitutions that articulate every possible problem indicate mistrust rather than congregational health" (2006, 311). Secondary matters, such as the process of selecting leaders, are defined in the bylaws because this location allows them to be more easily amended.[5] Second, do not belabor the drafting of such documents. Much energy can be wasted in reinventing the wheel. Appoint a small group of trusted persons to draft the documents; make sure that they fulfill any local legal requirements, and then submit them to the congregation for approval. Conflicts over minute details can kill momentum in the church. Make use of sample documents, and adapt them as necessary to the local circumstances.

Finally, adopt a procedure of receiving new members that, on the one hand, informs them of the vision, beliefs, practices, and expectations of members of the church and, on the other hand, examines the level of commitment of the candidate to both Christ and the local congregation. Membership interviews or classes can also provide good opportunities to discuss financial support and service opportunities in the church. Do not underestimate the importance of a well-informed and committed membership for the health of the church. Leaders of a small church plant can be so excited about persons who want to join that they jettison better judgment. Raising the bar for membership will actually increase the quality of the church in the short term and the numerical growth of the church in the long term.[6] The first practice in Milfred Minatrea's list of essential practices of missional churches is "Have a high threshold of membership." He notes these characteristics:

- Missional churches are concerned for nominal church members.
- Membership is not casual.
- Members are unified in community.
- The church has clear expectations for members.
- Members have clear expectations of the church. (Minatrea 2004, 29–40)

Formal documents cannot prevent conflict and are no guarantee of spiritual life or health. They may aid the church in being the church, but the church

5. For example, in the U.S. a constitution must fulfill certain governmental requirements, but bylaws need not.

6. See, for example, the landmark study by Dean M. Kelly, *Why Conservative Churches Are Growing* (1977).

should not become a slave to them. More important is the faithful living out of the church's calling under the guidance of the Holy Spirit, consistent with biblical teaching, and in an atmosphere of love and trust.

Achieve Full Financial Autonomy

Financial autonomy is one of the important marks of church maturity. This means that the church reaches a point where local believers are able and willing to cover the ongoing expenses of ministry and does not need to draw on outside resources to sustain itself. If the church has received any outside funding, now it should be discontinued and made available for new church planting. The church should moreover take up its responsibility of financially contributing toward mission efforts and outside needs. In chapter 18 we shall discuss with greater detail the use of resources and funding.

In apostolic church plants the majority, if not all, of ongoing expenses such as rents, materials, and salaries should be borne by local believers from the very start. Their financial commitment should grow with the church. Just as in other aspects of apostolic church plants, so too with finances: from the outset local sustainability is a key. Apart from minimal start-up funds, ministries should be initiated only as local believers with local resources are able to sustain them. In this way unhealthy dependencies are avoided and locally sustainable reproduction will be possible. As needs arise, believers are challenged to meet those needs from their own resources. They will have a truer sense of ownership if they are financially committed to supporting the ministry.

Personal finances are a sensitive subject in most cultures, but the matter of stewardship and giving to support the ministry must be clearly and biblically taught early on in the church plant as expenses arise. Outside funds from a denomination or mission organization may serve to launch evangelistic efforts and give initial impetus, but ultimately local believers should learn the joy of supporting their church ministries and outreach. Sometimes a church-operated business will be opened as a source to fund ministry, but this is generally to be avoided (see chapter 19). The biblical pattern is that God's people support God's work with their own sacrificial gifts and offerings. In many parts of the world, giving is done in kind, not cash: food or other goods and services are given to support the work of the ministry. We have observed how in the Congo church members volunteer time to tend a garden that provides food for the pastor.

As opportunities arise to expand ministry, usually expenses also increase: rent, materials, evangelistic efforts, training events, and the like. This becomes a great occasion to challenge the congregation to higher levels of financial commitment. Appeals to guilt or mere obligation rarely generate adequate motivation. People tend to give to a vision. They are more willing to sacrifice joyfully and in faith when they sense that God is at work and that their gifts will make a difference in advancing his cause. Even in situations where local expenses are minimal, giving should be encouraged to support compassion ministry or other mission-related efforts. As members are encouraged to pray and give, they can also discover the joy of giving and will experience what Jesus taught, "It is more blessed to give than to receive" (Acts 20:35).

Conclusion

In conclusion, the church's structuring process is not primarily about "settling down" but rather positioning itself for more effective ministry and reproduction. Healthy churches become reproducing churches with kingdom impact. At this point the church-planting team is already in the process of phasing out as ministries are primarily conducted by local believers. The focus of the church planters is now not only to reproduce leaders and workers at the local level but to prepare those who will be part of launching the next church plant. In the words of Tom Steffen, "Success is much more than having a successor, Rick Warren would argue; it is instituting a structure. That is, establishing basic ministry principles and processes so that the ship keeps on course no matter how thick the fog becomes when the expatriates leave or when new national leadership succeeds existing national leadership. Wise church planters structure for servant-based multiplication and the trauma of departure, not control or premature departure" (2001, 187).

14

Reproducing

....
....
....

Strengthening and Sending

Though the reproduction of new congregations begins here, multiplication at every level of ministry should have been built into the church from the start. Reproduction begins by teaching new believers how to share their faith, teaching disciples how to disciple others, teaching leaders how train up new disciples and other leaders, and reproducing cells as the spiritual building blocks of the church. Reproduction thus becomes part of the very DNA of the church. With the birthing of new *congregations*, kingdom impact is also multiplied and whole *movements* can be launched. A single congregation, no matter how large, will eventually plateau in size and be limited in its ability to reach new people groups and bring the gospel to the ends of the earth. Reproduction is not only the natural outgrowth of every living organism but also God's desire for the church, be it through the planting of daughter churches, the planting of pioneer churches at greater distance, or partnering with others who launch new kingdom communities.

Overview of Phase

Biblical Examples

Acts 13:1–3: The church at Antioch sends its best leaders as missionaries

Acts 9:31: The church(es) in Judea was (were) multiplied*

Acts 19; Colossians 4:12–13; Revelation 2–3: The church at Ephesus gives rise to a cluster of churches in Asia Minor

Key Steps

1. Sustain evangelistic thrust
2. Prepare the church for reproduction
3. Determine the location and approach of possible daughter church or pioneer church plants
4. Launch the daughter or pioneer church plant
5. Send cross-cultural missionaries
6. Participate in common efforts with other churches

Critical Issues

1. Avoid slipping into maintenance mode
2. Launch the first daughter or pioneer church plant well
3. Continue multiplication through evangelism and equipping of leaders
4. Be willing to take steps of faith in obedience to the Great Commission

*The Western and Byzantine texts read "So the churches . . . were multiplied" (Bruce 1977, 208). The object of multiplied in Acts 9:31 is not the disciples but churches. The dispersed Jerusalem church is sometimes considered collectively, but Paul referred to it as "churches" (Gal. 1:22; 1 Thess. 2:14). Note that this *multiplication* occurred after the dispersion and a time of spiritual strengthening and growth.

Counterintuitive Convictions in Moving to Reproduction

Before discussing the various tasks of this phase, we address several convictions that are essential to a church's becoming a reproducing church. These convictions move church reproduction from an obligation to a passion and joy. They should already have become part of the church's ethos during the previous phases, but now they will be put to the test at a new level as the church anticipates this move. These convictions are counterintuitive—they go against what one would normally expect. Therefore they must be taught and lived continually.

Success Is Defined by Impact, Not Size

As we noted in chapter 1, the churches we seek to plant must be kingdom communities that have an impact on lives, families, communities, and beyond. The goal cannot be merely large numbers of people attending church services or meetings without experiencing the transforming lordship of Jesus Christ. In some ways large churches can have more immediate community impact than small churches because of their greater visibility and resources. But smaller churches that multiply can ultimately have greater kingdom impact as more lives, families, and communities come under the gracious and powerful influence of Jesus Christ.

Every true church wants to see more people transformed by the gospel. As people become devoted followers of Jesus Christ, they become responsible, serving members of the local church. In this sense it is good that every church wants to grow. But if it is to reproduce, the church's vision must be greater than merely reaching more individuals. Even being the largest church in the city or state is too small a vision. The vision must include depth—lives and whole communities that are touched by the gospel.

Growth Is Measured by the Capacity to Release, Not Retain

One of Milfred Minatrea's nine essential practices of missional churches is "Measure growth by capacity to release, not retain" (2004, 111). If churches are to reproduce, significant resources, both personal and financial, must be allocated to the cause. A high level of commitment and sacrifice will be necessary. Every church will always have need for more workers and resources. Giving some of these away to launch a new church is costly. Not only will the needs in the mother church remain, but the resources to meet them will, in the short term, actually be *fewer*. A church will be willing to make such sacrifices only if it is convinced that growth is not measured by attendance, buildings, and budgets but by reproduction that increases overall kingdom impact. This is the spirit that characterized the church of Antioch as it released its beloved leaders Barnabas and Paul[1] for the wider mission to which God had called them (Acts 13:1–3).

One can only imagine the joy in the Antioch church when Paul and Barnabas returned to report on the fruit of their mission and the churches that had been planted (Acts 14:26–28). Reproducing churches everywhere have since discovered that there is much greater joy and satisfaction in seeing workers mobilized and released, new churches birthed, communities and people groups reached with the gospel, and a movement launched, than in merely growing a single larger church. Minatrea rightly adds, "Missional churches are not simply releasing members to start churches. Their focus is on starting church-starting movements. Releasing members to start new churches is addition. Releasing members to start church-planting churches results in movements" (2004, 122).

Giving up members and resources to launch new church plants does not mean that the mother church cannot continue to grow. Indeed countless examples can be given of churches that have not only planted numerous daughter churches but have continued to grow and become megachurches. The measure of success is not size in itself but rather obedience to God's leading resulting in kingdom impact. This vision involves selflessness and a great step of faith, which leads us to the next point.

Acting in Faith Is Prudent, Not Seeking Security

Whenever a church gives away workers and resources to launch a new church plant, faith is exercised: believers trust God to prosper the plant as well as fill

---

1. Paul had worked in the church of Antioch at least one year before departing on the mission with Barnabas to Cypress and Galatia (Acts 11:26). Barnabas would have been there somewhat longer.

the gap left in the mother church. Our natural human tendency is to gravitate to the secure and predictable. But in the kingdom of God, opting for the secure and predictable can result in severing a church from dependency on God—the spiritual lifeline of the church. One of the sins of the church in Laodicea was self-sufficiency (Rev. 3:17). Steps of faith keep a church dependent on God.

There is a difference between a prudent step of faith and "bungee-jumping-without-a-cord" (Williams n.d., 3). A fine line divides a bold step of faith in God from a foolish leap, testing God. The difference is often spiritually discerned. However, if God has blessed a church with growth in the early phases, it is a reasonable act of faith to trust God for continued growth as the church releases and reproduces for greater kingdom impact. Jesus himself taught that the kingdom *will* grow and spread as a tiny mustard seed becoming a large tree and as the unseen yeast leavening the whole lump of dough (Matt. 13:31–35). Results will not be calculable in proportion to initial appearances but in proportion to God's supernatural working. It is only prudent to trust God for such results.

Begin with Multiplying Disciples and Leaders, Not Programs or Institutions

Neil Cole has said, "If you can't reproduce disciples, you can't reproduce leaders. If you can't reproduce leaders, you can't reproduce churches. And if you can't reproduce churches, you can't reproduce movements" (quoted in Williams n.d., 4). The multiplication of disciples provides the source of leaders who are necessary to launch new congregations. This principle applies to a house church multiplication as well as large church multiplication, in every part of the world and in any context. Sometimes we want to see large results without giving attention to the basic necessities. Basic discipleship is, however, the fundamental building block of reproduction, because church reproduction is not primarily about reproducing institutions or programs but about reproducing spiritual life. That life begins with evangelism and the new birth, which grows in discipleship, develops to maturity with strong leadership, and functions organically in cells. When these reproduce, the infrastructure for natural reproduction and multiplication is in place. Overlooking or attempting to bypass this fundamental principle will result in anemic reproduction, if there is any reproduction at all.

Simple Beginnings, Not Big Budgets and Large Numbers

Churches that wait until they reach a certain size or until they can raise a certain amount of extra funds before reproducing will rarely ever do so. The local needs never seem to be adequately met, and the threshold to launch typically increases with time. Reproducing churches are less concerned about fully meeting local needs, because they know that this will never be possible! Over and over again, research confirms that reproducing churches find ways to plant new churches that are not dependent on large budgets or large memberships. This is not only true of grassroots house church movements in the Majority World, like those described by David Garrison (2004a), but also in Western contexts. For example, Robert Vajko reports on a church in Grenoble, France, that was able to plant six daughter churches without giving any extra funds to do so. He concludes, "I discovered that as soon as a group bases its church multiplication on how much money is available, they stop planting churches" (2005, 297).

This is, of course, possible only when the new churches are primarily lay led (with perhaps assistance from the mother church pastor) or have bivocational pastors, and when inexpensive or free meeting places (such as homes or public venues) are used for the initial phases. Creative approaches can be taken. For example, mother and daughter church can share the services and expenses of one paid pastor. In the greater Munich area, retired pastors with energy and vision gave initial leadership to several church plants, costing the plants only the reimbursements for their basic ministry expenses.

It is sometimes recommended that a church reach a "critical mass" before reproducing. It is reasonable to guard the mother church from being too severely weakened in the process. However, what constitutes a critical mass will vary and may be fewer members than suspected. Vajko's (1996) study of reproducing churches in the greater Paris area showed that most churches planted daughter churches giving only twelve to fifteen members to the launch team. For house churches, a critical mass in the mother church might be fewer then twenty persons; for churches with lay leaders but needing to pay rent, the critical mass may be forty persons; for churches with paid pastors and a mortgage, the critical mass might be one hundred. Highly attractional and program-oriented churches often "launch large" with a core launch group of one hundred or even two hundred persons. Since the average church has fewer than two hundred members, this approach is an option for very few. Much will of course depend on the overall strategy and church structure. But no matter what the church size or budget, church reproduction will *always* involve a step of faith beyond the safe, predictable, and calculable, a step that stretches the resources of the mother church. This spirit of faith and vision, not size or budget, characterizes reproducing churches.

Messy and Unpredictable, Not Neat and Calculable

This principle is not an argument against careful and prayerful planning. Rather, it is a reminder that a daughter or pioneer church plant will encounter surprising breakthroughs as well as unexpected setbacks. There will be spiritual opposition and many unanticipated turns of events. Not every attempt at reproduction will meet with visible success. Often opposition comes hand in hand with opportunity, as Paul wrote of his ministry in Ephesus: "A great door for effective work has opened to me, and there are many who oppose me" (1 Cor. 16:9). As a movement grows, local government or religious authorities may take notice and create problems. As people are reached for Christ, they often bring broken lives and relationships into the church. They may have many personal or relational dysfunctions that inhibit the building of a healthy and trusting fellowship. Satan may incite division, false teaching, and conflict. All of these challenges were faced by the early church, and we can expect to experience them today. Yet the first Christians also experienced the grace and transforming power of God in the midst of the challenges. We can count on the same God to be at work in our efforts.

Furthermore, the church-planting team must be flexible—on the one hand remaining faithful to the ultimate vision of launching a reproducing movement with kingdom impact, while on the other hand responding creatively to opportunities and unexpected developments. God may open doors to minister to people groups or subcultures that were not part of the original vision. He may at the same time close doors that seemed to be the most strategic. Here again we can learn from the Pauline missionary band as they attempted to move in the direction of Asia and then to Bithynia, but were hindered each time by the Holy Spirit. Only with the Macedonian vision did God's plan became clearer (Acts 16:6–10). The beginnings in Philippi, the first church planted in Macedonia, were meager (a women's prayer meeting) and filled with spiritual and political opposition (harassment by an evil spirit and imprisonment, Acts 16:11–38). Yet in spite of its unpromising beginnings, the Philippian church became one of Paul's dearest partner churches, contributing to his support needs (Phil. 4:14–15). The best of plans must remain open to the leading of the Holy Spirit and respond to circumstances as they arise.

For a summary of the essential traits of reproducing churches, see case study 14.1.

Tasks of the Reproduction Phase: Strengthening and Sending

Sustain Evangelistic Thrust

Church planting is hard work not only for the church planter and initial launch team, but for all the committed members during the early years. Often by the time the church has matured to a point of considering reproduction, the members are weary and want to rest and enjoy the fruits of their labors. Care for new believers and their assimilation into the life of the church demand increasing attention and energy. Many will have the impression that there is work enough just sustaining the gains that have been made during the young life of the church. Such concerns and fatigue are fully understandable but can lead to stagnation and spiritual lethargy if allowed to become the dominant spirit.

The vision of evangelism, discipleship, kingdom impact, and church multiplication must be continually refreshed and refocused if growth is to be sustained and reproduction is to become a reality. The passion for seeing lost persons reconciled to God and transformed is best kept before the congregation by ongoing teaching, vision casting, evangelistic emphases, training, and outreach efforts. Regular testimonies of new believers can be a great stimulus.

New believers themselves are often the best evangelists. Their faith is fresh, their testimony compelling, and their zeal uncontainable. Unlike most who have been Christians for years, they still have many close relationships with non-Christian friends, relatives, and colleagues with whom they can naturally share their faith or whom they can invite to evangelistic events. Not having been immersed in a Christian subculture, they still speak the language and think in terms of the contemporary culture. They can thus potentially communicate the Christian message in ways more easily understood by their peers. Such new Christians should be equipped, mobilized, and encouraged to maintain healthy relationships with unbelievers and share their faith. They too are often the best candidates to form the missional team when the first daughter or pioneer church plant is being launched. What they may lack in maturity they make up for in enthusiasm, energy, and understanding of the unreached.

> **Why Do[...]
> R[...]**
>
> Robert J. Vajko (1996; 2005) studied churches from several denominations in France and identified fourteen qualities that all reproducing churches evidenced:
>
> 1. A vision for reproduction
> 2. Willing to take risks
> 3. A spirit of self-giving
> 4. Growing themselves
> 5. Know how to plant daughter churches
> 6. Sensitive to the Spirit of God
> 7. Finances not central
> 8. Care for the training of their own church planters
> 9. Leadership base multiplied
> 10. A Pauline vision
> 11. Receptive areas sought
> 12. Homogeneous populations targeted
> 13. Creativity is encouraged
> 14. Clear principles

Prepare the Church for Reproduction

A vision to plant a daughter church does not develop accidentally or automatically. As we have noted above, the leadership must cast the vision for reproduction and multiplication not only by instilling these as core values but also by explicit teaching and vision casting. Dietrich Schindler recommends, based on his twenty years of church planting and studies in Germany, that

sion for reproduction be "time released" like the tiny capsules that begin releasing their medication early on and continue over time. "Time release is the discipline of setting the date of the next church plant shortly after the current church has been launched" (Schindler 2008, 322). Vision tends to "leak" over time and be lost. The spiritual needs of the city, region, nation, and world must be continually held before the congregation. The Great Commission, taking steps of faith, and God's heart for the lost should be recurrent teaching themes. At a church leadership retreat followed by a congregational meeting, these questions might be prayerfully considered:

What are the biblical reasons to start another church?

How does church reproduction fit into our calling and mission?

What is God doing that indicates this may be the time to begin reproduction?

What obstacles are there to reproduction? How can we overcome them?

How can we mobilize more workers and resources to start another church?

What steps of faith are appropriate at this time?

Where are the spiritual needs greatest and what opportunities has God opened up to us?

The church must be spiritually prepared for reproduction, just as women prepare physically and mentally for giving birth. The vision and plans for church reproduction must be bathed in prayer for discernment, that the Lord of the harvest would raise up workers (Matt. 9:38) and that God would open doors of opportunity (Col. 4:3). The church can expect increased spiritual opposition when considering such a move. Bible studies on Joshua taking the land, Nehemiah building the walls, or Haggai on spiritual priorities and sacrifice to restore the temple can be helpful to challenge and prepare the church for bold steps of faith for Christ's kingdom purposes.

Careful preparation is especially important for a church's first effort to reproduce. The mother church has no previous experience to build on. If the first effort fails or encounters serious difficulties, the congregation may develop a negative attitude toward church reproduction that will be difficult to overcome. On the other hand, if the first effort succeeds, it will be considerably easier to motivate the church to plant additional churches in the near future and build on that experience.

Determine Location and Approach for Possible Church Plants

Two strategic questions must be answered as a young church considers launching its first church plant: location and church-planting approach. Though we consider them separately, the two decisions are closely interrelated.

Determining the Location of the Church Plant

Broadly speaking, either the new plant will be local by way of cell division (also known as the mother-daughter church plant), or the new church will be a pioneer plant in a new, more distant location. If it is a pioneer church plant, then the steps of preparation and planning discussed in chapters 9 and 10 can be followed to determine the focus people and build the church-planting team. Unreached communities or people groups where the spiritual need is greatest can be identified. Evangelistic efforts might be conducted in various communities, and the most responsive could be chosen for the new church plant. One of the most common ways to reproduce through pioneer planting happens when members of the church move to another city or new community. They can become the catalyst for a pioneer church plant in that location, much like the Jerusalem Christians who were scattered by persecution and planted churches throughout Judea and Samaria (Acts 8:1; 11:19–21). Today church members may be scattered for reasons such as famine, war, economic opportunity, available jobs, or housing.

Location can also be determined when members of the church have relatives in a distant community who are believers or open to the gospel. Sometimes members in the church have come from distant towns where they still have many relatives and friends. Such contacts can become key persons in opening the door for a church plant in that community. This can be particularly important in more traditional societies, where outsiders may have difficulty gaining access to the community but extended family is always welcome.

If a number of persons from the mother church are commissioned for a more local plant, a somewhat different approach will be taken. One of the simplest ways of determining the location for the plant is to map out where the present members of the church currently live. Often one or more cell groups already meet in a particular district of the city or region and can serve as a potential core launch team for the new church. As a next step, the spiritual needs of the communities where such groups exist can be assessed. Communities that have very few or no churches would be given priority over those that already have churches.

Neighborhoods undergoing population growth might also be given priority over those that are in decline. Also, when several church members relocate in a nearby community, that community can become a potential location for a church plant. For example, housing in the city of Munich became so expensive that larger families with only one wage earner were forced to move to more affordable housing in suburbs or villages. A plan was devised to plant churches in towns along the commuter rail routes surrounding Munich, with such believers constituting the core groups. Several churches were planted in this manner.

A community might also be targeted where there is a critical social need that the potential church plant could address. For example, a middle-class church in Manila partnered with expatriate missionaries to plant a church in a poor squatter district, bringing both material and personal resources to the task. In addition to evangelism and Bible studies, community services such as preschool educational programs and tutoring were launched.

DETERMINING THE APPROACH

In chapter 7 we outlined various approaches to both pioneer church planting and church reproduction. The planting church will want to prayerfully consider these options. The long-term goal to launch a multiplying movement should always be kept in mind. Some approaches multiply well in one context but not in another. For example, house church networks may multiply best in situations where there is considerable governmental or religious opposition or where extended family networks become the bases for house churches. The multisite approach is most effective in urban settings, where more program-oriented churches have access to many resources and where people have high expectations of quality and professionalism.

Furthermore, the regional strategies discussed in chapter 7 should be considered as part of a larger plan for multiplying churches in a region. Such longer-term planning and vision place the immediate church plant in a larger perspective. It is wise to consider such regional church-planting plans with other churches and possible partners in the area, so as to coordinate efforts, develop synergy, and demonstrate unity in the cause of Christ.

Launch the Daughter or Pioneer Church Plant

If a daughter church is being planted, then members living in the target community typically form the church-planting team. Others may be recruited to move to the location or participate at a distance. This team will meet regularly over several months to pray, plan, and grow together. Many of the preparatory tasks described in chapters 9 and 10 will be undertaken. Chapter 16 explains how to build the team. Several resources are available for launching a daughter church in the North American context (e.g., Logan and Ogne 1995; Harrison, Cheyney, and Overstreet 2008), and these may be adapted to other cultural contexts. The leadership of the new plant will be critically important. If a community is targeted but the believers there lack the necessary leadership skills, then someone with such skills should be recruited to the team. Leaders of the mother church can assist in the ministry of the daughter plant, or an apostolic church planter may assist. However, if multiplication is to occur, new leaders must be prepared to lead the new work under the coaching of an experienced church planter. They can begin meeting in the target community for outreach events and occasional worship services. At the appropriate time a commissioning service can be held in the mother church to bless and celebrate the launch.

Launching a pioneer church plant will be more challenging. A church planter or launch team may be recruited from the sponsor church, but because the pioneer plant is often at a considerable geographic distance from the sponsor, the team will need to relocate to live in the focus community and find employment there. More preparatory research may be necessary if the launch team is unfamiliar with the community or if a new ethnic group is to be reached. The steps outlined in chapters 9 and 10 can be followed.

Meanwhile, members of the initial apostolic church-planting team will have already phased out of all key ministry responsibilities in the first church plant. They may now assist the new daughter or pioneer church plant, either directly or in a coaching role (illustrated in figure 14.1). Other possible roles for the apostolic church planter are explored below. This process of reproducing churches should continue repeatedly, with each generation of church plants continuing to reproduce and plant multiple churches (figure 14.2). The movement can be considered to be multiplying only when a third or fourth generation of churches has been planted, evidencing that the DNA of reproduction truly characterizes the movement.

Send Cross Cultural Missionaries

Thus far we have spoken of church reproduction mainly in terms of local or regional church planting within the same culture as the initial church plant. But the vision for church reproduction must include a vision for the world and the unreached peoples who live without a viable and understandable gospel witness.

Figure 14.1
Church Reproduction

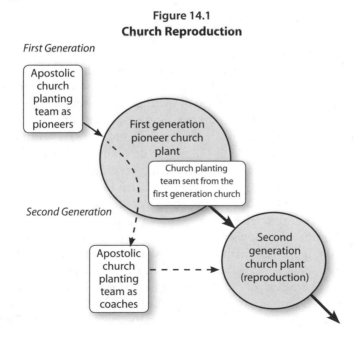

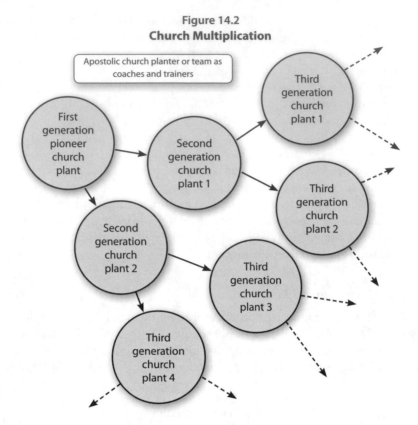

Figure 14.2
Church Multiplication

For a young church plant such a vision may seem overwhelming or even presumptuous. However, many new congregations include in their early vision statements, core values, or prayer goals the desire to become a missionary-sending church. The vision can be stimulated by inviting visiting missionaries to speak, by sending members on short-term mission trips, by including world mission themes in biblical teaching and preaching, by regular prayer for missionaries and global needs, and by making available to the congregation mission-related literature. Most of all, the church should pray that the Lord of the harvest raise up global harvest workers from within the church (Matt. 9:38).

As God calls members of the congregation to cross-cultural mission work, they can be sent out through a mission sending agency, with the church contributing to their financial support together with other supporting churches. Or, as is increasingly the case with Majority World missionaries, the missionary may be bivocational, earning the majority of financial support through secular employment. Advocates of "business as mission" call for Christian businessmen and women with international assignments or projects to see these as a means of both economic development and missional engagement. Christians in the Philippines have developed a whole strategy for world evangelization by mobilizing for mission Christian Filipinos who live and work in some 180 countries (cf. Pantoja, Tira, and Wan 2004).

As the church plant becomes a full participant in fulfilling the Great Commission by sending and supporting its own, this will be a sign of having come of age as a mature and full participant in the global body of Christ. However, the church will also experience great joy in knowing that it not only has been a recipient of missionary effort but is now a contributor so that others might benefit likewise.

Participate in Common Efforts with Other Churches

A spirit of independence tends to dominate American attitudes toward all of life, and it is often reflected in the way local churches relate to one another. However, as noted in chapter 3, the apostle Paul linked the churches he planted with one another in various ways. Today such partnerships and relationships are no less important. They may come in the form of associations, denominations, movement networks, local evangelical alliances, or common mission and diaconal efforts. There are many ministries such as theological education, missionary sending, and Christian media that a single church can rarely sustain alone.

Such partnerships and cooperation are also a sign of unity with the larger body of Christ (John 17:11, 20–23). This spiritual unity does not necessarily entail structural union but does involve a spirit of fellowship, cooperation, and common cause. An overemphasis on planting churches among homogeneous, strictly defined people groups can lead to ethnocentrism and even reinforce divisions within the larger church. A spirit of unity across ethnic, national, and confessional lines must be intentionally instilled in a church plant (Gal. 3:28; Eph. 2:11–22; cf. LOP 1, 1978; Padilla 1982). Ken Baker describes this as a move from being "evangelistically strategic" to "kingdom strategic" (2005, 166).

Alliances with other churches have the added benefit of stimulating church reproduction. For example, Robert Vajko discovered in France that "churches that are part of a fellowship of churches tend to reproduce themselves more than independent churches. My study of reproducing churches showed that the most reproductive churches, not surprisingly, were a part of a movement that encouraged reproduction" (2005, 299). This may be less the case in other contexts, but the general principle applies: synergy emerges when like-minded churches work together in mutual encouragement and vision. The total effect becomes greater than the sum of its parts.

Furthermore, as Tom Steffen notes, "an Association of Churches provides a second level of leadership that circulates among the churches, providing encouragement and challenge" (2001, 184). It also can help churches remain faithful to Scripture, hold forth a vision for continued mission, and negotiate conflict that a single local congregation is unable to resolve alone. Much as the Jerusalem Council and the apostles provided practical and theological guidance for first-century churches, church associations or denominations can provide stability and guidance for a movement. They can also help churches resist becoming overly dominated by a strong leader and can encourage small churches that are struggling or have weak leaders. One of the most strategic moves an association can make is to establish a regional church-planting or missionary-training center (see chapter 17).

Of course, church associations all too often evolve into self-justifying bureaucracies that consume resources and lack movement-promoting character and vision. Mission organizations have at times imposed denominational structures and offices that reflect the sending denominations but are poorly suited to the needs of the churches. Association structures should grow organically as needed, with clearly defined goals and in response to the felt needs and vision of the national churches themselves. Movement leaders should be those with the highest level of trust and respect of the local believers.

The Apostolic Church Planter Role: From Multiplier to Memory

Though Paul was the model apostolic church planter who continually moved on, entrusting the pastoral leadership to local elders, leaving the churches he planted was not easy. Sometimes he was driven from town by persecution (e.g., Acts 14:5–6; 19–20), but other times he departed willingly with tears (Acts 20:36–38). In Acts 21:1 Luke describes the team's departure as having "torn ourselves away from them." Any church planter who has invested much time, energy, and prayer in the people of the church will relate to these passages. The planter is in many ways a spiritual father or mother to the believers, and a unique bond grows between them. And yet the apostolic planter will move on, as did Paul with his team.

What will the church planter do after becoming a "memory," departing from the church plant? First, following the example of Paul, he or she will maintain contact with the church and not sever all relations. One must maintain a certain distance so as to allow local leaders to truly lead, yet those leaders may seek the counsel of the planter from time to time. Steffen (2001, 190–91) lists these healthy ways to maintain the relationship:

- prayer
- correspondence
- wise and discreet financial assistance
- subscription to culturally appropriate literature
- culturally appropriate books, tapes, or videos

- assistance in schooling
- periodical visits
- e-mails
- partnerships and networks for training

As the planter departs, several options exist for his or her continued ministry.[2] Some who are of a more pioneering spirit will choose to recruit partners from the church plant to help plant another church. Others with strong teaching gifts may choose to develop a ministry of equipping national church planters. That might occur by informally mentoring or coaching new church planters, producing culturally appropriate materials to aid evangelists and church planters, offering training seminars, or establishing a church planter training institute. Yet others with administrative gifts may choose to assist with the formation of a regional association of churches, development of missionary-sending structures, or building the infrastructure of the emerging movement (though this would be an option only after numerous churches had already been planted). The church planter ceases to be a multiplier and becomes a memory only in relation to the church just planted. The planter remains a multiplier in the broader sense. In each of these cases, the church planter continues to reproduce himself or herself in the next generation of church planters and to facilitate the ongoing development of the movement.

2. Steffen (2001, 190) also lists these options that missionary church planters might consider after departing from the plant: (1) change ministry roles, (2) retire, (3) begin a new church plant in the same culture in another unreached area (normally with a national participating with the expatriate), (4) begin a new church plant outside the culture in another unreached area, and (5) work under the association of churches to reach specific goals.

Part IV

CRITICAL
FACTORS

15

The Personal Life
of Church Planters

Church planting is an exciting—but often exhausting—venture of faith that touches every part of the lives of church planters. A study of 528 mission agencies found that nearly three quarters of all missionary attrition was due to preventable causes. About one quarter of that preventable attrition had diverse personal causes, 13 percent related to marriage and family, and 6 to 9 percent resulted from team problems (Brierly 1997, 89). The obvious conclusion: mission work in general and church planting in particular have a very high degree of impact on one's personal, marital, and family life. Furthermore, many church planters, being highly task oriented, have a tendency to overlook personal challenges and neglect some dimensions of their personal lives. Most church-planting books fail to address the personal dimensions of church planting, but our observation is that planters are just as likely to fall short because of personal inadequacies or an inability to work on a team as they are because of a flawed strategy. Jay Pinney, Quebec coordinator for Church Planting Canada, writes:

> While there are a growing number of rich resources which relate to the methodology of church planting, little is focused directly upon the church planters and the stresses which they and their families undergo as they attempt to plant churches. Though the church planter himself is an essential component of the church plant, the planter's personal and spiritual life has yet to receive adequate attention in current literature and training. In addition, while the whole concept of coaching is now in the spotlight and enjoying a great deal of attention in both Christian

Figure 15.1
Key Factors Resulting in Effective Church-
Planting Leadership

and secular circles, there are surprisingly few tools available to help coaches to effect change in the area of the planter's personal and family life. (2006, 8)

We devote this chapter to personal dimensions and the next chapter to teams. Resources for further study are found in sidebar 15.3 at the end of this chapter.

Church Planter Competencies

Church planters need special preparation, and studies have been done in North America to determine which competencies make church planters effective (e.g., Graham 1987; Ridley 1988; Thompson 1995 and 2007; Hertzberg 2008; Hertzberg and Lonsway 2008).

General Competencies

Figure 15.1 illustrates three broad categories for which adequate preparation is essential, based on the research of J. Allen Thompson:[1] spiritual life dimensions, church-planting skills (including knowledge), and personal and interpersonal abilities. These are listed in order of priority and importance.

1. J. Allen Thompson (1995, 2007) conducted research for his doctoral dissertation with North American church planters and leaders of assessment centers. The study identified twenty-one key qualities, and the qualities mentioned most often as critical to church-planting success were spiritual qualities.

Although Thompson did his research primarily in North America, these three basic categories also surface in the profile of an effective apostolic cross-cultural church planter (Taylor and Hoke 2003).

Table 15.1 compares the findings of Thompson with those of Charles Ridley, showing much overlap in the specific competencies they find most important. The *personal* competencies in table 15.1 should be considered important whatever the planting approach, even though the *skill requirements* will vary with the church planter role (pastoral, apostolic, or catalytic) and people group to be reached. We will discuss additional skills and competencies that apostolic and cross-cultural planters need.

Table 15.1
Church Planter Competencies:
A Comparison between the Findings of Ridley and Thompson

Church Planter Competencies according to Ridley (1988)	Church Planter Competencies according to Thompson (1995 and 2007)
Intrinsically motivated	Call
Spousal cooperation	Family commitment
Exercises faith	Spirituality, integrity, spiritual disciplines, godly character, person of prayer
Visioning capacity, creates ownership of ministry	Leadership, church-planting skills, dynamic, philosophy of ministry
Reaches the unchurched and lost, effectively builds relationships	Preaching, evangelism, discipling
Uses giftedness of others	
Builds group cohesiveness	
Committed to church growth	
Flexible, adaptable, demonstrates resilience	Conscientious, likable, sensitive, flexible, resilient, healthy self-image

A synthesis of these studies and personal observations leads us to conclude that the most important qualities for effective church planting, regardless of approach and people focus, are (1) God's call, (2) godly character, (3) strong spiritual dynamics (prayer, listening to God's voice, etc.), (4) spousal support, (5) a mission-specific skill set,[2] (6) emotional intelligence and adaptability, and (7) spiritual gifts that fit the task. If these foundations are in place, God will continue shaping the worker in service (Grady and Kendall 1992; Ridley 1988; Thompson 1995, 2007; Taylor and Hoke 2003).

2. Ridley's list in table 15.1 is used by church associations and church planting networks as a starting point. We recommend that proven ability to practice, motivate, and equip others in evangelism and discipling (present in Thompson's list) be included in any church planter profile and assessment tool.

Additional Competencies for Apostolic or Cross-Cultural Church Planting

In the 1990s two major cross-cultural planter profiles were developed, prompted by alarm over the high attrition rate of workers and in the hopes of improving their preparation and training (Taylor 1997; Hoke and Taylor 1999). Personal maturity and cross-cultural adaptability were identified as important factors in effectiveness and longevity (Taylor 1997, 184–249). Apostolic ministry among a different people group also requires evangelistic and entrepreneurial ability (initiating and gathering abilities) and cultural adaptation skills and proclivities such as flexibility, resourcefulness, and self-learning (Taylor and Hoke 2003). Effective cross-cultural leadership comes from the ability to adjust one's leadership style to the situation or culture, rather than from a set personality or pattern of behaviors. Because of the phase-out dimension and role changes required (Steffen 1997), cross-cultural workers need to be able to lead not only from in front but also coming alongside local apprentices and leaders. Furthermore, generational and people group distinctives should be taken into account.[3] Finally, one should never forget that no single church planter will have all the abilities; the team's competency set should be considered as well.

Spiritual Foundations

Calling and Confirmation

No amount of study, training, and experience can substitute for the call, leading, and power of the Holy Spirit in the lives of church planters. The assurance of God's appointment gives a tremendous amount of confidence and staying power. Since God speaks to people in different ways, one does not necessarily have to receive a "heavenly vision" as Paul did from a specific direction-setting event. That conviction can come at the outset in a rather dramatic way or progressively through a process of studying Scripture, reflection, and discussion with others. Luke Greer (2009, 328–32) points out that there are biblical precedents for both: the "obvious call" (Peter's call to Cornelius) and the "subtle call" reflected in James's summary phrase "it seemed good to the Holy Spirit and to us" after much deliberation (Acts 15:28). But candidates must have a genuine, settled, and enduring conviction (that is shared with their spouse, if married) of God's leading that is affirmed by their local church body (see McQuilkin 2002).

3. Generic church-planter profiles are time sensitive, because culture evolves and urban environments are increasingly pluralistic and diversified. Thus Thompson updated his 1995 study for North America in 2007, and Taylor and Hoke revised their 1998 cross-cultural profile in 2003. For example, personal integrity is now specified as a critical trait, whereas a few generations ago it would have been assumed (Thompson 2007).

Spiritual Maturity

Like Paul and Barnabas, lead church planters should be chosen from among those who have already demonstrated the spiritual maturity, spiritual disciplines, and ministry skills of an effective church leader. God's timing must be sought as well as his call. The Lord sovereignly prepares his servants through formative experiences that serve as foundational building blocks, shaping their character and drawing them to himself. He may take them through many crucibles of life and sacrificial service. These are his most effective teachers.

A deepening spiritual walk with God is required if one is to withstand pressure, respond graciously to opposition, and trust God in unpredictable circumstances. Wilderness experiences are often part of the maturing process. "Isolation is often used by God to teach important leadership lessons that could not be learned while [we are] experiencing the pressures of normal ministry context" (Clinton 1988, 161). There may initially be a "wrestling with God" that results in deeper intimacy with God, new patterns of dependence, greater humility and patience, and new ways of responding to emotional pain. If the potential church planter has not learned from such trying times, the initial shock of language and culture learning may be too great to bear. One Latin American leader offered this advice to cross-cultural church planters: "Don't come with ready-made agendas and plans, but come to learn." Another said: "Work with a spirit of prayer, trust, humility, respect, and, above all, with the infilling of the Holy Spirit." These character qualities require maturity and spiritual sensitivity.

Prayer and Spiritual Disciplines

The practice of spiritual disciplines should be well established. In many cross-cultural settings, church planters must nurture their spiritual life without the support of an established local church. Many find they must develop new or deeper patterns of spiritual disciplines because those practiced at home are inadequate on the church-planting battlefront. Research on one hundred effective church planters by Dick Grady and Glenn Kendall (1992) found that prayer is the number-one factor for success in church planting. The church planter who has not established an effective prayer life and ministry will not go far.

A church planter in Quito, Ecuador, made this troubling observation: "While we devote much time, energy and money to rallies and crusades, we have neglected the apostolic method of church growth: prayer and the ministry of the Word" (Mateer 1988, 146). Church planters need to be alert to the needs, character flaws, and spiritual openings of those they are working with and to intercede with focus and persistence. Often God's direction comes from this kind of listening and observing prayer.

Prayer is linked to evangelism as well (Eph. 6:18–20). Intercession is not merely the means to effective service—it is the heart and soul of a church-planting ministry. One church-planting mission asked its teams to devote 10 percent of their ministry day to various forms of prayer—for each other, for the new believers, and for unbelievers. The prayer ministry they developed included evangelistic prayer walks, prayer vigils, and days of prayer with fasting. Practical guides to developing a prayer life and ministry are found in sidebar 15.3 at the close of this chapter.

Spiritual Gifts in Church Planting

Church planters must also be men and women who rely on the Holy Spirit and use their spiritual gifts to reach the lost and build the church. Two comments are in order here: First, God uses *a variety of gifts* to plant his church, just as he uses many gifts to edify his church. Second, *some gifts have special relevance* to church planting, as suggested in table 15.1. Any list is suggestive, not exhaustive (Sawatsky 1991; 1997). In chapter 8 we identified and described the gifts that are most critical at each of the church-planting phases:

  launching—evangelistic and apostolic gifts
  establishing—teaching and shepherding gifts
  structuring—leadership and administration gifts
  reproducing—evangelistic and apostolic gifts

These are all primarily leadership gifts. We discover the role other gifts have when we look at biblical examples. A constellation of gifts prepared each team for the function God gave it (see table 15.2).

Table 15.2
Functions and Spiritual Gifts on a Church-Planting Team

Church Planter Function	Biblical Examples	Spiritual Gifts
Church foundation-layer	Paul, Peter, Barnabas, and Epaphras	Apostolic (cross-cultural gift), evangelism, preaching, leadership, faith, encouragement
Church waterer/developer	Apollos, Timothy, and Titus	Teaching, administration, encouragement, counseling
Church-planting assistant	Priscilla and Aquila	Evangelism, helps, hospitality, mentoring, teaching, encouragement

Church Foundation Layers

Paul and Peter represent the "foundation-layer" type who had the apostolic gift. Both were evangelists who mastered persuasive preaching. Barnabas, an evangelist along with Paul (Acts 13:2–14:28), was known for the gift of encouragement (Acts 4:36–37). He came alongside others to initiate them in ministry (Acts 11:25–26) and served as a bridge builder between people and groups (Acts 15:1–4, 12, 22–35).[4] Epaphras began the work in Colosse (Col. 1:7) and is also associated with Hierapolis and Laodicea (Col. 4:12–13). He demonstrated the gift of faith through his intercessory prayer (Col. 4:12).

Church Waterers or Developers

Apollos, a Jew from Alexandria, was discovered by the Pauline team in Ephesus. He was an accomplished student of the Old Testament and an eloquent preacher who had accepted Jesus as Messiah. With further instruction, he was prepared to use his abilities to persuade and instruct others in the faith. He developed, or "watered," the church in Corinth (1 Cor. 3:6) and apparently helped Paul in Ephesus (1 Cor. 16:12). It appears that Apollos never undertook pioneer church planting but devoted his efforts to strengthening the established works.

Timothy is another example of a "waterer." Having helped Paul evangelize several cities such as Corinth (Acts 18:5; 2 Cor. 1:19) and Berea, he remained to strengthen the believers while Paul went on to Athens (Acts 17:14). Later he returned to Thessalonica to affirm the faith of the new disciples there (1 Thess. 3:1–3). Finally, he ministered for an extensive time in Ephesus (1 Tim. 1:3–4). Titus and other of Paul's coworkers might also be considered waterers (Titus 1:5).

Church-Planting Assistants

The contributions of assistants or team members, though sometimes little noticed, should never be underestimated. In chapter 3 we give other examples, so here we highlight Priscilla and Aquila. They probably had the gifts of helps, hospitality, and, most certainly, teaching and encouragement (Acts 18:2–3, 26; 1 Cor. 16:19). They did the work of evangelism but also had the ability to come alongside others to contribute to their formation (Acts 18:26–27). Paul calls them "my fellow workers in Christ" (Rom. 16:3). Priscilla, the wife, is listed first, a fact that underlines her vital contribution. She and Aquila were valuable and flexible coworkers in Corinth (Acts 18:2–26), Ephesus (1 Cor. 16:19), and later Rome (Rom. 16:3). In Romans 16 Paul greets a number of people who assisted him at some time in his ministry. Their importance can be seen in the descriptors he uses: "servant of the church" (v. 1), "fellow workers" (vv. 3, 9), "dear friend," (vv. 5, 9), "outstanding among the apostles"

---

4. Barnabas also had an apostolic gift (Acts 14:14). Although he initially functioned as a foundation-layer in Cyprus, his place of origin, he later returned to consolidate the work there and continued John Mark's formation (Acts 15:39).

(v. 7), "approved in Christ" (v. 10), hard workers (vv. 6, 12), and "a mother to me" (v. 13).

Gift-Mix for Church Planting

Gifts from each category in table 15.2 should be present in a church-planting team. Those of evangelism, teaching or preaching, leadership or administration, and the missionary (apostolic) gift should be present to launch a cross-cultural or urban project (Sawatsky 1991). In the following chapter we will consider further what gift mix a church-planting team might need. Nevertheless, God will not be limited to a formula. He can give additional gifts, bring in new team members, or raise up national leaders with what is needed. God uses many kinds of church planters working synergistically through the Holy Spirit: vocational and lay workers, entrepreneurs and consolidators, and strong leaders and humble helpers. Henry Blackaby concurs: "It is time to release God's people as the Holy Spirit directs them and to encourage them to do what they did in the New Testament: proclaim God's Good News to all whom He will send them and in all places He will lead them; to believe and to look for God to draw those being saved and add them together, forming them into new churches."[5]

Spiritual Battle

Church planting is not a business, nor a profession. Church planters could be compared to the frontline troops in a spiritual battle being fought to regain the territory of their King. Jesus assures them that neither Satan nor the world will prevail against his advance (Matt. 16:18–19; 1 John 4:4). Church planters strive to set captives free through the gospel (John 8:32) so that they are transferred from the kingdom of darkness to the kingdom of our Lord and Savior Jesus Christ (Col. 1:13). They must learn to discern Satan's strongholds and rely on God's power and weapons to overcome them (Eph. 6:10–20). Spirit-empowered apologetics are needed to expose his deception and confront his lies. Church planters must count the cost and work diligently, wrestling in prayer as Epaphras did (Col. 4:12). The stakes are high and eternal, and those who engage in this battle must know how to use their spiritual armor, walk in *Christ*, battle in *his* power, and appropriate *his* resources to accomplish *his* will.

Those who have weathered the spiritual battle and experienced victory over darkness become more alert to and adept at responding to Satan's treacherous and devious ways. They learn to anticipate his strategies and expect his lies.

5. North American Mission Board Website, www.churchplantingvillage.net/site/c.iiJTK ZPEJpH/b.886067/ (accessed March 10, 2009).

Church planters must also go on the offensive to help others find freedom in Christ from spiritual bondage. A common weakness among Westerners is a functionally materialistic worldview. They believe in Satan and demonic influences but act as though rational persuasion and friendship alone will bring people to Christ. They don't know how to respond to or recover from direct spiritual attacks. Here are some situations church planters should be prepared to face:

- helping believers understand and walk according to their identity in Christ
- integrating freedom in Christ and worldview transformation in discipleship (see "Special Issues in Discipling" section of chapter 11)
- discerning the source of debilitating habits and helping people find freedom from them
- assessing a person's spiritual influences and practices
- having a plan to help seekers with demonic oppression or overt demonic possession

Some further reading is suggested in sidebar 15.3 at the end of this chapter. However, one does not learn to act wisely and decisively in these situations through reading alone. Seeking the help of veterans and those with the gift of discernment constitutes the best form of preparation. Also, it is always better to confront cases of possible demonic possession with a prayer team.

The Church Planter's Emotional Life

Inherent Difficulties

Elmer Towns calls church planting in the modern world "getting a church started in the face of insurmountable obstacles with limited resources in unlikely circumstances" (quoted in Klippenes 2003, 13). How do you prepare for the unknown and the humanly impossible? Leslie Andrews lists some very real and unique missionary stressors: "Among these are such things as cross-cultural living and communication in a second language; social and geographical isolation; political unrest; communication and conflict with co-workers, friends and family; work obligations and roles; and limitations of time and resources" (quoted in Eenigenburg 2008, 423).

Many factors contribute to general missionary stress and burnout (Taylor 1997; Foyle 1987), and it is beyond the scope of this book to examine them all. Most fall in one of the following categories: (1) multiple new circumstances and changes, (2) a lack of resources and helpers, (3) a loss of support systems, (4) the inherent difficulties of starting a new church, and (5) opposition or lack of recognition. In some ways church planting is like starting a small business with volunteers when the market analysis indicates that most people are not interested in your product. Church planters often feel like intruders and are frequently misunderstood by those they are attempting to reach. Finally, role changes are intrinsic to church planting (Steffen 1997), and church planters have to be designers, developers, managers, leaders, and trainers regardless of their natural bent. For all these reasons and many more, church planting is a complex, demanding, but rewarding ministry that requires emotional intelligence, fortitude, and resilience.

Emotional Resilience

When church planters move into their new place of ministry, they leave many things behind including church, extended family, and other emotional support systems. One of the qualifications for church planting is emotional resilience (Ridley 1988)—the ability to sustain oneself emotionally and physically through setbacks, losses, disappointments, and failures. Emotionally resilient people are adaptable and willing to accept change with few external props. They adjust to the challenging and rapidly changing environment of a growing ministry. When opposition and difficulties arise, they are not devastated but rather bounce back from even the most difficult circumstances to press on, finding strength within. They have their moments of discouragement but are nonetheless perseverant workers and unyielding servants of the cross.

Self-Management

Church planters often lack the external structure and supervision that pastors have. They seldom have a group equivalent to a church board to oversee and guide them. Many work out of the home without regular working hours or well-defined responsibilities. Consequently, some struggle to use their time and resources effectively. Sometimes they spin their wheels in indecision or procrastination and tend to fall back on the comfortable confines of their home or office instead of being out in public places meeting new people and sharing Christ.

Church planting involves both project development and people development. It is hard and complex work that requires long hours, focus, and the discipline to stay on task. Church planters also need clear goals and self-control if they want to see any real progress. Before they begin their first assignment they should have demonstrated an ability to effectively manage their time, families, and resources at home. Jesus turned his face toward Jerusalem and never lost sight of the reason he came. For some following his lead in this respect may be almost instinctive, but for most it is learned behavior. Self-management requires a realistic assessment of one's strengths and limitations and the cultivation of healthy habits and boundaries to keep moving toward the goal. The first healthy habit is the discipline of prayer.

Marital and Family Life

In the United States about one-half of marriages end in divorce.[6] Marriages are subject to formidable pressures in a society bent on instant gratification. Any Christian marriage will go through seasons of increased stress, but in church-planting ministry there are some rare and uniquely intense stressors. As church planting progresses through various phases, the planter's marriage and family life will be challenged in different ways, especially in the first years of ministry.

Stress from Initial Changes

Church planting usually requires relocation and crossing cultures to reach people from different backgrounds. *Culture shock* is defined as "an adjustment reaction syndrome caused by multiple and interactive stress in the intellectual, behavioral, emotional and physiological levels of a person recently relocated to an unfamiliar culture and is characterized by a variety of psychological distress" (Befus 1988, 387). Simply put, it is a product of the cumulative stress of exchanging a familiar culture for a strange one with few support structures. People in cultural transition go through four stages: the honeymoon stage, the crisis stage, the recovery stage, and cultural adjustment (Oberg 1960).[7] Case study 15.1 illustrates the crisis stage.

These changes, coming all at once, precipitate the adaptation process but can strain the marital relationship. Husbands and wives experience church planting differently. Often the husband's role is well defined because the entire process of selection and preparation has focused primarily on *his* gifts and training. If the wife's role does not appear to be as critical or clear, she will struggle more with role-related stress. The husband is more satisfied when he can begin church-planting activities, while she must stay at home with the children, having little time to devote to anything else. In some cases, on the other hand, the wife learns the language more rapidly and builds

6. Based on nondifferentiated 2005 Census Bureau information. Census Bureau estimates vary between 43 and 50 percent.

7. Culture shock is normal, but cross-cultural adaptability assessments can be used to identify excessive risk. The Cross-Cultural Adaptability Inventory measures four areas: perceptual acuity, emotional resilience, flexibility/openness, and personal autonomy. It is generally used *before* a cross-cultural ministry begins. While not necessarily predictive, it can be used to obtain an indication of how people might react in stressful situations. The Cerny Smith Adjustment Indicator is primarily used to see how people are adjusting to a new cultural environment *while* they are experiencing cross-cultural stress.

Case Study 15.1

A church planter's wife describes a particularly difficult day during her first winter in Quebec: "On the way home there was a terrible snowstorm. I could barely see through the windshield. All the street signs were in French. Then I noticed the red and blue bubbles of a police car behind me. I pulled over. He babbled something. I assumed he wanted to see my registration and license. He kept repeating something and motioning with his hands to the back of the car. I got out and looked—it looked fine to me! I had no idea what he was talking about and tears began to appear. He wrote something down on a scrap of paper and let me go. I drove home crying and trembling uncontrollably. I felt like a helpless child. I couldn't understand the simplest things. When I got home, my husband read the note which said my taillight was burned out and that it had to be fixed within a certain number of days. I felt trapped. I wanted to go back to Florida. I hated it here. I missed my friends. I missed my job. . . . I cried many evenings during the long, cold winter. I tried to share my feelings with my husband. But he didn't experience the same difficulties; he had his job, the language, co-workers, and us. Once he said, 'At least you're not in Africa.' I felt like I was being a baby" (Wilson 1996a, 18–10).

relationships more naturally, especially if she is more relationship oriented. When spouses have such different needs and perceptions, marital harmony becomes difficult to maintain. And as the illustration from Quebec shows, there is added marital stress when the spouses enter the adaptation phase on an unequal footing.

Lack of Boundaries between Home and Ministry

Another difficulty is the "fishbowl effect," when day-to-day activities are scrutinized by neighbors and the sense of privacy is lost. Westerners working in tribal settings have particular difficulty with this, because people who live collectively in extended families do not appreciate their need for privacy. Sometimes it is especially hard to accept overexposure of one's children. The natural reaction would be to pull away into a more private lifestyle, but parents realize the importance of their example and witness as a family and want to develop new relationships. They know that hospitality and a home-based ministry are essential in church planting. The tension is not easily resolved.

The lack of boundaries manifests itself in other ways as well. If an office is not available, church planters must learn how to work from the home. Children may be expected to share their toys and their space every Sunday if the church meets in the workers' home. Boundary issues seem only to increase as the ministry grows. Time with the family can become a scarce commodity as the work of mentoring disciples and leaders is added to evangelism and community formation. Healthy families will accept their need for "time out" and establish the habit of a family day off.

Individuals in people professions (teachers, doctors, social workers, and pastors) who do crisis intervention, family counseling, and emergency-room care have especially high levels of stress and anxiety (Hart 1999). Church planters who care for people in crisis, the destitute, hurting families, and couples on the brink of divorce fit into this category. They may face these emergencies with little preparation or training. Usually they see God's powerful intervention and manage to help, but their involvement can nevertheless take a toll on their personal and family health. Although emergencies are by definition impossible to predict or control, workers can learn to manage their lives and schedules as health professionals do.

Boundaries are needed in the area of finances as well. A quandary is created when economic disparity exists between the missionary's lifestyle and that of the general population. There are many requests for financial help from both Christians in need and people from the community. What does a church planter do when several have lost their jobs and want help, or when a couple wants to borrow money because they cannot afford medicine for their daughter? Where does one draw the line? In response to such pressures, the church-planting family must learn how to set reasonable boundaries in four areas:

Space—How will the home be used for ministry? What parts will be off limits to outsiders?

Time—What evenings will be devoted to meetings and visits, and which ones will be set apart for family? What day will be the family's sabbath?

Relationships—How will the spouse at home develop friendships? Do the teenage children have Christian friends? Whom can the couple confide in about ministry problems? How will the children be protected from "overexposure"?

Resources—Will family finances be used to help the needy in the church, and if so, under what conditions? How willing are family members to share their car and personal belongings?

Couples new to church planting need to seek the Lord together and consult with experienced colleagues to guide them through some of these challenges. The following questions can be used as a discussion guide:

1. How healthy are our communication patterns? Are we able to practice active listening, solve problems together, and resolve conflicts without hurting each other?

2. Do we set boundaries to protect our marriage and family?
3. Are we setting time aside regularly to get refreshed and just have fun together?
4. Will we have the support we need (prayer, friendship, mentors)?
5. Are we both willing to make sacrifices to see that we make it together?
6. Do we enjoy working together as a team in ministry?
7. Are we prepared for spiritual battle?
8. Have we considered the educational options for the children and come to agreement?
9. What will we do to provide spiritual nurture and Christian friendship for our children?

Women in Church Planting

Women make up an important part of the church-planting force, whether they are unmarried or work alongside their husband. They also face some unique challenges. Some religious systems, particularly in Muslim and tribal cultures, have distinct patterns of worship and practice for women that tightly restrict cross-gender communication. Paul worked in meaningful partnerships with women assistants such as Priscilla (Acts 18–19) and Euodia and Syntyche (Phil. 4) and local workers such as Lydia (Acts 16), Nympha (Col. 4:15), Phoebe, and others (Rom. 16) in an age when women were rarely found in leadership positions (Meeks 1986, 23–24; Banks 1994, 124–25). Women and men can work together in creative partnerships in church planting today as well, but there are difficulties that must be faced.

ROLE INEQUITIES

Women are sometimes expected to contribute without being given a real voice in team decisions. One female church planter changed missionary organizations because as a single woman and medical professional she had a full ministry load but no vote in team meetings. Frustration over role inequities is aggravated when the woman is serving in an Islamic state, where public roles for women are anathema, or in patriarchal and *machista* cultures where a woman's education, intelligence, and "voice" are not taken seriously. Even when women are treated with respect, they may have a harder time finding their place in a church-planting context. Often these tensions begin as minor irritants, but if they are not dealt with openly and fairly, they can develop into full-blown festering sores.

UNREALISTIC EXPECTATIONS

While some women feel like second-class citizens, others suffer from unrealistic expectations when they have to juggle children and a full ministry load. If women are full partners in church planting should they not also receive equal support and training? This means planning child care and including their agendas in team discussions. During her visits with church-planting wives, Linda Wilson (2003) often asked them to list the key issues and challenges they faced. The same ones came up time and time again, even though the women were serving in different countries (see sidebar 15.1).

Karol Downey (2005) suggests that both women and men would benefit from understanding ministry broadly as service to God in *every* sphere of life: family, church, and the outside world. This will help them find and maintain balance with less unwarranted guilt. Missionary organizations can also contribute by clarifying their role expectations of women, providing broad ministry opportunities according to gifting, recognizing and affirming the great contributions of women, and having experienced women involved in prefield preparation and coaching visits to the field (ibid.).

When women are accepted fully as coworkers and empowered to use their gifts and abilities in the work, kingdom impact is multiplied: the missionary force is expanded; women in Muslim and Buddhist societies can be reached; local women are discipled and trained; the quality of decision making and ministry is enhanced by women's unique insights; the priesthood of all believers is demonstrated; and people are attracted as they see how women can be equals in Christ (Zoba 2000). Sidebar 15.3 at the end of this chapter suggests further reading on this subject.

Sidebar 15.1

Most Challenging Issues Women Face in Church Planting

1. Adjusting identity and roles
2. Dealing with loneliness and discouragement
3. Building evangelistic contacts
4. Counseling believers with little training
5. Training leaders in the church
6. Coping with financial disparity and expectations of nationals
7. Raising children cross-culturally
8. Developing boundaries
9. Organizational rules and requirements
10. Gender role expectations and restrictions

Source: Based on Wilson 2003, 362–66.

Bivocational Church Planters

The expression *bivocational work* refers not to a church-planting method per se but to the way some missionaries and church planters financially sustain themselves. Bivocational workers, sometimes called *tentmakers* or *dual role/ career workers*, have a secular job or business to supplement or fully finance their church-planting endeavors. They must be competent in both roles, integrate them, and manage them along with family responsibilities. In chapter 4 we examined the handicap that is applied to church multiplication when full salaries are considered the norm, and in chapter 18 we will outline some "best practices" concerning finances and church planting. Here we want to look at some of the reasons for bivocational ministry, identify challenges, and make some brief recommendations.

A Growing Phenomenon

The apostle Paul literally worked as a tentmaker part of the time. The Moravian missionaries—the strongest missionary force of their day—were entirely bivocational (Langton 1956; Ward 1992). Today tentmaking has become a significant factor in missions, especially in creative-access places where traditional missionaries cannot obtain visas. It also has been adopted by several associations as an intentional strategy for saturating U.S. cities and rural regions.[8] In international missions, much of the relevant literature falls under the categories of "tentmaking" and "business as missions" (BAM, whose goal is broader than evangelism and church planting).[9] The tenth anniversary of the Overseas Professional Employee Network (OPEN), led by Patrick Lai, was celebrated in 2009. According to Forman Justin, OPEN Network has about two hundred tentmakers from all over the world working in the 10/40 Window (as of May 2009) and exists to upgrade, serve, and facilitate overseas professionals and BAM workers, especially in places and among peoples where there is little or no correct understanding of Jesus's life and work.[10]

8. For example, the North American Mission Board of the Southern Baptists writes, "We agree with Dr. Henry T. Blackaby that unleashing and equipping laypeople is our best strategy to reach North America for Christ: 'It is time to release God's people as the Holy Spirit directs them and to encourage them to do what they did in the New Testament. . . . If the "laypeople" ever catch God's pattern for using them in church planting, the nation and world could come to hear God's Good News in our generation!'" (www.churchplanting village.net/site/apps/nlnet/content3.aspx?c=joJMITOxEpH&b=4693097&ct=6105925; accessed February 5, 2010).

9. "'Tentmaking' refers principally to the practice of Christian professionals, who support themselves financially by working as employees or by engaging in business. In this way they are able to conduct their ministries without depending upon donors and without burdening the people they serve" (LOP 59, 2005). BAM, however, considers the development of business *in itself* as mission—a means of economic development and kingdom impact broader than evangelism and church planting. "Business as mission is about for-profit businesses that have a kingdom focus" (ibid.). Still, the growing BAM literature can be helpful to tentmaker church planters. Books and training resources on BAM have proliferated in the twenty-first century— for example, Rundle and Steffen 2003; Lai 2005; Baer 2006; Steffen and Barnett 2006; Johnson and Rundle 2010.

10. Justin Forman, "OPEN Network Conferences Come to Pennsylvania + Oregon," www .businessasmissionnetwork.com/2009/09/open-network-conferences-come-to.html (accessed February 5, 2010). OPEN has also made a resource bank website available to those who register: www.opennetworkers.net/.

Church Planting with Bivocational Teams

Opinions differ as to the desirability or feasibility of conducting God's kingdom business concurrently with "for-profit" business. Yet tentmaking is rarely questioned on missiological grounds. In fact, how can one expect local church planters in unevangelized countries to work bivocationally if cross-cultural church planters are unable or unwilling to do so? "We must avoid communicating that professional pastors and missionaries are the only, or even the best, way to reach the world for Christ" (Ott 1993, 287). The case for lay church planting does not exclude theologically trained workers who are salaried but recasts them as catalysts, equipping agents, and guardians of the faith in church-planting movements (Garrison 2004a).[11] In sidebar 15.2 we summarize some of the reasons for bivocational teams in church planting (see also Garrison 2004a, 189–91).

Bible schools and theological seminaries will not furnish enough workers to complete the Great Commission or to sustain church-planting movements. Only reproducing local churches committed to the harvest can provide them. For multiplication to take place, we need new models of effective partnership between teams of lay workers and specially trained full-time workers who have equipping roles.

A survey and study was conducted of 450 bivocational field workers from nine different countries from many organizations and denominations over a period of six years. It is significant that although most workers surveyed were bivocational *by necessity*—they could not have entered the ministry site with a religious visa—almost two-thirds of practitioners saw *practical benefits* as well (Patrick 2007). To make full use of those benefits, we must also understand and address some of the life challenges and ministry dynamics that tentmakers must face.

Unique Challenges

Stan Guthrie (2001, 84) identifies some unique challenges of tentmaking based on early attempts at tentmaking ministry:

> Too often in recent years, however, this missions "magic bullet" has misfired, sometimes hitting devoted supporters of the approach squarely in the foot. Between the boldface letters of hype, increasing numbers of astute observers in churches and missions agencies have become aware of tentmakers overseas wracked with guilt because of their double identity, or sent home broken and defeated thanks to a lack of training in spiritual or cross-cultural ministry, or an inability to balance the demands of their secular job with their spiritual ministry.

11. Theological institutions can then focus on shaping leaders of leaders, theologians, and equippers. See Gupta and Lingenfelter 2006, 1–24, for a case study on the benefits of identifying the unique roles of formal and nonformal education and linking them to multiply missional workers.

Sidebar 15.2

The Case for Bivocational and Lay Church Planters

Theological Basis. Bivocational church planting is grounded in the doctrines of the *priesthood, ministry, and gifting of all believers* and reflected in New Testament practice. Movements of lay mobilization advance the Great Commission and allow theologically trained pastors to return to the equipping role described in Ephesians 4:11–13.

Historical Precedent. This follows the pattern of the early church.

> In the early days the faith was spontaneously spread by informal evangelists, and had its greatest appeal among working classes. . . . There was no distinction in the early Church between full-time ministers and laymen in this responsibility to spread the gospel by every means possible. . . . It was axiomatic that every Christian was called to be a witness to Christ, not only by life but by lip. (Green 1970, 175)

> If a clerical class had been established in the first century and the expansion of the gospel had been entrusted to this special group, it is unlikely that Christianity would have spread as it did (ibid., 166–93).

Equipping Context. The local ministry context is the best training ground for frontline workers like evangelists and church planters. Sherwood Lingenfelter, a professor and seminary dean, concludes (with Paul R. Gupta):

> Formal education is ill suited and cannot effectively equip evangelists, church planters, and apostolic leaders for ministry. We are limited for the same reason that we do not train carpenters, masons, and airplanes mechanics through formal education. The skills and the work . . . can be understood and mastered only through practice, through experiential learning. (Gupta and Lingenfelter 2006, 23)

Churches must take the primary responsibility of preparing new workers through church-based training and other combinations of formal and nonformal learning.

Increased Relevance. Clergy are, to some degree, set apart from the members of the congregation by their training and status. While this might facilitate their leadership and ministry within the church, it often puts a distance between them and those on the outside. Bivocational workers identify better with the people, speak their heart language, use an incarnational lifestyle, practice more hospitality, and actively witness through word and deed (Patrick 2007, 171–73). In their for-profit work they share common spaces with those they are trying to reach, so that evangelism is more natural and integrated with life.

Economic Viability. In many places financial resources are too limited to sustain church planting through salaried workers. Even in affluent areas, funds are usually allocated to pastors and their staff before evangelists and church planters. The use of lay workers permits the mobilization and deployment of more local workers and makes funds available for missions and ministry outside the local church.

Steven Rundle, an associate professor of economics, found that deficiencies in the early wave of tentmaking fell into one of three categories: (1) inadequate training in Bible, theology, and cross-cultural evangelism resulting in gaps in ministry competencies, (2) role ambivalence and tension between the two vocations, producing identity and integrity struggles (thus the label "schizo-phrenic tentmakers"), and (3) the failure to create a profitable business, which adversely affected both business and ministry (Rundle 2000).

SERVING TOO MANY MASTERS

The immediate concern becomes how to effectively manage two major voca-tions—plus marriage and family in many cases—and the multiple expectations that go with them. The need for sabbath rest and boundaries between work and family may become more important even as they become more difficult to achieve. Time pressures can appear almost overwhelming; flexibility, resiliency, and good time management are critical to survival. Yet this challenge is not insurmountable. Research indicates that workers who successfully prioritized spiritual disciplines scored more highly in effectiveness (Patrick 2007, 171). And it should be noted that the for-profit work serves a dual purpose, since church planters *must* find common spaces with the unchurched. The bivocational role provides natural social networks with more people, including contacts for evangelism (Davies 1986; Patrick 2007). Furthermore, since there is no clear demarcation between sacred and secular spaces in the bivocational worker's life, connections can occur along natural lines rather than forced, artificial lines that require more effort and yield inferior results (Davies 1986, 96).

ATTITUDINAL CHALLENGES

Motivation is adversely affected when being bivocational is treated as second class, or when respect and more tangible forms of support or recognition are withheld. Ed Stetzer quotes a Japanese church planter with a strong aversion to bivocational ministry: "Never take [a] secular job to meet [a] financial need. I don't personally believe in part time ministry. If one is no[t] confident enough that the Lord provides [for the] needs of [the] worker, one should not take [up] ministry in the first place" (Stetzer 2003a, 260). Tentmakers must be able to articulate, and sometimes defend, their calling and philosophy of ministry.

Not all tentmakers are successful, and some struggle with a sense of guilt, feeling inadequate in both realms of business and church planting. Douglas Davies claims that a sense of liminality—being chronically in transition—is another part of a bivocational worker's identity struggle (1986, 100). Bivoca-tional church planters can suffer from achievement anxiety, always feeling they are in process with few accomplishments and performance markers to point to. When tentmakers fail at their business, or never take it seriously, they hurt their credibility and jeopardize their presence as a Christian witness. "Those who live 'out of sync' with their peers have a hard time interacting successfully with them because they are not understood or respected" (Niles 2000, 306). Thus they are under pressure to be successful at both ministry and business! "A struggling business has a shorter life expectancy, which burdens the family as well as the entire ministry" (Rundle 2000, 294). This challenge points to the need for realistic expectations. The time frame needed to start a church must take into consideration the requirements of this dual role.

Recommendations for Bivocational Church Planting

IMPROVE SELECTION AND INCREASE PREPARATION

Tentmaking is not for everyone. It requires a certain type of person—brave, relational, multitasking, flexible, hospitable, resilient, and adept at personal evangelism and cross-cultural communication. Mans Ramstad exemplifies this skill/attitude mix: "We know the difficulties involved in meeting such objectives in our 'restricted access' nation. We have endured police interrogations and always feel the oppressive weight of police surveillance. But the dangers and difficulties are not enough to dissuade us from the primary importance of evangelism and church planting" (1996, 416). The profile of aspiring tentmakers must include entrepreneurial skills and specialized work skills for the profit role as well as cross-cultural ministry training for the church-planting role. Tentmakers should also work toward professional competence, a good employment fit, and a positive attitude in their workplace, treating it as a part of their ministry rather than a means to an end (Niles 2000). A trainer working with bivocational church planters in African creative-access groups includes a module on designing a viable business plan in his basic training for planters.

SELECT THE FOR-PROFIT ROLE CAREFULLY

Of course, having a secular employment is a ministry advantage only if the for-profit role is congruent and amenable to the building of personal relationships and church planting. The fact that tentmakers find a good fit professionally is not necessarily a predictor of church-planting fruitfulness. Bivocational workers, like other Christians, can get caught up in their professional role to the detriment of their church-planting activities. Patrick observes "We need to admit that tentmakers may become so focused on our work platform that we will not be effective in ministry. Our motivation needs to be God-centered, not self-centered" (2007, 170). The for-profit work should, if at all possible, (1) involve credible employment, (2) be amenable to building relationships, (3) be a good personal fit, and (4) allow time for the ministry role.

WORK IN TEAMS WITH CLEAR PURPOSE AND ACCOUNTABILITY

Because of their constraints, there is a greater incentive for tentmakers to work in teams where responsibilities can be shared.[12] Each member can concen-

---

12. Ninety-three percent of those surveyed (Patrick 2007, 172) worked on a team.

trate on the dimension for which he or she is gifted and prepared. In Patrick's investigation, those who were part of teams with members from more than one country were found to be more effective in spite of the difficulties of cross-cultural understanding and communication (Patrick 2007, 172).[13] Frequent meetings—once or twice a week—were also a condition for fruitfulness (ibid., 174). Teams should provide regular means of holding each other accountable, since "laborers who have someone holding them accountable in ministry at least once a month have a better probability of being effective" (ibid.). The team must have a clear common purpose and strategy to which all members contribute. "Workers who have a clear strategy for planting a church are very effective, while workers who do not . . . are normally ineffective" (ibid.). Ramstad concurs:

> It's not easy to figure out in what ways we are evangelists and church planters, and in what ways we are Christians with secular vocations. But people who are supported with gifts and prayers from a home church must have a clear under-standing about three things: 1) why they are going overseas; 2) what they are going to do to serve the causes of evangelism and church planting; and 3) how they will specifically work toward those objectives. Many tentmakers want this kind of accountability, but others do not. (1996, 419–20)

Establish Ongoing Training and Support Systems

Clearly, recognition and moral support are important factors in the sus-tainability of bivocational work. Christy Wilson (1997, 142) recommends that tentmakers "not be like 'loose canons' around the world" but work through or in collaboration with reputable missionary organizations. Those who do are more likely to join a ministry team and receive prefield orientation, coaching, and logistical support as they face the hurdles ahead. Training for cross-cultural ministry should not be neglected, since there is a direct positive correlation between that training and church-planting effectiveness (Patrick 2007, 169). Although most bivocational workers have some training (Bible college, seminary education, focused missiological training courses, or short-term trips), they con-tinue to need training once they are on the field—especially those working with non-Christians in the 10/40 Window (Patrick 2007, 170). That ongoing training can be informal (mentoring and coaching) and nonformal (theological education by extension and web-based instruction). Fortunately, there are distance educa-tion institutions that make theological and ministerial education accessible and affordable. Furthermore, tentmakers should be given special consideration for educational grants, skill acquisition opportunities, and other forms of linkage or social capital. They also benefit by being linked with colaborers as part of a learning community or peer-coaching group like OPEN.[14]

13. Some pros and cons of multicultural teams are addressed in chapter 16.
14. OPEN facilitates "huddles" of bivocational workers who have a common ministry focus group or geographic focus. Tentmakers may be able to interact face to face, but more often

Sidebar 15.3

Selected Bibliography on the Personal Life of Church Planters

Call, spiritual maturity, and prayer

Blackaby, H., and Richard Blackaby. 2001. *Spiritual Leadership: Moving People on to God's Agenda*. Nashville: Broadman and Holman.

Hunt, T. W. 2002. *Life Changing Power of Prayer*. Nashville: Lifeway Church Resources.

Hunt, T. W., and Catherine Walker. 1997. *Disciple's Prayer Life: Walking in Fellowship with God*. Nashville: Lifeway Church Resources.

Sills, M. David. 2008. *The Missionary Call*. Chicago: Moody.

Spiritual battle

Anderson, Neil T. 2000. *Victory over Darkness: Realizing the Power of Your Identity in Christ*. Ventura, CA: Regal Books.

———. 2006. *The Bondage Breaker. Overcoming Negative Thoughts, Irrational Feelings, Habitual Sins*. Eugene, OR: Harvest House.

Cross-cultural stress and adaptation

Foyle, Marjorie. 1987. *Overcoming Missionary Stress*. Kent, UK: MARC Europe.

Jones, Marge, and E. Grant Jones. 1995. *Psychology of Missionary Adjustment*. Springfield, MO: Logion.

Loss, Myron. 1983. *Culture Shock: Dealing with Stress in Cross-Cultural Settings*. Winona Lake, IN: Light and Life.

Women in church planting

Janssen, Gretchen. 1989. *Women on the Move: A Christian Perspective on Cross-Cultural Adaptation*. Yarmouth, ME: Intercultural Press.

Kraft, Marguerite G., ed. 2003. *Frontline Women: Negotiating Cross-Cultural Issues in Ministry*. Pasadena: William Carey Library.

Kraft, Marguerite G., and M. Crossman. 1999. "Women in Mission." *Missions Frontiers*, August, 13–17.

Bivocational church planters

Johnson, C. Neal, and Steve Rundle. 2010. *Business as Mission: A Comprehensive Guide to Theory and Practice*. Downers Grove, IL: InterVarsity.

Lai, Patrick. 2005. *Tentmaking: Business as Missions*. Waynesboro, GA: Authentic.

Steffen, Tom A., and Mike Barnett, eds. 2006. *Business as Mission: From Impoverished to Empowered*. Pasadena, CA: William Carey Library.

---

they meet online. The program for each huddle is designed along practical issues that overseas professionals face on a regular basis. The intent is not only to learn from each other but also to support and build one another up. Prefield training events are beginning to be offered as well (OPEN 2009).

FURTHER STUDY AND EFFORTS ARE NEEDED

Tentmaking is no panacea, yet the majority of the world's unreached people groups reside in countries that restrict missionary access, so the need for bivocational workers from many countries and backgrounds will only increase. Rick Love affirms: "Training workers like Paul—who have integrated identities and combine credible tentmaking with fruitful disciple making—is the challenge of the 21st century" (2008, 36). Tentmaking by both local and cross-cultural workers should be embraced prudently but very intentionally by those who are so called and qualified. Carefully crafted and coordinated strategies, along with dogged perseverance, are needed to carve out effective tentmaking ministries in the Americas, Europe, and other places where the church has neglected lay mobilization and bivocational church planting. Creative and synergistic partnerships between lay teams and full-time theologically trained workers should be explored. For example, a German pastor with a passion for church planting has been empowered and released to devote 50 percent of his time to work with church-planting interns and guide new church-planting teams. As a catalytic planter, he is working with Bible school graduates and lay leaders to form the teams.

Conclusion

Although this discussion of life issues that church planters face is cursory due to space limitations, their importance should not be underestimated. This chapter should encourage church planters to strive for personal growth, balance, and a healthy integration of personal and ministry dimensions. Effective coaching takes both equally into account (Logan and Carlton 2003). Planters can be proactive in this by growing in self-awareness, establishing goals, having a mentor or coach, and joining a learning community of peers. Sidebar 15.3 offers a selection of reference works that are representative of many other excellent resources for further study in these areas.

16

Church-Planting Teams

Until recently literature on church planting did not give much attention to the role of teams. Even though, as we observed in chapter 3, teams were central to the mission of the first apostles, the popular notion arose that a cross-cultural church planter needed to be a rugged individualistic pioneer. Beginning in the last quarter of the twentieth century, however, there has been a shift toward community and teamwork. Even the business world is moving away from a culture of individualism to a culture of teams. Along with this shift, there is a growing interest in teams in missionary circles.[1] We can offer only a brief overview of the topic here.[2]

An extensive study on teams in the workplace (Katzenbach and Smith 1993, 1–8) produced some interesting results: a demanding performance challenge tends to bring a team into being. In this sense, the most effective and productive teams are not created in a vacuum but *arise out of need*. Most organizations intrinsically prefer individual or group accountability, but companies with strong performance standards seem to spawn more "real teams" than those that *promote* teams per se. Teams seem to work better when they have a clear task that requires a variety of perspectives and skills. They rarely work in the upper echelons of corporate leadership, because of the independent spirit

---

1. This is evident by the number of articles published. In the *Evangelical Missions Quarterly* alone we find Waldron 1971; Bacon 1978; Dyer 1986; Lukasse 1986; Allen 1991; Mackin 1992; Love 1996; O'Donnell 1999; Stetzer 2003b; Zehner 2005; Ellis 2005.

2. For a thorough discussion on missionary church-planting teams, see books such as Daniel Sinclair, *A Vision of the Possible: Pioneer Church Planting in Teams* (2006), and Trent and Vivian Rowland, *Pioneer Church Planting: A Rookie Team Leader's Handbook* (2001).

and time restraints of most executives. Church planting, however, is without a doubt a complex and challenging task that requires a variety of perspectives and skills, one in which "real teams" can be expected to thrive.

Definitions

Some experts distinguish two broad categories of teams: formal, long-term teams and informal, temporary teams like the working group, committee, or other forms of provisional small groups (Lanier 1993; Katzenbach and Smith 1993). In church planting there are people who work together to a certain degree without uniting behind and devoting significant time to a single, long-range purpose. They may use teamwork but do not constitute a *church-planting team* in the sense that we will use the term. While some of the principles in this chapter may apply to informal, low-commitment teams, we will focus on teams that have a formal and specific commitment of several years to a church-planting venture.

A *team* is a group of people with complementary skills who are committed to a common purpose and work together in agreed-upon ways to achieve that purpose, holding each other fully and jointly accountable for the team's results. The key elements are as follows:

- complementary rather than having the same profile
- committed to a common purpose (in our case planting churches)
- deciding how they will work together to achieve that purpose (plans)
- working collaboratively in the execution of the purpose and plans
- holding each other accountable for results

Stephen Macchia (2005, 41) fleshes this out for Christian ministry teams:

> A Christian ministry team is a manageable group of diversely gifted people who hold one another accountable to serve joyfully together for the glory of God by:
> - sharing a common mission
> - embodying the loving message of Christ
> - accomplishing a meaningful ministry
> - anticipating transformative results.

Thus *teaming* is the cooperative and coordinated effort of a group of persons acting together for a common cause. A *church-planting team* is a group of Christians who work together purposefully, under Christ, to start one or more new churches. Such teams come in many shapes and forms, as Johan Lukasse observes: "A church planting team is usually made up of career missionaries or short-term workers helping a missionary church planter for one or two years. In some cases, the team is a mix of career missionary couples and nationals. Sometimes, the team lives as a community. At other times, families are spread over a specific area of, for example, a town and operate from a central place such as an existing church building" (1986, 2). The members can be expatriates or national workers, or both—and either full-time workers or tentmakers. Church-planting teams that include national workers should not be confused with the local leadership team that emerges in the next phase of the church-planting process.

The Need for Church-Planting Teams

Many missionary organizations involved in church planting, especially those working among resistant populations such as Muslims and nominal Christians, use teams as a major element of their strategy. Frontiers Missions uses teams as the basic building block of its church-planting efforts among Muslims. Eric Adams and Tim Lewis elaborate: "[The field team] is the primary vehicle within Frontiers to penetrate Muslim people groups in restricted access countries with church-planting activities. Because the team structure is the key element through which the overall objective of the organization is accomplished, the whole of the Frontiers movement is organized around this fundamental unit. Each team forms around a leader with a vision and a strategy for penetrating a particular Muslim people group or segment of a Muslim city" (Adams and Lewis 1990, 1).[3]

Johan Lukasse, former general director of the Belgian Evangelical Mission, found that in Belgium "it takes team effort to root churches in hard soil." He summarizes the fruits thus:

> We began working with our first church planting training team in 1972. In one year a church was started. A second smaller team followed up that effort and in two years there were 50 adults attending with three elders and two deacons. That church produced a second congregation two years later, a third one four years later, and still another church some time after that. We have used this . . . approach because we have found it to be biblical, practical, and effective. Although we have made mistakes, and the Lord still has much to teach us, we have been able to start 15 churches in eight years. (1986, 134–35)[4]

3. A team approach to church planting continues to be favored by Frontiers Missions and most missions to Muslim and other unreached people groups. See also Livingstone 1993 and Sinclair 2006.

4. Lukasse adds, "When it comes to planting church with a team of people, I still believe that it is one of the best ways of working. We need to consider different kinds of teams however. The principles are very applicable as I explained at that time, the activities and how the team members operate is probably quite different, as we live in this post-modern time" (2006).

Ramón Carmona planted five churches in Colombia and remained to pastor the fifth one in Cartagena so that it would become an incubator congregation that sends out teams to start new works. He believes that the three biggest hindrances to effective church planting are lack of a clear call, inadequate church-planting strategy, and *an inability to work on a team* (our emphasis). He says: "Lone rangers need not apply. . . . It's very important that the missionary be a team player, prepared both to serve and to learn" (quoted in Tone 2000, 11).

Advantages of Church-Planting Teams

There are clearly advantages and disadvantages to teams. One major benefit is that multiple perspectives are available for problem solving. "Recent research by Deborah Gruenfeld of Stanford's Graduate School of Business suggests that teams encompassing at least two separate points of view on a particular question make better decisions because the pressure of the minority forces the majority to think more complexly and consider diverse evidence. Gruenfeld gained some of her evidence by analyzing decisions made by the US Supreme Court" (Snyder 2004).[5]

Ben Sawatsky (1987) studied the teams in Acts, as well as contemporary church-planting teams from five mission organizations, to identify the characteristics of healthy and effective urban church-planting teams. Sidebar 16.1 summarizes the *team member advantages* that Sawatsky found.

There are also *ministry advantages* in relationship to the work of church planting. Teams provide balance and cross-training. Some businesses are shifting from management-driven production (which emphasizes control) to team-based production (which requires empowerment).

- Teams are most often empowered to seek solutions, give input, and assess the output. The teams accept this responsibility willingly, and the results have been surprisingly successful.
- Absenteeism has become less of a problem in a team environment.
- According to surveys, customer satisfaction has improved.
- Decisions are made much more quickly.
- Problems are resolved at the source.
- Tasks are completed in a more harmonious manner.
- Morale remains high. (Norman 1996, 1)

5. The study Snyder (2004) refers to is Deborah H. Gruenfeld and Preston Jared, "Upending the Status Quo: Cognitive Complexity in US Supreme Court Justices Who Overturn Legal Precedent," *Personality and Social Psychology Bulletin* 26 (August 2000).

Furthermore, the work tends to be more stable because it is based on common commitments rather than on the personality or vision of one individual (Waldron 1971). Sawatsky (1987, sec. 6, 19–21) adds the following practical ministry-related advantages of working with a team:

1. Greater boldness in team evangelism
2. Greater power through team corporate prayer
3. Greater creativity through team planning
4. Greater productivity through team ministry
5. Ministry rather than personality centered

Lukasse describes the synergistic advantage of teamwork in church planting:

> Once in the community, the church planting team goes into action. First, each team member joins at least one or two social or cultural groups—such as sports—but only one team member to a club. As a result, they will be able easily to contact and penetrate that part of the population. This is a natural way of getting close to all levels of society and opens tremendous doors. Second, members begin to follow a program of different evangelistic approaches. During this time, they can build relationships and get to know people. Some also do additional research into the local situation to complement the initial work done prior to the selection of the target area. (1986, 136–37)

Possible Disadvantages of Church-Planting Teams

Disadvantages of the team approach can also surface: It takes time and effort to build and maintain healthy interpersonal relationships, and it is not easy to keep the group focused enough to accomplish team goals effectively. A team approach requires more personnel and finances. Even though the Belgian Evangelical Mission believed in teams, it had to adjust its strategy. Lukasse writes: "The strategy of BEM changed because as time went on we couldn't motivate sufficient people to join the church planting training teams. We were forced to look to other ways and methods" (Lukasse 2006, 1).

Sidebar 16.1

Team Member Advantages

1. Complementing gifts
2. Development of gifts
3. Stronger support system
4. Opens ministry door to many more
5. Security in time of crisis
6. Protection against temptation
7. Provides on-the-job training
8. Ensures accountability
9. Diminishes loneliness
10. Allows each to focus on areas of strength
11. Intensifies sense of vision
12. A team can tackle a bigger project

Source: Sawatsky 1987, sec. 6, 14–18

Some degree of conflict invariably takes place in the team-building process. Differences in philosophy of ministry and competition for team leadership often arise early on, and personality tensions can threaten the most committed team. Inequities on the team can also create problems. There is a tension between the desire to treat all team members equally and the awareness that some contribute more because of their hard work or abilities. Frustration may mount when a team member rides on the coattails of more gifted or more dedicated members; or jealousy may surface when one team member rises above the rest.

Team members can have different expectations regarding what each one should contribute to the group and its mission. Often these expectations are unspoken until they erupt in a heated discussion. Some teams stifle individuality; others give it too much place. Either extreme will hurt relationships and hinder productivity. Teams can become ingrown and even narcissistic. Exclusive and absorbing relationships, detrimental to interdependent teamwork, can develop when teams do not maintain a missional focus.

Some teams begin well but later slip into a dysfunctional pattern. This usually begins with a lack of trust and manifests itself eventually in a lack of productivity. When there is a lack of trust, team members hold back from full commitment and mutual engagement. They rarely, if ever, fully commit themselves to decisions and ministry initiatives, though they may indicate agreement during meetings. Without real commitment, team members avoid accountability and begin to function independently. They spend energy maintaining superficial harmony and avoiding conflict. Even the most focused and driven members will hesitate to discuss actions and behaviors that might seem to threaten the good of the team. Finally, the failure to hold one another accountable leads to a neglect of results (Lencioni 2002, 187–90).[6]

Further difficulties arise when a team of expatriates becomes concentrated in one geographic area. The church that emerges from their work can have a very "foreign" feel, and the initiative of local believers can be stifled or overpowered by all the foreign professionals. Furthermore, if the expatriate team members fail to build relationships with national believers or fail to consult them when making decisions, the team may become insular and give nationals the impression that they are not needed or that they have little to contribute. Damaris Zehner warns that even multicultural expatriate teams can become like the mission compounds that were separated from nationals by walls: "a tiny foreign culture in the midst of the mission field" (2005, 363).

In conclusion, "teams are *not* the solution to everyone's current and future organizational needs. They will not solve every problem, enhance every group's

6. According to Lencioni (2002, 188–90), the following dysfunctions build on each other: (1) absence of trust, (2) fear of conflict, (3) lack of commitment, (4) avoidance of accountability, and (5) inattention to results.

results. . . . Moreover, when misapplied, they can be both wasteful and disruptive" (Katzenbach and Smith 1993, 24). On the other hand, healthy teams can provide a community and increased effectiveness for church planters. In doing so, they become a mighty instrument to extend Christ's church.

Lessons from Pauline Teams

In chapter 3 we took note of several ways that team ministry contributed to the apostolic mission: new missionaries were apprenticed, messengers were sent out as needs arose, and more could be accomplished through the use of complementary gifts. We are not suggesting that today's church-planting teams be identical to Pauline teams, but rather that we can learn from these precedents and glean valuable principles. First of all, Paul's leadership is instructive. Today, many church-planting teams attempt to function democratically, seeing their leader as a coordinator without much authority. While understandable, this cultural adjustment can lead to stagnation when it comes to church planting. The biblical precedent underlines the wisdom of having clear and consistent spiritual authority that comes from a distinct spiritual calling and gifting.

A second lesson is the value of being a *missional* team. A church-planting team does not exist to meet the needs of its members or to establish a church that suits their tastes. Team members should be chosen, deployed, and released based on the needs of the mission. At times team members must forgo ministries they enjoy for ministries they find difficult. Later they relinquish control and turn over ministries to national leaders so that the church can be indigenous and multiply. This requires a missional focus from beginning to end.

Is the Pauline pattern of using the team as a training ground for new workers applicable today? Some studies indicate that team members can naturally integrate performance and learning if they have a high degree of commitment to the task, complementary abilities, and a sense of community (Katzenbach and Smith 1993). Initially the team leader will model ministry functions and mentor team members. Peer mentoring can also take place based on the strengths of individual members. In the next stage, as apprentices mature in Christ, missionaries and national apprentices can learn from each other and, together, develop culturally appropriate ways of witness, worship, and service. This creates a learning community in which everyone is a teacher and learner to some degree. Wise leaders of church-planting teams will exploit the equipping potential of the team, even when it means cutting back on some personal ministry.

Paul's teams were flexible and fluid, with members who could function either independently or jointly according to need. Missionary church-planting teams, particularly those that use the apostolic model, should see teaming as a dynamic concept rather than a static one. The team comes into being, grows, diminishes, changes methods, disperses, comes back together, and finally disappears. Team members are inclusive, not cliquish, in spirit; they can work as a large group or break into subgroups as needed.

Given fallen human nature and the dysfunctions that teams experience, it is remarkable how positive and productive church-planting teams in Acts appear to have been. It is clear that the Holy Spirit was assembling and leading these teams to fulfill his mission. He selected the workers, called them, set them apart, led them on their way, and empowered them to preach the gospel (Acts 13:2–9). They had a sense of divine destiny and guidance as a team (Acts 14:26–27). Church-planting teams today must, in the same way, be convinced that they are put together by God and carried by him in the work of the gospel. This requires that they consult him together each step of the way, maintain lives and families that are pleasing to him, and give him the glory. Finally, they must have godly leaders chosen by God himself.

Leaders of Church-Planting Teams

A church-planting team should have an able leader who inspires trust because of his or her character and competence. But what do you do when there is no leader whose experience, calling, or gifting clearly set him or her apart from the others? One church-planting team rotated the leadership function from month to month among its members, both women and men, for two years. With time, this team proved to be as dysfunctional as a body without a head, and after years of church-planting activities, it disbanded before the church was planted. There is no way to sidestep the need for competent leadership. Some of the most successful teams are those that come together on the field after competence in church-planting leadership has been demonstrated. This leads us to favor the formation of teams in which the leader has the final word in the selection of team members, has their trust, and is confident in their loyalty.

One of the most important lessons we gained working with teams over the last twenty years is the importance of the leader's experience. Many teams whose leader lacked experience in church planting or knowledge of the new culture have experienced crisis. Leaders who themselves are learning for the first time how to plant a church or how to minister in a new cultural setting will have difficulty leading others through the same process. When it is not possible to recruit a leader with experience in the culture of ministry, which is often the case in a pioneer situation, the leader should have experience in cross-cultural ministry in another similar setting.

How does the team leader exercise authority? There are many models of leadership and just as many cultural variants. Table 16.1 contrasts two of the most common patterns: the organizational and the organic leadership patterns (Lanier 1993, 7, 14):

Table 16.1
Organizational versus Organic Leadership

Organizational leadership pattern	Organic leadership pattern
Positional	Functional
Power-based	Gift-based
Permanent authority	Limited authority
Insists on allegiance	Establishes trust
Assigned by directors	Accepted by team members
Makes decisions	Builds consensus
Guards leadership functions	Shares leadership functions

Source: Summary of material from Lanier 1993, 7, 14.

Although the organizational pattern has been used effectively in some church-planting efforts, missionary church-planting teams should favor the organic pattern because of the need for flexibility, mobility, and role changes leading to phase-out.[7] Leaders must be ready to delegate responsibilities and share power with teammates and emerging national leaders. *After all, their primary aspiration is not to direct the team but to advance the church-planting mission.* They facilitate fruitful teamwork by helping the team identify and use complementary spiritual gifts. Such leaders prefer to use consensus but are able to make the difficult decisions when needed. They inspire a shared vision and maintain direction and focus by clarifying values and priorities. They have the emotional intelligence and flexibility to foresee needs, adapt to challenges, and influence change. Finally, they know teammates' strengths and weaknesses and promote teamwork and creativity without neglecting results. We see several examples of this organic leadership pattern in Scripture. This should not surprise us, because although God often begins a mission by calling an individual, rarely does he end there; he equips and empowers that individual to gather others to accomplish the mission.[8]

Junias Venugopal (1997) studied operational and disbanded missionary teams to determine factors contributing to effective teams. He discovered that teams that failed to discuss their expectations of ministry and team roles ended up in conflict. Authoritarian-hierarchical or laissez-faire leadership styles, poor communication, and lack of consensus decision making also

7. However, the organizational pattern is often used in the cellular multiplication of urban cell-churches. Moses's restructuring of the Hebrew tribes according to Jethro's advice (Exod. 18:24–26) is used as a model for this.

8. This can be illustrated in the life of Moses (Exod. 17:8–10; 18:24–25), David (1 Sam. 22:1–2), and Nehemiah (Neh. 2:11–18).

contributed to conflict. On the other hand, praying together was a mark of teams that were more cohesive. Effective team leaders give attention to clarity of expectations, balance authority and participation in their leadership style, and promote prayer.

> While maintaining accountability to the International Bureau, Frontiers Missions grants the team leader extensive autonomy and authority for his field out of the conviction that decisions pertaining to church planting among Muslims should be made as close to the field of activity as possible in approaching the task, leadership development, entrepreneurial zeal and a greater willingness to risk as well as better team ownership and morale in what is often an oppressive and hostile environment. Because the Muslim world is often volatile, the ability to quickly adapt the operations of the local team to changing field conditions is extremely valuable. (Adams and Lewis 1990, 4)

Understanding the purposes of the Pauline teams (see chapter 3) sheds light on the main functions of team leaders. Within the organic leadership pattern, they have a *coordinating function* inasmuch as they help the team reach optimum fruitfulness using their spiritual gifts (members as associates). They have a *delegating function* when they assign major responsibilities and send team members on assignments (members as representatives). They have an *equipping function* when they provide members with training opportunities and personal mentoring (members as apprentices). Finally, they have a *directing function* when they assign tasks and hold members accountable for their work (members as assistants).

What are the qualifications of missionary team leaders? They must be spiritually mature and meet the biblical qualifications of an elder. They must be humble and have a servant spirit. Paul writes to the Corinthians: "Not that we lord it over your faith, but we work with you for your joy" (2 Cor. 1:24). Team members need a shepherd, not a controlling ruler (1 Pet. 5:3). Yet they function best with a leader who is not afraid to exercise authority appropriately.

Team leaders must have a clear sense of calling, know their mission, and articulate it effectively. They should have an entrepreneurial spirit and good visionary leadership. Because of the complexity and difficulty of the task, they must be people of prayer who consult God, discern his leading, and then move forward with faith and determination. They must have team-building skills, be able to maintain morale, and inspire members in the face of opposition and discouragement. They must be hardworking, patient, and perseverant.

Leaders should understand the culture of their ministry focus people and the church-planting task sufficiently to lead with confidence. It is preferable that they have ministry experience among the people group. Team leaders should understand their gifts and abilities and choose members who will fulfill specific functions. They will deliberately and wisely choose people who complement them, are loyal to them, and will remain committed to the mission through difficult times. Finally, they must be team players who believe that the team can accomplish more together than each individual can independently (Eccles. 4:9–12). Armed with these qualities and convictions, they willingly help the team develop, resolve conflicts, and serve with their eyes on the Lord.

Multicultural Teams

With the increasing participation of African, Asian, and Latin American churches in mission, missionary teams are becoming more and more international and multicultural in composition. This development positively reflects the global nature of the church of Christ in the twenty-first century and also brings practical benefits. Multicultural teams counteract the perception of cultural superiority, favor mutual learning, model unity and diversity in the body of Christ, and can open doors to diverse communities in urban settings. A broader pool of resources can be brought to the task. They send the message that Christianity is not a Western religion. Furthermore, members from different ethnic backgrounds bring broader perspectives to decision making and can relate in different ways to the local people. Multicultural teams can also decrease suspicion.[9]

But such teams also present great challenges, as members from diverse cultures often bring conflicting expectations, values, and leadership styles with them. Team relationships can be difficult enough to navigate without the added dimension of cross-cultural misunderstanding and conflict.[10] Leanne Roembke lists assumptions that typically cause problems on multicultural teams: "1) the majority culture or the culture of the team leader rule the team culturally, 2) English is the team language, 3) only men do the leading, 4) only the wives carry responsibility for the family and household, 5) the salaries are fixed in the home country without respect to the host country, 6) leadership is from the top down" (2000, 109).[11]

Yet the goal of a healthy multicultural team is achievable with proper orientation, mature and sensitive leadership, an attitude of servanthood, patient

9. Ed Stetzer illustrates this point: "For example, a group of West African Ashanti missionaries seeking to reach the predominantly Muslim Wala in northwest Ghana will be viewed with suspicion. The Wala would be suspicious since the Ashanti have historically dominated the area. However, if an Ashanti missionary is teamed with a West African Fanti, a Korean, and, even better, a Wala, the team's reception will tend to be much more positive" (2003b, 500).

10. The leader of a major international mission agency confessed in a private conversation with one of us that so much energy was being consumed in trying to resolve conflict in that mission's multicultural teams that in many cases the work had come to a standstill or was moving backward. They were also a poor testimony to onlookers. These teams were so dysfunctional and counterproductive that the mission was considering discontinuing them altogether.

11. Roembke's work *Building Credible Multicultural Teams* (2000) is one of the most helpful guides on this subject.

communication, and a desire for ongoing learning. The team must patiently work through questions such as the use of finances, lifestyle and standard of living, the extent to which they will pool their resources, decision-making processes, core values, and team language. Roembke (2000, 175) suggests that input should be received from members of the host culture, and generally the values and language of the host culture should receive priority in such matters.

The leader should keep three essentials in mind when building and facilitating a multicultural team: cultural understanding, commitment to community, and complementary gifts.[12]

Cultural Understanding

Mutual understanding is needed in all human relationships, but particularly in church-planting teams. Unless team members learn to share their expectations, opinions, and aspirations and seek to understand those of their team members, there is little hope that the team will survive long enough to be productive. A large part of communication is nonverbal, and cues are easily misinterpreted. The chance of misunderstanding them is heightened on multicultural teams.

Disagreement over lifestyle issues—such as standard of living or the way a couple corrects their children—can arise on a regular basis. Some cultures value frank and direct communication while others find it offensive and prefer to use suggestive language. Leadership style invariably becomes an issue on multicultural teams. Whether the style is facilitative, authoritative, or collaborative, leadership expectations and boundaries must be clearly discussed and agreed upon. A common problem (Cho and Greenlee 1995) is that team members from different cultures may have difficulty agreeing on what ethical behavior is biblically forbidden, what is clearly approved, and what is subject to interpretation. Even if they agree that certain behaviors are ethically ambiguous, they may have difficulty accepting them on the team. Other sources of cultural tension can be time consciousness, decision-making patterns, the degree of community, and privacy issues. Unfortunately the nature and timing of these misunderstandings cannot be predicted, so processes to deal with them must be in place ahead of time: Here are some practical suggestions:

1. Allow for additional time in the team-building phase (discussed below).
2. Make sure all agree with the conflict resolution agreement and live by it (also discussed below).

12. For a fuller discussion, see "Selection, Training, and Formation of Multicultural Teams," chapter 5 in Roembke 2000 (197–217).

3. Empower all team members to call a special meeting to clear the air, and encourage them to do it as soon as possible when tension arises.
4. Make use of an external team facilitator who is gifted in cross-cultural communication when the team leader feels it would be preferable.
5. Take additional time for team evaluation and relational checks during team retreats (see section on team health and maintenance).

Commitment to Community

According to Yong Joong Cho and David Greenlee (1995, 179), the most important factor in the survival of multinational teams is fostering what community psychologists have called a "sense of community."[13] David McMillan and David Chavis (1986) define four elements necessary for a high sense of community within a particular reference group.

1. The element of membership: the feeling of belonging or sharing a sense of personal relatedness.
2. The element of influence: the sense of having influence over a group and being influenced by that group.
3. The element of fulfillment of needs: the belief that one's needs can be and are being met through the collective resources of the group.
4. The element of shared emotional connection: the commitment and cohesion that grows out of the experience of shared history.

It can be quite a challenging and time-consuming process for a multi-cultural team, or any team, to develop this sense of community. But when team members commit themselves to grow together through this process, the benefits can be great. Members of healthy multicultural teams understand each other's cultural values, practice serving one another, give preference to one another, and are willing to make changes for the sake of mutual edification. Lester Hirst's study of urban church-planting teams found that high "others-orientation" is essential to effectiveness. "On a church-planting team, a team member with high team orientation would be a person who values others and who is willing to sacrifice personally in order that others succeed. This *others*-orientation enables team members to work in cooperation together, for the benefit of all, and toward the goals established by the team" (1994, 144).

However, Venugopal's (1997, 42–44) research revealed two dangers of *excessive* group cohesion: first, "social loafing"—when members work less hard

13. This can be defined as "the perception of similarity to others, an acknowledged interdependence with others, a willingness to maintain this interdependence by giving or doing for others what one expects from them, (and) the feeling that one is part of a larger dependable and stable structure" (Sarason 1974, 157).

because they believe that they are dispensable and others will fill the gap; second, "groupthink"—when the desire for group harmony and unanimity overrides the motivation to consider alternative ideas or courses of action. Commitment to community must not be an excuse for allowing these dysfunctions to develop. Members must be held accountable for fulfilling their individual responsibilities, and creative ideas and independent thinking must be encouraged.

Complementary Gifts and Roles

In chapter 15 we examined gifts that equip team members to accomplish the primary functions of church planting: cross-cultural competency, evangelism, teaching, preaching, leadership, faith, encouragement—and others that have a less direct role but are nevertheless important. Just as all the gifts are needed in the church, so all can be used in church planting. Whether the team is multicultural or monocultural, team members will want to understand their gifts, share them with each other, and help each other use them to plant the church together. All members will have certain roles in common such as sharing Christ, discipling new Christians, and leading a small group, but they will be most effective and satisfied when their primary role flows from their area of giftedness.

After seeing several church plants struggle in Mexico City because an important spiritual gift was lacking, one team leader identified the minimal constellation of gifts needed to plant the church. This new lead church planter determined which of those he and his wife had and which were lacking and proceeded to recruit new team members to supply the needed gifts. The team members also focused on helping new believers discover and develop their spiritual gifts, believing that God would distribute his gifted people to fulfill his kingdom purposes.

What might an optimal constellation of spiritual gifts for a church planting team look like?

Figure 16.1 illustrates an ideal balanced configuration of complementary spiritual gifts on a church-planting team.[14] We should not forget that God assembles teams according to the needs of the situation and that many configurations are possible. Our responsibility is to work toward a viable, balanced team with the best possible mix of gifts and talents, realizing that the perfect team has yet to be assembled.

14. This is an optimal constellation, and teams should not be discouraged if some gifts are lacking. Rather they should look to local believers to supply what is lacking. When there is a full team of expatriates well endowed with spiritual gifts, they should work with several church plants, equipping local believers for the work of the ministry. In this way a single church plant will not appear too foreign or be so filled with expatriate workers that local people feel no need to volunteer.

Figure 16.1
Spiritual Gift Constellation
for a Church Planting Team

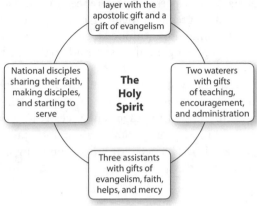

Team Conflict

Even after the leadership question is resolved, conflict is inevitable—and it can be devastating. Much time, money, and training are invested when a missionary team is deployed. When it comes apart, the material cost is great, the strategic setback can be serious, and the damage can be irreversible. Whatever the initial issue of disagreement, conflict grows when members are unprepared for it and fail to manage it with understanding and skill. When biblical commands are not obeyed, a destructive cycle of taking sides and collecting injustices will lead to open confrontation or to the resignation of some members (Shawchuck 1983). When conflict reaches a heightened stage, even if members choose to forgive and reconcile, it becomes difficult to rebuild trust and preserve the team.

Team members need a sound theology of conflict. Norman Shawchuck (1983) points out that, although unavoidable, not all conflict is sinful or harmful (Eph. 4:26–32).[15] Church planters who work on teams should not be afraid of conflict. Rather they should prepare and learn how to manage it in order to minimize the damage and maximize the gains. They can profit from understanding their approach to conflict and learning to develop other responses.[16]

15. Even the spiritually mature have conflicts. The apostle Paul engaged in conflicts over doctrine (Acts 15:1–2), a personnel decision (Acts 15:38–39), and the inconsistency of other apostles (Gal. 2:11–13). Yet Paul resolved these conflicts and restored good relationships with his coworkers.

16. Robert Blake and Jane Mouton (1968) identify five primary responses to conflict: competing, avoiding, collaborating, accommodating, and compromising. Jesus seems to have used

The timing of conflicts on church-planting teams is unpredictable. They can arise over deeply rooted character issues or strongly held values and beliefs. They can also develop out of seemingly insignificant misunderstandings. However, they often arise as the team works through its goals, strategies, and methods—things that involve personal preferences and personality style. Bruce Tuckman (1965) found that teams typically go through four stages before becoming productive: forming (honeymoon stage), storming (working through differences), norming (agreeing on processes and goals), and performing (see figure 16.2).[17]

These stages tend to be cyclical, and conflict can arise at any time; nevertheless, informed team members can learn to manage it rather than succumbing to it. "Anticipating these four stages enhances team dynamics, reduces the pain of team life, and helps us persevere so that we can be fruitful in our ministry" (Love 1996, 312). The need for a team-building plan that includes conflict resolution becomes evident.

Team Building

Team building is not needed only to prepare for conflict and avoid problems. Just as a couple goes through a period of engagement to prepare for married life, a team can benefit from a period of three to six months of structured team formation to prepare for life together. During this time the priority is on team relationships and plans, although members may engage in some ministry activities.

The context for team building is important. Some teams come together for team-building meetings near a sponsoring church before going to the field. Others wait until they arrive in their ministry context and begin right away. A third, and usually preferable, approach is to assemble the church-planting team around an experienced church planter toward the end of language and culture acquisition but before members are caught up in ministry obligations. A mentor or facilitator should be available to help the team debrief, observe their relational dynamics, and help them with decision-making and conflict resolution patterns.

The leader should develop a plan for team building, in consultation with the church-planting mentor, and then discuss it with the team. Two primary goals are building relationships and agreeing on a team growth plan. The plan should also have clear objectives like those that follow:

---

all of these. He confronted the disciples for their lack of faith and for jockeying for position (Matt. 16:8; Mark 10:35–38). Yet he also chose to resolve conflict at times (John 8:3–11) and to avoid it on some occasions (Luke 4:28–30). He also taught his disciples how to deal with private personal offenses (Matt. 5:23–24, 38–40; 6:14–15; 18:15–17).

17. Those who work with group dynamics have also identified these four stages in small group development. See Tuckman 1965 and Tuckman and Jensen 1977.

Figure 16.2
Team Conflict Cycle

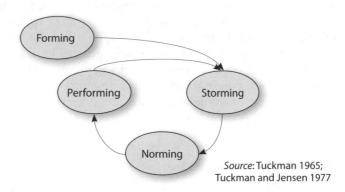

Source: Tuckman 1965;
Tuckman and Jensen 1977

1. To know each other, accept each other, build trust, and develop esprit de corps
2. To clarify the mission and vision of the church-planting effort
3. To study the ministry focus people together
4. To agree upon the key values, common commitments, and early goals
5. To make conflict safe by agreeing on a conflict management and resolution plan
6. To identify the major gifts and abilities of each member and work toward his or her initial roles
7. To express dreams, fears, and expectations openly and develop healthy patterns of communication
8. To agree on when and how meetings will take place and how decisions will be made
9. To allow a member who does not fit the team to leave with dignity at the end of the team-building period
10. To describe leader and follower responsibilities
11. To commit under God to love each other, support each other, and work together

Teams that solidify relationships and agree on goals before becoming immersed in the task of church planting tend to find greater joy in service, model community more consistently, and become more productive. When team formation is completed, members know each other better, trust each other more, and have begun building an esprit de corps from their common values and commitments. "Because each team has a unique leader and MOU [memorandum of understanding], many different field models are created with unique adaptations to the field context and personality of the team" (Adams and Lewis 1990, 2).

Extending the team-building period beyond a few months can be counter-productive. The team members may spend too much time building relationships and lag behind in language learning, cultural adaptation, and relationship building with their neighbors. As a core group of believers emerges, the team might overwhelm the few local believers, stifle their initiative, and give the group a foreign feel. Local workers can get the impression that they are not needed or have little to contribute. When possible, the missionary team should be involved in several church plants simultaneously, leave room for local disciples to develop, and find fellowship and friendships with local believers just as their children do.

Team Health and Maintenance

Many teams set out to plant a church, but not all succeed. Those that do manifest healthy, mutually supportive relationships and complementary roles based on spiritual gifts. The team leader is the guardian of the team's health and values. But all team members should feel responsible to gauge team health and work toward strengthening it. Teams can survive with less, but they will rarely reach their potential without a plan that includes the following four types of team maintenance.

1. *Regular team meetings* (two to four times a month). Members take time to check in, share, and pray for each other. They can all suggest items to be put on the agenda. They discuss issues that affect the team and make plans together.

2. *Special family gatherings* for fellowship and enjoyment (several times a year). This can be a meal or an activity, but "business" is avoided. Families take turns planning and hosting these gatherings. Since the team members are away from their relatives, these gatherings can meet a need during holidays such as Christmas.

3. *Team retreats for assessment and longer-range planning* (at least annually). During these retreats the team celebrates victories, assesses team relationships and productivity, and reviews goals. Retreat time can be used to plan when members will have time off to visit their families and supporting churches and discuss other matters that cannot be covered in the weekly team meeting. Retreats can also provide a chance to receive special teaching and training, discuss sensitive issues, and incorporate new team members.

4. *Visits to team families* (as needed). The team leader personally meets with each couple or single on the team. He or she should have the pulse of the team, something that is difficult to get in the context of the larger group settings alone. Meeting with individual families provides an opportunity to inquire about personal things such as physical and emotional health, to hear any concerns, and to express appreciation and affirmation.

Conclusion

Having a team is neither a panacea nor a guarantee for church-planting success. It may be preferable to delay a project rather than launch without a team, or with one that is not healthy or productive. The five critical factors that must be in place for a team to be healthy and productive are (1) a common purpose, (2) an accepted leader who is both competent and trustworthy, (3) satisfactory community among team members, (4) a functional division of labor within the group, and (5) agreement on how to work together (Waldron 1971).

Teams are particularly important for opening pioneer church-planting works; but even when a project is being launched in one's own culture, the team approach should be given serious consideration, especially with a view to church multiplication. Members can model kingdom relationships and equip leaders for the new church and future ones. With its constellation of gifts, the team serves as a synergistic work force and mobile group of trainers. It is still, in the final analysis, a vehicle that God uses in important ways to extend his church worldwide.

17

Developing Servants, Leaders, and Planters

Every church planter faces the challenge of not having enough workers for the ministry. New believers seem to mature more slowly than one would wish. All too often they just don't seem very gifted. And yet every church planter also realizes that if the church is to grow, become truly indigenous, and reproduce, then local workers and leaders must emerge. This challenge is not new. In fact Jesus himself faced it! We read in Matthew 9:35–38:

> Jesus was going through all the cities and villages, teaching in their synagogues, proclaiming the gospel of the kingdom and healing every kind of disease and every kind of sickness. Seeing the people, He felt compassion on them, because they were distressed and dispirited like sheep without a shepherd. Then He said to His disciples, "The harvest is plentiful, but the workers are few. So ask the Lord of the harvest to send out workers into His harvest field."

As Jesus was inundated with the needs of people seeking his help, his analysis concludes that a greater exercise of his immediate supernatural power is not the ultimate solution. The lack of laborers is the problem. And the answer begins with prayer. Church planters will make prayer the starting point of their quest to develop, empower, and release workers for the harvest.

Making Equipping a Priority

Church planters are often eager evangelists and entrepreneurs who thrive during the launching phase of the church plant. But as we have seen, the gifts necessary to launch are not the same as the gifts needed to strengthen and multiply. As the church grows and seeks to reproduce, increasing emphasis must be placed on equipping local believers for ministry. The apostle Paul makes very clear in Ephesians 4:11–13 that a key to growing the church to maturity is leaders equipping "God's people," that is, ordinary believers, for service. This equipping must go beyond mere teaching of biblical truth to practical identification of spiritual gifts and their development in the service of Christ and the church. Equipping is broader than mere skills training. Its aim includes not only the cognitive and behavioral domain but also the affective (relating to emotions, attitudes, and values). A team of leaders and workers must be equipped with Christian character, convictions, and values. "Effective ministry emerges out of the quality of character—not out of technical competence. Until the Lord has shaped the vessel, it will not serve His purpose" (Elliston and Kauffman 1993, 165).

Early along in the church plant a spirit of empowerment needs to be instilled in the whole approach to ministry. The church-planting team members are not the only ones qualified to serve, nor only those who have formal theological training; but every believer is gifted by God and able to serve others (Rom. 12:4–8; 1 Cor. 12). As Peter writes, "Each one should use whatever gift he has received to serve others, faithfully administering God's grace in its various forms" (1 Pet. 4:10). Every believer developing and employing these gifts will be a key to growing and maturing the church, and ultimately to healthy church reproduction. The church planter's role shifts from being motor and model to being mobilizer and mentor. In most churches key ministry functions such as teaching, preaching, counseling, and visitation are reserved for highly trained professionals. However, as long as the launching of new church plants depends on highly trained and fully paid church planters, church multiplication will be very slow. Mobilization of the whole church for ministry must empower lay leadership in all aspects of pastoral and church-planting functions.

John Maxwell delineates three different levels at which mobilization normally occurs (see table 17.1). "Nurturing" involves caring for the basic needs of the entire congregation; it tends to be maintenance oriented and thus by itself seldom leads to growth. "Equipping" tends to be task oriented, helping many develop and exercise their gifts, with an emphasis on skills. "Developing" occurs with only a few, and emphasis is laid on personal character and leadership. All three levels are important. Pastoral church planters tend to focus on nurture, in keeping with their pastoral gifts. But apostolic church planters with multiplication in view will focus on the equipping and developing levels so that local believers can nuture the congregation. They will also be looking for those gifted to become the next generation of church planters.

Table 17.1
Levels of Mobilization

Nurturing	Equipping	Developing
Care	Training for work	Training for personal growth
Focus is on need	Focus is on task	Focus is on person
Relational	Transactional	Transformational
Service	Management	Leadership
Maintains leadership	Adds leadership	Multiplies leadership
Establishing	Releasing	Empowering
Helping	Teaching	Mentoring
Need oriented	Skill oriented	Character oriented
What people want	What the organization needs	What people need
A desire	A science	An art
Little or no growth	Short-term growth	Long-term growth
All	Many	Few

Source: Maxwell 1995, 112.

From Disciples, to Servants, to Leaders

Christian leaders do not spring up overnight like dandelions. They are more like a solid oak tree that grows with patience, sinking deep roots and extending strong branches. Before attempting to develop leaders per se, we must begin with developing faithful disciples who grow in servanthood and demonstrate qualities necessary for leadership.

Disciples

The process of developing leaders begins with the follow-up of the first new believers as they are made into faithful disciples of Jesus Christ. In the Great Commission Jesus calls the church to make disciples by not only going and baptizing, but also by teaching them to obey all that he has commanded us (Matt. 28:19–20). Milfred Minatrea identifies one of the marks of missional churches as "teaching to obey" rather than merely to know. "Missional churches are not satisfied simply to transfer biblical knowledge. Their goal is members' obedience to spiritual revelation. It is not what they know, but what they live that counts" (2004, 54). George Patterson has developed materials for planting churches based on obedience-oriented discipleship (Patterson and Scoggins 1993; O'Connor 2006).

Servants

Of course learning to serve is part of the most fundamental discipleship. Here the disciple grows in the ability to pass on to others whatever he or she has learned. One learns to serve in simple ways wherever needed, for it is in serving that one develops a servant heart. Equipping is most effective when skills are applied to meeting immediate needs in the church. The personal development of the believer must be in service to the church and Christ's larger kingdom purposes (1 Cor. 12:7). One of the many problems the church in Corinth faced was that members were using their spiritual gifts to edify themselves and not the church!

Patterson warns, "Beware of traditional educational objectives which focus on educating a man. Biblical educational objectives seek to edify the church" (1981, 606). By integrating equipping with actual ministries and acts of service, ministry training becomes training in service. Oswald Sanders, quoting Stephen Neill, explains why this is so important: "If we set out to produce a race of leaders, what we shall succeed in doing is probably to produce a race of restless, ambitious and discontented intellectuals. To tell a man he is called to be a leader is the best way of ensuring his spiritual ruin." Sanders adds, "The need is not so much for leaders as for saints and servants, and unless this fact is steadily in the foreground, the whole idea of leadership training in Christian leadership becomes dangerous" (Sanders 1989, 180). Developing true servant-leaders will mean focusing mainly on meeting the needs of others in a Christlike spirit of humility (Phil. 2:1–8). Our conviction is, *Train a servant, and you will get a leader*. Of course God has not called or gifted every servant to become a leader in the church or mission. But *through* service in specific tasks of ministry character and gifting become evident, and a humble, serving character is more likely to be developed.

Leaders

With time the church planter will need to focus attention increasingly on developing those persons who will become the future leaders and missionaries of the church. A leader will always be a servant, but the difference between the leader and the worker is that the leader *leads*! Leaders are not merely helpers; they are not only effective and faithful in service; they are more than managers who can get things done. Rather, they lead by giving guidance to others and helping them discover and attain their potential in service. The multiplication of churches is built on multiplying disciples, workers, *and* leaders.

We observe this in Jesus's ministry. Initially he ministered to the masses, but as his days on earth drew to a close, he devoted more and more time to being alone with the disciples. In selecting such persons, the place to begin is prayer. Recall that Jesus prayed and fasted all night prior to calling the twelve apostles (Luke 6:12–13). Paul and Barnabas appointed elders in the churches with prayer and fasting (Acts 14:23).

The qualifications for church leadership include many character qualities (e.g., 1 Tim. 3:1–10; Titus 1:5–9) that are not always evident in the young believer. Biblical values of leadership must be taught. On the one hand, local cultural expectations of leaders may or may not be in alignment with biblical expectations of leaders. On the other hand, cross-cultural church planters need to be cautious that they are not imposing foreign cultural standards for leaders that are not necessarily biblical (see, e.g., Thornton 1984).

There are two factors that are especially essential in identifying potential leaders in whom a church planter should invest: *faithfulness* and *giftedness*. Paul instructed Timothy, "And the things you have heard me say in the presence of many witnesses entrust to *reliable men* who will also be *qualified to teach others*" (2 Tim. 2:2, emphasis added). We look for faithfulness in service in the small tasks and responsibilities that have been entrusted to the person in question. Have they been responsibly carried out? If yes, then we entrust more to that person and invest more time in his or her development.

We learn from Jesus's parable of the talents that faithfulness in small things is a prerequisite to being entrusted with greater things: "His master replied, 'Well done, good and faithful servant! You have been faithful with a few things; I will put you in charge of many things. Come and share your master's happiness!'" (Matt. 25:23; cf. Luke 16:10; 19:17). Furthermore, we equip in alignment with gifting. To do otherwise will lead to frustration and possibly harm. There will be many who are faithful in carrying out tasks but who are not gifted to teach others or to lead. Therefore in addition to the more general prerequisite of spiritual maturity, we look to invest in potential leaders who have demonstrated faithfulness in service *and* an appropriate giftedness for leadership in the church and mission.

Methods for Equipping Workers in the Local Church

Imagine for a moment that you have contracted a handyman to remodel your basement. When he arrives to begin work and opens his toolbox, you notice that he has a wide variety of hammers: sledgehammer, claw hammer, tack hammer, ball peen hammer, rubber hammer, wood hammer, and more. In fact, his has *nothing but* hammers. You would become more than a bit concerned about his ability to do the job. We should be no less concerned when in the church only a limited number of equipping tools are available or used. Unfortunately, that is the situation in many churches where only one or two methods are adopted, such as formal classroom teaching or individual discipleship. It is little wonder that so many churches have failed to truly mobilize the congregation for ministry. Equipping servants and leaders will demand a wide array of teaching and development methods. Many books have been written on leadership development in the church, and church planters should familiarize themselves with that literature. We highlight here just a few approaches that we have found to be helpful.

Levels of Leadership and Models of Equipping

Before deciding on a set of equipping methods, one must consider the type of service or leadership for which the person is being equipped. Different methods are appropriate for different tasks and roles.

New believers need to understand the basics of Christian living: how to live obediently as a follower of Christ, to read and apply the Bible, to pray, to share their faith, to begin ordering their life under Christ's lordship, to serve others in simple ways, to stand strong in the face of opposition or trials, and so on. This will not take place primarily in a classroom, though Bible study will play an important part. Rather the approach will be mostly informal, in daily life, walking alongside other mature Christians, observing them, hearing their stories, and following their examples.

Volunteer workers who desire to serve the church or community and employ their spiritual gifts will need more specialized equipping that is geared to the development of the particular practical skills that are needed to be effective. Such volunteers become ministry team members and leaders, cell group leaders, or house church leaders. Workshops and seminars can offer a good starting point for developing such skills, but the primary approach will be mostly hands on. Apprentices in ministry need on-the-job coaching in addition to seminars or workshops to develop their potential. Ongoing training in ministry teams or small group leader meetings will offer continued motivation and strengthening of ministry skills. Those who become ministry team leaders or cell group leaders will need additional coaching and instruction to enable them to lead others and help them achieve their potential as followers of Christ. Cell group leaders will need to acquire rudimentary skills of pastoral care and spiritual oversight. Ministry team leaders will need to learn how to recruit and equip others to join their ministry team and develop their spiritual gifts. Wise church planters will, together with the local church leaders, map out a comprehensive equipping plan to focus strategically on specific ministry needs, and equip to those needs (see sidebar 17.1).

Those exercising primary leadership of larger churches and church-planting teams need still deeper character and greater biblical understanding. At this level higher standards of maturity become essential, as such persons become role models and are entrusted with the spiritual care of others. Leaders face complex challenges and make decisions that have an impact on many lives and whole movements. Thus they need the ability to discern issues and solve problems with biblical insight and cultural discernment. Learning about theology,

Equipping Plan for the North Munich Evangelical Free Church

1. Ongoing equipping of small group leaders during the monthly small group leader meeting
   Goal: Equipping and multiplication of small group leaders
   Objectives: Leading Bible studies, counseling, visitation
2. Mentoring of two men in the church
   Goal: Leadership development
   Objectives: Disciple a newer believer for future leadership and promote growth of a current church elder
3. Training workshops two to three times per year for special ministry skills
   Goal: Recruitment of new workers and development of others. Focus on introduction to basic skills
   Objective: Plan workshops for lay preaching, preparing Bible studies, personal evangelism, counseling, etc.
4. Coaching a ministry team leader
   Goal: Multiply leaders who can train their team members
   Objective: Meet with worship team leader to help plan the worship team meetings
5. Character formation of the church elders
   Goal: Spiritual development of elders
   Objective: Semiweekly breakfast meeting with elders to discuss personal growth and pray; no church business!
6. Small groups as primary context for discovering and developing spiritual gifts
   Goal: Recruit new workers on basis of spiritual gifts
   Objective: Work with small group leaders on how to promote this in their groups

biblical interpretation, church history, counseling, world missions, and other subjects will broaden the leaders' horizons and give new perspectives.

Initially such training can happen through informal seminars, mentoring, or personal reading programs. But realistically, most church planters alone will not be in a position to equip leaders at this level. While formal approaches to teaching, such as Bible school courses or seminary, are common avenues for such equipping, many will not be able to follow this route. Several church-based training programs have been developed to equip leaders locally at higher levels. Other educational delivery means such as distance learning, correspondence courses, and theological education by extension should also be considered, especially for those unable to attend traditional residential schools.

If the goal is to multiply churches primarily through lay or bivocational church planters, then nontraditional equipping will be the best route. Regarding the development of leaders for church-planting movements Garrison warns, "Avoid the temptation to pull new local church leaders away from their churches for years of training in an institution. A decentralized theological education which is punctuated by practical experience is preferable" (2000, 44). Such an approach reduces the tendency toward overprofessionalization of ministry, keeps the learner in the context of ministry, and makes application of learning more immediate and relevant. A failure to attend to theological grounding of such leaders ultimately would make even the most dynamic movement susceptible to instability and false teaching. Biblical and theological equipping of leaders is not optional.

Finally, every movement will need *movement leaders*, *strategists*, and *theologians* who provide visionary leadership, see beyond the immediate issues, discover creative solutions to challenges, provide in-depth biblical teaching and theological reflection, and develop biblically contextualized practices. They are the movement pacesetters and decision makers. A church-planting movement does not need many of these types of leaders, but they are necessary for the long-term health, depth, and continued growth of a movement. They need the highest level of training and must have the freedom to experiment on the front lines of ministry as well as to reflect in the quiet of the study. Once a sound theological foundation has been laid, further equipping of such leaders will be more a matter of mentoring and encouraging the kind of creative thinking and critical reflection necessary to discover fresh ways of building the church and Christ's kingdom.

One of the most helpful books on lay mobilization and leadership development is Edgar J. Elliston's *Home Grown Leaders* (1992). Elliston points out that the different levels of leadership in a movement require different approaches to equipping and development (see table 17.2). Because many missionaries and pastors have received formal training at a Bible school or seminary, the tendency is to attempt to equip leaders at all levels with school-oriented approaches, which are strong on theory but often weak on praxis. One size does not fit all. An equipping plan must take into consideration the responsibilities, skills, depth of character, and biblical understanding necessary to be effective at the anticipated level of leadership.

Key Methods of Equipping

As indicated above, we must move beyond the formal school approach to equipping. Table 17.3 outlines three other equipping models: workshops, equipping in ministry teams, and individual instruction (mentoring, coaching, and modeling). Each has its strengths, weaknesses, and appropriate application. Selection of the best method will depend on the equipping goals, the participants, and the available resources.

Table 17.2
Development Distinctives for Each Type of Leader

Curricular issues	Type 1 and 2	Type 3	Type 4	Type 5
Purpose	Small group leadership	Small congregation leadership	Large congregation or small Christian agency leadership	National/international leadership in administration, teaching, or writing
Content	Specific skills and limited knowledge	Generalizable skills and knowledge, management skills	Knowledge of theories and theory application	Knowledge of theories and theory construction
Timing	Short cycle, at convenience of the learner	Long cycle, at convenience of the institution	Short cycle, at convenience of the learner	Short cycle, at convenience of the learner
Resources	Limited amount needed, usually available from the learner and the community being served	Resource intensive, many resources needed, often outside subsidies needed	Moderate resources needed	Low to moderate resources needed
Costs	Minimal	High	Moderate	Low
Delivery system	Informal, modeling, apprenticeships	Formal, highly structured	More non-formal, less structured	Informal mentoring, apprenticeship
Control	Partially external to the learner	Largely external to the learner	Increasingly self-selected	Self-selected or chosen by agency served
Spiritual formation	Focus on foundations and on doing	Focus on moving from doing to being	Focus on converging status, role, and giftedness	Focus on convergence

Source: Elliston 1992, 35.

Workshops

Workshops are typically conducted on a weekend or several evenings. The central feature of workshops is that participants actually *work*; these are not "listening-shops" (what is often called a workshop is in fact just another lecture). True workshops emphasize practical application, with the participant actively engaging in the skill being taught by using the concepts learned. An

Table 17.3
Three Models for Equipping Workers in the Local Church

	Workshops	In Ministry Teams	Individual Instruction
Format	Group training whereby the trainer teaches and leads participants in application exercises; nonformal, structured	In the context of regular ministry team meetings; informal or nonformal, some structure	Intentional one-on-one meetings: modeling, coaching, mentoring; informal, minimal structure
Purpose	Development of initial ministry knowledge and skills, or expansion of the same	Ongoing development of ministry skills and team effectiveness	Individual character formation or development of specific skills
Participants	Suited for both recruitment and training of new workers as well as development of experienced workers	Members of the ministry team who are already involved in serving	A few carefully selected persons with high potential and demonstrated faithfulness; future leaders
Time	Short-term: several hours, often on a Saturday or over several evenings	Ongoing: time is set aside for training at the regular team meeting	Short or long term: trainer and trainee meet as needed until the trainee reaches the desired skill or maturity level
Content	Mainly skills oriented, with necessary theory to perform the ministry; *knowing*	Mainly process oriented, dealing mostly with current cases and issues arising from the ministry; *doing*	Modeling and coaching are more skill oriented. Mentoring is more character oriented; *being*
Methods	The trainer presents material or demonstrates the skill. Participants then practice the skills or apply knowledge; *know → do*	Case study, problem solving, readings, practical assignments, evaluation of ministry; *do → know → do*	Primarily personal (one-on-one) instruction, guidance, counsel, discipleship; *be ⟷ do ⟷ know*
Advantages	• Well suited for introducing specific tasks and skills • Efficiency: many workers can be trained in a short time • May be led by qualified outside experts • Easily repeated or standardized	• Direct application of training to current ministry • Need oriented, relevant • High motivation of participants • Minimal extra time demand on participants • Training is ongoing • Group learning	• Maximum potential for character formation • Highly effective • Leads to multiplication of leaders/workers
Limitations	• Transfer of learning from workshop to actual ministry may be limited • Minimal character formation	• Difficult to use outside resources • Limited time and intensity • Often irregular participation	• High time commitment • Possible with only a few persons • Dependent on gifts and skills of the instructor • Often unsystematic

example would be a preaching workshop, in which a facilitator walks the participants through the steps of sermon preparation and each participant actually prepares a sermon following those steps. Workshops are a great way to introduce new, inexperienced workers to a particular ministry. Coaching can follow to further hone the skills.

In Ministry Teams

As ministry teams are formed, they usually meet regularly for planning. Such meetings become ideal opportunities to provide ongoing equipping. Our experience has been that if a meeting typically lasts two hours, the first hour can be devoted to equipping and the second hour will be adequate for planning. There are several advantages to this approach: participants do not need to devote additional time to training sessions, and they are already engaged in ministry, thus motivation is high and application of learning immediate. Such equipping can be geared to the challenges the group is currently facing. This is the approach taken in the ongoing equipping and guidance of cell group leaders, house church leaders, children's workers, youth workers, counselors, and so on.

The leadership team in particular is an important venue for such equipping. The leadership community should be a safe place with the following objectives:

- coordination of cell ministry through joint instruction and direction
- encouragement by sharing victories and providing positive models
- providing support and prayer for those facing difficulties
- receiving feedback from fellow leaders in order to make adjustments
- a group context for problem solving, brainstorming, role playing, and curbing individualism
- specific training in ministry-related skills or issues
- strengthening accountability through reporting
- building relationships between leaders
- fostering a team spirit

Individual Instruction

Individual instruction has the advantage of being personalized, but it cannot be done with many people. Typical methods include modeling, coaching, and mentoring. *Modeling* involves simply performing a task with explanation, which the learner imitates and for which she receives feedback. The simple equation is (1) I do it, you watch, (2) you do it, I watch, (3) you do it alone, (4) you teach someone else to do it. Clearly this approach is suitable only for fairly basic skills and tasks. Role playing is often used to model a skill, such as how to share the gospel. Informally, leaders are, of course, always modeling what it means to live as a Christian.

Coaching will be addressed further below, in the discussion of coaching church planters. Coaching tends also to be task oriented, but more complex tasks are learned. Much as an athletic coach shares techniques, guides exercises, and observes the player in action, ministry coaching focuses primarily on the performance of the learner. It usually occurs over a longer period but is limited in scope and lasts only until the skill or task is mastered.

Mentoring is a learning partnership in which an experienced leader as mentor builds an ongoing relationship with the mentee. Mentoring is closer and more intense than modeling or coaching. It also has more comprehensive objectives: not only building skills and sharing knowledge but also shaping character. Mentoring has become commonplace in professional development in business and education to help employees grow, learn the corporate culture, acquire skills, receive counsel, and adjust to change. "Mentors provide a personal connection in an often impersonal and threatening world" (Daloz 1990, 220). The interactive mentor model has been used to supplement or replace the supervisor model (Caldwell and Carter 1993). Church-planting mentors listen to mentees, pray for them, model faithful life and ministry, set the pace, hold them accountable, and give them constructive feedback. Mentoring offers the greatest potential for character development.

The Equipping Context: In-Service Training

In-service training emphasizes the importance of immediate application and experiential learning. After all, "it's not what the teacher does that provides the learning. Rather it is what the learner does" (Elliston and Kauffman 1993, 207). Ted Ward and Samuel Rowan (1972, 19-20) underline four valuable aspects of learner-centered in-service education: (1) Learning proceeds best as learners associate new information with the information they already have. (2) Learning (retention) depends on the use of the newly acquired information very soon after it is acquired. (3) Learning depends on the perceived importance of the information (how it relates to the learners' purpose and goals). (4) Learning (retention and accuracy) is increased when learners are informed promptly whether their use of the new information is appropriate.

In-service training also allows the trainer to see apprentices in action and identify problems early on. Few leaders fail because of a lack of knowledge. Rather, leaders often have relational and character problems that are rooted in unresolved attitude and value issues. These problem areas should be identified and addressed as early as possible in the equipping process, to avoid future pitfalls. The classroom model does little to identify and resolve such underlying issues.

Recruiting and Training the Next Generation of Planters

If our goal is to launch a church-planting movement, one thing is clear: not only leaders but also church planters will need to be equipped and *multiplied*. Workers must be recruited *from* the harvest *for* the harvest, not merely from churches external to the emerging movement. Planters must be equipped in a manner that leads to the multiplication of planters, not merely the addition of planters as is typically the case in most training programs.[1]

Recruiting from the Harvest for the Harvest

In chapter 3 we pointed to an important lesson for church planters drawn from Paul's mission: recruit the next generation of church planters from the churches that you are planting! Church multiplication is achieved when church planters are recruited from the newly formed churches. They must be trained in a manner that is reproducible so that they can also train others. This is a great challenge, because often young church plants are small and are reluctant to surrender gifted workers for fear that the church will suffer. But the Antioch church's sending off two of its most gifted and beloved leaders, Paul and Barnabas (Acts 13:1–3), became the pattern that churches of the Pauline mission followed.

Today rapidly growing church-planting movements have discovered this principle. They rarely wait for seminary graduates or additional missionaries from the outside to come along to fuel the leadership of the movement. Workers, planters, and missionaries are "home grown" in the local church. House church movements may use the simple MAWL approach (see figure 17.1), while larger churches may operate church-based training programs and church-planting residencies (all to be described below). Common to both approaches is intentionality of recruiting and equipping the next generation of workers from among those who are being led to Christ.

Church Planter Selection and Assessment

In North America and elsewhere, attention is being increasingly given to church planter selection, training, and coaching. Not everyone who volunteers to become a church planter is necessarily gifted for such a ministry. The selection process often begins with an assessment of potential church planters. Church planter assessment seeks to discern the readiness and giftedness of

1. Wolfgang Simson (2001, 108–9) points out that traditional formal ministerial training usually leads to the same number of graduates each year. This number barely keeps up with the number of retired pastors or those who have left ministry. If an actual increase in the number of churches and church planters is the goal, models as described below that can be easily reproduced and lead to multiplication of workers and churches must be adopted.

potential candidates. Evidence is mounting that church planters who were positively assessed have a greater likelihood of success and tend to plant larger churches than those planters who were not assessed (e.g., Mannoia 1994, 67; Stetzer 2006, 82; Gray 2007, 59–60). Assessment may take place at an assessment center, where candidates participate for several days in an intense evaluation process including interviews, testing, and simulation games. Other assessment approaches depend more heavily on recommendations, personality tests, and behavioral interviews by a trained team.

The most commonly used standard for assessment is based on a 1984 study by Charles R. Ridley (1988), who identified thirteen key behavioral characteristics necessary for effective church planters:

1. Visioning capacity
2. Intrinsically motivated
3. Creates ownership of ministry
4. Relates to the unchurched
5. Spousal cooperation
6. Effectively builds relationships
7. Committed to church growth
8. Responsive to community
9. Utilizes the giftedness of others
10. Flexible and adaptable
11. Builds group cohesiveness
12. Demonstrates resilience
13. Exercises faith

Though the study was done among white North American males, many believe that the characteristics have cross-cultural validity because they describe functions that church planters must perform effectively to be successful in any context. Ridley has created several practical guides for those wanting to develop a church planter assessment program (Ridley 1988; Ridley and Logan 1998 and 2002; Ridley and Moore 2000).

Other personal characteristics are important in the assessment process, such as spiritual maturity, life experience, education, and community and denominational fit (see also chapter 15). For example, Allen Thompson's (1995) study found the following characteristics to be important:

- spiritual: prayer, integrity, spiritual disciplines, affirmation of God's influence, family oneness, godly character, and recognition of limitations
- skills: leadership, evangelism, preaching, philosophy of ministry, and discipling
- personal: conscientiousness, resiliency, flexibility, likableness, self-image, sensitivity, and dynamism

In many contexts, movements will not have the luxury of being highly selective in commissioning church planters. The above studies were conducted in Western contexts and assume that the church planter is planting a traditionally structured church; thus their findings may not apply to non-Western contexts, nontraditional approaches, and grassroots movements. One study of Hispanic church planters in Miami, however, revealed similar characteristics of effective church planters, the most important being (1) adaptability to ministry contexts, (2) multicultural sensitivity and skill, and (3) ability to develop relationships personally and within a congregational community (Tucker 2006). Another study of cross-cultural missionary church planters in the Philippines found that, in addition to general spiritual qualities, these skills are important:

1. Teach the Bible in the local language
2. Effectively witness in the local language
3. Effectively use the indigenous church-planting approach
4. Use leadership skills with Filipino groups
5. Give an effective evangelistic invitation in the local language
6. Disciple one on one and in small groups
7. Plan strategy for planting a church
8. Evaluate one's own ministry

Additionally, communicative competencies involved several more skills of the effective church planter:

1. Establish personal relationships with Filipinos
2. Solve personal relationship problems with Filipinos
3. Carry on conversations on general topics in the local language
4. Understand Filipino values (Gopffarth 1993)

Regardless of cultural context or church model, both common sense and careful research confirm that wise selection and assessment of church planters contributes to greater stewardship of resources and more effective church planting. This includes appropriately matching personality, spiritual gifts, and experience with the task.

Church Planter Training and Internships

Not only the assessment but also the training of church planters is an important factor in planting healthy reproducing churches and sustaining a movement. Many experienced and effective missionary church planters have transitioned into the role of church-planting trainer or coach of national church planters, thus leveraging their impact. In North America, opportunities abound for church planter training. Many seminaries offer courses on church planting and related subjects, but most seminaries train primarily for nurturing, teaching, and pastoral ministry and less for missional church leadership (Robinson 1992, 32). As Robert Vajko sadly observes, "When leaders enroll in a formal educational institution, they often tend to look at their education as an entrance into a more established church where they can be adequately cared for financially" (2005, 297). Thus, as a supplement to more formal ministerial training, many denominations, movements, and some local churches offer nonformal church training programs. For example, church planter boot camps are typically intensive one-week workshops that focus on practical planning and preparation for the launch of a church plant. Organizations such as ChurchSmart[2] and networks such as Acts 29,[3] NEXT,[4] and New Thing[5] offer a plethora of high-quality seminars, boot camps, publications, resources, and support systems to train and assist church planters. Similar networks and organizations are being formed internationally. For an excellent overview and examples of the many approaches to church planter training being done in North America, see Glenn Smith's monograph "Models for Raising Up Church Planters" (2007). Here we focus on grassroots training, modular training, church-based residencies and internships, nonformal regional training, and coaching.

Grassroots Church Planter Training

Rapidly growing grassroots church-planting movements have seemingly little time or need for such church planter training. Relatively new believers spontaneously start new cell groups that develop into house churches. But the impression is deceptive. Their method of training is often profound in its simplicity. For example, David Garrison outlines one approach with the acronym MAWL: "Model, Assist, Watch, and Leave. Model evangelism and church planting; Assist local believers to do the same; Watch to ensure that they are able to do it; Leave to go and start the cycle elsewhere" (2004a, 344). The church planter teaches largely by example, with minimal theoretical instruction or planning. He or she models what is expected from the lay evangelists in the first house church, then assists them with the first daughter church and watches while they start a third-generation church on their own (figure 17.1). When the third-generation church is planted without assistance, the multiplication process is fully under way. House church leaders are taught basic skills of interpreting and applying the Bible as well as caring for the needs of believers. The primary emphasis is on evangelism.

2. See www.churchsmart.com.
3. See www.acts29network.org.
4. See www.nextchurches.org.
5. See www.newthing.org.

Figure 17.1
Reproduction Cycle

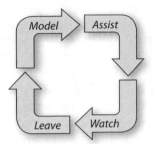

Source: adapted from
Garrison 2004, 44

MODULAR CHURCH PLANTER TRAINING

With modular training, church planters are brought together regionally on a regular basis for training and encouragement. In the 1990s the New Church Incubator system was developed by Robert Logan and Steve Ogne (1991b), whereby church planters and their lay leaders from several church plants come together monthly for encouragement, prayer, and training on various practical topics. Between meetings each church plant is assigned a coach, who helps the team members implement their learning. This concept has been used widely in Western contexts. A similar example is the Bulgarian Bible League, which brings together planters from around the country for five modules over a two-year period. Topics such as vision, practical tools, spiritual character, administration, and Bible study are presented, and planters are given specific assignments. Trainees receive at least two on-site visits from trainers, and those already launching a church plant receive additional visits (Appelton 2008, 2). Vineyard churches of German-speaking Europe have adopted modular church planter team training involving five weekends over eighteen months. These cover the topics of vision, planning, team building, evangelism, and discipleship (Vineyard Dach 2009). A great advantage to this approach is that trainees do not need to relocate their families or surrender jobs to receive the training. The training is also in-service, as trainees are often already engaged in a church plant or serving in a local church. This increases learner motivation and makes implementation of principles and plans immediate.

CHURCH-BASED CHURCH PLANTER TRAINING RESIDENCIES
AND INTERNSHIPS

Several larger churches in North America have raised their commitment to church multiplication and training church planters to an exciting new level. Growing from the vision to launch a movement and to share their experience, they have pioneered their own church planter training programs, often including a church-planting residency or internship. These are usually not seen as a replacement for formal ministry training (such as seminary) but as a practical, hands-on, in-service approach to testing, acquiring, and honing particular skills necessary for planting churches. Often the program also includes other elements such as character building and fund-raising.

One of the most impressive of such programs is offered by Hill Country Bible Church in Austin, Texas (2009). Numerous applicants are assessed for their church-planting potential, and then four or five are received into a one-year church-planting residency. A personally tailored learning plan for each resident is formulated. Participants receive instruction from subject matter experts, and, most important, they are coached in evangelism, discipleship, cultural exegesis, project management, budgeting, speaking, and leadership skills. Not only do they assist in a current church plant, but as the residency progresses they begin preparation for a new church plant that they themselves will lead. This entails recruiting participants from the sponsor church to form their missional core team, formulating a strategic plan, raising funds, and making evangelistic contacts in the focus community. In fact, with their team, they are held accountable to build at least two hundred relationships with unbelievers in the community. By the time that these church-planting residents have completed the twelve-month program (and not all do), the likelihood of their church plants succeeding is very high. It is a great investment in training, and the spiritual dividends are also great.

Another church excelling in training church planters is NorthWood Church near Fort Worth, Texas (Roberts 2008, 137–50). Its nine-month church-planting internship program takes in over a dozen interns who have been assessed for high church-planting potential. Another pioneer in church-based church planter training is Redeemer Presbyterian Church in New York City, whose program deals with the following topics:

- call and competencies of the church planter
- vision, values, and mission of the church
- research: demographics and ethnographics
- contextualized philosophy of ministry
- action plan
- leadership structures
- linking the gospel to your community
- renewal dynamics for church planting and growth
- small groups
- preaching in the context of church planting (Redeemer Church Planting Center 2009)

Most such church-based church planter training programs include a full system of recruitment, assessment, training, coaching, resourcing, partnering, and ongoing training. They are usually led by a full-time director and administrative assistant. Residents (or interns) often receive funding; thus these programs are expensive to operate. They often depend on considerable outside funding from foundation grants and private donors (Williams n.d., 4).

Nonformal Regional Church Planter Training

Hindustan Bible Institute (HBI) offers an outstanding example from India of creative and effective church planter training and mobilization (see Gupta and Lingenfelter 2006). In addition to its formal degree programs, HBI began a two-year nonformal program to multiply church planters, the Missionary Training Institute (MTI). Three principles guided the plan: (1) find students with a passion for evangelism and church planting, (2) repeat foundational information in Bible and practical ministry to ease learning for those with little formal education, and (3) have trainees apply teaching by teaching others—that is, they immediately teach what they have learned by reaching and discipling others in the villages. An on-site training program was developed to help evangelists actually plant churches. The average number of churches planted by each trainee grew from 1.5 in 1991 to 3 churches in 1993, and by 2003 to 4.5 churches (ibid., 38). During this time over 500 church planters were trained through MTI, who planted some 2,300 churches with a total membership of 110,000 (ibid., 50–53).

The key factors contributing to the success of the movement included (1) the opening of the nonformal program, which was accessible to those unable or unqualified to undertake formal study but gifted for church planting; (2) the practical, in-context, experiential learning approach; (3) regular evaluation, repetition of learning, on-site mentoring; and (4) empowerment of the trainees to teach and mobilize converts for church multiplication. In moving from addition to multiplication, training planters to intentionally disciple new believers who could in turn disciple others was critical (ibid., 52). Eventually cross-cultural church planters were trained to reach various ethnic groups of India using the apostolic approach laid out in chapter 5. As in many other programs that train grassroots church planters, vocational skills, hygiene, and basic medicine are also taught to help them be bivocational, support themselves, and remain healthy.

Another example of a regional church planter training center comes from Myanmar (Burma). From 1996 to 2007 five churches with a total membership of under one hundred grew to thirty-six churches with 835 members primarily from Buddhist backgrounds. The church planter training center offers a certificate and a diploma. "All church planters begin as evangelists. When a group has been gathered, the evangelist is then promoted to probationary pastor. Only when the group continues to grow and mature is the leader confirmed as a pastor" (Tanner 2009, 154). Though all the leaders at the center have degrees in theology, they received specialized training in evangelism and church planting in Australia.

A final example of training teams for church planting among Muslims also comes from Southeast Asia. Planters are recruited who have already received general biblical and practical training for ministry in Bible schools and seminaries. They are then brought to one of several regional training centers for specialized church planter training. For a six-month period they attend classes two days a week, and on the other days they participate in a local church-planting team to apply what they are learning. Teams of four or five persons are then formed and sent out to launch new church plants. Periodically the teams come together in their regions for fellowship, to report on their work, and to receive ongoing equipping.

Coaching and Encouraging Church Planters

Another significant factor in equipping effective church planters is ongoing coaching or mentoring. As the new church planter actually enters into the adventure of church planting, many challenges will be faced that were unanticipated or never addressed in the training. Application of church-planting principles, problem solving, and gaining fresh perspectives on one's situation do not come automatically. Thus some form of ongoing assistance is considered essential in the overall equipping of church planters. Offering advanced seminars is one way to address the need. But usually more personal guidance and counsel geared to the church planter's individual situation will be more effective. The long-term development of church planters must include more than task-oriented problem-solving skills. It must also include the personal development of the church planter. Dealing with discouragement and personal limitations, building on one's strengths, and celebrating one's victories are the primary goals for which church planters usually need coaching during the first year or two of ministry.

The importance of mentoring and coaching has been widely recognized in nearly every discipline, particularly management, education, and sports. Church-planting leaders everywhere agree that ongoing encouragement and counsel of church planters is essential. Sherwood Lingenfelter summarizes the importance of personal mentoring of church planters in India associated with HBI: "Training without mentoring by the pastor or another leader usually doesn't succeed. This was true at all levels of HBI mobilization training. Pastors did not know how to plant second and third churches without leader or peer mentoring" (Gupta and Lingenfelter 2006, 98). Though empirical evidence is somewhat mixed regarding whether coaching of the church planter leads to faster church growth,[6] there can be little doubt that personal encouragement and sharing of wisdom through coaching will contribute to overall effectiveness.

Sometimes a distinction is made between mentoring, which gives particular attention to personal development, and coaching, which focuses more on skills. But whether the term *coach* or *mentor* is used is not as important as the intentionality with which a more experienced church planter offers personal assistance to a less experienced one. Of course the concept of mentoring is as old as the Bible itself and can be found in the examples of Moses and Joshua, Elijah and Elisha, Barnabas and Paul, and Paul and Timothy. However, practical resources to assist church planter coaches have become available only recently.

Space doesn't allow us to explore church planter coaching in detail. We refer the reader to some of the various resources and guidelines for coaching that are available. For example, John Whitmore in *Coaching for Performance* (2009) uses the acronym GROW as a guide for each coaching session:

- define and clarify Goals
- examine one's Realities in terms of the given situation and obstacles to achieving the goals
- explore Options for overcoming obstacles and attaining goals
- Will: what will the coachee actually do as next steps to reaching the goals?

Robert Logan and Sherilyn Carlton in *Coaching 101* (2003) outline a similar "5R" approach to coaching:

- Relate
- Reflect
- Refocus
- Resource
- Review

An accompanying *Coaching 101 Handbook* is also available (Logan and Reinecke 2003a), and *Developing Coaching Excellence* (Logan and Reinecke 2003b) offers written and audio training for coaches based largely on the 5Rs. *Empowering Leaders through Coaching* (Ogne and Nebel 1995) is an espe-

---

6. Stetzer (2006, 102–3) found that the frequency of meeting with a coach improved the size of the church plant. A study by Gray (2007, 146), however, did not show coaching of the church planter to be a significant factor when rapidly growing and struggling church plants were compared.

cially helpful tool, including print and audio resources, evaluation guidelines, preparation questions, and worksheets. A variety of online resources also are available to coaches such as www.coachu.com and www.coachnet.org.

Most such tools emphasize that the coach should give few answers and ask more questions based on well-honed listening skills. The coach thus seeks to assist the coachee in discovering his or her own path for achieving goals and finding solutions to issues being faced. The objective is to avoid the church planter's becoming dependent on the coach, and instead to help the church planter develop in his or her own character, skills, and problem-solving ability. She or he should learn not only to be an effective church planter but ideally to also become a coach of others.

Cross-cultural coaching, where coach and coachee are from differing cultures, involves additional challenges of communication that can create differing expectations and misunderstanding. For example, the relatively nondirective coaching methods preferred by North Americans may be found confusing. Overly task-oriented relationships may be experienced as dissatisfying. Coaches should become familiar with standard works on cross-cultural communication and management. Coaching in small groups, sometimes called coaching clusters, is another approach found to be helpful. While this style of coaching is less individual, the group members exercise a measure of peer coaching and accountability that adds a valuable dimension to the experience.

Whatever particular approach one takes, effective coaching must be based on a genuine caring relationship, be intentional, involve regular meetings, and include some level of accountability. This will demand commitment from both parties. Most advocates and practitioners of church planter coaching recommend at least monthly coaching meetings, and more frequent contact will likely increase effectiveness, especially during the early phase of the church plant. The goal is for the coach to help the planter realize his or her full potential and become a reproducing church planter.

18

Partnerships and Resources
in Church Planting

The concept of partnerships in missions, although greatly in vogue, is far from new. For example, in the eighteenth century John Williams took the gospel to the Pacific Islands and established a base on the island of Rarotonga. In the years that followed he translated the Bible into Rarotongan, developed a training center, and built a vessel to transport evangelistic teams of Rarotongans. "Under his supervision, evangelism was carried out almost entirely by native teachers, most of whom had very limited training. . . . Nevertheless, they courageously left their homes and tribal security, and entered into strange surroundings and learned unfamiliar languages, risking their lives to bring the gospel to their fellow islanders" (Tucker 1983, 211). This partnership was a key factor in the evangelization of the South Seas and, by 1834, only eleven years after he landed on Rarotonga, "no island of importance within 2,000 miles of Tahiti had been left unvisited" (Hardman 1978). Making disciples from Jerusalem to the ends of the earth has frequently given rise to a wide variety of international and intercultural partnerships.

The gospel must travel from one people group to another, and it only makes sense that the recently evangelized collaborate with those who brought them the gospel to reach other unevangelized groups. Furthermore, no church or association of churches has access to all the unreached people groups of the world or enough resources and wisdom to fulfill the Great Commission on its own. Christopher Little observes, "The International Partnership Movement

(IPM) has debatably become the most influential force affecting the global church today. . . . It is gaining more momentum as organizations, churches, and individuals, both Western and non-Western, are jumping on board" (2005, 2). This is largely attributable to the globalization of missionary efforts and the maturing of new sending nations from the Southern Hemisphere. The new missionaries often want to work in creative collaboration with existing Western missionary organizations from a position of equality and respect. Paul Gupta, writing primarily about the situation in India, underlines the value of such collaboration: "As a trainer, consultant, and facilitator, [an expatriate] may serve the national church to develop a church planting movement, or to equip that movement with essential leadership skills and resources to grow mature, dynamic Christians and churches. As expatriate churches and mission organizations adjust their vision and *redefine their role to partner with national churches, they may have a greater impact for the kingdom of God than was ever possible through 'pioneer' efforts*" (Gupta and Lingenfelter 2006, 198, emphasis added).

Partnerships include efforts such as short-term teams, compassion and relief efforts, and financial assistance to national workers. Today partnerships appear in many forms:

- an expatriate missionary alongside national workers
- cooperation between mission agencies from various nations
- international congregation-to-congregation partnerships
- local churches sending international short-term teams to partner with missionaries or local churches
- direct support of national workers by a local church or mission agency
- collaborative efforts between associations or denominations

However, partnerships in mission are so commonly and sometimes uncritically practiced that they can produce unintended negative consequences. We will look at diverse types of partnerships, common dangers, and some "best practices" to avoid disappointments and the misuse of God's resources in global church planting.

Definitions and Assumptions

In this chapter we focus on partnerships that intentionally pursue church planting. A *church-planting partnership* is a voluntary collaborative association to plant one or more churches. When such a partnership is healthy, it contributes to the reproduction of healthy indigenous churches through the sharing of resources and ideas in complementary relationships of mutual respect and trust.[1] We explore various types of partnerships that integrate cooperative disciplemaking and compassionate social action and contribute to the multiplication of healthy kingdom communities (see chapter 19).

All churches can be involved in partnership. With many churches in Africa, Asia, and Latin America sending missionaries, the language of *sending and receiving* must be used and heard in an entirely new light. The *sending church versus receiving church* paradigm falls short because it gives the impression that some churches remain receiving churches indefinitely. The language of partnership breaks down this false dichotomy. For the sake of simplicity, we will use the term *expatriate* for the partner who travels cross-culturally and *local* for the partner where the new church is being planted. Expatriate church planters involved in the partnership will be called the *missionary team*.

Biblical and Practical Reasons

There are some convincing biblical reasons for partnering in missions. The acceleration and advance of the Great Commission must remain the primary goal. Paul and Timothy could count on the Philippians in their effort to reach other communities with the gospel (Phil. 4:10–18), and Paul expected the church in Rome to help him take the gospel to Spain after he had visited it for a while (Rom. 15:24). Partnerships facilitate the planting of new kingdom communities by strategically bringing together complementary gifts and resources.

Partnerships also have a qualitative impact by demonstrating reciprocal care, respect, and support. The Philippians demonstrated generosity by giving sacrificially (Phil. 4:10–19) and sending Epaphroditus to care for Paul's physical needs (2:25–30). Paul in turn sent Epaphroditus home to alleviate their concern (2:28) and encouraged them with his letter. The partnership between the Pauline team and Gentile churches to bring famine relief to the Jerusalem church was also intended to build greater unity between Jewish and Gentile churches (1 Cor. 16:1–4; 2 Cor. 8–9).[2]

When partnerships are healthy, they empower rather than control. Paul implies that he avoided baptizing many Corinthian believers so that they should not form a Pauline party (1 Cor. 1:14–15). The leaders of the Jewish church chose not to impose their cultural norms on the Gentile churches (Acts 15).

---

1. A vast literature has been produced on the topic of dependency and financial support of national workers, fueling a vigorous debate. See for example McQuilkin 1999 and Bennett 2000. Daniel Rickett (2000) discusses healthy interdependency and accountability in missionary efforts. Our approach will be to avoid the polemics and propose positive ways of using resources in church-planting partnerships.

2. Richard Longenecker (1964, 228–29) argues that both goals were present but that Paul's decision to go to Jerusalem with the offering indicated his preoccupation with a growing estrangement between Jewish and Gentile Christianity.

No one should have to sacrifice their cultural identity to be part of a partnership. The goal is that both entities, although different, preserve their cultural distinctives, learn from each other, and contribute something significant to the common goal according to their respective abilities.

These voluntary collaborative associations use diverse gifts, resources, and ideas *synergistically*. Paul incorporated into new teams the strengths and cultural savvy of coworkers recruited from churches he had previously established.[3] Ecclesiastes 4:9–12 lists several benefits of partnership: greater returns, protection, help in time of need, warmth, and strength. Furthermore, the mandate to be wise stewards of time, talent, and treasure calls partners to regularly evaluate their kingdom impact and fruitfulness (Luke 16:8–12).

Other Partnership Benefits

Working together helps to overcome the enormity of the task of world evangelization and permits good stewardship of the diverse resources needed for so great a task. This becomes even more important when we consider the rise of new agents in world evangelization. At the turn of the twenty-first century the number of missionaries from the Southern Hemisphere approached that of traditional Western churches (Jaffarian 2004) or may even have surpassed it (Keyes 2003). Also, the practical matters of training, deployment, and ongoing outreach can be more effectively addressed through the skillful cooperation of everyone involved.

Partnerships can also function as learning communities. Those from newer sending nations offer fresh perspectives, additional energy, and greatly needed personnel but seek to learn from the experience of established missionary organizations in areas such as developing support structures and care for long-term effectiveness. The flow of ideas and strategies is increasingly going from East to West (e.g., cell and house church movements, spiritual warfare, ways of reaching postmodern pagans), as can be seen by the example in case study 18.1.

Partnerships allow more personnel to be involved. "Short-term mission is, paradigmatically, a form of collaborative partnership in witness and service with Christians who are already present locally" (Priest and Priest 2008, 66). Thus short-term missions (STMs) expose literally millions of Christians to cross-cultural service and witness. Historian Eliseo Vílchez sees enormous potential in this volunteer movement: "In the context of religious globalization, STMs arise as one of the strongest instruments of contemporary mission and of the religious transformation that the whole world is experiencing" (quoted

3. Review chapters 3 and 16, on church-planting teams, to see how intentional Paul was about his teamwork.

Partnership as a Learning Community

An American church planter worked in Central Asia for seven years without a single convert in spite of his experience, dedication, and support from churches back home. He was successful in developing many friends among Uzbeks but brokenhearted to the point of tears because none had come to faith in Christ. A Korean missionary joined him. This man had fewer resources but greater boldness and a deeper understanding of traditional cultures. He explained that by making so many friends the American was failing to live up to Uzbek expectations of friendship and hospitality. The two set aside friendship evangelism to focus on finding receptive "men of peace" (Luke 10:6) and initiated spiritual discussions with them intentionally and immediately. This approach was the key to unlocking several homes for the gospel and starting two church plants. Several more new churches began in these homes because Bible studies with the "first respondents" in each village were done openly to allay suspicions and over time other family members joined in. The Korean missionary understood the cultural patterns and helped the American to adapt his approach. On the other hand, the American brought the resources of a team and was able to take the lead in the establishing phase. The value of partnership as a learning missional community should not be underestimated.

in Paredes 2007, 250). Cross-cultural experiences and relationships broaden a person's perspective and break down stereotypes.[4]

The long-term contribution of these STM partnerships to church multiplication cannot be taken for granted, however. Most trips last less than two weeks; most teams are made up of inexperienced youth and target countries with tourist appeal (Priest and Priest 2008). Since very few teams go to places in the 10/40 Window,[5] the net effect is, at best, to strengthen existing ministries rather than to expand into new unreached areas (ibid.). Nevertheless, we believe that strengthening the quality of STMs and designing them in the context of long-term church-planting partnerships can bring about positive lasting contributions. Practical suggestions will be given throughout this chapter.

It should be noted as well that the contribution of kingdom partnerships goes beyond functional benefits. When partnerships palpably demonstrate Christ's love before the world, they serve as testimony to the power of the gospel and constitute a sign that the kingdom is at work. Sameh Maurice ex-

4. See the following works for more detailed studies of STM teams. Rickett 2000 and Livermore 2006 offer contrasting points of view. Robert Priest (2008) has compiled the most quantitative research and offers a balanced perspective.

5. "The 10/40 Window" designates those counties that lie geographically between the 10th and 40th parallels in Asia and Africa. Most countries that are least reached with the gospel are located in this region.

presses their intrinsic theological value: "We believe very much in partnership. We believe in the oneness of the Body of Christ; that a local church by herself can do very little. Churches together can do more and more. [We believe] that the united Body of Christ can do the impossible; [it] can do what Christ Himself can do. This is why we invite the church world-wide to partner with us in many projects" (Maurice 2005).[6]

Types of Partnerships

Church-planting partnerships are diverse and dynamic. They are living things and should be treated as such. Each is shaped by a distinct vision, the available resources, and the maturity and giftedness of those involved. Some add more players as they evolve. Their structure is determined by the number and identity of the partners. Most are between two (dyadic partnership) or three parties (tripartite partnership), but some involve more than three (complex partnership).

Dyadic partnerships, also called congregation-to-congregation, link a local church with an expatriate church or a missionary team. These are the simplest, most common type. Many agreements to send STM teams fall in this category. These teams bring added energy, credibility, and resources at critical moments of the church-planting effort, helping the new church overcome natural growth barriers. These are usually long-term collaborative efforts in which the missionary functions initially as "broker" and then unselfishly serves the interests of partnership as an encourager, adviser, and problem solver. Carl Brown's (2007) research demonstrated that the competence and commitment of this person has a great impact on the success of the partnership and church-planting project.[7]

We call a collaborative effort that involves more than two associates a *complex partnership* (see figure 18.1). The effort may bring together several expatriate churches and a local missionary team to help an international church-planting project. Usually the number of partners grows with the scale of the project. Sometimes the partnership is between regional entities. For example, a group comprising dozens of North American Evangelical Free churches (a district) is partnering with an association of Mexican churches in many church projects, using STM teams for training, evangelism, and construction to strengthen existing plants and launch new ones. An experienced missionary couple serves as facilitator and catalyst by preparing the projects, orienting the teams, and participating in many of the projects.

6. Sameh Maurice was pastor of Kasr-El-Dobbara church in Cairo, Egypt, at the time of this interview (November 18, 2005).

7. See also Hiebert 2006 on the mediatory role of the missionary in today's globalizing world.

Figure 18.1
A Complex Partnership

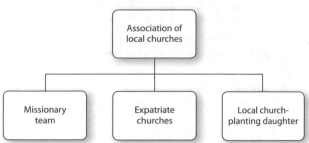

Key factor: partnership specialists who nurture relationships and build systems

Interdenominational coalitions of local churches that partner together to support a church-planting project have also been formed. For example, in the greater Milwaukee area a consortium of several churches have joined together to support work in Indonesia. In order for this to function well, the facilitators must be specialists who view this as a primary ministry. They develop tools, best practices, and systems to see these sometimes complicated partnerships through difficult stages to positive church-planting outcomes.

Partnerships can also be distinguished by their ministry emphasis. Even those that focus on church strengthening and reproduction may utilize a wide variety of means. Evangelistic and discipleship efforts are often part of a church-planting partnership but they are not the only, nor necessarily the primary form of involvement. Sidebar 18.1 lists just some of the ways that STM teams can partner with a church-planting effort.

Guidelines for Healthy Partnerships

Church-planting partnerships have great potential, but they are costly in terms of manpower and energy. Thus they should be handled wisely, in accordance with the following guidelines.

Have a clear purpose. The primary objective must be prayerfully agreed upon. Through prayer, the Holy Spirit often accomplishes things that neither partner had expected. Partners International found that to increase the effectiveness of its partnerships, it needed a greater focus on the end result of the partnership, so it began joint evaluations of the qualitative and quantitative fruit of the partnership (Downey 2006).

Clarify expectations. The nature of the partnership, financial arrangements, decision making, and a host of other matters should be openly discussed at the outset. Partners from different cultures may understand the meaning and

Sidebar 18.1

Ways to Involve Short-Term Mission Efforts in Church Planting

- Construction projects: church buildings, playgrounds, housing, community centers
- Community service such as digging wells, clean-up efforts, agricultural development, assisting in schools, orphanages, hospitals
- Neighborhood canvassing, literature distribution
- Street theater, drama, sports outreach, pantomime, music, showing films
- Evangelistic English-language camps, English tutoring
- Medical and dental clinics, community health education
- Presentations in local schools
- Camping and camp ministries
- Leadership development, teaching, training seminars
- Prayer ministry, prayer walks
- Professional development seminars such as continuing education for doctors, school-teachers, business leaders, development workers
- Environmental projects
- Logistical and technical assistance with large evangelistic campaigns

purpose of a partnership differently. For example, more relational cultures may view the partnership as a collaborative friendship, whereas those from an urban business culture would see it primarily in terms of the church-planting task (Brown 2008). Oscar Muriu (2007) points out that Americans tend to be confident and direct and like to solve problems, while Africans tend to be more reserved and indirect, thus the partnership suffers unless American STM members value the opinions of the local people over their preconceived ideas.

Remain flexible. Relationships evolve, circumstances change, and unexpected developments arise. A written partnership agreement may be viewed by one partner as a temporary guide that is tacitly open to renegotiation as situations change, while the other may see it in more rigid contractual terms. Even when expectations are clearly spelled out, arrangements may need to be adapted to suit new realities. Fundamental principles should not be compromised, but flexibility in nonessentials will contribute to greater effectiveness and satisfaction on all sides. Overly stringent policies and timelines should be avoided.

Include a bicultural mediator. In a fallen world we can expect unmet expectations to cause tension. And where there are cultural, linguistic, economic, and other differences, the potential for misunderstanding is great. Inexperienced partners often underestimate this challenge. Again, a bicultural and bilingual mediator, such as a mature missionary, is invaluable to negotiate the relationship, help each party understand the other's idiosyncrasies, and fairly represent both parties.

Grow the partnership with patience. In Spanish *relación de socios* (relationship of associates), the expression used for partnership, implies a peer relationship of equality and trust. Some North Americans tend to be very results oriented and can have unrealistic expectations about how quickly trust can be developed and how long it takes to plant a healthy church.[8] Partners should take time to get acquainted, share vision, and build trust. Then they can build on that foundation with mutual respect, appreciation, and understanding. Partnerships that have built a bridge of trust and established healthy communication patterns are more likely to survive.

Seek to empower and make the benefit mutual. "In true partnership, each member seeks to build and empower the other" (Hiebert and Larsen 1999, 59). Partners International defines partnership as "collaboration without control" (Downey 2006, 200) and describes its ethos as "empowering locally-led ministries to carry out God's work in culturally-appropriate ways in partnerships of mutual trust" (ibid., 202). The goal of an empowering partnership is always to give with an open hand, looking to the common goal. Any attitude of superiority, control, or paternalism will do great damage, but a two-way exchange of resources, strengths, insights, hospitality, and values helps to keep a partnership healthy and interdependent. The ultimate focus is on God's glory and the growth of his kingdom.

Establish a fair decision-making process. Sometimes the partner with more resources can intentionally or unintentionally dominate decision making.[9] Local believers may feel powerless for fear that if they propose a different course of action the support they count on will be withdrawn or the partnership will be dissolved. Or they may acquiesce but not follow through. Decision-making processes should respect the interests of all partners and guard the integrity of the local work from inappropriate outside influence (Collins 1995).

Exercise wisdom regarding financial assistance. One of the most common sources of conflict in partnerships is the use of money. Difficulties may come from an overly cautious and stingy spirit on the part of the wealthier partner, or unhealthy dependencies can result when financial subsidies are unwisely administered or dominate the relationship. While the investment and benefit of the partners need not be equal and should not be compared, it is expected that all partners will make sacrifices and reap kingdom dividends. We'll return to this point below.

8. American congregations have a "tendency to focus on programs that have immediate payoffs" (Wuthnow 1997, 199).

9. On the importance of power and authority in partnerships, see Davies 1994, 46. Carl Brown (2007) discovered that even simple decision-making processes are a key factor in the health and effectiveness of intercultural church-planting partnerships.

Practical Steps for Each Partnership Stage

Partnerships, like most relationships, have a life span. Healthy ones are entered into prudently and concluded graciously. Even though the joint project ends, the relationship continues. But that relationship changes as the partners release each other from their mutual commitments related to the church-planting effort. This is why we call the final phase "culmination and release" (see figure 18.2).

In the *exploration and conception stage* churches decide to explore the formation of a church-planting partnership. Partnerships can be initiated by an established church that wants to send STM teams cross-culturally or by the leader of a new ministry seeking outside help to launch it. Alternatively, a third-party missionary organization, seeing the benefit of partnerships, may bring together a local church and an expatriate church (or churches) that have compatible goals, values, and interests.

The choice of a partner should be made prayerfully, based on clear goals and criteria. Relational compatibility between leaders is also important. Potential partners should seek to understand each other's culture, situation, and history. Three factors that commonly contribute to a precipitous and unhealthy partnership are a pressure to perform well, the overwhelming needs of the work, and the adrenaline rush of a new and exciting experience (Lederleitner 2007). It is preferable not to make promises and agreements until sufficient common ground is evident.

Figure 18.2
Stages in Partnerships

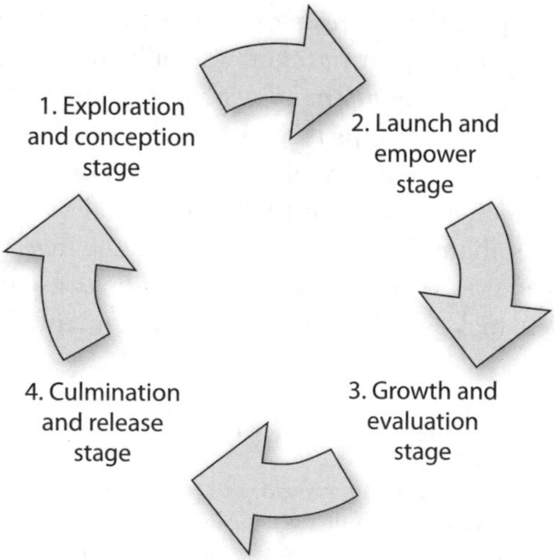

1. Exploration and conception stage

2. Launch and empower stage

3. Growth and evaluation stage

4. Culmination and release stage

During the *launch and empower stage*, the focus moves from selecting the right partner to establishing common goals and plans. Dialogue should be facilitated by the kind of bicultural mediator described earlier. The point persons representing each partner should also be competent and mature people of unquestionable integrity who ideally have had some prior cross-cultural experience.

An initial trial project is conducted. Afterward the facilitator and point persons debrief together. The joint evaluation serves to affirm the partnership, make adjustments to it, or bring it to a gracious conclusion. Between STM trips, partners keep in touch and work on the next steps in their common effort. Ways to sustain the partnership between STM trips should be explored. These may include sustained personal correspondence, extended ministry assignments, and visits that go in both directions.

In the *growth and evaluation stage*, the church plant takes shape and a local leadership team emerges. Partnerships require energy, attention, and flexibility—especially in this phase. The role of STM team members changes as they seek to complement and enhance the work of the local disciples. A focus on the purpose is maintained by asking, "What is needed to take the church plant to the next level?" and, "How do we overcome obstacles and move the work forward together?" STM teams should encourage the new church toward stewardship of gifts and resources. If outside resources have been used, a gradual transition to reliance on local resources must occur in this phase. Changes, problems, disappointments, and unfulfilled expectations are addressed immediately and openly (remembering that in some cultures this is more difficult). The facilitator and point persons consider how setbacks can be redeemed and become learning experiences. During the joint evaluations even the smallest advances are underlined and affirmed.

In the *culmination and release stage*, there is a healthy rhythm of cooperative ministry. This pattern may involve repeated seasonal ministries, such as English-language camps in the summer and leadership training during the winter months. Relationships are increasingly comfortable, and responsibility for ministry plans now lies squarely on the shoulders of the local ministry team. Fellowship is enjoyed, mutual respect and accountability are bearing fruit, and victories are celebrated.

However, just as the partnership appears to climax, a healthy conclusion must be prepared. If there is no plan to complete the project, inertia will most likely lead to frustration and an unpleasant termination. A sense of abandonment can arise unless relationships are affirmed and continued even as the joint mission comes to a close. The partners may cooperate in planting yet another daughter church or join hands in an entirely new work. The partnership can evolve into a mutually edifying sister-church relationship by means of informal friendships, occasional visits, and special cooperative projects.

Strengths and Weaknesses of Partnerships

Healthy partnerships are not without cost. Nor are partnerships always successful. Just as conflict between Paul and Barnabas led to a painful parting of ways (Acts 15:36–41), so today church-planting partnerships have the potential for both fruitfulness and frustration. It is wise to establish early in the relationship a pattern of evaluation in which all parties participate. It is helpful to draw out concerns by making evaluation natural and constructive criticism safe. We have seen that in church planting the benefits are multifaceted and come from the relationship: mutual learning and growth as well as visible results. Honest assessments should take all of these into consideration.

As we stated earlier, every partnership is unique; however, certain common criticisms emerge, and we have summarized and grouped them according to their source. Here they are from three perspectives: those of expatriate churches, local indigenous churches, and traditional missionaries.

Perspective of Expatriate Churches

Besides wanting to advance church planting and to increase their own involvement in missions, expatriate churches often expect personal growth to take place in the lives of STM members. Some even think of STM trips as a type of boot camp that transforms lives. Randy Friesen (2005) found, however, that the greatest cognitive and attitudinal changes occurred during the first short-term experience but that regression occurred in most cases after a year.[10] Strangely, most participants experienced a *decline* in spiritual disciplines, moral purity, and local church involvement in the year following their mission trip. Likewise, Kurt Ver Beek's (2006) study of STM construction projects in Honduras found that there was no evidence of significant change in participants' lives or giving patterns as a result of the experience. Friesen (2005) found that these trips are more likely to enhance a participant's practice of spiritual disciplines if a sufficient foundation is already there. So it would be a mistake to send people who are not spiritually mature on STM trips in the hope of jolting them toward maturity through exposure to difficult conditions.[11] If participants are not sharing their faith and exercising a positive influence at home, it would be ill-advised to expect them to do so in a foreign context. The rule of thumb is,

10. This study involved 116 STM participants ages eighteen to thirty who took part in one of five STM trips ranging from one month to a year between September 2001 and August 2002. For other cautions about STMs, see Livermore 2006.

11. The study also reported: "Short-term mission participants with extensive pre-trip discipleship training experienced significantly higher change scores than those without training . . . related to personal communication with God (prayer), the Bible as a guide for life, the value of Christian community, relationship with the local church and evangelism" (Friesen 2005, 453).

the greater the maturity at the outset of an STM, both spiritual and personal, the greater the potential of positive impact will be. Also, lasting changes in participants are more likely when guidance, debriefing, follow-up, and other subsequent service opportunities are added.

Local Indigenous Church Perspective

Often the local churches are enthusiastic about the contributions of lay volunteers from other countries. They come at their own cost, demonstrate sacrificial service, and make significant contributions. They may help to attract unbelievers, use their professional skills, improve community relationships, offer leadership training, and develop infrastructure (buildings, roads, wells, bridges). At times the expatriate partners contribute financially even after the STM trip. They may sponsor orphans, contribute to educational or medical projects, offer scholarships to seminary students, and financially support church planters.

Robert Priest (2007) surveyed 551 evangelical pastors in Lima, Peru, and found that 58 percent had hosted STM teams and those that did were over-whelmingly positive about the experience. He summarizes, "When short-term mission trips are underpinned by humble service, sacrificial stewardship, and wise leadership, they potentially make important contributions to the global church" (187). STM participants' primary contributions were not in evange-lism but in resource sharing, building credibility, and opening doors.[12]

Oscar Muriu offers a candid counterbalancing perspective. He finds that STM members are often poorly informed about the world, overly self-con-fident, ill-prepared for cross-cultural ministry, and as a result less effective than they could be. "Short-term experiences have their place, but they need to be more carefully constructed. All too often a church says: 'We'd like to come for a short term experience.' Then they say, in so many words, 'We're going to do A, B, C, D, and we're in charge'" (Muriu 2007, 97). He prefers to call these trips *short-term learning opportunities*.[13] Latin Americans have not held back their criticisms either. The following is representative of several contributors to a journal issue devoted to the matter: "There is a latent and, in my humble opinion, inevitable danger of 'religious tourism' that will hap-pen to the extent that prior preparation and subsequent assessment of STM groups is disregarded. That is, the further we are from serious planning and

12. Nationals desire and teams brought *linking social capital*, that is, relationships that create opportunities, generate goodwill, and enhance the credibility of struggling local church plants.

13. Todd Poulter (2006, 452–53) argues that metaphors like "selling the vision," "getting them on-board," and "transferring ownership," when used regarding local believers, are condescending and hurtful. It is preferable for sending churches to be involved in the cocreation of projects in community with the local believers.

coordination with local churches, the greater the risk of investing millions of dollars in 'religious tourism' that could well be used in more effective ways for establishing the Kingdom" (Cerron 2007, 31).

Traditional Missionary Perspective

Traditional missionaries[14] may have mixed feelings about STM trips and the partnerships that sustain them. They see the educational and motivational value of exposing thousands of people to the country and cause to which they have dedicated their lives. Occasionally a participant returns for a longer-term stay or helps to send others.[15] At times traditional missionaries find themselves in the position of brokers caught between conflicting interests or goals. They can also feel overwhelmed by the sheer volume of work that STM trips require. Like leaders of the local churches, they find that STM members need cultural orientation and practical preparation and feel responsible to help them succeed.

Some missionaries are also concerned about the amount of resources used by STM that would otherwise go to longer-term church planting or development efforts. "Short-term trips, lasting two weeks or less, drew about 1.6 million Americans to foreign mission fields last year, according to a survey by Robert Wuthnow, a sociologist of religion at Princeton University" (MacDonald 2006). The median cost of a participant's STM trip abroad is somewhere between $1,000 and $1,500 (Priest and Priest 2008, 57). This would mean that a whopping $1.6–2.4 billion are spent on STM trips from the United States yearly. Ver Beek's (2006) study found that the average cost of a home built by STM teams was $30,000, while a home of the same quality built by local Christian Honduran organizations costs only $2,000. Such figures give us pause and require us to consider the stewardship in such endeavors. The impact on giving to missions is impossible to calculate, since in most cases participants contribute themselves, receive help from family, and raise the balance of the funds from their own pool of friends and relatives (ibid.). Furthermore, some STM participants will become donors to long-term efforts and recruit others.

Another concern is the amateurism of volunteers on STM teams. The criticism is warranted to the degree that it is provoked by the immaturity of participants or their lack of preparation for the task. But Garrison (2004a, 261–66) reminds us that the word *amateur* literally means *one who does it out of love* rather than for pay and that many volunteers are highly skilled professionals who can relate to local believers and residents through and because of their career. "This conveys a powerful message to the new believers" (ibid., 262).

14. By *traditional missionary* we mean a full-time missionary, usually sponsored by a Western missionary organization.

15. Friesen (2005, 452) found that a year after returning from a STM trip, almost equal numbers had become less interested in long-term missions as those who became more interested in long-term service as result of their experience.

Concluding Comments

These diverse perspectives, taken together, encourage us to channel this lay-volunteer movement toward greater long-term effectiveness. More is not necessarily better. STM ministries should be seen as a supplement rather than a substitute for traditional church-planting missions. The consensus seems to be that partnerships using STM teams are beneficial if they contribute to long-term goals already in place and are well managed by partnership coordinators so that the expectations are clear and the long-term missionary staff is not sidetracked or overwhelmed. Better selection, orientation, and training are all needed. Costs need to be carefully examined and managed.

The STM movement was not planned by the missionary establishment and will not be curtailed by its reservations. We must not forget that, arguably, most New Testament church planters were in a sense short-term missionaries who had other means of livelihood. Both short- and long-term missionaries can be dismissive or inconsiderate of each other. When all partners recognize each other's strengths and use them collaboratively toward a clear mission, the greatest fruit is borne.

There are times when Christian leaders and churches should move ahead without looking to form a partnership. If STMs become the modus operandi of missions, undesirable partnerships may be created and bold kingdom initiatives may be stifled. However, healthy, empowering partnerships bring joy even where there are challenges. They exude energy, motivate participants, and produce visible results. No partnership is without its problems, but healthy ones produce a cooperative synergy that allows partners to grow and become more effective for the kingdom.

Financial Factors and Church Multiplication

"Church Planting Movements thrive on indigeneity. They must have internal momentum if they are to rapidly multiply through a people group. One of the surest ways to cripple a Church Planting Movement is to link reproduction to foreign resources" (Garrison 2004a, 267). What financial practices will contribute to fresh waves of church multiplication?

Relying on Lay Workers

Church multiplication occurs most rapidly where church planting does not require theologically trained and ordained pastors but is led by teams of lay or bivocational workers. As we saw in chapter 15, this is the New Testament pattern. Not that the apostles did not receive help from established churches—they did. But they did not rely on that help as a precondition to church planting. The Moravian missionary movement exemplifies what God can do through workers trained in local churches. "The proportion of [Moravian] missionaries to home communicants has been estimated at 1:60 compared with 1:5000 in the rest of Protestantism" (Norman 1978, 676).

Lay movements are still possible today. The fastest-growing grassroots movement in Peru at the turn of the twenty-first century, the Movimiento Misionero Mundial, attributes part of its remarkable growth to the fact that it works with the people and resources that God provides locally. MMM church planters begin with house churches led by lay workers and offer leveraging funds for biblical training or meeting places only on rare occasions when workers distinguish themselves as effective evangelists and shepherds. The financial help is temporary, and the new church body must rent or purchase its building. Rodolfo Cruz adds that freedom from dependence on outside resources has allowed the churches to finance movement-wide projects like television broadcasts, missionary efforts, and regional evangelistic campaigns using predominantly local funds.[16] This does not mean that pastors should never be salaried but that this will take place at a later stage, when the local body of believers is in a position to call and support a full-time worker. Other churches may choose to continue to be led by bivocational elders and invest their funds in church extension and missions.

Apostolic Lifestyle

Extension works can usually be started by local teams of lay workers who do not have to uproot their families and find other jobs. However, to launch a cross-cultural work in a more distant region, church planters must often move and be supported by churches or find other employment. In many countries there is not a strong enough financial base to support the missionaries who are needed, so new paradigms of missionary support must be explored. Planters must also adjust their expectations, embrace a simple and sacrificial lifestyle, and be willing to find an additional source of revenue if needed—following the example of Jesus and his apostles.

Peruvian pastor Samuel Nieva speaks of the proliferation of grassroots churches among the poor of Lima, in places where one would least expect them: "They don't start thinking of all the problems, that they need benches, a pulpit . . . they just start to build. Money can be raised through 'polladas' [chicken roasts], clothing sales and other devices" (Berg and Pretiz 1996, 217). Church-planting movements grow in the midst of subsistence living and strong opposition (Garrison 2004a). This is convincing evidence that church multiplication need not be resource driven.

On the other hand, the paucity of resources should not be an excuse for inadequate preparation. Initial seed money can make a big difference. When

---

16. Personal interview with Rodolfo Cruz, president of the Movimiento Misionero Mundial, in October 2005.

asked, "Why do church planters fail most often in Latin America?" many church-planting leaders mentioned a lack of funds and lack of denominational support as primary causes. Preparation and planning should never be a substitute for sacrifice and dependence on God. Many supporting churches cannot rely on fixed giving, nor can they afford inflexible budgets with financial commitments to buildings, salaries, and programs. They need to operate on limited and unstable assets, with flexibility and a high degree of ownership by members, constantly determining what God is calling them to do and then praying and working together to bring it to pass. In chapter 4 we used the example of a small grassroots movement in Colombia that supports workers without outside subsidy. It has found creative ways to support church planters who live sacrificially on an average of $300–400 U.S. dollars a month. Many remain single by choice. Some live in simple quarters attached to a church building or live with church families. Most receive about one-third of their support from family and friends, one-third from their local church, and one-third from a joint missions fund to which all the churches contribute. Others have part-time work.

Postponing Costly Programs and Purchase of Buildings

Great wisdom is needed when a young church is considering the use of outside funds to purchase or erect a building. Historically, churches have not needed real estate to flourish. Missionaries who come from congregations that own real estate sometimes assume that buildings are an important ingredient of church life. However, new believers in some societies are rejected by family and lose their jobs when they follow Jesus. Others live from day to day, growing most of their own food, and cannot afford a home, let alone a church building. Thus church planting can slow or comes to a halt when there is an expectation that each Christian community should have a special building of its own. The organic reproduction of the church is compromised. This does not mean that meeting places are unimportant. The healthy pattern is for churches to start out with what they have and as they grow in maturity and means, acquire property later. In church multiplication movements, where church buildings are used at all, they are generally simple structures erected with local materials and resources. Otherwise the attitude can quickly develop that only outsiders can build churches and that locally constructed church buildings are inferior.[17]

Teaching Stewardship of Life and Resources

Good stewardship of life and resources will be part of the DNA of any healthy church-planting movement. All along the way, giving will be an im-

17. Examples of the misuse of resources for buildings can be found in Wood 1998, 9, and in Saint 2001, 54–55.

portant part of any church plant. The giving of self and of material gifts, the sacrifice of luxuries, and the sharing of resources are all necessary. Pastor Oscar Muriu of Nairobi Chapel warns of importing approaches that are primarily resource driven and therefore not a model that can be used by resource-poor nations. "We can design new models that do not depend on money" (Muriu 2007, 96).

The first church-planting movement points to community practices that cultivate the generosity and stewardship needed to empower the mission regardless of economic status:

1. Community is real, built on relationships of love and trust (Acts 4:32).
2. Sharing is voluntary, not forced (Acts 4:32).
3. There is an ethos of grace, not law (Acts 4:33).
4. All that Jesus commanded is taught, including stewardship of life and belongings (Matt. 28:20; John 13:14–17).
5. The leaders set an example of generosity (Acts 4:36–37).
6. There is freedom in giving, but honesty is required (Acts 5:1–10).
7. Fairness in distribution is overseen by spiritual servants (Acts 6:1–7).

Outside resources can help and are not antithetical to church multiplication. After all, in the pioneering stage there is no church and all resources—human, strategic, technological, and financial—must come from the outside. But they should be handled with wisdom so that those resources do not stand in the way of the multiplication of healthy, self-supporting, reproducible congregations.

The Sharing of Financial Resources in Church Planting

Strong arguments have been made representing various extremes regarding the use of outside resources in missionary church planting. Some advocate that no financial assistance should be given from the outset, so that the church does not become dependent on outside finances and learns to sustain and reproduce itself based on local resources. The apostle Paul never brought financial assistance to the churches he planted (Allen 1962a, 49–61), and this has been the practice in most rapidly growing indigenous church-planting movements (Garrison 2004a). Numerous examples can be cited of broken relationships, resentments, misappropriation, manipulation, and hindrance of the advance of the gospel because of financial dependencies and the unwise use of funds.

Others assert no less passionately that the sharing of wealth between congregations is a Christian obligation (e.g., Rowell 2007). Paul wrote in 2 Corinthians 8:13–14, "Our desire is not that others might be relieved while you are hard pressed, but that there might be equality. At the present time your plenty will supply what they need, so that in turn their plenty will supply what you need. Then there will be equality." The traditional three-self goal of self-propagating, self-governing, and self-supporting has been challenged as a Western pragmatic and individualistic construct not found in the Bible. Financial help is not viewed by these advocates as a necessary evil but rather as a more equitable distribution of resources.

The answer, as in so many such debates, is that both are correct in part. An all-or-nothing, either-or approach will seldom have the best results. We do indeed have an obligation to share wealth and to pool different types of assets for kingdom advance. At the same time, we need to share resources in ways that empower and do not control, in ways that do not create indifference on the part of the recipients or condescension on the part of the giver. This requires that we keep the larger picture of church multiplication and the advance of the gospel in view.

Furthermore, each situation must be considered individually. Local circumstances, cultural norms, and a variety of other factors must be taken into account when determining the wise use of funds in any given situation. David Maranz (2001) gives an excellent discussion of the complexities of financial matters in Africa. Members of local African cultures have very different views from those of Americans on several key issues: saving and spending, paternalism and partnership, independence versus interdependence, accountability and accounting systems.

Beyond warning of the dangers of dependency or praising the benefits of resource distribution, we want to examine positive practical uses of finances in church-planting partnerships. The question is how to use such resources wisely for the long-term development of the work and demonstrate solidarity as interdependent parts of the global church. Here are seven different ways in which financial aid can be given and corresponding instructions for the wise use of each approach.

Launching Funds

Here assistance is given in order to launch a new effort or movement where local resources are limited. This might be called jump-starting a project (see case study 18.2). Where there are few or no Christians, outside resources in the form of sending a missionary, supporting a national church planter, funding evangelistic efforts, or renting temporary facilities are usually necessary. Initial production of literature, Bibles, or other materials may also be needed. The purchase of simple forms of transportation, such as bicycles or mopeds, for church planters might also fall in this category.

Launching funds are usually limited in both amount and duration. Like the jumper cables used to start an automobile, support is removed once the church plant is "running." The funds are intended to help start but not to sustain the

Case Study 18.2

Encounter with God Project, Lima, Peru

One of the most impressive and successful examples of funding for a launch was the Encounter with God project of the Christian and Missionary Alliance in Lima, Peru. A launching grant of $300,000 was provided, and a comprehensive evangelistic and church-planting strategy, including local refunding of the project, was implemented. Funds were used for evangelistic outreach, advertising, the purchase of properties, and construction of church buildings (Mangham 1987; Turnidge 1999). The movement grew from one church with 117 members in 1973 to twenty churches and 9,127 members in 1987. By 1997 there were thirty-eight churches with 15,870 members and a weekly attendance of 25,000. Though the Lima project has inspired many similar attempts to launch church-planting movements in other countries, none have matched the remarkable results of the original project.

movement. Normally this kind of funding should go to one-time projects, not to ongoing salaries. If the precedent is set that launching funds are *always* necessary for a church plant to begin, then the growth of the church-planting movement will be limited to the availability of such outside funds. Church-planting movements prosper to the extent that local resources and indigenous ways are found to plant and reproduce churches. So when launching funds are provided, one must consider from the outset how the approach will be locally sustainable and reproducible in the long run. Sometimes launching funds for future church plants can be generated locally in the churches that have already been planted.

Lengthening Funds

Lengthening is giving that encourages and extends the giving capacity of local believers. It is most commonly accomplished through some form of matching grants. This has the advantage of stimulating (and ensuring) local ownership and commitment to a project. The matching grant may be 5:1 rather than 1:1, depending on what is realistic in the given context. The important thing is that the local contribution is indeed raised locally—that is, members of the church plant are indeed providing the funds to match the grant and other outside sources are not being tapped for that purpose.

The use of matching-fund grants is suitable for onetime projects such as buildings or the purchase of equipment. Caution should be used so that buildings do not turn into prestige objects of local pastors, or even into a means of stealing congregations, as has occurred in India and other parts of the world.[18]

18. Rajamani Stanley, Roger Hedlund, and J. P. Masih write of so-called church planting wherein congregations started by other denominations are enticed with an offer to construct a

Matching funds for salaries of local church planters or pastors can quickly become problematic. Such an approach tends to reinforce the expectation that a paid pastor is necessary and will always be provided by outside sources. Church multiplication is threatened when too great an emphasis is placed on buildings or professionally paid workers.

Leveraging Funds

"Leveraged giving" enhances impact and increases return by investing in ministries that in turn influence many other ministries. The most common form of leveraged giving is investment in leadership development. Increasingly, training centers for national church planters are being sponsored. Often these are schools that provide bivocational preparation, that is, vocational training in a trade or skill as well as ministry preparation. Those who complete such training become self-supporting tentmakers who earn income with the trade or occupation they have learned and plant churches alongside of their secular work. Other forms of leveraged giving that serve to advance church planting include the sponsoring of theological education by extension, production of Christian literature, creation of a microenterprise ministry, development of discipleship materials, and Bible translation.

Linking Funds

"Linking giving" makes it possible for newly planted churches to organize and be linked with other churches and Christians regionally, nationally, and internationally. Such projects could include sponsorship of regional church-planting workshops, an area church-planting director or coach, or the travel costs of leaders who meet together for training, fellowship, and encouragement. Support for denominational offices or the international travel of movement leaders would fall into this category. While even budding church-planting movements can normally be expected to cover local expenses through local giving, they rarely have adequate funding for such projects.

Loving Funds

In the final chapter we will revisit the relationship of compassion ministries and church planting. It can and should be symbiotic—that is, they should enhance each other and have a greater impact together than they would separately. Sponsorship of compassion ministries that are associated with a church

church building, "In South India today there is evidence of a deliberate strategy of such congregation stealing. This is a careful plan of building in an area where another group has gathered a congregation but has not yet acquired a building." This gives donors a false impression of dramatic church growth (Stanley, Hedlund, and Masih 1986, 299).

plant is an important and practical way to demonstrate the love of Christ and the church's commitment to serve the community. The gospel cannot easily be ignored when it is proclaimed in a holistic manner, in word and deed. Compassion projects and their funding should be discussed carefully with local leaders.

A problem can arise when local church leaders discover that outside funds can more easily be raised for compassion ministry than for evangelism or other ministries. For example, the young church might begin to operate an orphanage as a source of income and end up neglecting evangelism and discipleship. Both are legitimate and important, but balance can easily be lost and integrity in use of funds may become compromised (Stanley, Hedlund, and Masih 1986; Yost 1984).

Lending Funds

"Lending giving" occurs when a onetime grant is given to create a revolving fund that finances loans for church-planting projects. Once the finances are secured, it becomes a revolving fund. As funds are borrowed and repaid, they continue to be available to help finance future projects. Most commonly such projects include loans for church buildings or major capital investments. Whatever the project, it must be one that has the promise of generating future funds, so that the loan can be repaid. In less affluent countries repayment rates are seldom 100 percent, and this must be factored into the program.

Loans to finance small industries or microenterprises of local Christians may indirectly benefit a church-planting project but are best managed separately from church-planting funds. Job programs and seed funding for small businesses may be appropriate ministries of economic development. But it is generally best to finance the church and ministry through the gifts and offerings of members and keep business enterprises independent of the direct management and ownership of the church.

Lingering Funds

Lingering funds are subsidies for the church plant that continue indefinitely with no clear plan for reduction. This is a practice that we generally discourage because it usually creates unhealthy dependencies and resentments when the funding must eventually be reduced or discontinued. The reduction of such funding can also create tension and hardship. Frustration is often experienced by both the receiving church and the sponsor. The system of gradually reducing subsidies by an annual percentage (for example, subsidy is reduced 20 percent per year and local believers increase funding 20 percent per year) until the subsidy is discontinued has often worked well in affluent contexts. However, such approaches seldom work harmoniously or effectively when there is significant economic disparity between the partnering churches. But why is financial dependency wrong? Indeed no church should be fully independent of other churches. New Testament examples fall primarily in the categories of occasional financial assistance and famine relief, not ongoing sustenance (1 Cor. 16:1–4; 2 Cor. 8). Wealth can and should be shared in times of need, but the goal is that each provides for his or her own under normal circumstances (for example, even younger widows were expected to provide for themselves; 1 Tim. 5:8–11).

When we take a practical view, strategic stewardship must be of paramount concern. So long as one church is receiving assistance, those same resources cannot be used to launch new church plants in needier areas. If the goal of reaching the unreached is to be achieved, then every church must be viable and self-sustaining under normal circumstances so that it can eventually become a giving and sending church. Lingering support is susceptible to sponsor manipulation and to the undermining of local decision making, initiative, and ownership. A survival mentality, or worse, a poverty mindset, can set in. One person has called this an "ecclesiastical welfare system" (Elder 2003).

Concluding Guidelines

We conclude this section on financial resources with a summary of practical guidelines for the strategic investment of outside resources.

Give in ways that eventually lead to church multiplication based on local resources. This means that financial support is focused on short-term projects, training, leadership, and regional coordination in ways that permit a ready transition to locally based leadership and financing. Church plants should learn how to reproduce using local resources.

Prioritize efforts that have no natural local constituency to support the ministry. For example, it is reasonable to expect that even a small, poor congregation with a lay pastor would be able to pay its ongoing expenses through the tithes of its members. Church-planter training centers and compassion ministries, on the other hand, at least in the early phases of a movement, do not have an immediate constituency to support them.

Avoid giving in ways that stifle local initiative or create long-term dependencies. Support of national evangelists and church planters is not the golden key to world evangelization, as some have suggested. The practice is fraught with difficulties and if unwisely carried out can actually hinder a movement (Ott 1993). Such approaches are seldom locally sustainable or reproducible.

Do not give the impression that ministry depends on money, buildings, or paid professionals. Through the history of the church the gospel has advanced under the most adverse circumstances. Full-time paid workers can be very helpful, but they are not essential to church health and multiplication. The same can be said of church buildings. Some of the most dynamic church-planting movements have been largely lay led using simple means and meeting places. Wealthy churches must be generous without giving the impression that where there is no money ministry cannot progress.

Know the local culture, customs, and needs, and listen to local leaders. Unfortunately, outside financial assistance can lead to dominance by those who understand local needs and customs least. Giving should empower local people, respect their judgment, and be done in ways that consider the needs and objectives of all partners.

19

Planting Churches
with Kingdom Impact

If we are to plant churches that are truly a witness to, a sign of, and a foretaste of the kingdom of God, then they must address human needs and concerns that are broader than narrowly defined evangelism and discipleship. This will especially be the case when we are planting churches among the poor, oppressed, and illiterate. Their needs simply cannot be ignored. Our concern cannot be merely the number of churches that are planted but must also extend to the quality of churches we plant and their influence on lives and communities. They must not only proclaim the message of God but also manifest the character of God. They must be churches with kingdom impact.

The kingdom of God will not come in fullness until Christ returns. But where Christ reigns in this age, there the kingdom is, in the midst of this world. The kingdom of God is characterized by righteousness, peace, and joy in the Holy Spirit (Rom. 14:17). Christ's reign begins in the unseen dimension of the new birth, when one is born again by the Spirit of God and submits to the lordship of Christ in one's life (Matt. 7:21; Luke 9:23; John 3:3–5). His reign transforms the life of the believer, which in turn shapes the life of the community of believers, the church, and the church in turn has an impact on the world in which it is situated. This is what we mean by kingdom impact: *the church's influence in all its relationships by reflecting and advancing the righteousness, compassion, justice, and restoration of all things under Christ's reign.* In the coming kingdom we will enjoy the glorious presence of God and the absence of death, suffering, sorrow, and injustice. All things will be made new (Rev. 21:1–5). In this age the church is an imperfect foretaste of that coming kingdom. And even though the church's ability to transform a world that has not yet submitted to Christ's reign will be limited, its presence as salt and light should be a witness to that kingdom, drawing men and women to its goodness and glory. We want to plant churches with this kind of kingdom impact.

In this chapter we briefly describe the three dimensions of kingdom communities: the Great Commission, the Great Commandment, and the Great Calling. Then we will discuss practical questions of getting started in community impact, integrating church planting and service ministries, and some of the pitfalls of service ministry, economic development, and church planting. Finally, we'll briefly address church planting among the very poor.

Three Dimensions of Kingdom Communities

The church is the earthly community of God's called-out people who are to manifest the lordship of Christ over every aspect of their lives. The transforming work of God must ultimately encompass all dimensions of life: personal, familial, social, economic, and political. In chapter 1 we noted that churches experiencing Christ's transforming power and manifesting his lordship can be called *kingdom communities*. Zac Niringiye has said, "Kingdom community is both the means and the goal of the proclamation of the good news of the Kingdom of God" (2008, 18). Kingdom communities have three dimensions, which while distinct in focus are all interrelated in practice.

The Great Commission: Evangelism and Discipleship

Given all that has been said thus far in this volume, this point might well go without saying. The Great Commission is unequivocal: "Therefore go and make disciples of all nations, baptizing them in the name of the Father and of the Son and of the Holy Spirit, and teaching them to obey everything I have commanded you" (Matt. 28:19–20). This will involve sending, proclaiming, baptizing, teaching, gathering into congregations, and in turn sending, thus multiplying disciples and churches among all peoples. The church can never rest until from every people, nation, tribe, and tongue there are those who have been purchased by the blood of the Lamb and entered into the fellowship of the King of kings (Rev. 5:9–10). The church is birthed in the gospel, and it is with the gospel that the church goes into the world empowered by the Spirit. Whatever else churches are, they must be gospel-centered communities. Any church that no longer preaches the gospel and makes disciples has forfeited its birthright. Only as individual lives are transformed by the power of the gospel will community transformation be truly possible.

The Great Commandment: Love in Action

When Jesus was asked what the greatest commandment is, he answered, "'Love the Lord your God with all your heart and with all your soul and with all your mind.' This is the first and greatest commandment. And the second is like it: 'Love your neighbor as yourself.' All the Law and the Prophets hang on these two commandments" (Matt. 22:37–40). We will return below to the first half of this answer, loving God. But loving God and loving neighbor are inseparable. "If anyone says, 'I love God,' yet hates his brother, he is a liar. For anyone who does not love his brother, whom he has seen, cannot love God, whom he has not seen" (1 John 4:20).

Practical, sacrificial love, even toward even those who hate us, is a reflection of the very character of God (Matt. 5:43–44). We cannot *not* love! Through the ministry of the church (and church plants), love will be demonstrated in works of compassion, justice, upholding human dignity, and meeting needs of the whole person. We will be compelled to do so because we care about people as more than mere souls in need of eternal salvation. The earliest Protestant mission works included medical, educational, and various compassion ministries hand in hand with evangelism and church planting.

Urban churches and those working among the poor readily recognize that evangelism, discipleship, and church planting cannot be separated from ministries that address the daily social, economic, and physical needs of the people. Evangelicals have long advocated holistic mission that emphasizes the importance of ministering to the whole person, body, soul, and mind, and addressing societal ills.[1] Yet even advocates of holistic ministry, such as Tetsuano Yamamori of Food for the Hungry, include church planting as a part of a total urban strategy to minister to the poor (Yamamori 1998, 9). The Thailand Report on Christian Witness to the Urban Poor states, "We believe the basic strategy for the evangelization of the urban poor is the creation or renewal of communities in which Christians live and share equally with others" (LOP 22, 1980, 16)—that is, kingdom communities. Much of this chapter is devoted to examining the relationship between such ministries of love and service and the work of church planting.

The Great Calling: Worship and Glorification of God

The worship and glorification of God is the ultimate end of all mission effort. In the famous words of John Piper, "Missions exists because worship doesn't. . . . Worship, therefore is the fuel and goal of missions" (1993, 11). Worship is the goal because when all else passes away, worship will be the oc-

---

1. For a further evangelical discussion of holistic ministry, see LOP 33, "Holistic Mission," from the 2004 Forum for World Evangelization, available at http://www.lausanne.org/documents/2004forum/LOP33_IG4.pdf.

cupation of the church for all eternity. It is our Great Calling, from eternity past into eternity future, as expressed (with added emphasis) in Paul's opening words in Ephesians 1:

> He predestined us to be adopted as his sons through Jesus Christ, in accordance with his pleasure and will—*to the praise of his glorious grace*, which he has freely given us in the One he loves. . . . In him we were also chosen, having been predestined according to the plan of him who works out everything in conformity with the purpose of his will, in order that we . . . might be *for the praise of his glory*. . . . Having believed, you were marked in him with a seal, the promised Holy Spirit, . . . *to the praise of his glory.*

Worship is also the fuel of missions, as Christopher Wright explains: "We could say that mission exists because praise does. The praise of the church is what energizes and characterizes it for mission" (Wright 2006, 134). Only as the church draws its strength, inspiration, and motivation from its relationship with the risen Christ is it able to be mobilized for fruitful mission to God's glory and realize the first two dimensions of the Great Commission and the Great Commandment (John 15:5–8).

If nothing else, churches we plant should be worshiping communities. Not only do they gather for corporate worship—praise, prayer, offerings, hearing the Word of God, and celebration of baptism and the Lord's Supper—but their daily lives are considered an offering to God (Rom. 12:1). Wherever they are—in the workplace, at home, in the community—they are a sweet fragrance to the glory of God (2 Cor. 2:14–15; 1 Pet. 2:12). Believers live in anticipation of that day when we will be gathered with all the saints from every people, nation, tribe, and tongue to worship and serve the Lamb of God for all eternity (Rev. 7:9–17). This is the Great Calling of the church.

These three dimensions—the Great Commission, the Great Commandment and the Great Calling—constitute the fullness of what it means to be the church, the people of God's choosing, a kingdom community. Different churches will evidence them in different measure, yet all must be present and each contributes to the other.

Perhaps one of the best evangelical statements on the relationship of evangelism and social action was formulated at the International Consultation on the Relationship between Evangelism and Social Responsibility (1982) in Grand Rapids, Michigan, sponsored by the Lausanne Committee for World Evangelization. The resulting report (LOP 21, 1982) concluded that social action is a *consequence of, a bridge to, and a partner of evangelism.*

> Evangelism, even when it does not have a primarily social intention, nevertheless has a social dimension, while social responsibility, even when it does not have a primarily evangelistic intention, nevertheless has an evangelistic dimension.

Thus, evangelism and social responsibility, while distinct from one another, are integrally related in our proclamation of and obedience to the gospel. The partnership is, in reality, a marriage. (LOP 21, C)

Consider this example from Latin America:

> The largest evangelical church in Caracas, Venezuela, is La Iglesia Evangélica Pentecostal Las Acacias. It began by reaching out to the city's people—by offering telephone counseling. The response was overwhelming. The people reached by phone formed a congregation that eventually bought a huge old cinema seating 2,000 and occupying an entire city block. The Spirit-filled evangelistic witness of the church is clear and uncompromising. The church is helping meet the needs of the surrounding depressed neighborhoods with medical and legal services, marriage and family counseling. Most recently, they helped establish a drug rehabilitation center, the Hogar Nueva Vida. The Las Acacias Church lives and serves in the light of the two great realities—the spiritual and the physical. The Christ of this church is the Lord of both the spiritual "heavenlies" as well as the nitty-gritty pain-filled and hungry "real" world. (Berg and Pretiz 1992, 151)

This is a church having holistic kingdom impact. In what remains of this chapter we'll focus more narrowly on ministries of compassion, social service, and community and economic development as they relate to church planting.

Determining Needs and Getting Started

For our purposes we will refer to compassion, economic development, justice and other similar ministries as *service ministries*. We will not attempt to address the enormous literature and many principles of holistic ministry; we can offer only a summary. Here are a few of the many options for service ministry:

- clothing and food programs
- medical and dental clinics or services
- legal counsel and advocacy
- crisis, marriage, family, trauma, addictions, and other counseling
- literacy, tutoring, education, and school programs
- vocational training and employment opportunities
- disaster relief
- prison, orphan, hospital, and other institutional services or visitation
- community development and public health education
- addictions, divorce, single parent, and various other self-help groups
- economic development, microloans, rotating funds, cooperatives
- environmental education, projects, and advocacy

The church-planting team will need to carefully assess several factors as it considers how to begin a service ministry: community needs, available expertise and resources, level of commitment, and possible partnerships. Church planters should not underestimate the demands of such ministry and the pitfalls related to it. They must anticipate how the service ministry will be balanced with the many other demands of church planting. Thus it is wise to assess carefully what is realistic and effective.

Wherever church planters work, human need abounds. It will be crying out when one works among the poor, but even among the more affluent, needs are not far under the surface. Indeed the sensitive church planter may be overwhelmed when confronted by the magnitude of need and hardly know where to begin. But rushing ahead without a plan and careful preparation can lead to disaster. Following are a few basic steps.

1. *Begin with the community.* What do the local people see as their greatest needs? How do they identify root causes of the need, and what solutions have they attempted or proposed? Who are the key decision makers or gatekeepers in the community who need to be included? This is important because the perception of needs and solutions of an outsider may differ greatly from those perceived by the local people (see Tembo 2003). Speak with community leaders, and listen carefully to ordinary citizens, but avoid prematurely creating any false hopes or imposing solutions. Of course felt needs are not always real needs, so here also discernment is necessary.

2. *Start with small efforts.* Begin by prayerfully identifying one or two needs that can be reasonably addressed. Prison, hospital, or orphanage visitation requires relatively little technical skill or financial resources. Sponsoring a short-term team that does a community cleanup project, runs a dental clinic, or builds a playground would serve as a relatively manageable project for a small church—one that can make a considerable difference in people's lives but will not overwhelm the church as it is being planted. Such programs will also instill in the young church a DNA of caring and serving the community. These are great ways to involve sponsor congregations in the church plant and to build community relations. Smaller projects and events allow the church to gain experience and grow the service ministry. Local press coverage of such projects can win the church much favor in the public eye.

3. *Evaluate local resources and assets to meet the need.* Long-term solutions must be based on local initiative and resources. Often the church-planting team can come alongside already existing efforts or works. This develops trust and a spirit of cooperation while not overtaxing the energy and resources of the fledgling church plant. For example, consider volunteering at a local clinic instead of opening a new one. A failure to coordinate efforts, even between Christian development and relief organizations, can be wasteful and counterproductive and lead to unnecessary competition. On the other hand, one

may discover unaddressed community needs, and the church could initiate a new effort to meet them.

4. *Carefully assess the level of expertise, resources, and commitment that the church plant can realistically bring to the effort.* Making a commitment to a project that cannot be completed raises false hopes and creates ill will. Attempting to launch a program that lacks adequate professional leadership can likewise cause more harm than good, negatively affecting local economies, the environment, or the social, psychological, or physical well-being of individuals. If the church plant is considering involvement in a larger program, it should obtain, in advance, professional advice to ensure that it is prepared to address the need in ways that will genuinely help. Think the ministry through to the end. For example, starting a prison visitation ministry will often entail ministering to prisoners after they have been released and helping them to find jobs, housing, and reintegrate into normal life. Is the church prepared for this as well?

5. *Consider partnering with one of the many experienced Christian service ministries or NGOs.*[2] Organizations such as World Relief, Samaritan's Purse, Compassion International, Tearfund, and many others often cooperate with local initiatives and churches. Involvement may range from providing Christmas packets, to funding a school meal program, to launching a full-orbed and fully staffed development project or clinic (see case study 19.1). Such relief and development organizations bring resources, expertise, and experience that would be impossible for a fledging church plant to provide alone. In such partnerships the expectations of all parties should be clearly spelled out in advance. For example, will the NGO expect reports, letters from sponsored children, or names and photos that could jeopardize the work in a sensitive context? What level of volunteerism or commitment will the NGO expect of the church and local people? What happens after the NGO departs? Churches should also be cautious that they not become subject to what Ian Wallace (2002, 135) calls the "open pipe syndrome": churches become a convenient conduit for distributing aid to the poor but in the process become overwhelmed or distracted and actually suffer.

6. *Plan with local sustainability in view.* The old adage "Give a man a fish and you feed him for a day. Teach a man to fish and you feed him for a lifetime" is all too true. Long-term sustainability must be part of the larger plan. Ultimately people should be taught how to meet their own needs, apart from outside assistance, though in extreme situations this may not be possible. In one case a primary health care team refused to use x-ray or other expensive equipment as part of a community health educational program, because they

---

2. An NGO is a nongovernmental organization; those mentioned here are devoted to community development, relief, or meeting social or physical needs. Some, such as the Red Cross and various organizations of the United Nations, are secular in nature. Others, such as Samaritan's Purse and Food for the Hungry, are Christian.

Case Study 19.1

Earthquake in Chincha

The following report by ReachGlobal missionary Meredith McAllister describes in a prayer letter a response to the 2007 earthquake in Chincha, Peru, that illustrates a multifaceted partnership between a local church and various partners to meet the immediate and long-term needs of the people, spiritually and physically:

"Peru experienced a 7.9 scale earthquake on Aug. 15, three hours south of Lima. Our first response involved gathering and sending relief to be distributed through a local church in Ica. 'El Shaddai' church turned into an NGO for the first two months following the earthquake, becoming a distributor of choice for several secular businesses due to their trustworthy reputation. We also had the opportunity of hosting Jonathan Olford, a Christian psychologist who developed a seminar called 'His Presence in Crisis' to help the church reach their community in crisis. Three of us translated for him, presenting to 50 pastors and leaders in the city of Chincha, and over 100 in the city of Ica. Many local leaders have been overwhelmed as they try to respond to this crisis which has affected their own homes, families, and churches directly. . . . Now we are involved in a second, more complicated phase, reconstruction. After investigating several options, we have decided to move forward with a community in Chincha (city of 40,000, one of three hardest hit) called Salto de la Liza. Food for the Hungry has a comprehensive plan involving reconstruction of 60 plus homes, which will hopefully multiply as builders are trained in seismic-resistant construction techniques."

knew that such equipment would not be available to those communities later (Seale 1989). Such an approach will sometimes mean settling for less and seeking creative low-tech solutions. Locally sustainable projects build community self-esteem as people become self-reliant and are not continually dependent on outsiders for their well-being. All too often development projects have fallen by the wayside as soon as outside assistance is withdrawn. Thus a plan to recruit and train local people from the very start will be needed—people who can gain the skills needed to sustain the ministry and who will help the community to make the ministry its own.

7. *Focus more on empowerment than on aid.* In many urgent situations, such as famine relief, immediate action in the form of aid is necessary to save lives. But ultimately people must be empowered to master their own challenges independent of outside assistance. As one writer states it, development must seek "to change their outlook from one of being clients of others and victims of situations, to one of agents of their own development; from being fatalistic to being hopeful; from being helpless and self-pitying to being industrious and self-affirming" (McCauley 2007, 16–17). The gospel of Jesus Christ empowers

like nothing else, elevating human dignity, giving hope, engendering personal responsibility, and transforming root values.

8. *Integrate the spiritual dimension naturally with the service ministry.* Most Majority World cultures see life holistically, whereas Western cultures tend to bifurcate the physical and spiritual realms of life. Western missionaries are sometimes reluctant to include spiritual care with physical or social care. Of course we must never use a person's need or vulnerability as an occasion to manipulate or coerce. But church planters should in an appropriate and natural way make known that they are moved by the love of Christ to meet the needs of the entire person, body, soul, and mind. It may be as simple as stating up front, "We are a Christian organization. We are here to serve everyone regardless of faith, but you should know that we do it because of the love God has put in our hearts. We will pray for you and will share with you more about the love of God in Christ if you wish." In a remote region of Rwanda, two medical clinics were operated: one by a Christian mission, the other by a secular NGO. Though the medical services offered by both clinics did not differ, local people preferred the Christian hospital, even when the distance was greater for them. When researchers investigated, the reason repeatedly given was "At the Christian clinic they also pray for us!"[3]

Practically Relating Service Ministry to Church Planting

How does service ministry organizationally relate to church planting? Each of the scenarios below involves the provision of a channel to practically demonstrate the love of God and communicate the gospel. Service ministries give credibility to the church plant, win the goodwill of the community, and can be a source of new believers and opportunities for believers to serve the neighborhood in practical ways. Conversely, the church plant can provide the spiritual home, counsel, and discipleship for those ministered to through the service ministry. The church plant can also provide counsel and encouragement for workers in the service ministry. In this and other ways service and church planting often go hand in hand.

Ways of Relating Service Ministry to Church-Planting Ministries

Practically speaking, there are several ways that service ministries can relate to church planting. Each can be effective under certain circumstances, and each has its own challenges.

3. Recounted in personal conversation with Walter Rapold, former missionary to Rwanda.

INCIDENTAL

One possibility is that the church plant organizes or sponsors occasional projects or events to meet local needs. Examples include a weeklong medical clinic staffed by a visiting short-term team of health experts,[4] distribution of Christmas packets among the poor or families of prisoners, occasional clothing distribution, job fairs, and infant care seminars. Such services require limited time, expense, expertise, and energy to be effective. They meet needs and produce goodwill in the community, but they need not overwhelm the church-planting team. Especially in the early stages of a church plant, such an approach is realistic and can lay the foundation for broader, longer-term services that can be developed as the church grows in size and resources.

FULLY INTEGRATED

Here an ongoing service ministry and church-planting ministry are fully integrated and thus may share staff and have a common budget, leadership team, board, or sponsors. The service ministry is typically under the authority of the church planter or pastor (with responsibility often delegated) and may take place on church premises or be carried out by church staff or volunteers. The identification of the service and the church plant in this case is overt, immediate, and desired. The witness to Christ is to be holistic. The work of the Salvation Army is perhaps one of the most thoroughgoing examples of this in that often church planting and service to the poor are combined. For another example, see case study 19.2.

For many, if not most, Majority World church planters such a holistic approach is entirely natural. It's simply impossible to minister to people's spiritual needs without also addressing their other daily needs. Full integration works well with service ministries such as soup kitchens, HIV/AIDS education, or after-school tutoring programs that require minimal administration, resources, or specialized skill. These can usually be carried out with volunteer workers or minimally trained staff.

However, more complex and demanding ministries such as drug rehabilitation centers, orphanages, clinics, or vocational training centers can become problematical when fully integrated with the church plant. The demands of the work can easily overshadow the needs of the church plant and overwhelm workers attempting to serve both. Such ministries also usually require skills that typical church planters do not possess. As we will note below, economic development programs can become especially problematic when church leaders become responsible for businesses, distributing microbusiness loans, and the like.

4. For a practical guide in conducting short-term medical teams see Dohn and Dohn (2006).

Full Gospel Church—Purral Alto

In 1991, Pastor Rocha came to pastor a small church consisting of a dozen women in Purral Alto [Costa Rica], a typical slum. Families here live in small, one-room squatter shacks made of scrap lumber and corrugated tin. Most residents were underemployed, and educational opportunities for their children that could serve to break the cycle of poverty were inadequate. The greatest difficulty for the pastor was to convince the church that his vision to develop a holistic ministry would work.

Once the church bought the vision, it moved to develop a kindergarten for the children in the community. This soon led to a nutritional program for the children. For many the kindergarten gave them their only decent meal of the day. This resulted in good public relations with the community so that the church could reach out and initiate other positive relationships.

After the success of the kindergarten, the pastor formed a two-fold path to (1) develop the church quantitatively and qualitatively, and (2) further develop the community. To accomplish the first goal, members were formed into cell groups. The leaders who emerged in these groups formed the leadership core of the church. Through their participation in cell groups community members became aware of the other programs available through the church. Over time the church has been able to offer (1) a dental clinic supplied with equipment donated by a local hospital and voluntarily staffed by professionals, (2) a computer lab to develop computer literacy for children and adults, (3) a sewing workshop designed to teach women a marketable skill, and (4) a program to teach English as a second language.

Besides community development, the church has attended to its own growth and now has 175 members. It is currently developing an apostolic team to plant a new church.

The church's social outreach has been assisted by its utilization of government funds made available when a government representative saw the impact the church was having on the community. However, the majority of the capital to initiate and maintain its programs has come from the church members themselves (Armet 1997, 19–20).

FULLY SEPARATE

In this model the service ministry operates independently of the church plant. There may be some small overlap of staff or volunteers. Service ministry workers may attend the church plant, and the church planter may give spiritual input to the service ministry. But the service ministry operates independent of the church plant organizationally, financially, and in staffing. Sometimes the service ministry deliberately has no public identification with the church. This is intentional for practical reasons: the legal status of the service work might be threatened if associated with a church or mission, or if there would be a problem of "rice Christians" or other dangers described below. Often

Case Study 19.3

Relating Service Agencies and Local Churches

The issue group Holistic Ministry at the 2004 Forum for World Evangelization and Tetsunao Yamamori, former president of Food for the Hungry, offer these principles for the relationship of local churches and service agencies:

1. The role of the service agency is that of an apprentice. As a part of the body of Christ the members of the service agency must work from within the church so as to learn and to face the local issues of holistic mission.
2. The role of the service agency is that of a facilitator. The service agency should place itself beside the church in order to enable the church to carry on its holistic mission.
3. The role of the service agencies is that of a catalyst. Despite the increasing number of churches with a vision for holistic mission, there are still many in need of help to get a wider vision of their task. The service agency exists to encourage these churches to become involved with their respective communities.
4. The role of the church is that of a pioneer. The role of the service agency as an apprentice, a facilitator, and a catalyst can only be fulfilled when there is a local church in the community. If no church exists, the service agency will have to choose between not working in that community and making strategic plans to plant a church either alone or in cooperation with a church from another community (LOP 33, 2005, 23).

the service ministry is sponsored or operated by a Christian NGO that is financially and organizationally entirely independent of the church plant. This allows each ministry to focus and finance its work effectively and in its field of expertise, while informally complementing one another.

OVERLAPPING

Here the service ministry and church-planting work are neither fully integrated nor fully separated but have considerable overlap in workers, budget, public identification, and so on. Such overlapping ministries may face challenges. For example, ministries may compete for energy, resources, or the loyalty of volunteers and sponsors. Also, lines of authority may be unclear.

GENERATIVE

In this case one ministry is already present and over the course of time generates the other. For example, the staff of a Christian relief agency end up leading many people to Christ where there is no church; this results in the planting of a church. Sometimes the relief workers attempt to lead the church plant alongside their service work. More often a church planter or church-planting team is recruited to take over the plant. Conversely, a church plant may discover a great need in the community, for example, youth drug abuse. As the new ministry develops, it remains within the framework of church ministry. However, meeting the need may go beyond the resources of the church plant such that the ministry takes on a life of its own. Therefore an independent ministry is created, such as a foundation with its own budget and legal status, and is able to recruit its own staff, raise its own funds, and pursue the ministry with single-minded focus. In a generative relationship it is important to clarify lines of authority and responsibility as the newer ministry becomes more independent.

In general it can be said that the more institutionalized the service work becomes (such as a hospital or orphanage), the more difficult it is to integrate it organizationally with the church-planting ministry. Only well-established churches can normally run such services—and that not without challenges. Ian Wallace, of the department for international and rural development at the University of Reading, notes that whatever the relationship between church and service, "it is difficult to do well, either for the poor, or for the church itself" (2002, 136). On the other hand, the more grassroots the work is the easier it is to fully integrate—for example, a church-based program for AIDS orphans that assists adoptive or extended families in their care.

Avoiding Pitfalls in Service and Church-Planting Partnerships

We cannot discuss all the challenges of service ministry but will focus on potential pitfalls of partnering them with church planting. While the exercise of compassion and various social ministries should be a natural outflow of the gospel, practically speaking the relationship can be a complicated one.

Producing "Rice Christians"

This problem is age old and well known: people often become Christians for the sake of what they will personally gain, be it a bowl of rice, an education, or a small business loan. Sometimes such persons eventually become committed Christians; often, however, they fall away from the faith when the assistance or benefit ceases. To a certain extent this problem is unavoidable where poverty and injustice reign, and we must remember that God alone can judge motives. In church planting, discernment must be exercised so that numbers are not bloated by persons seeking material benefit. This is one reason that some have advocated full separation of service ministry from church-planting ministries.

However, the danger of creating rice Christians is probably less than often feared. Viv Grigg, an advocate of holistic ministry to the urban poor, makes this statement: "Of over a hundred churches planted among the poor, I have seen only two that came into being through the giving of aid" (1992, 247).

He goes on to state that aid may arouse interest but rarely leads to a spiritual breakthrough. It is not unusual, even in Western contexts, for persons who initially show interest in Christianity with questionable motives to eventually become sincere followers of Christ. Any exercise of love risks abuse, but that does not mean we should stop loving.

Leadership Drain

One of the disturbing trends observed in the global South is that many of the national church's most gifted leaders have left church ministry to take positions of leadership in NGOs and parachurch ministries. This happens in part because these works offer a handsome salary, a vehicle, and benefits and seek leaders who will shepherd and teach their staff. The church cannot offer a comparable salary and benefits. Of course such works want and need national leaders who are people of integrity and Christian maturity. But many feel that this has become a significant problem draining the church of its best leaders. Churches need strong leaders too! The need here is for balance. Ideally NGOs and parachurch ministries should adjust their pay scales so that they are not unreasonably disproportionate to pay in church ministry.

Burnout and Diffusion

Service ministries demand not only financial but also considerable human resources. Where service ministries partner with church planting, the service ministry can drain a disproportionate amount of energy and resources from the ministry of evangelism and discipleship. Church plants in most situations begin with small numbers of believers. If they are expected to volunteer service in typical church ministries and a service project as well, they may become overwhelmed and burn out.

Often the pastor of the church plant exercises leadership in the service ministry as well. This can lead the pastor to neglect the ministry of prayer and the Word for the sake of the service work. For example, when a church in India operates an orphanage, the pastor is often responsible for both ministries. Administration and fundraising for the orphanage can consume the pastor's energy, causing the church plant to suffer. According to one report, "In a majority of cases the pastor devotes himself to the buying and banking and supervising of the orphanage, and his sheep suffer without good spiritual food" (Stanley, Hedlund, and Masih 1986, 296).[5] The early church resolved this tension by appointing deacons alongside the elders, so that each group

5. Sadly ironic situations can arise: "The orphanage explosion is so widespread that now there is competition for orphans. A good percentage of children in the orphanages are not really orphans at all" (Stanley, Hedlund, and Masih 1986, 296).

could focus on the ministry for which God had called and gifted them (Acts 6:1–6).

Wallace describes the problem of the community development "tail" wagging the church "dog":

> "Picture a small Anglican diocese in a poor Latin American country which launches a major initiative to purchase land and resettle displaced Indian communities upon it. This quickly attracts the interest of several para-church and secular agencies and a large programme develops. The church remains small and lacking in resources. Its development department soon has 20 or more expatriate staff, shiny vehicles and two-way radios. It is soon apparent that the project director has more power than the bishop does!" (Wallace 2002, 135).

Evangelism and discipleship can, of course, take place *through* the exercise of service ministries. The Western church has often assumed that discipleship is a matter of studying the Bible and personal spiritual disciplines, somehow apart from practical service. Serving in a compassion or development ministry can be a vehicle for learning spiritual disciplines, an opportunity to share one's faith with unbelievers, and a place to exercise obedience, use one's spiritual gifts, and be salt and light in the community. But realistically, the larger the service work grows, the more it can become all-consuming in the ministry of the church and can hinder healthy church plant development.

Superficiality or Naiveté

Church planters may be tempted to undertake a service ministry without having considered the depth of the need, the cost of attempting to meet it, and the expertise necessary to be effective. It is better to take on small projects of limited scope and duration than to make promises that cannot be kept. Bruce E. Swanson (1993) notes several helpful principles; here are a few of them:

- Identify a need that you can really do something about.
- Get involved with the community's problem personally before trying a large-scale program.
- Don't offer a "home-grown" answer to the need.
- Be willing to work with the community's need over the long haul.

Those specially trained for service ministry, such as physicians or social workers, are seldom also trained in church planting. Similarly, church planters are seldom qualified to lead professional service ministries. When they do so, usually one ministry suffers and commitments are divided. Thus it is best to have qualified persons devoted primarily to their given ministries (see case study 19.4).

Case Study 19.4

Primary Health Care and Church Planting

Paul Seale (1989) describes a project in the Philippines in which the development of primary health care was a vehicle for church planting. The goal was to train local people in prevention-oriented health care over a fifteen-month period. At each site a church was to be planted through evangelism, discipleship, and establishing home Bible studies with contacts made in the health care program. A team was composed of a church planter and a physician along with several assistants with medical experience. Several small towns with inadequate health care were targeted where the team itinerated regularly. Three-day "medical crusades" were also held in remote areas.

Parallel to the medical clinics and education, evangelistic preaching and evening worship services were conducted. In one of the remote areas 150 people made professions of faith, and a church began to self-organize under lay leadership even though the people were largely illiterate. After the medical program was phased out, local churches took over the follow-up of new believers in the various towns. Ultimately two churches were planted.

Because those responsible for the church-planting aspect of the plan were from neighboring churches, Seale notes a particular challenge they faced: "While such programs may be excellent evangelistic efforts, a great deal of energy is required to orient their activities towards planting a new church in an area outside their own church's district" (357). The health care team members who visited the towns weekly over thirteen months eventually took responsibility for the church planting. This was facilitated through their extended personal contacts.

Seale goes on to recommend various changes for such programs. For example, he considers it "critical to pair a health worker with an evangelistic worker whose primary responsibility is church planting" (358). But the strength of the general approach is evident. "The great advantage of our medical program, as opposed to other church planting methods, was that we could begin work in new communities where there were no previous contacts. Traditionally, church planters in the area depended on contacts gained through friends or family of church members, and such contacts are not always easy to come by" (357).

In conclusion, Seale writes, "Past medical missionary programs show that, except for the least responsive areas, compassionate Christian medical care will bring an evangelistic harvest. Too often, however, such programs have been dominated by medical personnel with good intentions but limited expertise in evangelism and church planting. Tremendous opportunities for evangelism and church planting are lost because we do not devote adequate time and enough people to plan and carry out church planting" (359–60). This confirms our recommendation that wherever service ministries team up with church planting, it is important that qualified personnel for *both* ministries are involved and able to devote themselves single-mindedly to their particular ministry.

Bait-and-Switch

Service ministries are a testimony to the love of Christ and the righteousness of God. But they should never be used merely as bait to draw people to what is in reality an evangelistic event. Depending on the nature of the service, it may be fully natural to share the message of the gospel as part of the service ministry. For example, it would be entirely appropriate for an orphanage to have worship or Bible instruction for the children. Hospitals have chaplains. A lecture series on child rearing might discuss the spiritual development of a child. However, insisting that people hear a gospel message before they may receive medical treatment would be inappropriate. Advertising a seminar on financial planning and then spending ten minutes on finances and twenty minutes sharing the gospel is likely to do more harm than good. One could of course invite people to hear the presenter's testimony *after* the seminar, so that no one feels tricked. Where one draws the line on such matters will vary. The basic principle is integrity. Service ministries should be done because they are the right thing to do, and they may be done in the name of Christ, but not as a lure to trick or coerce people into hearing the gospel.

Economic Development and Church Planting

Economic development programs that seek to provide employment, stimulate local economies, offer microloans to fund small businesses, and the like can be extremely helpful to local Christians and others. They can also provide a platform for church planters to work in places where public evangelism and church planting are prohibited by law. Such undertakings are a legitimate form of Christian ministry in themselves (see Yamamori and Eldred 2003 for numerous case studies). Strategies combining business efforts with financing of churches have a long history in Protestant missions going back to the work of William Carey (Stanley 1992). A sizable literature on the topic of "business as mission" is now available.

However, if not done well such economic development programs can also become a minefield of difficulties that waste resources and create jealousy, animosity, conflict, and mixed motives. All this will set back the church plant and can, in worst-case scenarios, create ill will in the community or torpedo the church plant. Not a few church planters have naively become involved in such programs, only to end in misunderstanding, discouragement, pain, and abuse. The integration of economic development and church planting is fraught with its own set of challenges. Again, we cannot enter a full discussion of economic development, business ventures, or microloan programs. But here are just three guiding principles for the church planter.

Guidelines for Church Planters

The first principle is to *have qualified and informed persons leading the effort*. They must not only have good business understanding but also be somewhat acquainted with local customs and business practices. The greater the level of involvement and resources, the more important is the involvement of qualified and experienced persons who can make wise and sometimes hard decisions. Spiritual leaders are not always good business leaders. Trying to plant a church while also overseeing a business venture or microloan program will normally mean that one or the other suffers.

Second, it is normally best to *have a board of directors or foundation, separate from formal church leadership* that is responsible for the administration of the service. As noted above, mixing church and business is complicated. Decisions regarding distribution of funds, managing loan repayment, or offering employment to some but not others become complicated by personal and family loyalties. Hard feelings and jealousies quickly arise. In collectivistic cultures the danger is compounded as family or clan loyalties will often trump sound business decisions. A church planter or spiritual leader who is responsible to both spiritually counsel *and* keep congregants financially accountable will inevitably become embroiled in conflict.

Finally, *consider carefully the worldview of local people regarding possessions, work ethic, and money*. This is likely to be quite different from that of an expatriate church planter or development worker. David Maranz's *African Friends and Money Matters* (2001) offers a marvelous description of the depth and complexity of these differences in the African context. Those administering an economic development program should be well informed of such matters. Ideally the board of directors will include persons who understand the local expectations and practices, as well as those who can represent the interests and expectations of sponsors.

Inadvertently Promoting Materialistic Values

Though it is certainly a noble endeavor to increase the standard of living of those who have little, some forms of economic development can actually promote unbiblical materialistic values. Missionaries have been accused of being a great secularizing force in the Majority World, in part because they bring a materialistic worldview with them. Continually emphasizing projects aimed at improving a people's economic standing can send the wrong message (see Power and Power 1998). An attitude of entitlement can quickly arise where funding seems easy to come by. Local people can begin to expect ever more microloans, job opportunities, or development benefits. Christians and non-Christians alike can become angry or disillusioned when such are not forthcoming or when there is not enough to go around for everyone in the community.

Jim Yost did development work alongside church planting in a remote area of Irian Jaya with the Sawi people. He noticed that church growth declined significantly with the introduction of community development such as planting fruit trees, animal husbandry, and making fishnets. One of the reasons he identified was that people became more interested in material well-being than spiritual well-being. They also tended to follow the lead of the missionary: if the missionary gives priority to development, so will the local people. He tells how operating a small store for the local people conveyed the message that he was really there to operate a business and not to work with the church. His conclusion is perhaps extreme but nevertheless worthy of consideration: "Let me suggest that no church planting missionary involve himself in community development unless he absolutely has to. If you want a development project in your area, bring in a development specialist to do it. Don't risk confusing your image with the people." He continues, "Non-Christians then think that becoming a Christian means getting something done for you" (Yost 1984, 356, 358).

Such experiences should not discourage church planters from helping people improve their lives, earn an honest living, feed their families, and provide for ministry needs. There will always be risk of abuse and failure in any worthy endeavor. But such endeavors should also not be undertaken hastily or naively.

Financing Church Plants through Church-Operated Businesses

The promotion and funding of business endeavors is sometimes conceived with the goal of providing direct income for a church plant. In some cases the business is owned and operated by the church.[6] At first glance this may appear to be a practical and efficient way to finance the needs of the church plant, especially in places where poverty prevails and members of the church have little expendable income. However, making business ventures a major source of direct income for a church plant is to be strongly discouraged for several reasons.

First, the Bible clearly teaches the principle of stewardship: God's work is to be supported by the gifts and offerings of God's people. Even the poor can give of what they have, and the impression should not be given that ministry just happens without personal sacrifice. Believers must be taught the joy and responsibility of giving to support God's work. Second, the church is not a business and should not become a business-operating enterprise. Conflicts of interests soon arise—how to develop spiritual ministry and how to run a profitable business. The energy of the church can become consumed with the business venture. Third, most church planters are not trained in business

---

6. This is not to be confused with the situation of a church planter operating a small business in a tentmaking arrangement to provide his or her personal support, keeping the business clearly separate from the church.

management. Time and again we have seen church planters become involved in business ventures for which they have little understanding and less training. If the business fails, misunderstanding and hardship for employees can result, potentially discrediting the gospel. Finally, most businesses—especially larger ones that can generate significant income—are subject to market fluctuations, technological advancements, and other factors that can quickly turn a profit-making business into a money-losing fiasco, actually draining church funds. This has been the case with agricultural projects established in Africa to support church ministries.

A separately owned and operated business venture, independent of church authority, that provides local believers with employment is the better way. Believers should at the same time be taught good stewardship and giving to support the needs of the church. The church must remain first and foremost a spiritual community of faith and not become encumbered or compromised through entanglement with operating a for-profit business, even if the profits are devoted to supporting ministry.

Church Planting among the Very Poor

Often the poor are the most responsive to the gospel. Here we are speaking of the *very* poor who not only have much less than the average person but are destitute. The destitute poor are those barely able to survive, who live day by day not knowing where their next meal might come from, or who are severely exploited. Such groups include the homeless, refugees, and residents of shantytowns, slums, and squatter settlements. They are often ill, malnourished, overworked, and sleep deprived, and are exposed to crime and abuse.

Attempts to plant churches among such people face the challenge not only that the people are physically destitute but that they are often also hopeless and uneducated, lacking a sense of self-worth and initiative. They may respond positively to the gospel but remain in a mentality of dependency and inadequacy. The needs for security and survival dominate their day and must be taken seriously. Most established churches do not welcome such persons into their fellowship. And if welcomed, the poor seldom feel comfortable in such churches. Although not the ideal, often there is no alternative but to plant churches focusing specifically on reaching the very poor.

Church-planting teams working among poor populations must have great patience, a strong sense of God's calling, and a commitment to long-term ministry. A delicate balance must be found of workers on the one hand identifying with the focus people (including in a low standard of living) and on the other hand providing for their own personal health, safety, and stress relief to avoid burnout and discouragement. One should not underestimate the level of stress that workers in such circumstances face.

Generally speaking, an incarnational approach to ministry will be necessary: the church planter will adopt a standard of living near to that of the people, living in the community, identifying with their lives on a daily basis. This will build trust, demonstrate solidarity, and model Christlike service. Such workers should consult Viv Grigg's *Cry of the Urban Poor* (1992), one of the few practical guides to church planting in a context of extreme poverty.

A church-planting team can easily reinforce feelings of inadequacy and dependency among the poor by paternalistically treating them as helpless charity cases. Church-based programs must seek rather to empower the people, helping them to understand and realize their potential in spite of their circumstances. Even the poorest and the least educated can pass on to others what they have received. From slum dwellers, refugees, and street gangs natural leaders often emerge who have potential for spiritual leadership.

Churches planted among the poor can sometimes do astonishing work. Liberia is a country ravaged by civil war during 1989–1996 and 1999–2003. An entire generation of young people received no schooling. In the capital city of Monrovia, Hope Evangelical Free Church, a church plant with barely fifty, mostly poor attendants, operates a primary school for over two hundred children. Makeshift reed mats divide the small clay-bricked structure into four cramped classrooms without electricity or running water. The majority of the children meet in open-air "classrooms" because the building cannot accommodate them. Though the school is primitive by Western standards, Pastor Luke is proud of his church's accomplishments. The members built everything themselves with little help from outsiders and nothing from the government. Teachers of large classes lack the most basic materials and are paid barely enough to purchase rice for the month. When asked how they can do the seemingly impossible, Pastor Luke replied, "We have to. Our children are the future of the country and they must be educated, whatever it takes." Hope EFC is not unusual. Similar one-room church-based schools can be found across Liberia. These are churches having kingdom impact because their members have refused to be merely victims. They have a biblically inspired hope and sacrificial dedication to do whatever it takes to make a better world.

The Gramin Pachin Mandal is a remarkable indigenous church-planting movement among the poorest of India's poor, the Bhangis, who are the lowest of the Dalits (sometimes called outcasts or untouchables). Their jobs include removing human waste, eliminating dead animals, and cleaning sewers. They often live from the spoiled or leftover food of others. A movement to Christ was launched among them in 1984 that by 2004 had grown to some 700,000 baptized believers and totaling as many as 1.5 million counting children and baptismal candidates! The story is one not only of explosive growth and extraordinary contextualization of the gospel but also of holistic ministry. For example, article 19 of the Gramin Pachin Mandal articles of faith reads, "It is an absolute religious duty of believers to rely on themselves economically"

(Pierson 2004, 45). A full-blown educational program has been developed from primary through university level. "This is a logical result of their recovery of dignity and selfhood before God. It is also necessary if Dalits are to escape from poverty" (ibid., 52). Many of the men have obtained better jobs in construction, and women have learned clothing manufacture. Others have become entrepreneurs. These are truly kingdom communities devoted to spiritual, mental, physical, and economic transformation.

Epilogue

....
....
....

In 1774 a man named John Chapman was born in Massachusetts. By the time he was twenty-five he had started apple orchards in New York and Pennsylvania. As the Northwest Territories were opened up for settlement, John became one of the first to explore the region that is now Ohio, Michigan, Indiana, and Illinois. For fifty years he roamed the land, and everywhere he went he planted apple seeds and grew apple trees. Johnny understood the multiplication principle that "Twiggy" (from the prologue) learned. He planted strategically, with an eye to future markets, and seldom did he make a poor choice: many towns emerged near his nursery sites. It is said that some of his "seedlings may have crossed the great plains in covered wagons to produce their bountiful fruit in the western states." He became known as "the Apple Man" or Johnny Appleseed. As one person wrote of him: "Somewhere, somehow, he had caught a vision of the wilderness blossoming with apple trees, orchard after orchard of carefully nurtured trees, whose fragrant blossoms gave promise of a fruitful harvest for the settlers."[1]

There was a price to pay to realize this vision. With perseverance John endured the hardships of itinerant wilderness life as he worked to make his dream come true. It wasn't quite as simple as dropping a few seeds by the roadside wherever he went. In a systematic fashion, he would clear the weeds and brush, select a good, loamy piece of ground in an open place, make a protective barrier to keep out animals, and carefully plant the seeds in rows. He strove for the best possible fruit by always seeding rather than grafting or budding as others were doing.

---

1. This quotation and part of this account of John Chapman's life are taken from www .millville.org/workshops_f/Dich_FOLKLORE/WACKED/story.html (accessed on January 15, 2007). See also "The Story of Johnny Appleseed," www.swedenborg.org/jappleseed/history .html (accessed May 25, 2009) and "Johnny Appleseed: A Pioneer Hero," *Harper's New Monthly Magazine* 64 (1871): 830–31.

John didn't abandon his fledgling nurseries. He returned when he could to care for the young trees, repair the fence, tend to the soil, and plant more seedlings. But his vision was to move on and launch new nurseries to prepare for future colonies of settlers. So he spent most of his time on the frontier. He was not quite the loner he is purported to be. At times he took others with him, and when he could he left the nurseries in the care of a neighbor who protected the trees and sold them on shares. He knew his calling and left most of the cultivation to others.

Elias[2] could be compared to Chapman. He started a church in Liberia, but his vision was for much more. Elias believed that young people can be equipped to start and lead simple fellowships of believers. Within a decade, primarily through his training and coaching ministry, that first church grew to a movement of sixteen congregations. Some are house churches; others meet in rented buildings; one is a mobile church in the marketplace that is reaching drug addicts. Not unlike John Chapman, Elias is an agronomist. Under his leadership this group of churches has purchased a twenty-acre parcel of land that will produce food for needy families. A well will provide water for the farm and drinking water for the nearby village. And on the land a training center for disciples, leaders, and workers is being built.

Then Elias heard a challenge to touch the lives of millions of people with the gospel in the next decade. Along with his friends he wrestled with questions like "What part of the Great Commission is our responsibility?" and "How can we work together to do our part as Africans to reach the unevangelized of Africa?" An indigenous African mission was formed, and its leaders decided to target six African unreached people groups and train fifteen hundred church-planting missionaries.

Elias traveled to explore opportunities to begin new church plants in numerous other districts of Liberia, including Muslim-dominated areas: "There is a need to continue to engage these communities until the gospel takes root there." He is now devoting himself full time to the training of leaders who will serve as catalysts for church multiplication. His mission has already sent out tentmaking workers who have started churches among Muslim people groups in neighboring countries. As I write, he and his friends are launching church multiplication training for sixty pastors and church planters in another West African country. Later this year they will be sharing the vision of church multiplication with nine hundred pastors in central Africa.

Apostolic church planters, like Johnny Appleseed, begin by planting seeds. They invite many others to join them in the hard work of growing orchards of kingdom communities. They believe that they are seminal agents in a master plan to extend Jesus's reign until all have heard his message. Our prayer is for God to raise up many like Elias who will contribute to movements of healthy, reproducing churches.

2. The name in this account is a pseudonym for a real person.

Works Cited

Adams, Eric, and Tim Lewis. 1990. "New Mission Structures for Church Planting," *Mission Frontiers*, December, www.strategicnetwork.org/index.php?loc=kb&view=v&id=4753&fby=e16d4680d785ae386ddb7a4dc4179056&fti=new%20mission&(accessed February 6, 2010).

Allen, Frank W. 1991. "Your Church-Planting Team Can Be Booby-Trapped." *Evangelical Missions Quarterly* 27, no. 3 (July): 294–97.

Allen, Roland. 1962a [1912]. *Missionary Methods: St. Paul's or Ours?* Grand Rapids: Eerdmans.

———. 1962b [1927]. *The Spontaneous Expansion of the Church and the Causes Which Hinder It*. Grand Rapids: Eerdmans.

Anderson, Neil T. 2001. *Steps to Freedom in Christ: A-Step-by-Step Approach*. Ventura, CA: Regal.

Anderson, Rufus. 1869. *Foreign Missions: Their Relations and Claims*. New York: C. Scribner.

Andrews, Colin E. 2009. "Contextualization in a Glocalizing World." *Evangelical Missions Quarterly* 45, no. 3 (July): 314–17.

Appelton, Joanne. 2008. "Preparing to Plant: Calling, Equipping, and Enabling Church Planters in Europe." European Church Planting Network Concept Paper 3, www.ecpn.org/content.php?section_id=9&content_type_id=59 (accessed April 14, 2009).

Armet, Stephen. 1997. "Holistic Church Planting among Latin America's Urban Poor." *Urban Mission* 14, no. 4 (June): 17–22.

Arn, Win. 1986. "How to Use Ratios to Effect Church Growth." In *Church Growth: State of the Art*, edited by C. Peter Wagner, Win Arn, and Elmer L. Towns, 97–103. Wheaton: Tyndale House.

Arnold, Clinton A. 1996. *The Colossian Syncretism: The Interface between Christianity and Folk Belief at Colossae*. Grand Rapids: Baker Books.

Bacon, Dan. 1978. "Should Mission Boards Send Teams as Well as Individuals?" *Evangelical Missions Quarterly* 14, no. 2 (April): 95–99.

Baer, R. Michael. 2006. *Business as Mission: The Power of Business in the Kingdom of God.* Seattle: YWAM.

Baker, Ken. 2005. "What Do You Do When Sin Seems Ignored?" *Evangelical Missions Quarterly* 41, no. 3 (July): 338–43.

Banks, Robert J. 1994. *Paul's Idea of Community: The Early House Churches in Their Historical Setting.* Peabody, MA: Hendrickson.

Barna, George. 1999. *The Habits of Highly Effective Churches.* Ventura, CA: Regal.

Barrett, David B., Todd M. Johnson, and Peter F. Crossing. 2008. "Missiometrics 2008." *International Bulletin of Missionary Research* 32, no. 1 (January): 27–30.

Bate, Fr. Stuart. 1994. "Inculturation: The Local Church Emerges." *Missionalia* 22, no. 2 (August): 93–117.

Beaver, Pierce. 1981. "The History of Mission Strategy." In *Perspectives on the World Christian Movement*, edited by Ralph Winter and Steven Hawthorne, B58–72. Pasadena, CA: William Carey Library.

Beckham, William. 1995. *The Second Reformation.* Houston: Touch.

Befus, Constance P. 1988. "A Multilevel Treatment Approach for Culture Shock Experienced by Sojourners." *International Journal of Intercultural Relations* 12, no. 4 (Winter): 381–400.

Bennett, Robertson. 2000. "Open Letter to Robertson McQuilkin." *Evangelical Missions Quarterly* 36, no. 2 (April): 210–14.

Berg, Clayton L., and Paul E. Pretiz. 1996. *Spontaneous Combustion: Grass-Roots Christianity, Latin American Style.* Pasadena, CA: William Carey Library.

Berg, Mike, and Paul E. Pretiz, 1992. *The Gospel People of Latin America.* Monrovia, CA: MARC and World Vision International.

Bibby, Reginald. 1987. *Fragmented Gods.* Toronto: Irwin.

Blackaby, Henry, and Richard Blackaby. 2001. *Spiritual Leadership: Moving People on to God's Agenda.* Nashville: Broadman and Holman.

Blake, Robert R., and Jane S. Mouton. 1968. *Corporate Excellence through Grid Organization Development.* Houston: Gulf.

Bosch, David. 1991. *Transforming Mission. Paradigm Shifts in Theology of Mission.* Maryknoll, NY: Orbis.

Bowers, Dan. 2005. "Globalization and the Missionary Potential of International Churches." *Evangelical Missions Quarterly* 41, no. 3 (July): 284–90.

Bowers, W. P. 1987. "Fulfilling the Gospel: The Scope of the Pauline Mission." *Journal of the Evangelical Theological Society* 30: 185–98.

Brierley, Peter W. 1997. "Missionary Attrition: The ReMAP Report" in *Too Valuable to Lose*, edited by William D. Taylor, 85–103. Pasadena, CA: William Carey Library.

Bright, Bill. 2007 [1965]. *The Four Spiritual Laws.* Peachtree City, GA: Campus Crusade for Christ.

Britt, David. 1997. "From Homogeneity to Congruence: A Church-Community Model." In *Planting and Growing Urban Churches,* edited by Harvie Conn, 135–49. Grand Rapids: Baker Books.

Brock, Charles. 1994. *Indigenous Church Planting: A Practical Journey.* Neosho, MO: Church Growth International.

Brown, Carl M. 2007. "Exploratory Case Studies and Analysis of Three Intercultural Congregation-to-Congregation Partnerships." PhD diss., Trinity International University.

———. 2008. "Friendship Is Forever: Congregation-to-Congregation Relationships." In *Effective Engagement in Short-Term Missions,* edited by Robert Priest, 209–37. Pasadena, CA: William Carey Library.

Brown, G. Thompson. 1994. "Why Has Christianity Grown Faster in Korea Than in China?" *Missiology* 22, no. 1 (January): 77–88.

Bruce, A. B. 1971 [1894]. *The Training of the Twelve.* Grand Rapids: Kregel.

Bruce, F. F. 1965. *The Acts of the Apostles: The Greek Text with Introduction and Commentary.* Grand Rapids: Eerdmans.

———. 1969. *New Testament History.* New York: Doubleday.

———. 1977. *Commentary on the Book of Acts.* Grand Rapids: Eerdmans.

Caldwell, Brian, and E. M. A. Carter, eds. 1993. *The Return of the Mentor: Strategies for Workplace Learning.* London: Falmer.

Carle, Robert D., and Louis A. Decaro Jr., eds. 1999. *Signs of Hope in the City: Ministry of Community Renewal.* Valley Forge, PA: Judson.

Cerron, Francisco. 2007. "Short-Term Missions: An Initial Assessment from Experience." *Journal of Latin American Theology* 2, no. 2: 21–32.

Chaney, Charles L. 1982. *Church Planting at the End of the Twentieth Century.* Wheaton: Tyndale House.

Chaves, Mark, Mary Ellen Konieczny, Kraig Beyerlein, and Emily Barman. 1999. "The National Congregations Study: Background, Methods, and Selected Results." *Journal for the Scientific Study of Religion* 38, no. 4 (December): 458–76.

Chester, Tim. 2000. "Church Planting: A Theological Perspective." In *Multiplying Churches,* edited by Stephen Timmis, 23–46. Fearn, Ross-Shire, UK: Christian Focus.

Cho, Paul Yonggi. 1981. *Successful Home Cell Groups.* South Plainfield, NJ: Bridge.

Cho, Yong Joong, and David Greenlee. 1995. "Avoiding Pitfalls of Multicultural Teams." *International Journal of Frontier Missions* 12, no. 4 (October): 179–84.

Ciesniewski, John. 2006. "How Much Does a New Site Really Cost?" www.new thing.org/news/articles/staff/124-how-much-does-a-new-site-really-cost (accessed January 30, 2010).

Clinton, Robert J. 1988. *The Making of a Leader.* Colorado Springs: NavPress.

Cole, Neil. 2004. *Cultivating a Life for God: Multiplying Disciples through Life Transformation Groups.* St. Charles, IL: ChurchSmart Resources.

———. 2005. *Organic Church: Growing Faith Where Life Happens.* San Francisco: Jossey-Bass.

Coleman, Robert. 1963. *The Master Plan of Discipleship*. Old Tappan, NJ: Revell.

———. 1987. *The Master Plan of Discipleship*. Rev. ed. Old Tappan, NJ: Revell.

Collins, Travis M. 1995. "Missions and Churches in Partnership for Evangelism: A Study of the Declaration of Ibadan." *Missiology* 23, no. 3 (October): 331–39.

Comiskey, Joel. 1999. *Groups of Twelve: A New Way to Mobilize Leaders and Multiply Groups in Your Church*. Houston: Touch.

Condon, John C. 1997. *Good Neighbors: Communicating with the Mexicans*. Yarmouth, ME: Intercultural.

Conn, Harvie M. 1979. "The Muslim Convert and His Culture." In *The Gospel and Islam: A 1978 Compendium*, edited by Don M. McCuny, 97–113. Monrovia, CA: MARC.

Cordelle, Steve. 2005. *The Church in Many Houses*. Nashville: Abingdon.

Costas, Orlando. 1979. *The Integrity of Mission: The Inner Life and Outreach of the Church*. San Francisco: Harper and Row.

Crow, Kenneth E. n.d. "The Life Cycle of Nazarene Churches." http://media.premierstudios.com/nazarene/docs/The%20Life%20Cycle%20of%20Nazarene%20Churches.pdf (accessed April 28, 2007).

Cymbala, James, and Dean Merrill. 2001. *Fresh Power*. Grand Rapids: Zondervan.

Daloz, Laurent A. 1990. "Mentorship." In *Adult Learning Methods*, edited by M. Galbraith, 205–24. Malabar, FL: Robert E. Krieger.

Davies, Douglas J. 1986. "Person, Power, and Priesthoods." In *Working for the Kingdom: The Story of Ministers in Secular Employment*, edited by J. Fuller and Patrick H. Vaughan, 93–101. London: SPCK.

Davies, Stanley. 1994. "Responding to Butler: Reflections from Europe." In *Kingdom Partnerships for Synergy in Missions*, edited by William D. Taylor, 43–48. Pasadena, CA: William Carey Library.

Denney, J. 1976 [1895]. *Studies in Theology*. Grand Rapids: Baker Books.

DeSilva, Ranjit. 1996. "The Missing Ingredient in Leadership Training." *Evangelical Mission Quarterly* 31, no. 1 (January): 50–56.

Dever, Mark. 2000. *Nine Marks of a Healthy Church*. Wheaton: Crossway.

Dietterich, Inagrace T. 2004. "Leading the Missional Church: The Shape of the Church." www.allelon.net/articles/article.cfm?id=141 (accessed January 30, 2010).

Dohn, Michael N. and Anita L. Dohn. 2006. "Short-Term Medical Teams: What They Do Well . . . and Not So Well." *Evangelical Missions Quarterly* 42, no. 2 (April): 216–24.

Downey, Karol (pseud.). 2005. "Missionary or Wife? Four Needed Changes to Help Clarify the Role of a Missionary Wife." *Evangelical Missions Quarterly* 41, no. 1 (January): 66–74.

Downey, Steven. 2006. "Partnership Re-visited." *Evangelical Missions Quarterly* 42, no. 2 (April): 200–204.

Duck, Arthur. 2001. "Attrition and Retention Factors in Three Pentecostal Churches in Curitiba, Brazil." PhD diss., Trinity International University.

Duclos, R. P. 1982 [1913]. *Histoire du Protestantisme français en Amérique du Nord* [The History of French Protestantism in North America]. Cap-de-la-Madeleine, Quebec: Éditions Impact.

Dudley, Carl S. 1979. "Churches in Changing Communities." In *Metro-ministry: Ways and Means for the Urban Church*, edited by David Frenchak and Sharrel Keyes, 78–91. Elgin, IL: David C. Cook.

Dudley, Carl S., and Nancy T. Ammerman. 2002. *Congregations in Transition*. San Francisco: Jossey-Bass.

Duewel, Wesley. 1995. *Revival Fire*. Grand Rapids: Zondervan.

Dyer, Kevin. 1986. "Crucial Factors in Building Good Teams." *Evangelical Missions Quarterly* 22, no. 3 (July): 254–58.

Eenigenburg, Susan E. 2008. "Preparing Missionary Couples for Cultural Stress." *Evangelical Missions Quarterly* 44, no. 4 (October): 422–29.

EFCA (Evangelical Free Church of America). n.d. "Ten Leading Indicators of a Healthy Church." www.efca.org/church-health/reachnational-church-health/ten-leading-indicators-healthy-church (accessed May 7, 2009).

Eiesland, Nancy L. 1999. *A Particular Place: Urban Restructuring and Religious Ecology in a Southern Exurb*. New Brunswick, NJ: Rutgers University Press.

Elder, Brett. 2003. "Dismantling the Ecclesiastical Welfare System." *Occasional Bulletin*, Evangelical Missiological Society, 15, no. 3 (Fall): 1–2, 5.

Ellis, Jordan. 2005. "Let's Get Real about Missionary Team Chemistry." *Evangelical Missions Quarterly* 41, no. 4 (October): 440–45.

Elliston, Edgar J. 1992. *Home Grown Leaders*. Pasadena, CA: William Carey Library.

Elliston, Edgar J., and J. Timothy Kauffman. 1993. *Developing Leaders for Urban Ministries*. New York: Peter Lang.

Elmer, Duane. 1993. *Cross-Cultural Conflict*. Downers Grove, IL: InterVarsity.

———. 2002. *Cross-Cultural Connections*. Downers Grove, IL: InterVarsity.

———. 2006. *Cross-Cultural Servanthood*. Downers Grove, IL: InterVarsity.

Engel, James. 1977. *How Can I Get Them to Listen?* Grand Rapids: Zondervan.

Engel, James F., and William A. Dyrness. 2000. *Changing the Mind of Mission: Where Have We Gone Wrong?* Downers Grove, IL: InterVarsity.

Evangelical Alliance Information and Resources Centre. 2006. "2005 Church Census." www.eauk.org/resources/info/statistics/2005englishchurchcensus.cfm#denomination (accessed April 28, 2007).

Farnsley, Arthur E. n.d. "A Quick Question: When Is Average Not Average?" http://hirr.hartsem.edu/research/quick_question9.html (accessed February 6, 2010).

Fee, Gordon D. 1987. *The First Epistle to the Corinthians*. Grand Rapids: Eerdmans.

Fee, Gordon D., and Douglas Stuart, 1982. *How to Read the Bible for All Its Worth: A Guide to Understanding the Bible*. Grand Rapids: Zondervan.

Felde, Markus. 1998. "Truly Vernacular Worship for the Sake of the Gospel." *International Review of Mission* 87, no. 344 (January): 39–47.

Ferguson, Dave. 2003. "The Multi-site Church: Some Strengths of this New Life Form." *Leadership* 24, no. 2 (Spring): 80–84.

————. 2007. "Reproducing Churches: Church Growth to Missional Movement." Presentation handout, 2007 Exponential New Church Conference, Orlando, FL, April 24–26.

Flemming, Dean E. 2005. *Contextualization in the New Testament: Patterns for Theology and Mission*. Downers Grove, IL: InterVarsity.

Fowler, Floyd J. 2009. *Survey Research Methods*. 4th ed. Thousand Oaks, CA: Sage.

Foyle, Marjorie. 1987. *Overcoming Missionary Stress*. Kent, UK: MARC Europe.

Freytag, Walter. 1961. *Reden und Aufsätze*. 2 vols. Munich: Kaiser.

Friesen, Randy. 2005. "The Long-Term Impact of Short-Term Missions." *Evangelical Missions Quarterly* 41, no. 4 (October): 448–54.

Garrison, David. 2000. *Church Planting Movements*. Richmond, VA: International Mission Board, Southern Baptist Convention.

————. 2004a. *Church Planting Movements: How God Is Redeeming a Lost World*. Midlothian, VA: WIGTake Resources.

————. 2004b. "Church Planting Movements v. Insider Movements." *International Journal of Frontier Missions* 21, no. 4 (Winter): 151–54.

————. 2005. "Global Church Planting: Something Is Happening." *Journal of Evangelism and Missions* 4 (Spring): 77–87.

Garrison, V. David. 1990. *The Nonresidential Missionary*. Monrovia, CA: MARC.

Gehring, Roger W. 2004. *House Church and Mission: The Importance of Household Structures in Early Christianity*. Peabody, MA: Hendrickson.

Gensichen, Hans-Werner. 1971. *Glaube für die Welt: Theologische Aspekte der Mission*. Gütersloh, Germany: Gütersloher Verlagshaus Gerd Mohn.

George, Carl F. 1991. *Prepare Your Church for the Future*. Grand Rapids: Revell.

George, Timothy. 1994. *Galatians*. Nashville: Broadman and Holman.

Gilliland, Dean S., ed. 1989. *The Word among Us*. Dallas: Word.

Glover, Robert. 1960. *The Progress of Worldwide Missions*. New York: Harper and Brothers.

Gobena, Iteffa. 1997. "Ethiopian Church Planting." *World Evangelization* 81 (December): 15–16.

Goldsmith, Martin. 1980. "Parabolic Preaching in the Context of Islam." *Evangelical Review of Theology* 4, no. 2 (October): 218–22.

Gómez, Jorge. 1995. "Protestant Growth and Desertion in Costa Rica: Viewed in Relation to Churches with Higher Attrition Rates, Lower Attrition Rates, and More Mobility, as Affected by Evangelism (i.e., Message and Method) and Discipleship Practices (including Church Discipline)." DMin diss., Columbia International University.

————. 1996. *El crecimiento y la deserción en la iglesia evangélica costarricense* [Growth and Desertion in the Costa Rican Church]. San José, Costa Rica: Publicaciones IINDEF.

Gopffarth, William. 1993. "A Study of the Functional Competencies of Southern Baptist Missionaries Who Originate Indigenous Churches in the Philippines." EdD diss., University of North Texas.

Grady, Dick, and Glenn Kendall. 1992. "Seven Keys to Effective Church Planting." *Evangelical Missions Quarterly* 28, no. 4 (October): 366–73.

Graham, Thomas. 1987. "How to Select the Best Church Planters." *Evangelical Missions Quarterly* 23, no. 1 (January): 70–79.

Gray, Stephen. 2007. *Planting Fast-Growing Churches*. St. Charles, IL: ChurchSmart Resources.

Green, Michael. 1970. *Evangelism in the Early Church*. Grand Rapids: Eerdmans.

Greer, Luke. 2009. "Sometimes It Just Seems Good: Another Look at Missionary Call." *Evangelical Missions Quarterly* 45, no. 3 (July): 326-32.

Grigg, Viv. 1992. *Cry of the Urban Poor*. Monrovia, CA: MARC.

Grover, Rick. 2004. "Urban Church Planting: The Call to the City." In *Church Planting from the Ground Up*, edited by Tom Jones, 40–51. Joplin, MO: College.

Gupta, Paul R., and Sherwood G. Lingenfelter. 2006. *Breaking Traditions to Accomplish Vision: Training Leaders in a Church Planting Movement*. Winona Lake, IN: BMH Books.

Guthrie, Donald. 1973. *Galatians*. Grand Rapids: Eerdmans.

Guthrie, Stan. 2001. *Missions in the Third Millennium: 21 Key Trends for the 21st Century*. Rev. ed. Waynesboro, GA: Paternoster.

Hadaway, C. Kirk. 1982. "Learning from Urban Research." *Review and Expositor* 80, no. 4 (Fall): 543–52.

Hadaway, C. Kirk, Francis M. DuBose, and Stuart A. Wright. 1987. *Home Cell Groups and House Churches*. Nashville: Broadman.

Hardman, Keith J. 1978. "John Williams (1796–1839)." In *The New International Dictionary of the Christian Church*, edited by J. D. Douglas, 1052. Grand Rapids: Zondervan.

Harrison, Rodney, Tom Cheyney, and Don Overstreet. 2008. *Spin-Off Churches: How One Church Successfully Plants Another*. Nashville: Broadman and Holman.

Hart, Archibald. 1999. *The Anxiety Cure*. Nashville: Word.

Hempelmann, Heinzpeter. 1996. *Gemindegründung: Perspektive für eine Kirche von Morgen?* Giessen, Germany: Brunnen.

Herrington, John. 2009. "A City Movement." Presentation at Church Planting Week at Trinity Evangelical Divinity School, January 27.

Herron, Fred. 2003. *Expanding God's Kingdom through Church Planting*. New York: Writer's Showcase.

Hertzberg, Hutz H. 2008. "Personal Characteristics and Ministry Perceptions of Younger Evangelical Church Planters." PhD diss., Trinity Evangelical Divinity School.

Hertzberg, Hutz H., and Francis A. Lonsway. 2008. "Young Evangelical Church Planters." *Theological Education* 43, no. 2: 67–77.

Hesselgrave, David J. 1980. *Planting Churches Cross-Culturally. A Guide for Home and Foreign Missions*. Grand Rapids: Baker Academic.

———. 1991. *Communicating Christ Cross-Culturally*. 2nd ed. Grand Rapids: Academie Books.

Hesselgrave, David J., and Edward Rommen. 1989. *Contextualization: Meanings, Methods, and Models*. Grand Rapids: Baker Books.

Hibbert, Richard Y. 2008. "Stagnation and Decline Following Rapid Growth in Turkish-Speaking Roma Churches of Bulgaria." PhD diss., Trinity International University.

Hiebert, Paul G. 1982. "The Flaw of the Excluded Middle." *Missiology* 10, no. 1 (January): 35–47.

———. 1987. "Critical Contextualization." *International Bulletin of Missionary Research* 11, no. 3 (July): 104–11.

———. 1989. "Form and Meaning." In *The Word among Us*, edited by Dean S. Gilliland, 101–20. Dallas: Word.

———. 1994. *Anthropological Reflections on Missiological Issues*. Grand Rapids: Baker Books.

———. 2006. "The Missionary as Mediator of Global Theologizing." In *Globalizing Theology*, edited by Craig Ott and Harold A. Netland, 288–308. Grand Rapids: Baker Academic.

———. 2008. *Transforming Worldviews: An Anthropological Understanding of How People Change*. Grand Rapids: Baker Academic.

Hiebert, Paul G., and Eloise Hiebert Meneses. 1995. *Incarnational Ministry: Planting Churches in Band, Tribal Peasant, and Urban Societies*. Grand Rapids: Baker Books.

Hiebert, Paul G., and Sam Larsen. 1999. "Partnership in the Gospel: Misers, Accountants, and Stewards." *Direction* 28, no.1 (Spring): 55–62.

Hilary, Mbachu. 1995. *Inculturation Theology of the Jerusalem Council in Acts 15: An Interpretation of the Igbo Church Today*. Frankfurt am Main: Lang.

Hill Country Bible Church. 2009. Diagram of Church Plants. www.hcbc.com/templates/System/details.asp?id=28485&PID=212315 (accessed March 21, 2009).

Hirsch, Alan. 2006. *The Forgotten Ways: Reactivating the Missional Church*. Grand Rapids: Brazos.

Hirst, Lester J. 1994. "Urban Church Planting Missionary Teams: A Study of Member Characteristics and Experiences Related to Teamwork Competencies." PhD diss., Trinity Evangelical Divinity School.

Hoke, Stephen, and William D. Taylor. 1999. *Send Me: Your Journey to the Nations*. Pasadena, CA: William Carey Library and World Evangelical Fellowship.

Holste, Scott, and Jim Haney. 2006. "The Global Status of Evangelical Christianity: A Model for Assessing Priority People Groups." *Mission Frontiers* 28, no. 1 (January-February): 8–13.

Hopkins, Bob. 1988. *Church Planting*. Bramcote, UK: Grove Books.

Hull, Bill. 1988. *The Disciple Making Pastor*. Grand Rapids: Baker Books.

Hunter, Malcolm J. 2000. "The Nomadic Church: The Church in Its Simplest Form." *International Journal of Frontier Missions* 17, no. 3 (Fall): 15–19.

Jaffarian, Michael. 2004. "Are There More Non-Western Missionaries Than Western Missionaries?" *International Bulletin of Missionary Research* 28, no. 3 (July): 131–32.

Johnson, C. Neal and Steve Rundle. 2010. *Business as Mission: A Comprehensive Guide to Theory and Practice*. Downers Grove, IL: InterVarsity.

Johnstone, Patrick. 2001. *Operation World*. 3rd ed. Minneapolis: Bethany House.

Johnstone, Patrick, and Jason Mandryk. 2005. *Operation World*. 21st century ed. Waynesboro, GA: Paternoster USA.

Jones, Philip B. n.d. "Research Report: Executive Summary of Southern Baptist Congregations Today." www.namb.net/atf/cf/%7BCDA250E8–8866–4236–9A0C–C646DE153446%7D/Exec_Summary__stand_alone.pdf (accessed June 26, 2007).

Jongeneel, Jan. 1991. "The Missiology of Gisbertus Voetius: The First Comprehensive Protestant Theology of Missions." *Calvin Theological Journal* 26, no. 1 (April): 47–79.

Julien, Thomas. 2000. "Apostolic Church-Planting Team (ACT) Strategy (2.0)." Manuscript. Grace Brethren International Missions.

Kane, J. Herbert. 1976. *Christian Missions in Biblical Perspective*. Grand Rapids: Baker Books.

Katzenbach, Jon R., and Douglas K. Smith. 1993. *The Wisdom of Teams: Creating the High Performance Organization*. New York: HarperCollins.

Kee, Paul. 1991. "Retention among the 'Nso of Cameroon." MA thesis, Harding Graduate School of Religion.

Kelley, J. N. D. 1963. *The Pastoral Epistles*. London: Adam and Charles Black.

Kelly, Dean M. 1977. *Why Conservative Churches Are Growing: A Study in Sociology of Religion*. New York: Harper and Row.

Kendall, Glenn. 1988. "Missionaries Should Not Plant Churches." *Evangelical Missions Quarterly* 24, no. 3 (July): 218–21.

———. 1990. "Tiny Rwanda Shines as Example of Cluster Church Planting." *Evangelical Missions Quarterly* 26, no. 2 (April): 136–43.

Keyes, Larry. 2003. "A Global Harvest Force." In *Perspectives on the World Christian Movement: A Reader*, edited by Ralph Winter and Stephen Hawthorne, 744–47. Pasadena, CA: William Carey Library.

Kiddle, Martin. 1940. *The Book of Revelation*. London: Hodder and Stoughton.

King, Roberta. 2005. "Variations on a Theme of Appropriate Contextualization: Music Lessons from Africa." In *Appropriate Christianity*, edited by Charles H. Kraft, 309–24. Pasadena, CA: William Carey Library.

King, Steve. 2007. "Closing the Back Door." *Idea*, September-October. www.eauk.org/resources/idea/SepOct2007/closing-the-back-door.cfm (accessed June 1, 2009).

Kirk, J. Andrew. 2000. *What Is Mission? Theological Explorations*. Minneapolis: Fortress.

Klippenes, George. 2001. *Church Planter Boot Camp*. Minneapolis: Evangelical Free Church of America Press.

———. 2003. *Church Planter's Start Up Bootcamp*. Minneapolis: Evangelical Free Church of America Press.

Köstenberger, Andreas J., and Peter T. O'Brien. 2001. *Salvation to the Ends of the Earth: A Biblical Theology of Mission*. Leicester, UK: Apollos.

Kraemer, Hendrik. 1938. *The Christian Message in a Non-Christian World*. New York: Harper and Brothers.

Kraft, Charles H. 1979. *Christianity in Culture*. Maryknoll, NY: Orbis.

———, ed. 2005. *Appropriate Christianity*. Pasadena, CA: William Carey Library.

Kraft, Charles H., and Tom N. Wisley, eds. 1979. *Readings in Dynamic Indigeneity*. Pasadena, CA: William Carey Library.

Kreider, Larry, and Floyd McClung. 2007. *Starting a House Church*. Ventura, CA: Gospel Light.

Küng, Hans. 1967. *The Church*. New York: Sheed and Ward.

Ladd, George Eldon. 1974. *A Theology of the New Testament*. Grand Rapids: Eerdmans.

Lai, Patrick. 2005. *Tentmaking: Business as Missions*. Waynesboro, GA: Authentic.

Langton, Edward. 1956. *History of the Moravian Church*. London: Allen and Unwin.

Lanier, Don. 1993. *Team Assessment and Development: A Process for Improving Team Effectiveness*. Colorado Springs: Navigators.

Latourette, Kenneth S. 2003. *A History of Christianity*, vol. 1, *To AD 1500*. New York: HarperCollins.

Lederleitner, Mary Mallon. 2007. "The Devil Is in the Details: Avoiding Common Pitfalls When Funding New Partnership Endeavors." *Evangelical Missions Quarterly* 43, no. 2 (April): 160–65.

Lencioni, Patrick. 2002. *The Five Dysfunctions of a Team: A Leadership Fable*. San Francisco: Jossey-Bass.

Liefeld, Walter L. 1978. "Theology of Church Growth." In *Theology and Mission*, edited by David J. Hesselgrave, 173–87. Grand Rapids: Baker Books.

———. 1995. *Interpreting the Book of Acts*. Grand Rapids: Zondervan.

Lingenfelter, Sherwood G., and Marvin K. Mayers. 2003. *Ministering Cross-Culturally*. 2nd ed. Grand Rapids: Baker Academic.

Little, Christopher R. 2005. *Mission in the Way of Paul*. New York: Peter Lang.

Livermore David. 2006. *Serving with Eyes Wide Open: Doing Short-Term Missions with Cultural Intelligence*. Grand Rapids: Baker Books.

Livingstone, Gregory. 1993. *Planting Churches in Muslim Cities: A Team Approach*. Grand Rapids: Baker Books.

Logan, Robert E. 1988. *International Church Planting Guide*. Alta Loma, CA: Strategic Ministries.

Logan, Robert E., and Gary B. Reinecke. 2003a. *Coaching 101 Handbook*. St. Charles, IL: ChurchSmart.

———. 2003b. *Developing Coaching Excellence*. St. Charles, IL: ChurchSmart.

Logan, Robert E., and Sherilyn Carlton. 2003. *Coaching 101*. St. Charles, IL: ChurchSmart.

Logan, Robert E., and Steve L. Ogne. 1991a. *The Church Planter's Toolkit*. Pasadena. CA: Charles E. Fuller Institute of Evangelism and Church Growth.

———. 1991b. *New Church Incubator*. Fullerton, CA: Church Resource Ministries.

———. 1995. *Churches Planting Churches*. St. Charles, IL: ChurchSmart Resources.

Longenecker, Richard N. 1964. *Paul: Apostle of Liberty*. Grand Rapids: Baker Books.

———. 1971. *The Ministry and Message of Paul*. Grand Rapids: Zondervan.

———. 1981. "Acts." In *The Expositors Bible Commentary*, vol. 9, gen. ed. Frank E. Gabelein. Grand Rapids: Zondervan.

———. 2002. "Paul's Vision of the Church and Community Formation in His Major Missionary Letters." In *Community Formation in the Early Church and in the Church Today*, edited by Richard N. Longenecker, 73–88. Peabody, MA: Hendrickson.

LOP 1 [Lausanne Occasional Paper]. 1978. "The Pasadena Consultation: Homogeneous Unit Principle." Wheaton: Lausanne Committee for World Evangelization.

LOP 21. 1982. "Evangelism and Social Responsibility: An Evangelical Commitment." Wheaton: Lausanne Committee for World Evangelization.

LOP 22. 1980. "The Thailand Report on the Urban Poor: Report of the Consultation of World Evangelization Mini-consultation on Reaching the Urban Poor." Wheaton: Lausanne Committee for World Evangelization.

LOP 33. 2005. "Holistic Ministry." Wheaton: Lausanne Committee for World Evangelization.

LOP 43. 2005. "The Realities of the Changing Expressions of the Church." Wheaton: Lausanne Committee for World Evangelization.

LOP 54. 2005. "Making Disciples of Oral Learners." Wheaton: Lausanne Committee for World Evangelization.

LOP 59. 2005. "Business as Mission." Wheaton: Lausanne Committee for World Evangelization.

Loss, Myron. 1983. *Culture Shock: Dealing with Stress in Cross-Cultural Settings*. Winona Lake, IN: Light and Life.

Love, Rick. 1996. "Four Stages of Team Development." *Evangelical Missions Quarterly* 32, no. 3 (July): 312–16.

———. 2008. "How Do We Deal with the Baggage of the Past? Blessing the Nations in the 21st Century, a 3D Approach to Apostolic Ministry." *International Journal of Frontier Missiology* 25, no. 1 (Spring): 31–37.

Lukasse, Johan. 1986. "It Takes Team Effort to Root Churches in Hard Soil." *Evangelical Missions Quarterly* 22, no. 1 (January): 34–42.

———. 2006. "Update on the Use of Teams in the BEM [Belgian Evangelical Mission]." E-mail to Jim Reapsome, November 23.

Lyons, Carol. 2009. "The Story of God and Man: Narrations from God's Word for Building a Solid Foundation of Faith." Manuscript. Dar es Salaam, Tanzania.

Macchia, Stephen A. 1999. *Becoming a Healthy Church: Traits of Vital Ministry*. Grand Rapids: Baker Books.

———. 2005. *Becoming a Healthy Team: Five Traits of Vital Leadership*. Grand Rapids: Baker Books.

MacDonald, Jeffrey. 2006. "Rise of Sunshine Samaritans: On a Mission or Holiday?" *Christian Science Monitor,* May 25, www.csmonitor.com/2006/0525/p01s01-ussc .html (accessed June 16, 2009).

Mackin, Sandra L. 1992. "Multinational Teams: Smooth as Silk or Rough as Rawhide?" *Evangelical Missions Quarterly* 28, no. 2 (April): 134–40.

Malphurs, Aubrey. 1992. *Planting Growing Churches for the 21st Century*. Grand Rapids: Baker Books.

———. 2005. *Advanced Strategic Planning: A New Model for Church and Ministry Leaders*. 2nd ed. Grand Rapids: Baker Books.

Mangham, William F., Jr. 1987. "A Study of the History and Strategy of the Movement 'Lima to an Encounter with God,' 1973–1986." MA thesis, Columbia Biblical Seminary.

Mannoia, Keven W. 1994. *Church Planting: The Next Generation*. Indianapolis: Light and Life.

Maranz, David E. 2001. *African Friends and Money Matters: Observations from Africa*. Dallas: SIL International.

Mateer, Samuel. 1988. "The Missionary's Ministry Prayer." *Evangelical Missions Quarterly* 24, no. 2 (April): 144–48.

Maurice, Sameh. 2005. "From Now to Eternity." Author's transcript of interview from DVD. November 18. Middle East Christian Outreach (MECO).

Maxwell, John C. 1995. *Developing the Leaders around You*. Nashville: Thomas Nelson.

McCauley, Horace. 2007. "The Church and Development." *A.M.E. Zion Quarterly Review* 119, no. 4 (October): 16–19.

McConnell, Scott. 2009. *Multi-Site Churches: Guidance for the Movement's Next Generation*. Nashville: Broadman and Holman.

McGavran, Donald A. 1955. *The Bridges of God*. New York: Friendship.

———. 1980. *Understanding Church Growth*. Rev. ed. Grand Rapids: Eerdmans.

McIlwain, Trevor. 1987. *Building on Firm Foundations*, vol. 1. Sanford, FL: New Tribes Mission.

McMillan, David W., and David M. Chavis. 1986. "Sense of Community: A Definition and Theory." *American Journal of Community Psychology* 14, no. 1 (January): 6–23.

McNamara, Roger N., and Ken Davis. 2005. *The Y-B-H Handbook of Church Planting (Yes, But How?)*. Longwood, FL: Xulon.

McQuilkin, Robertson. 1999. "Stop Sending Money! Breaking the Cycle of Mission Dependency." *Christianity Today* 43, no. 3 (March): 57–59.

———. 2002. *The Great Omission*. Waynesboro, GA: Authentic Media.

Meeks, Wayne. 1986. *The Moral World of the First Christians*. Philadelphia: Westminster.

Metzger, Bruce M. 1971. *A Textual Commentary on the Greek New Testament*. London: United Bible Societies.

Miller, Darrow L., and Scott Allen. 2005. *Against All Hope: Hope for Africa*. Nairobi: Samaritan Strategy Africa Working Group of the Disciple Nations Alliance.

Minatrea, Milfred. 2004. *Shaped by the Heart of God: The Passion and Practices of Missional Churches*. San Francisco: Jossey-Bass.

Moffat, James. 1961. *The Book of Revelation*. Grand Rapids: Eerdmans.

Montgomery, Jim. 1989. *DAWN 2000: 7 Million Churches to Go*. Pasadena, CA: William Carey Library.

Moreau, A. Scott. 2006. "Contextualization That Is Comprehensive." *Missiology* 34, no. 3 (July): 325–35.

Morin, R. 1994. "La culture québécoise [Quebec culture]." *L'Action Nationale* 5 (May): 579–82.

Muriu, Oscar. 2007. "The African Planter: An Interview with Oscar Muriu." *Leadershipjournal.net*, Spring, www.christianitytoday.com/le/2007/002/3.96.html (accessed on January 22, 2009).

Murray, Stewart. 1998. *Church Planting: Laying Foundations*. Carlisle, Cumbria, UK: Paternoster.

Neeley, Paul. 1999. "Noted Ministry." *Evangelical Missions Quarterly* 35, no. 2 (April): 156–61.

Neighbour, Ralph W. 1990. *Where Do We Go from Here? A Guidebook for the Cell Group Church*. Houston: Touch.

Neumann, Mikel. 1999. *Home Groups for Urban Cultures: Biblical Small Group Ministry on Five Continents*. Pasadena, CA: William Carey Library.

Nevius, John. 1958 [1885]. *Planting and Development of Missionary Churches*. Nutley, NJ: Presbyterian and Reformed.

Newbigin, Lesslie. 1954. *The Household of God*. New York: Friendship.

———. 1989. *The Gospel in a Pluralistic World*. Grand Rapids: Eerdmans.

Nida, Eugene Albert. 1960. *Message and Mission: The Communication of the Christian Faith*. Pasadena, CA: William Carey Library.

———. 1974. *Understanding Latin Americans: With Special Reference to Religious Values and Movements*. Pasadena, CA: William Carey Library.

Niles, Nathan (pseud.). 2000. "Professional Tentmakers Open Doors for Ministry." *Evangelical Missions Quarterly* 36, no. 3 (July): 300–306.

Niringiye, D. Zac. 2008. "To Proclaim the Good News of the Kingdom," pt. 2. In *Mission in the 21st Century: Exploring the Five Marks of Global Mission*, edited by Andrew Walls and Cathy Ross, 11–24. Maryknoll, NY: Orbis.

Norman, J. G. 1978. "Moravian Brethren (Unitas Fratrum)." In *The New International Dictionary of the Christian Church*, edited by J. D. Douglas, 676. Grand Rapids: Zondervan.

Norman, Nathan. 1996. "The Value of Teams in the Workplace." *University Record*, October 8, www.ur.umich.edu/9697/Oct08_96/artcl15c.htm (accessed June 26, 2009).

Oberg, Kalvero. 1960. "Cultural Shock: Adjustments to New Cultural Environments." *Practical Anthropology* 7, no. 4 (July-August): 177–82.

O'Brien, Peter T. 1995. *Gospel and Mission in the Writings of Paul*. Grand Rapids: Baker Books.

Oborji, Francis Anekwe. 2006. *Concepts of Mission*. Maryknoll, NY: Orbis.

O'Connor, Patrick. 2006. *Reproducible Pastoral Training: Church Planting Guidelines from the Teachings of George Patterson*. Pasadena, CA: William Carey Library.

O'Donnell, Kelly. 1999. "The CACTUS Kit for Building Resilient Teams." *Evangelical Missions Quarterly* 35, no. 1 (January): 72–78.

Ogne, Steven L., and Thomas P. Nebel. 1995. *Empowering Leaders through Coaching*. St. Charles, IL: ChurchSmart.

Ollrog, Wolf-Henning. 1979. *Paulus und seine Mitarbeiter* [Paul and His Coworkers]. Neukirchen-Vluyn, Germany: Neukirchener Verlag.

Olson, Daniel V. A. 2002. "Do New Nazarene Churches 'Do Better' When Started Near Existing Nazarene Churches?" Report, Church of the Nazarene. www.nazarene .org/files/docs/NewstartProximity.pdf (accessed January 21, 2009).

OPEN [Overseas Professional Employee Network]. 2009. "Huddles." www.open networkers.net/huddles (accessed June 1, 2009).

Orr, E. 1970. *Evangelical Awakenings in India*. New Dehli: Christian Literature Institute.

Ortiz, Manuel. 1996. *One New People*. Downers Grove, IL: InterVarsity.

Osborne, Larry. 2008. *Sticky Church*. Grand Rapids: Zondervan.

Ott, Craig. 1993. "Let the Buyer Beware: Financially Supporting National Pastors and Missionaries May Not Always Be the Bargain It's Cracked Up to Be." *Evangelical Missions Quarterly* 29, no. 3 (July): 286–91.

———. 1994. "Evangelikale Christen in München." Manuscript. Report for Evange- lische Allianz and Kreis zur Einheit, Munich.

———. 2001. "Matching the Church Planter's Role with the Church Planting Model." *Evangelical Missions Quarterly* 37, no. 3 (July): 338–44.

Ott, Craig, and Stephen J. Strauss. 2010. *Encountering Theology of Mission*. Grand Rapids: Baker Academic.

Padilla, C. René. 1982. "The Unity of the Church and the Homogeneous Unit Principle." *International Bulletin of Missionary Research* 4, no. 1 (January): 23–30.

Pantoja, Luis, Jr., Sadiri Joy Tira, and Enoch Wan, eds. 2004. *Scattered: The Filipino Global Presence*. Manila: LifeChange, 2004.

Pao, David W. 2002. *Acts and the Isaianic New Exodus*. Grand Rapids: Baker Academic.

Paredes, Tito. 2007. "Short-Term Missions: What Can Be Rescued, What Can Be Criticized, and the Challenge of Contextualization." *Journal of Latin American Theology* 2, no. 2: 249–59.

Parshall, Phil. 1979. "Contextualized Baptism for Muslim Converts." *Missiology* 7, no. 4 (October): 501–15.

———. 1989. "Lessons Learned in Contextualization." In *Muslims and Christians on the Emmaus Road*, edited by J. Dudley Woodberry, 251–65. Monrovia, CA: MARC.

Patrick (pseud.). 2007. "Tentmaking Unveiled: 'The survey says.'" *Evangelical Missions Quarterly* 43, no. 2 (April): 168–75.

Patterson, George. 1981. "The Spontaneous Multiplication of Churches." In *Perspectives on the World Christian Movement: A Reader*, edited by Ralph D. Winter and Steven C. Hawthorne, 601–18. Pasadena, CA: William Carey Library.

Patterson, George, and Richard Scoggins. 1993. *Church Multiplication Guide*. Pasadena, CA: William Carey Library.

Payne, J. D. 2003. "Problems Hindering North American Church Planting Movements." *Evangelical Missions Quarterly* 39, no. 2 (2003): 220–27.

———. 2007. *Missional House Churches*. Colorado Springs: Paternoster.

PC(USA). 2005. "PC(USA) Congregations and Membership: 1995–2005." www.pcusa .org/research/compstats/cs2005/2005_table1.pdf (accessed February 6, 2010).

Peters, George W. 1970. *Saturation Evangelism*. Grand Rapids: Zondervan.

———. 1981. *A Theology of Church Growth*. Grand Rapids: Zondervan.

Pfister, Jürg. 1998. "Gemeindegründungsbewegung in Macenta, Guinea." Term paper submitted for the course Missionarische Gemeindegründung, Columbia International University, Korntal Branch Campus.

Pierson, Paul E. 2004. "The Gramin Pachin Mandal among Dalits in India." Chapter 3 in *Transformation from the Periphery: Emerging Streams of Church and Mission*. 2004 Forum for World Evangelization, Thailand, September 2004.

Pinney, Jay. 2006. "Essential Tools for Strengthening the Life and Ministry of Church Planters: A Training Manual." DMin thesis, Fuller Theological Seminary.

Piper, John. 1993. *Let the Nations Be Glad: The Supremacy of God in Missions*. Grand Rapids: Baker Academic.

Pobee, John S. 1981."The *Skenosis* of Christian Worship in Africa." *Studia Liturgica* 14, no. 1: 37–52.

Poulter, Todd. 2006. "Partnerships in Ministry: Moving from Misguided Metaphors to Sustainable Strategies." *Evangelical Missions Quarterly* 42, no. 4 (October): 452–56.

Power, Grant, and Nancy Power. 1998. "Promoting Urban Economic Transformation at the Grassroots." In *Serving with the Urban Poor: Cases in Holistic Ministry*, edited by Tetsunao Yamamori, Bryant L. Myers, and Kenneth L. Luscombe, 149–66. Monrovia, CA: MARC.

Priest, Robert J. 2003. " 'I discovered my sin!' Aguaruna Evangelical Conversion Narratives." In *The Anthropology of Religious Conversion*, edited by Andrew Buckser and Stephen Glazier, 95–108. Lanham, MD: Rowman and Littlefield.

———. 2007. "Peruvian Churches Acquire 'Linking Social Capital' through STM Partnerships." *Journal of Latin American Theology* 2, no. 2: 175–89.

———. 2008. *Effective Engagement in Short-Term Missions: Doing It Right*. Pasadena, CA: William Carey Library.

Priest, Robert J., and Joseph P. Priest. 2008. " 'They see everything, and understand nothing': Short-Term Mission and Service Learning." *Missiology* 36, no. 1 (January): 53–73.

Prill, Thorsten. 2009. "Expatriate Churches: Mission and Challenges." *Evangelical Mission Quarterly* 45, no. 4 (October): 450–54.

Quicke, Michael. 1998. Foreword to Stuart Murray, *Church Planting: Laying Foundations*. Carlisle, Cumbria, UK: Paternoster.

Rainer, Thom S. 1999. *High Expectations: The Remarkable Secret of Keeping People in Your Church*. Nashville: Broadman and Holman.

Ramsay, William Mitchell, Sir. 1963 [1904]. *The Letters to the Seven Churches of Asia and Their Place in the Plan of the Apocalypse*. Grand Rapids: Baker Books.

_____. 1982 [1895]. *St. Paul the Traveler and the Roman Citizen*. Grand Rapids: Baker Books.

Ramstad, Mans. 1996. "Making Tents or Building Churches?" *Evangelical Missions Quarterly* 32, no. 4 (October): 416–21.

Reapsome, Jim. 1995. "What Went Wrong in Rwanda?" *Evangelical Missions Quarterly* 31, no. 1 (January): 2.

Redeemer Church Planting Center. 2009. *Redeemer Church Planting Center Partner Program*. Brochure. www.redeemer2.com/rcpc/rcpc/Church_Planting_Brochure .pdf (accessed March 23, 2009).

Reinhardt, Wolfgang. 1995. *Das Wachstum des Gottesvolkes: Biblische Theologie des Gemeindewachstums*. Göttingen, Germany: Vandenhoeck und Ruprecht.

Rhodes, H., and A. Campbell. 1964. *History of the Korean Mission*. New York: United Presbyterian Church in the USA.

Rickett, Daniel. 2000. *Building Strategic Partnerships: A Practical Guide to Partnering with Nonwestern Missions*. Pleasant Hill, CA: Klein Graphics.

Ridley, Charles R. 1988. *How to Select Church Planters*. Pasadena: Fuller Evangelistic Association.

Ridley, Charles R., and Robert E. Logan. 1998. *Training for Selection Interviewing*. St. Charles, IL: ChurchSmart.

———. 2002. *Church Planter's Assessment Guide*. St. Charles, IL: ChurchSmart.

Ridley, Charles R., and Tweed Moore. 2000. *Evaluating and Reporting*. St. Charles, IL: ChurchSmart.

Riesner, Rainer. 1998. *Paul's Early Period: Chronology, Mission Strategy, Theology*. Grand Rapids: Eerdmans.

Robb, John D. 1990. "Prayer as a Strategic Weapon in Frontier Missions." Paper presented to the International Society for Frontier Missiology, September 13–15.

Roberts, Bob. 2008. *The Multiplying Church: The New Math for Starting New Churches*. Grand Rapids: Zondervan.

Roberts, Dayton. 1971. *Strachan of Costa Rica: Missionary Insights and Strategies*. Grand Rapids: Eerdmans.

Robinson, Martin. 1992. "Church Planting and the Kingdom of God." In *Planting Tomorrow's Churches Today*, edited by Martin Robinson and Stuart Christine, 15–58. Speldhurst, Kent, UK: Monarch.

Robinson, Martin, and Stuart Christine. 1992. *Planting Tomorrow's Churches Today*. Speldhurst, Kent: Monarch.

Roembke, Leanne. 2000. *Building Credible Multicultural Teams*. Pasadena, CA: William Carey Library.

Rowell, John. 2007. *To Give or Not to Give? Rethinking Dependency, Restoring Generosity, and Redefining Sustainability.* Atlanta: Authentic.

Rowland, Trent, and Vivian Rowland. 2001. *Pioneer Church Planting: A Rookie Team Leader's Handbook.* Littleton, CO: Caleb Project.

Rundle, Steven L. 2000. "Ministry, Profits, and the Schizophrenic Tentmaker." *Evangelical Missions Quarterly* 36, no. 3 (July): 292–300.

Rundle, Steven L., and Tom A. Steffen. 2003. *Great Commission Companies: The Emerging Role of Business in Missions.* Downers Grove, IL: InterVarsity.

Saint, Steve. 2001. *The Great Omission.* Seattle: YWAM.

Sanders, J. Oswald. 1989 [1967]. *Spiritual Leadership.* Chicago: Moody.

Sankey, Paul J. 1994. "The Church as Clan: Reflections on African Ecclesiology." *International Review of Mission* 83, no. 330 (July): 437–49.

Sanneh, Lamin. 1989. *Translating the Message: The Missionary Impact on Culture.* Maryknoll, NY: Orbis.

———. 1995. "The Gospel, Language, and Culture: The Theological Method in Cultural Analysis." *International Review of Mission* 84. no. 332 (January-April): 47–64.

———. 2008. *Disciples of All Nations: Pillars of World Christianity.* New York: Oxford University.

Sarason, Seymore B. 1974. *The Psychological Sense of Community: Prospects for a Community.* San Francisco: Jossey-Bass.

Sawatsky, Benjamin. 1987. "World Glass City Frontier Project: A Team Training Manual." Minneapolis: Evangelical Free Church of America.

———. 1991. "What It Takes to Be a Church Planter." *Evangelical Missions Quarterly* 27, no. 4 (October): 342–47.

———. 1997. "The Profile of a Cross-Cultural Church Planter." Teaching notes, EFCA Annual Cross-Cultural Church Planting School, Minneapolis.

Schindler, Dietrich. 2008. "Good to Great Church Planting: The Road Less Traveled." *Evangelical Missions Quarterly* 44, no. 3 (July): 330–37.

Schnabel, Eckhard J. 2004. *The Early Christian Mission.* Downers Grove, IL: InterVarsity.

———. 2008. *Paul the Missionary: Realities, Strategies, and Methods.* Downers Grove, IL: InterVarsity.

Schomerus, H. W. 1935. "Bildung von Kirche als Aufgabe der Mission." *Neue allgemeine Missionszeitschrift* 12, no. 9: 289–312.

Schwarz, Christian A. 1996. *Natural Church Development.* St. Charles, IL: ChurchSmart.

Scott, J. M. 1995. *Paul and the Nations: The Old Testament and Jewish Background of Paul's Mission to the Nations, with Special Reference to the Destination of Galatians.* Tübingen: J. C. B. Mohr / Paul Siebeck.

Seale, J. Paul. 1989. "Primary Health Care and Church Planting." *Evangelical Missions Quarterly* 24, no. 4 (October): 350–61.

Shawchuck, Norman. 1983. *How to Manage Conflict in the Church: Understanding and Managing Conflict.* Orland Park, IL: Spiritual Growth Resources.

Shenk, David W., and Erwin R. Stutzman. 1988. *Creating Communities of the Kingdom.* Scottsdale, PA: Herald.

Shorter, Aylward. 1988. *Toward a Theology of Inculturation.* Maryknoll, NY: Orbis.

Simson, Wolfgang. 1995. *Gottes Megatrends.* Emmilsbühl, Germany: C&P.

———. 2001. *Houses That Change the World.* Waynesboro, GA: Authentic Media.

Sinclair, Daniel. 2006. *A Vision of the Possible: Pioneer Church Planting in Teams.* Waynesboro, GA: Authentic Books.

Singh, Godwin R., ed. 1985. *A Call to Discipleship: Baptism and Conversion.* Delhi: SPCK.

Slack, James B., James O. Terry, and Grant Lovejoy. 2003. *Tell the Story: A Primer on Chronological Bible Storying.* Rockville, VA: International Center for Excellence in Leadership.

Smith, Glenn. 1995. "Urban Mission in the French North Atlantic." *Urban Mission* 12, no. 4 (June): 5–21.

———. 1997. "The Protestant Church in the Quebec Regions: Since 1960." Manuscript. Montreal, Quebec: Christian Direction.

———. 2007. "Models for Raising Up Church Planters." *Leadership Network,* www.leadnet.org/Resources_downloads.asp (accessed May 9, 2009).

Snyder, Bill. 2004. "Better Decisions through Teamwork." *Stanford Graduate School of Business News,* April, www.gsb.stanford.edu/news/research/ob_teamdecisionmaking.shtml (accessed June 23, 2009).

Snyder, Howard A. 1975. "The Church as God's Agent in Evangelism." In *Let the Earth Hear His Voice,* edited by J. D. Douglas, 327–60. Minneapolis: World Wide Publications.

Speer, Robert E. 1902. *Missionary Principles and Practice.* New York: Revell.

Spradley, James P. 1980. *Participant Observation.* Orlando, FL: Harcourt Brace Jovanovich College.

Stanley, Brian. 1992. "Planting Self-Governing Churches: British Baptist Ecclesiology in the Missionary Context." *Baptist Quarterly* 34 (October): 378–89.

Stanley, Rajamani, Roger Hedlund, and J. P. Masih. 1986. "The Curse of Money on Missions to India." *Evangelical Missions Quarterly* 22, no. 3 (July): 294–302.

Stauffer, S. Anita. 1996. "Worship and Culture: An International Lutheran Study." *International Review of Mission* 85, no. 337 (April): 183.

Stedman, Ray. 1972. *Body Life.* Glendale, CA: Regal Books.

Steffen, Tom A. 1996. *Reconnecting God's Story to Ministry: Cross-Cultural Storytelling at Home and Abroad.* La Habra, CA: Center for Organizational and Ministry Development.

———. 1997. *Passing the Baton: Church Planting That Empowers.* La Habra, CA: Center for Organizational and Ministry Development.

———. 2001. "Exit Strategy: Another Look at Phase-Out." *Evangelical Missions Quarterly* 37, no. 2 (April): 180–92.

Steffen, Tom A., and Mike Barnett, eds. 2006. *Business as Mission: From Impoverished to Empowered*. Pasadena, CA: William Carey Library.

Steffen, Tom A., and James O. Terry. 2007. "The Sweeping Story of Scripture Taught through Time." *Missiology* 35, no. 3 (July): 315–35.

Stetzer, Ed. 2001. "Closing the Back Door." *On Mission*, November-December, www.onmission.com/site/c.cnKHIPNuEoG/b.830375/k.6EA3/Closing_the_back_door.htm (accessed June 1, 2009).

————. 2003a. "The Impact of the Church Planting Process and Other Selected Factors on the Attendance of Southern Baptist Church Plants." PhD diss., Southern Baptist Theological Seminary.

————. 2003b. "Multicultural Teams in Church Planting." *Evangelical Missions Quarterly* 39, no. 4 (October): 498–505.

————. 2006. *Planting Missional Churches*. Nashville: Broadman and Holman.

————. 2007. "Church Squared: Churches across the Country Are Finding New Ways to Obey Acts 1:8—To Multiply to the Ends of the Earth; Is There an Equation That Works for Your Church?" *Outreach Magazine*, July-August, http://server.mbcworld.org/files/church%20planting/church%20squared%20by%20ed%20stetzer.pdf (accessed January 30, 2010).

Stetzer, Ed, and Phillip Connor. 2007. "Church Plant and Survivability Study." Center for Missional Research, North American Mission Board.

Steyne, Philip M. 1992. *In Step with the God of Nations*. Houston: Touch.

Strachan, Kenneth. 1968. *The Inescapable Calling*. Grand Rapids: Eerdmans.

Strauss, Steve. 2006. "Creeds, Confessions, and Global Theologizing: A Case Study in Comparative Christologies." In *Globalizing Theology*, edited by Craig Ott and Harold A. Netland, 140–56. Grand Rapids: Baker Academic.

Stricker, Barry, and Nik Ripken. 2007. "Muslim Background Believers and Baptism in Cultures of Persecution and Violence." In *Missions in Contexts of Violence*, edited by Keith Eugene Eitel, 155–73. Pasadena, CA: William Carey Library.

Sullivan, Bill M. 1997. *Starting Strong New Churches*. Kansas City, MO: NewStart.

Surratt, Geoff, Greg Ligon, and Warren Bird. 2006. *The Multi-site Church Revolution*. Grand Rapids: Zondervan.

Swanson, Allen J. 1986. *Mending the Nets: Taiwan Church Growth and Losses in the 1980s*. Pasadena, CA: William Carey Library.

Swanson, Bruce E. 1993. "Compassion Pre-evangelism: The Master Key to the Town." *Evangelical Missions Quarterly* 29, no. 1 (January): 6–9.

Sylvia, Ron. 2006. *Starting New Churches on Purpose*. Lake Forest, CA: Purpose Driven.

Tanner, John. 2009. "A Story of Phenomenal Success: Indigenous Mission Training Centers and Myanmar." *Evangelical Missions Quarterly* 45, no. 2 (April): 152–57.

Taylor, Mrs. Howard. 1959. *Behind the Ranges: Fraser of Lisuland Southwest China*. London: Overseas Missionary Fellowship and Lutterworth Press.

Taylor, William D., ed. 1991. *Internationalizing Missionary Training: A Global Perspective*. Grand Rapids: Baker Books.

————, ed. 1997. *Too Valuable to Lose: Exploring the Causes and Cures of Missionary Attrition*. Pasadena, CA: William Carey Library.

Taylor, William D., and Steve Hoke. 2003 [1998]. "General Profile of a Cross-Cultural Church Planter." Report for World Evangelical Alliance Missions Commission, Austin, TX.

Teeter, David. 1990. "Dynamic Equivalent Conversion for Tentative Muslim Believers." *Missiology* 18, no. 3 (July): 305–13.

Tembo, Fletcher. 2003. *Participation, Negotiation, and Poverty: Encountering the Power of Images; Designing Pro-poor Development Programmes*. Burlington, VT: Ashgate.

Tennent, Timothy C. 2007. *Theology in the Context of World Christianity*. Grand Rapids: Zondervan.

Terry, John Mark. 2000. "Indigenous Churches." In *Evangelical Dictionary of World Missions*, edited by A. Scott Moreau, 483–85. Grand Rapids: Baker Books.

Thompson, J. Allen. 1995. "Church Planter Competencies as Perceived by Church Planters and Assessment Center Leaders: A Protestant North American Study." PhD diss., Trinity Evangelical Divinity School.

————. 2007. "Church Leader Inventory: A PCA Qualitative and Quantitative Study." Lawrenceville, GA: Presbyterian Church of America.

Thornton, W. Philip. 1984. "The Cultural Key to Developing Strong Leaders." *Evangelical Missions Quarterly* 20, no. 3 (July): 234–41.

Tippett, Alan. 1967. *Solomon Islands Christianity: A Study in Growth and Obstruction*. London: Lutterworth.

————. 1971. *People Movements in Southern Polynesia: Studies in the Dynamics of Church-Planting and Growth in Tahiti, New Zealand, Tonga, and Samoa*. Chicago: Moody.

————. 1992. "The Cultural Anthropology of Conversion." In *Handbook of Religious Conversion*, edited by Newton Maloney and Samuel Southard, 192–258. Birmingham, AL: Religious Education.

Tone, Ralph. 2000. "No Lone Rangers Need Apply: The Call to Multiply Churches Takes a Team Effort." *Latin America Evangelist*, July–Oct., 10–11.

Towns, Elmer, Ed Stetzer, and Warren Bird. 2007. *11 Innovations in the Local Church*. Ventura, CA: Regal.

Travis, William. 1997. "His Word to His World: First Baptist Church Flushing." In *Planting and Growing Urban Churches*, edited by Harvie M. Conn, 231–34. Grand Rapids: Baker Academic.

Tucker, Eric. 2006. "Competencies of Effective Hispanic Church Planters in Miami, Florida, as Perceived by Reformed Hispanic Church Planters and Pastors." PhD diss., Trinity Evangelical Divinity School.

Tucker, Ruth A. 1983. *From Jerusalem to Irian Jaya: A Biographical History of Modern Missions*. Grand Rapids: Zondervan Academic.

Tuckman, Bruce W. 1965. "Developmental Sequence in Small Groups." *Psychological Bulletin* 63, no. 6 (June): 384–99.

Tuckman, Bruce W., and Mary Ann Jensen. 1977. "Stages of Small Group Development." *Group and Organizational Studies* 2 no. 4 (December): 419–27.

Turnidge, John E. 1999. "Developing a Reference Guide for Encounter with God Churches." DMiss project, Trinity Evangelical Divinity School.

Untener, Ken. 2005. "The Mystery of the Romero Prayer." www.larynandjanel.com/blog/prophets-of-a-future-not-our-own-oscar-romero (accessed May 20, 2009).

Vajko, Robert J. 1996. "Principles for the Design and Implementation of a Working Strategy for the Multiplication of the TEAM-Related Churches in France by the Daughter Church Method." DMiss Project, Trinity Evangelical Divinity School.

———. 2005. "Why Do Some Churches Reproduce?" *Evangelical Missions Quarterly* 41, no. 3 (July): 294–99.

Van Gelder, Craig. 2000. *The Essence of the Church*. Grand Rapids: Baker Books.

Venugopal, Junias V. 1997. "Individual Mender Adaptation for Effective Team Work: A Research of Operational and Disbanded Evangelical Missionary Teams." PhD diss., Trinity Evangelical Divinity School.

Ver Beek, Kurt Alan. 2006. "The Impact of Short-Term Missions: A Case Study of House Construction in Honduras after Hurricane Mitch." *Missiology* 34, no. 4 (October): 477–95.

Vicedom, Georg. 1965. *The Mission of God: An Introduction to a Theology of Mission*. St. Louis: Concordia.

Vineyard Dach. 2009. "Training and Coaching." www.vineyard-dach.net/churchplanting/training-coaching.html (accessed April 14, 2009).

Wagner, C. Peter. 1981. *Church Growth and the Whole Gospel*. San Francisco: Harper and Row.

———. 1990. *Church Planting for a Greater Harvest*. Ventura, CA: Regal.

Waldron, Scott. 1971. "Teams and Teamwork." *Evangelical Missions Quarterly* 7, no. 2 (April): 111–21.

Wallace, Ian. 2002. "Bringing Good News to the Poor: Does Church-Based Transformational Development Really Work?" *Transformation* 19, no. 2 (April): 133–37.

Walls, Andrew F. 1982. "The Gospel as the Prisoner and Liberator of Culture." *Missionalia* 10, no. 3 (November): 93–105.

———. 1985. "Culture and Coherence in Christian History." *Evangelical Review of Theology* 9, no. 3 (July): 214–55.

Wang, John. 2007. "Congregations in Transition: Contextualization in Urban Immigrant Communities." PhD seminar paper, Trinity Evangelical Divinity School.

Ward, Ted, and Samuel F. Rowan. 1972. "The Significance of the Extension Seminary," *Evangelical Missions Quarterly* 9, no. 3 (Fall): 17–27.

Ward, W. Reginald. 1992. *The Protestant Evangelical Awakening*. Cambridge: Cambridge University Press.

Warner, Stephen R. 1994. "The Congregation in Contemporary America." In *American Congregations*, vol. 2, edited by James Wind and James Lewis, 54–99. Chicago: University of Chicago Press.

Warren, Rick. 1995. *The Purpose-Driven Church*. Grand Rapids: Zondervan.

Wasson, Alfred. 1934. *Church Growth in Korea*. New York: International Missionary Council.

Wedderburn, A. J. M. 1988. *The Reasons for Romans*. Edinburgh: Clark; Wheaton: Tyndale House.

Whiteman, Darrell L. 1983. *Melanesians and Missionaries*. Pasadena, CA: William Carey Library.

———. 1997. "Contextualization: The Theory, the Gap, the Challenge." *International Bulletin of Missionary Research* 21, no. 1 (January): 2–7.

Whitmore, John. 2009. *Coaching for Performance*. 4th rev. ed. London: Nicholas Brealey.

Williams, Andy. n.d. "Church Multiplication Centers: Best Practices from Churches That Do High-Yield Church Planting." *Leadership Network*, www.leadnet.org/resources_downloads.asp?IsSubmit=true#churchmult (accessed April 14, 2009).

Williams, C. Peter. 1990. *The Ideal of the Self-Governing Church*. Leiden, Netherlands: E. J. Brill.

Wilson, David Dunn. 1996. "Colonies of the Kingdom: A Biblical Image of Church Planting." *Epworth Review* 23, no. 1 (January): 42–48.

Wilson, Eugene. 1998. "Equipping Quebecois Cell Leaders in a Cell Church in Montreal." DMin thesis, Westminster Theological Seminary.

———. 2001. "Plantación de iglesias del punto de vista de un movimiento" [Church Planting from a Movement Perspective]. Electronic document. Latin America Training Network, San José, Costa Rica.

Wilson, J. Christy, Jr. 1997. "Successful Tentmaking Depends on Mission Agencies." *International Journal of Frontier Missions* 14, no. 3 (July-September): 140–43.

Wilson, Linda. 1996a. "Culture Shock: What's Experience Got to Do with It?" MEd thesis, McGill University.

———. 1996b. "Women and Culture Shock." *Evangelical Missions Quarterly* 32, no. 4 (October): 442–49.

———. 2003. "Issues for Women in Church Planting." *Evangelical Missions Quarterly* 39, no. 3 (July): 362–66.

Wilson-Hartgrove, Jonathan. 2008. *New Monasticism*. Grand Rapids: Brazos.

Winter, Ralph D., Steven C. Hawthorne, Darrell R. Dorr, D. Bruce Graham, and Bruce A. Koch. 1999. "Finishing the Task." In *Perspectives on the World Christian Movement: A Reader*, edited by Ralph D. Winter and Steven C. Hawthorne, 531–46. Pasadena, CA: William Carey Library.

Wood, Rick. 1995. "A Church Planting Movement: The Key to Reaching Every People and Every Person." *Mission Frontiers* 20, nos. 5–6 (May-June): 8–15.

———. 1998. "Fighting Dependency among the 'Aucas': An Interview with Steve Saint." *Mission Frontiers* 20, no. 5–6 (May-June): 8–15.

Woodberry, J. Dudley. 1989. "Contextualization among Muslims: Reusing Common Pillars." In *The Word among Us*, edited by Dean S. Gilliland, 282–312. Dallas: Word.

Woolever, Cynthia. 2005. "The Other Half of Health: Patterns in Declining Churches." Paper presented at the Society for the Scientific Study of Religion annual meeting, Rochester, NY, November 4. www.uscongregations.org/pdf/cw-sssr-2005.pdf (accessed April 28, 2007).

Wright, Christopher J. H. 2006. *The Mission of God*. Downers Grove: InterVarsity.

Wuthnow, Robert. 1997. *The Crisis in the Churches: Spiritual Malaise, Fiscal Woe*. New York: Oxford University Press.

Yamamori, Tetsuanao. 1998. Introduction to *Serving with the Urban Poor*, edited by Tetsuanao Yamamori, Bryant L. Myers, and Kenneth L. Luscombe, 1–9. Monrovia, CA: MARC.

Yamamori, Tetsuanao, and Kenneth A. Eldred, eds. 2003. *Kingdom Business*. Wheaton: Crossway.

Yost, Jim. 1984. "Development Work Can Hinder Church Growth." *Evangelical Missions Quarterly* 20, no. 4 (October): 352–60.

Zadero, Rad. 2004. *The Global House Church Network*. Pasadena, CA: William Carey Library.

Zahniser, A. H. Mathias. 1997. *Symbol and Ceremony: Making Disciples across Cultures*. Monrovia, CA: MARC.

Zehner, Damaris. 2005. "Building Teams, Building Walls." *Evangelical Missions Quarterly* 41, no. 3 (July): 362–69.

Zoba, Wendy Murray. 2000. "A Woman's Place." *Christianity Today* 44, no. 9 (August): 40–48.

Index

442